Disabling Barriers – Enabling Environments

Disabling Barriers – Enabling Environments

Second Edition

Edited by
John Swain
Sally French
Colin Barnes
Carol Thomas

SAGE Publications
London • Thousand Oaks • New Delhi

First edition published 1993
This edition published 2004

SAGE Publications Ltd
1 Oliver's Yard
55 City Road
London EC1Y 1SP

SAGE Publications Inc.
2455 Teller Road
Thousand Oaks, California 91320

SAGE Publications India Pvt Ltd
B-42, Panchsheel Enclave
Post Box 4109
New Delhi 100 017

British Library Cataloguing in Publication data

A catalogue record for this book is available from the British Library

ISBN 0 7619 4264 5
ISBN 0 7619 4265 3 (pbk)

Library of Congress Control Number: 2003112200

Typeset by C&M Digitals (P) Ltd., Chennai, India
Printed in Great Britain by The Cromwell Press Ltd, Trowbridge, Wiltshire

Contents

List of Contributors

Paul Abberley is an Associate Lecturer for the Open University. He lives in South Dartmoor and has written a range of articles on disablement.

Colin Barnes is Professor of Disability Studies at the Centre for Disability Studies at the University of Leeds.

Martin Banton is a black disabled man. He is a trainer in Disability Equality and Race and Disability. He is currently undertaking a Social Work degree at the University of Coventry.

Len Barton is professor of Inclusive Education at the Institute of Education, University of London. He is the founder and editor of *Disability and Society*.

Peter Beresford is Professor of Social Policy and Director of the Centre for Citizen Participation at Brunel University. He is Chair of Shaping Our Lives National User Network and a long-term user of statutory mental health services.

Selina Bonnie has a Master's Degree in Disability Studies from the University of Leeds. Her particular research interests centre on sexuality, reproductive rights, bioethics and independent living for disabled people.

Helen Caplan is a freelance trainer and lecturer in disability issues and applied ethics. She has a particular interest in genetics, especially in relation to reproductive issues.

Liz Carr is a disabled woman from Nottingham. She is active in the disabled people's movement (including Direct Action Network). She is a founding member of Nasty Girls, the Disabled and Deaf Women's Comedy Group (www.nasty-girls.co.uk).

Paul Anthony Darke is a disabled writer and creator who works in collaboration with Marie Claire Darke, Walker Darke and Ann Whitehurst. For further information visit www.outside-centre.com.

Ken Davis played a leading role in the early organisational development of the disabled people's movement at national and at local level in Derbyshire.

John M. Davis   is co-ordinator of a BA course in Childhood Studies at the University of Edinburgh. He is also Director of the Children and Social Inclusion Consultancy in Edinburgh, and a visiting Senior Research Fellow at the University of Leeds.

Vic Finkelstein   is a retired lecturer at the Open University. He was the first chair of the British Council of Organisations of Disabled People and started several other disability organisations.

Sally French   is a Senior Lecturer in the Faculty of Health and Human Science at the University of Hertfordshire and an Associate Lecturer at the Open University. Her main area of interest is disability studies.

Maureen Gillman   is Principal Lecturer and Programme Director for post-qualifying social work education at Northumbria University. Her research interests include adult learning, family psychotherapy and disability.

Colin Goble   is a Senior Lecturer in Learning Disability Nursing in the School of Health and Social Care at the University of Greenwich. His interests include genetics, bioethics, intellectual impairment and the social model of disability.

Dan Goodley   is a Reader in Applied Disability Studies in the School of Education at the University of Sheffield. His research engages with the activism of disabled people with 'learning difficulties'.

Frances Hasler   is Chief Executive of the National Centre of Independent Living. Her career spans local, regional and national organisations of disabled people and mainly focuses on independent living issues.

Alan Hewitt   is the Working Together Co-ordinator at Connect, involving people with aphasia at all levels of policy, planning and practice.

Chris Holden   is a Lecturer in Social Policy at Brunel University. His research interests are in the political economy of the welfare state and globalisation.

Bill Hughes   is head of the Division of Social Sciences at Glasgow Caledonian University. His research interests are in the sociology of the body and disability studies.

Rachel Hurst   is the Director of Disability Awareness and Action, an international information network on disability and human rights. She is also Chair of the European Disability Forum's Human Rights Committee.

Rob Imrie   is Professor of Human Geography at Royal Holloway College, University of London. He is co-author (with Peter Hall) of *Inclusive Design:*

Designing and developing accessible environments (2001, Spon Press, London).

Ann MacFarlane is a leading Disability Rights and Equality Consultant, Trainer and Researcher. She specialises in independent living and direct payments and is actively involved in the Disabled People's Movement.

Geoffrey Mercer   is a member of the Centre for Disability Studies in the Department of Sociology and Social Policy at the University of Leeds.

Mike Oliver   is Emeritus Professor of Disability Studies in the Department of Sociology at the University of Greenwich.

Carole Pound   is Director of Therapy and Education at Connect, the communication disability network, an influencing organisation working with people living with stroke and aphasia.

Mark Priestley   is a Lecturer in disability studies at the Centre for Disability Studies at the University of Leeds and administrator of the international e-mail discussion group disability-research@iiscmail.ac.uk.

Donna Reeve   is a post-graduate research student in the Department of Applied Social Science at Lancaster University. Her research interests include the psycho-emotional dimensions of disability, identity and counselling.

Steve Robertson   is an NHS Research Fellowship student at the Institute of Health Research at Lancaster University. His research interests are in the area of identity, gender and health promotion.

Alan Roulstone   is Reader in Disability Policy at the University of Sunderland. His research interests are disability and employment policy and the experiences of disabled workers and job seekers.

Bob Sapey   is a lecturer at Lancaster University. His teaching and research interests are concerned with disability, technology and social work practice.

Mairian Scott-Hill   is a self-employed writer and editor, working at the interface of disability studies and discourse studies, and Honorary Senior Research Fellow at King's College, London.

Alison Sheldon   is currently working as a Research Fellow at the Centre for Disability Studies at the University of Leeds.

Gurnam Singh   is a Senior Lecturer in Social Work at Coventry University where he is a founder member of the Centre for Social Justice. He is an active participant in anti-oppressive struggles.

John Stewart   is Senior Lecturer in Social Policy and a Social Work Tutor at Lancaster University. He is currently researching wheelchair users' understanding of their social circumstances.

John Swain   is Professor of Disability and Inclusion at Northumbria University. His research interests include the analysis of policy and professional practice from the viewpoints and experiences of disabled people.

Carol Thomas   is a Senior Lecturer in the Institute for Health Research at Lancaster University. Her current research interests are in disability studies and the social aspects of cancer and palliative care.

Sian Vasey   has had a long involvement with the disability movement and the disability arts movement and is now the director of Ealing Centre for Independent Living.

Michele Wates   is a researcher, writer and disabled parent. She has been involved in building a peer support, information and campaigning network now based at the National Centre for Disabled Parents.

Introduction

The first edition of this book was compiled as a reader for the Open University (OU) course, 'The Disabling Society'. Between 1975 and 1994 the OU team produced a wealth of material that provided the basis for the development of disability studies courses and professional training schemes at both the undergraduate and postgraduate levels in mainstream colleges and universities across the UK, including the course readers *Handicap in a Social World* (Brechin et al., 1981) and *Disabling Barriers – Enabling Environments* (Swain et al., 1993). The latter became, arguably, the most widely used reader in disability studies, both in Britain and internationally.

So how have we approached the second edition? To begin with, some key characteristics of the first edition have been retained:

1 The main assumptions underlying this compilation remain unchanged – encapsulated by the title, that originally came from Vic Finkelstein. The focus is on disabling barriers faced by people with impairments in their interactions with a physical and social world designed for non-disabled living. It is also on the establishment of enabling environments and the control by disabled people of their own lives and their participation in the community.
2 Disability impacts on and finds expression in every aspect of contemporary social life. Disabling barriers permeate the physical and social environment: organisations and institutions; language and culture; organisation and delivery of services; and the power relations and structures of which society is constructed. Thus, a wide range of topics are covered – though we would not claim that it is comprehensive. As in the first edition, this is a collection of quite short, pithy and, we hope, challenging analyses of disability issues.
3 The contributors, and editors, are predominantly disabled academics and activists. Some chapters are written by well-established authors, but the book also provides a forum for new voices within this burgeoning arena.

So what has changed? The primary aim of this volume is to reflect changes over the past ten years – since the first edition. What, then, have been the major changes in the lives and experiences of disabled people – and in understandings of 'disability'? The first response has to be that the more things change, the more they remain the same (there's a French phrase). Despite major changes in legislation, for instance, the dominant picture remains one of discrimination, prejudice, injustice and poverty, often rationalised on the grounds of supposed progress for disabled people. Finkelstein's statement in the opening chapter of the first edition still stands:

> One set of facts immediately stands out when we look at the situation of disabled people. Government statistics ..., independent research projects ... and personal experiences show that on nearly every indicator of participation in mainstream life disabled people come out extremely badly; for example on employment statistics, income levels, suitable housing and access to public transport, buildings, information (newspapers, radio and television) and leisure facilities. (1993: 11)

It also remains true that any radical change in the prospects for a better quality of life for disabled people comes from one direction: disabled people have taken the initiative. The thrust for change is grounded in the analysis of the disabled people's experiences from their own perspective and their involvement in controlling their lives – collectively and individually. It is a scene of challenge by disabled people, developing their view of disability, their demands for change, their individual and collective activism and their identity within a disabling society. Perhaps it is not surprising, then, that the structure of the book remains the same – in five parts summarised below.

Yet the chapters in this volume reflect upon some key changes. Only two chapters have been retained, in slightly revised form, from the first edition. Recognising that any summary of social change will be selective and partial, we would pinpoint the following as key themes of change, each holding its own controversies and tensions:

1 Perhaps the most obvious changes in the past ten years, in Britain and internationally, are embodied in relevant policy relating to disabled people, particularly as expressed within legislation. A number of chapters in the first edition looked towards anti-discriminatory legislation. In Britain, we now have the Disability Discrimination Act 1995, the establishment of the Disability Rights Commission 2000 and, on a broader front, the Human Rights Act 1998.
2 A second change, we would suggest, has been not simply the quantitative growth of disability studies literature, but the variety of voices that can now be found in journals, books and on the Internet – almost a cacophony of personal experiences, research and analysis.
3 Perhaps above all is the changing social context and, in particular, the impact of the escalating processes of 'globalisation' and the political, economic, social and cultural interdependence of nation-states. The reverberations are multiple and complex, including the rise in political activism by disabled people's organisations at the international level.

These themes are addressed in different guises throughout this volume. The past ten years have seen substantial change and *Disabling Barriers – Enabling Environments* is being re-established in this new and ever-changing social world. Yet, for us as editors, a social model of disability remains the fundamental stance for the critique of changing theory, policy and practice. It is rooted in the history of the oppression of disabled people – a history of elimination, segregation, marginalisation, enforced dependency and social death – rationalised on the grounds of progress for disabled people. The aims of the first edition remain just as relevant, that is to:

• increase knowledge about the more active role that disabled people are playing in the community and how this can be supported;
• develop a greater understanding of the experiences and situation of disabled people from their own perspective; and
• further the involvement of disabled people in controlling their lives through the development of an understanding of citizenship and empowerment.

Part I: Perspectives of disability and impairment

Part I charts the continuing development of a social approach to understanding disability and impairment that emanates from the lived experience of injustice and the establishment of a collective identity of disabled people. These papers set the scene by providing a conceptual map for exploring the tensions inherent in understanding disability and impairment, approaching the issues from different directions. To bridge the first and second editions, the section begins with chapters by two of the editors of the first edition: Mike Oliver and Vic Finkelstein. Both assert and reaffirm the potency of the social model, first as a tool in breaking down the power relations and walls of discrimination within a disabling society, and second as a window through which to consider the state of humanity in the contemporary world.

Part II: In our own image

Part II addresses 'image' at its broadest – as encompassed by the notion of identity. The chapters contribute to the growing literature by disabled people and their supporters in writing their own history, creating their own images in literature and art, and developing their own accounts of disability that reflect their experiences and vested interests. Two related themes are apparent. The first is power in determining and controlling identities. Disabling images, themselves created and controlled by non-disabled people, are essentially founded on concepts of dependency, abnormality, individual tragedy and the colonisation of disability by professionals and policy makers as gatekeepers of services and support. 'In our own image' encapsulates disabled people's direct opposition to the dominant ideologies that would reduce, determine and stereotype disabled people. The second, and related, theme is commonality and diversity, and the politics of difference. This collection of chapters concerns the diversity of disabled people, different forms of oppression, and the affirmation of disabled identity in terms of gender, ethnicity, sexuality and impairment. Inherent in these analyses, and explicitly addressed by some authors, are questions of fragmentation and unity, commonality and difference that have taken on a particular significance in contemporary disability studies.

Part III: Controlling lifestyles

The disabling barriers analysed in Part III are those that prevent the full participative citizenship of disabled people, that marginalise and segregate people in every aspect of social life, that deny access to and participation in organisations and that preclude equal rights. 'Enabling' is crucially founded on disabled people's control in their day-to-day lives in the community, and the papers in this section are essentially concerned with processes of social inclusion. Perhaps not surprisingly, the range of topics covered closely reflects those in the first edition, including: independent living, housing, education, employment, leisure and ageing. New topics covered are an expression of the broadening of disability studies within a changing social context: technology, communication, family life and childhood.

Part IV: In charge of support and help

Part IV turns to the help and support provided for and by disabled people. Disabling barriers here are those faced by disabled people within the service providers' models (such as the medical model) for understanding, planning and evaluating services, and the understanding of disability in which these are grounded. The papers included here represent some ostensibly significant developments over the past decade, the establishment of direct payments being an obvious example. The primary concern, however, is the continuing critical analysis of the health and welfare services – the more things change, the more they remain the same. The first two chapters set the scene. The first is a revised version of the chapter, by Ken Davis, that opened this section in the first edition. He charts the 'care, cure and control' that still characterise the supposed 'support' perpetrated on disabled people in their role as clients. Vic Finkelstein then turns a similar light of analysis on service providers, arguing that so-called 'modernising' of services is disabling professionals as well as people with impairments. The 'partnership' advocated here is founded on disabled people's control of the decision making that defines the support they need and shapes and determines their lives. These themes reverberate in different ways through the remaining chapters in this Part.

Part V: Creating a society fit for all

Part V contains papers in which analysis is undertaken at the broadest level. The reader concludes by focusing on possibilities for creating full democratic participation within the context of a rapidly changing social world. The topics address themes of change over the past ten years, including: the escalating development of the information society; changing legislation; and developing technology, including the so-called biotechnological revolution. The chapters are about the possibilities that such changes strengthen disabling barriers and the exclusion, and elimination, of disabled people and provide the context for the resistance of disabled people and the development of enabling environments.

Overall we hope that this second edition takes forward thinking in understanding and analysing disabling barriers and the development of practice in creating enabling environments.

References

Brechin, A., Liddiard, P. and Swain, J. (eds) (1981) *Handicap in a Social World*. London: Hodder and Stoughton.

Finkelstein, V. (1993) 'The commonality of disability', in J. Swain, V. Finkelstein, S. French and M. Oliver (eds), *Disabling Barriers – Enabling Environments*. London: Sage.

Swain, J., Finkelstein, V., French, S. and Oliver, M. (eds) (1993) *Disabling Barriers – Enabling Environments*. London: Sage.

Part I
Perspectives of Disability and Impairment

1

If I Had a Hammer: The Social Model in Action
MIKE OLIVER

A little while ago Tony Blair made the following statement when he said that the Labour Government aim 'to take down the barriers that hold people back from fulfilling their potential'. It's tempting to suggest that we are all social modellists now. It certainly seems that it's not just disabled people who recognise the potential and usefulness of the social model. However, the rising popularity of the social model of disability has coincided with it becoming increasingly contested, not just in definitional terms but also in terms of its usefulness and applicability.

In this particular chapter I want to argue that, as the title implies, in the last 20 years we have spent too much time talking about the social model and its usefulness, and indeed its limitations, and not enough time actually implementing or attempting to implement it in practice. This criticism applies both to those disabled people active in the disability movement and the academics who have been central to the ongoing development of disability studies.

In order to develop this argument, first I will provide a brief history of the social model from my own personal perspective as someone who was centrally involved almost from the beginning. Second, 1 will discuss the main criticisms of the social model that have emerged from the movement and from disability studies. I do not intend to engage with external criticisms that have emerged from outside the movement or other parts of the academy. Third, I intend to discuss three examples of the social model in action in which, in one way or another, I have been centrally involved. Finally, as the title of this chapter implies, I will end with a plea for more action and less talk.

Origins of the social model

The social model stemmed from the publication of *Fundamental Principles of Disability* (UPIAS, 1976). This turned our understanding of disability completely on its head and argued that it was not our impairments that were the main cause of our problems as disabled people, but that it was the way society responded to us as an oppressed minority. My first encounter with, or my first attempt to use, this idea resulted in the development of this thing which has come to be called the social model of disability.

It emerged out of a course that I was teaching at the time, which was the first postgraduate course in what would now be called disability studies. It was based at the University of Kent in Canterbury and was aimed primarily at qualified social workers, although some occupational therapists and others including a few disabled people also enrolled. Essentially what I was seeking was to provide my students with a way of using the idea that it was society and not us that should be the target for their professional interventions and their professional practice. This idea was first introduced to the world outside Canterbury at a RADAR conference in 1982. It subsequently was developed in a book that I published in 1983 called *Social Work with Disabled People* (Oliver, 1983).

What happened next

As a consequence of this, and the emergence of disabled people's organisations in the 1980s (Campbell and Oliver, 1996), we saw the Disability Equality Training Movement take off. The social model became the prime idea for taking forward the idea of disability equality across a whole range of trainers and organisations. The next stage in the development of the social model came when it was adopted by the Disability Movement, and in particular the British Council of Disabled People. If you read the book by Jane Campbell and myself (*Disability Politics*, 1996) you will see quite clearly that the social model had a big part to play in developing the collective consciousness of disabled people who were trying to build the Disability Movement.

It was not just amongst disabled people that the idea developed. It gradually became incorporated into the state and there were a number of reports, the first one in 1988 called 'A Wider Vision for the Blind', which advocated and adopted the idea of the social model as the way forward in providing services for blind people. By the 1990s the social model was becoming colonised by a range of organisations, interests and people, some of whom had bitterly opposed it less than ten years previously.

Criticisms

From the Movement and disability studies itself there are five main criticisms that can be made of the social model. The first of these is that the social model ignores or is unable to deal adequately with the realities of impairment. This is based upon a conceptual misunderstanding, because the social model is not about the personal experience of impairment (Oliver, 1996) but the collective experience of disablement (Oliver, 1990). This criticism has sometimes been turned into personal attacks and some have suggested that it is only fit white men in wheelchairs who are able to ignore their impairments.

As a severely disabled tetraplegic, who every day of my life needs to make the necessary arrangements to be able to get up in the morning and go to bed at night and indeed use the toilet, I find such suggestions galling, particularly when they come from non-disabled people or those disabled people who have no idea what it's like to be at the mercy of state services for personal survival, let alone social functioning. Of course white men in wheelchairs are aware of the limitations that our impairments impose, and of course we struggle with that, and of course that creates difficulties for us. As I've indicated in the past, however, the limitations that our impairments impose upon us are an inadequate basis for building a political movement.

A second related criticism suggests that our subjective experiences of the 'pains' of both impairment and disability are ignored by the social model. Again I find this criticism partial and hard to countenance. If I simply focus on my own work, I co-wrote a book on male experiences of spinal cord injury (Oliver et al., 1988) and undertook a further study on the experiences of ageing with a disability (Zarb and Oliver, 1993). More generally I find it difficult to accept that the social model is not based upon disabled people's experiences. Indeed, it emerged out of the experiences of a number of disabled activists in the 1970s.

The third criticism of the social model argues that it is unable to incorporate other social divisions, that is, race, gender, ageing, sexuality and so on. The fact that the social model has not so far adequately incorporated these dimensions does not mean that it is unable to. I sometimes think the people who criticise the social model on these grounds are precisely the ones who should actually be trying to forge the social model in action in dealing with issues of race and gender and sexuality and age. In my view it's not that the social model cannot cope with these, it's that its critics have spent most of their time criticising the social model for its perceived failures rather than attempting to apply it in practice.

A fourth criticism of the social model centres on the issue of 'otherness'. It argues that it's not the physical and environmental barriers that we face, but the way our cultural values position disabled people as 'other'. This criticism is buttressed by the recent developments in the theory of postmodernism and ideas about representation being crucial to disabled people. It is wrong to suggest that, in principle, the social model ignores cultural values but, more importantly, I would wish to point out that at the moment most disabled people in the world live in abject poverty, don't have enough food and drink, and that the two main causes of impairment in the world are war and poverty. As a consequence of this, to try to move disability politics exclusively into the realm of the politics of representation is fundamentally misguided and inappropriate when so many disabled people continue to experience life-threatening material deprivation.

The final criticism of the social model is that it is inadequate as a social theory of disablement. Now the problem with this is that I don't think that those of us who developed the social model have ever claimed that it was a theory, and indeed most of us have explicitly said that the social model is not a theory of disability. A recent collection (Corker and French, 1998) spends a lot of time in the first and last chapters criticising what they call 'social model theorists' for their inadequacies before finally acknowledging that the social model is not a theory. It seems unnecessary to criticise the social model for not being something it has never claimed to be.

The battle for the social model

The criticisms discussed above should not be seen merely as academic disputes, however heated and vitriolic they have become at times. They have also been part of the political terrain over which disability activists have fought in the last ten years. There have been those who have been critical of the alleged formal or informal policing that has supposedly taken place. For example, the journal *Disability and Society* has been accused of only publishing papers on the social model that were ultimately sympathetic to it. Recently I did a count and from the first edition in 2000 until the last in 2002, we published more than 20 papers which sought to criticise, refine, review or even abandon the social model.

There is, of course, no dispute that some disability equality trainers were, as indeed were some racism awareness and sexism awareness trainers, over-zealous in their enforcement of the social model and perhaps spent their time trying to make non-disabled people feel guilty that they were not disabled. However, that is clearly a problem with the application of the model, not a problem of the model itself.

Further, there is no doubt that the Disability Movement itself may sometimes have been over-sensitive about its big idea. That has to be seen in the context of the way in which, throughout our history, our big ideas have been taken by others, used and indeed even claimed for their own. We have seen some of that in respect of the social model. Speaker after speaker from non-representative organisations claimed the social model as their own in the Trafalgar Square demonstrations of 1994. The Disability Rights Commission, established in 1997 by Government, claims to be guided in everything it does by the social model of disability.

This has recently led some parts of the Disability Movement to attempt to reclaim the social model, whatever that means. My argument is that we don't have the time, the energy or the resources to reclaim it, even if such a thing were possible. That would reduce disability activism to the kind of intellectual masturbation that academics sometimes engage in. Instead we need to develop and promote political strategies that are in line with the principles of the social model. Never mind yet more talk about how we might reclaim it, let's get on and use it. Let's not waste the gift that was bestowed upon us by those disability activists who were struggling against the oppressive structures that kept disabled people out of society in the 1970s.

The social model in action

For the remainder of this chapter I will focus on three projects that I have been involved in over the last 20 years which have attempted to use the social model in practice.

The first project was my attempt to reconstruct social work with disabled people in accordance with the social model principles. It was an attempt to provide a counter to individualised casework, which was prevalent at the time and which positioned disabled people as tragic victims in need of personalised therapeutic intervention. My book (Oliver, 1983) was an attempt to switch the target for social work intervention away from impaired individuals and onto the disabling society.

The British Association of Social Workers adopted it in 1986 as the way ahead in developing a relationship between disabled people and social workers, but in reality this failed to materialise. Since then disability issues have remained a poor relation in all of the equalities of social work training. Disabled people's needs have also remained very low down the agenda of most social services departments. There is little doubt that the hegemony of the individual model still exists within social work and, indeed, the other professions as well.

The social model, then, has had no real impact on professional practice. Consequently there is little doubt that social work itself has largely failed to meet disabled people's self-articulated needs (Oliver and Sapey, 1999). In my book in 1983, I predicted that if social work was not prepared to change in terms of its practice with disabled people, it would eventually disappear altogether. Given the proposed changes by the New Labour government in respect of modernising social services, it seems likely that that prediction is about to come true. We can probably now announce the death of social work, at least in relation to its involvement in the lives of disabled people.

As I have already indicated, the social model of disability became the first big idea of the Disability Movement. When Jane Campbell and I did our research on the movement, it was clear that the reason for this was that it provided a shorthand way of linking up the many diverse experiences that people with a whole range of different impairments had had. Prior to the late 1970s and early 1980s, disabled people's attempts at self-organisation had always floundered on the conflicts between the specific impairments and the different experiences of disablement that they generated.

The social model was a way of getting us all to think about the things we had in common, the barriers we all faced. Of course, some of those barriers were impairment specific; for example, blind people might have information barriers, people with mobility restrictions might have access barriers, deaf people communication barriers and so on. Nevertheless, the social model became a way in which to link up all of those kinds of experiences and enabled the movement to develop a collective consciousness which enabled it to expand at a rapid rate throughout the 1980s.

In the 1990s we have seen the emergence of rights and independent living as big ideas which sit alongside the social model. This coupled with the increasing contestations about what constitutes the social model has led some activists, notably Vic Finkelstein, to claim that the Disability Movement has lost its way and needs to return to the grass roots. What is clear is that, as we move into the twenty-first century, the social model of disability is no longer the glue that binds together the Disability Movement in the way that it did in the 1980s. The social model has somehow been relegated to the back burner in the Movement, and its radical potential has been put on hold while the leadership of the Disability Movement has become involved in parliamentary campaigns to improve our rights and to give us the services necessary to live independently.

The third social model project I have been involved in was a recent piece of work that I undertook with Birmingham City Council (Oliver and Bailey, 2002). In 1996 the City Council had adopted the social model in principle as a way of guiding their services for disabled people. Like many organisations who endorse the social model, when it was reviewed in 2001 some five years later nothing had happened. It had obviously had absolutely no impact on the way the City Council thought about or did things to, with and for disabled people.

In 2001 I was commissioned to provide a report suggesting ways in which the City Council could take forward its renewed commitment to the social model. I worked with a disabled colleague Peter Bailey and after extensive data collection, visits, meetings and consultations, we produced 24 recommendations. Only one of these was impairment specific, and that was one about the acceptance of British Sign Language as a language. Whether ultimately our report will improve the lives of disabled people in Birmingham is unknown at this particular time; nevertheless, that is the only basis on which it can be judged. There is little point in asking whether the social model was an adequate framework for revamping disability services in Birmingham or whether we accurately translated the principles of the social model as recommendations for action. The real test will be in five or ten or fifteen years' time in terms of the impact that it has had, or not had, on the lives of disabled people in Birmingham. The key question that will need to be asked is whether the social model is an adequate tool for improving the lives of disabled people.

Conclusion

Throughout this paper I have argued that the social model of disability is a practical tool, not a theory, an idea or a concept. Further, I have suggested that we have spent too much time discussing it rather than attempting to use it to produce social and political change. If we imagine that throughout human history the carpenters and builders of the world had spent their time talking about whether the hammer was an adequate tool for the purpose of building houses, we would all still be living in caves or roaming the plains. Finally, I have tried to demonstrate that we do have a hammer in the Disability Movement and that, if properly used, the social model of disability could become the hammer of justice and freedom for disabled people 'all over this land'.

References

Campbell, J. and Oliver, M. (1996) *Disability Politics: Understanding Our Past, Changing Our Future*. London: Routledge.

Corker, M. and French, S. (eds) (1998) *Disability Discourse*. Buckingham: Open University.

Oliver, M. (1983) *Social Work with Disabled People*. Basingstoke: Macmillan.

Oliver, M. (1990) *The Politics of Disablement*. Basingstoke: Macmillan.

Oliver, M. (1996) *Understanding Disability: From Theory to Practice*. Basingstoke: Macmillan.

Oliver, M. and Bailey, P. (2002) *Report on the Application of the Social Model of Disability on the Services Provided by Birmingham City Council*. Birmingham: Birmingham City Council.

Oliver, M. and Sapey, B. (1999) *Social Work With Disabled People* (2nd edn.). Basingstoke: Macmillan.

Oliver, M., Zarb, G., Moore, M., Silver, J. and Salisbury, V. (1988) *Walking Into Darkness: The Experience of Spinal Cord Injury*. Basingstoke: Macmillan.

UPIAS (1976) *Fundamental Principles of Disability*. London: Union of the Physically Impaired Against Segregation.

Zarb, G. and Oliver, M. (1993) *Ageing with a disability: What do they Expect After all These Years*. London: Rivers Oram.

2 Representing Disability
VIC FINKELSTEIN

'Thought must be divided against itself before it can come to any knowledge of itself.'

Aldous Huxley (1894–1964). British novelist. *Do What You Will.*

New beginnings

Towards the end of the 1960s there was a rapid and radical growth in disabled people's organisations. Campbell and Oliver suggest that this development was not merely numerical, but expressed the new way in which disabled people began to see themselves and their place in society. This, they say, can be seen in their:

> challenge to dominant social perceptions of disability as personal tragedy and the affirmation of positive images of disability through the development of a politics of personal identity ... the development and articulation of the social model of disability, which, by focusing on disabling environments rather than individual impairments, freed up disabled people's hearts and minds by offering an alternative conceptualisation of the problem. ...
>
> The origins of these fundamental changes, it seems to us, can be found in the 1960s with the coming of the 'age of affluence', when disabled people began to organise around issues of income, employment, rights and community living rather than institutional care. It continued in the 1970s with the passage of the Chronically Sick and Disabled Persons Act (1970) [CSDPA] and the formation of the Union of the Physically Impaired Against Segregation (UPIAS). (Campbell and Oliver, 1996: 20–21)

One of the first of the new breed of organisations was the Disablement Income Group (DIG). This was founded in 1965 and focused its main energies on campaigning for a national income to compensate for disability. From its beginning it had massive support from disabled people and their friends. However, it soon became apparent:

> that hopes had been raised which could not be met by the struggles in hand ... These frustrated expectations raised increasing doubts about the nature of our struggles. ... It started to become clear, as some of us had warned at the time, that 'charters' such as the CSDPA did not herald a new age for disabled people. Rather did it mark the end of an era in which physically impaired people could naively continue to believe that able-bodied people would solve our problems for us. (Leaman, 1981)

Criticism of DIG with its 'single issue' (incomes) campaign led Paul Hunt and friends to call for a new type of organisation based on a comprehensive interpretation of disabled people's needs. Paul Hunt's views had been shaped during the residents' struggle in a Cheshire Home for the right to exercise some democratic control over the running of the 'home' and for alternatives which would enable disabled people to live in the community. The problem was that in the 1960s 'severely disabled people' were regarded as incapable of functioning independently in the community. It was clear that moving into the community required both accessible public facilities and appropriate support systems. The campaign for greater community accessibility and appropriate support systems could not be comprehended without radically rethinking the prevailing interpretation of 'disability'.

The need for a radical rethink was started by the Union of the Physically Impaired Against Segregation (UPIAS), who concluded that the problems faced by disabled people were not caused by personal impairments but by the way society was exclusively arranged for able-bodied living:

> It follows from this view that poverty does not arise because of the physical inability to work and earn a living – but because we are prevented from working by the way work is organised in this society. It is not because of our bodies that we are immobile – but because of the way that the means of mobility is organised that we cannot move. It is not because of our bodies that we live in unsuitable housing – but it is because of the way that our society organises its housing provision that we get stuck in badly designed dwellings. It is not because of our bodies that we get carted off into segregated residential institutions – but because of the way help is organised. It is not because of our bodies that we are segregated into special schools – but because of the way education is organised. It is not because we are physically impaired that we are rejected by society – but because of the way social relationships are organised that we are placed beyond friendships, marriages and public life. Disability is not something we possess, but something our society possesses. (Leaman, 1981)

Thus started the new way of representing disability.

Interpretations, models and theories

At an early stage in developing UPIAS, and during my long discussions with Paul Hunt prior to his call for a new type of organisation of disabled people, we explored different interpretations of disability. We saw this as the beginning of a new theory:

> ... the Union from its inception spent much time reconsidering the prevailing *interpretations* of the nature of disability. The result of this groundwork was that ... [we] were able to state unequivocally that, 'our own position on disability is quite clear ... In our view, it is society which disables physically impaired people. Disability is something imposed on top of our impairments by the way we are unnecessarily isolated and excluded from full participation in society. Disabled people are therefore an oppressed group in society'. (UPIAS, 1976; my emphasis)

Because this was early days in grappling with the new interpretation of disability we also, in the same *Fundamental Principles* document, rather loosely referred to our interpretation as providing us with a social theory of disability which could guide our struggle against oppression:

> the ... struggle proposed by the Union is logically developed from a social theory of disability. (UPIAS, 1976)

What was consistent in our view, however, was that our interpretation of 'disability' led us to focus on the nature and workings of society, *not* our personal or individual attributes (which we saw as related to impairments). We had started to redefine the meaning of disability:

> ... it is society which disables physically impaired people. Disability is something imposed on top of our impairments ... (UPIAS, 1976)

Since those early days there has been, perhaps not unsurprisingly, an escalation in disability models and definitions; and with this has come growing confusion between different 'interpretations', 'models' and 'theories' and their focus of attention.

In this chapter I will attempt some clarity amidst the uncertainties. I start with two negative assertions:

- the social interpretation of disability does *not* provide an explanation of disability; and
- disabled people are *not* the subject matter of the social interpretation of disability.

I have used the term 'interpretation' rather than 'model' or 'theory' because this is where we, in UPIAS, started trying to make sense of the meaning of disability.

Interpretations

At an early stage in re-thinking the meaning of disability, members of UPIAS began debating 'why were we in this situation' and we confronted a crude but fundamental choice:

- either our tragedy is that the impairments we possess make us incapable of social functioning; or
- our society is so constructed by people with capabilities for people with capabilities and it is this that makes people with impairments incapable of functioning.

The agreed UPIAS interpretation was that, although it may be a personal tragedy to have an impairment, at the social level it is the construction of the social and physical environment that disables us (prevents us from functioning). The central issue in our campaigns for a better life, therefore, ought to be concerned with issues around emancipation rather than problems in attaining adequate compensation for the possession of a 'disability'.

In the early 1970s disabled people were encouraged to talk about our awful experiences (an approach nowadays promoted by those who wish to 'rectify' the original social model of disability as if this was something new!). The conceptual problem was never a lack of concern or interest in the effects of 'impairment', but an unwillingness to concentrate beyond the personal and on to the way society disables us. UPIAS concluded that there was an urgent need to promote the new and different interpretation of disability.

With this in mind, a simple way of presenting the new interpretation of disability was needed and in 1975 I wrote the story about a village where the population all used wheelchairs (Finkelstein, 1975). The idea was to show how such a society would, without intent, disable people who were not wheelchair users. The story (and the subsequent television version that I wrote, *Very Cross Roads*) have been shamelessly plagiarised and my focus on the development of a dynamic disability relationship frequently distorted. The disabling factors are often simply presented as physical barriers, stereotyped attitudes and inadequate personal 'care' (or professional) services. 'Disabling barriers' are to be overcome with access regulations for buildings, transport and so on; 'discrimination' is to be overwhelmed with civil 'rights' legislation; and the quality of 'care' is to be tackled with promoting standards for 'excellence' in social 'care'.

Interpretations, then, are simply a very early stage in trying to make sense of a complex situation.

Models

It was Mike Oliver, however, who was most successful in promoting a clearly expressed version of the UPIAS interpretation in the public arena (Oliver, 1981, 1983). This interpretation of disability he identified as a social model of disability. Mike's work on the social model of disability gained wide general acceptance over a lengthy period of time.

Models are constructed so that an object can be looked at in different ways and under different conditions. Models are artificial and do not explain anything. Model aeroplanes, for example, are constructed to see how they might behave in a wind-tunnel. The model aeroplane will not explain the laws governing flight, although they might provide the insight from which such laws are inspired. A good model can enable us to see something which we do not understand because in the model it can be seen from different viewpoints (not available to us in reality) and it is this multi-dimensioned replica of reality that can trigger insights which we might not otherwise develop. Mike's social model of disability has provided the disability movement with an invaluable tool that has strengthened our insight into the struggle for emancipation.

Nowadays most people probably refer to the social model of disability in a much more vague, confused and sometimes totally alien way to Oliver's original version (for example, Rachel Hurst (2001) refers to the 'social or rights model of disability' and confuses the social model with a legalistic model of disability).

Models, then, are the next stage in gaining insight into a complex situation.

Theories

In UPIAS we felt that our struggle for emancipation needed to be informed by theory. We had always hoped that we would have time to develop and debate such a theory. But it was not to be. The disability movement still awaits an explanation of the social laws that make, or transform, people with impairments into disabled people. Such a theory will be built on a clear hypothesis. I'll come back to this point.

Theories, then, are a later stage in trying to provide an explanation of a complex situation.

Changing models

In February 2000, Greater London Action on Disability (GLAD) added a new dimension to the growing confusion about the social model of disability in their conference 'Reclaiming the Social Model of Disability'. Amongst the key points from the conference we are told that:

> We need to produce an updated social model of disability that: includes a positive statement about us; recognises our diversity and difference; recognises institutionalised discrimination; talks about choice; recognises that not all the things that exclude us are about society's barriers; and talks about barriers (attitudes and access). (GLAD, 2000)

and:

> We need to consult widely on this new definition. (GLAD, 2000)

Apart from the confusion between models and definitions, in my view this conference was not about reclaiming the social model of disability. It was rather about promoting an updated version or, in Tom Shakespeare's (1993) wonderful expression, rectifying the social model of disability. In the absence of speakers who can promote, defend and elaborate the original radical version, the GLAD conference presented a one-sided and, in my view, ineffectual return to the narrative case file approach to disability that historically has always held back progress towards emancipation.

Jenny Morris, one of the speakers, for example, says:

> The social model of disability gives us the words to describe our experiences of inequality. (GLAD, 2000)

In fact, the radical social model of disability gave us the words to describe the way society is constructed so that we become disabled:

> It can be ... seen in the development and articulation of the social model of disability, which, by focusing on disabling environments rather than individual impairments, freed up disabled people's hearts and minds by offering an alternative conceptualisation of the problem. (Campbell and Oliver, 1996)

It was an outside-in approach to our situation; words to describe our experiences of inequality are an inside-out approach (that is, a case file approach). The former is a 'materialist' approach and the latter an 'idealist' approach. The idealist approach is perfectly at home with the 'rights' approach. In Jenny's words:

> The social model helps us to understand what needs to happen in order that we can access our human and civil rights. (GLAD, 2000)

I don't agree. Models, of course, provide insight rather than understanding and the radical social model of disability has to do with the creation of a society which enables us to be 'human' – not just access our 'rights' within an existing competitive market economy.

Similarly, Nasa Begum, also speaking at the conference, focuses on inside-out experiences and says:

> ... it is vital we claim the social model as a tool for understanding the discrimination and prejudice we face, and for helping to explain our experiences in society. (GLAD, 2000)

Dealing with discrimination by promoting legislation for civil rights involves a legalistic approach to emancipation. If my two negative assertions have any validity, then the campaign for disability rights does not depend on, nor is it a reflection of, the social model of disability. This is why the US 'Americans with Disability' Act is not informed by a radical social model of disability. The fact that the social interpretation of disability embraces civil rights does not make it a rights model.

Changing ourselves

The prevailing view that it is personal impairments that disable us is reinforced every day by the media, 'care' assessments, medical forms and so on. In order to locate the problem in the disabling society it is necessary, therefore, to break the impairment – disability link. However, 'impairment equals disability' is a core value of the modern 'body-perfect' culture and extremely resistant to change. To many, breaking the link is rejected simply because it is incomprehensible; somewhat like the rejection 'flat-earthers' might have made when faced with a challenge to their long-established view.

Perhaps an example of a non-disability dynamic social relationship might throw light on the way the radical interpretation of disability works. 'Parenthood' indicates a particular social relationship. To be a mother (or read father in this context) you must be a female (male). However, being a female does not make you into a mother. Being a mother presupposes a female physique, but it is only a special relationship to another person (child) that transforms the person into a mother, as well as quite independently still remaining a female. This special relationship with a child captured in the identifier 'mother' is given substance by the social context in which it takes place. This context is historically determined, dynamic and changes over time with the ebb and flow of a society's evolution.

There was a time when cultural emphasis of the parenting relationship was so ingrained that you could not separate the personal attribute from the social status, for example, a person was not thought of as a 'real' female (male) until becoming a mother (father). Nowadays with the growth in single parent families, wage-earning parents unable to provide daytime child care and same sex partnerships, for example, many adults have to take on both mother and father roles from time to time. Clearly, the parenting relationship terms are undergoing further profound changes.

Similarly, I see the modern meaning of disability in the UK as involving a unique dynamic relationship between people with certain personal attributes (impairments) and the particular social and physical environment in which they function. The socio-economic system at the same time, of course, defines the meaning of gender, race, class and so on. In the same way that the identity and attributes of being a mother (or father) in the parenting relationship are not applicable in every social situation (for example, at a place of employment), disability should always be interpreted dynamically within a particular social context.

Changing humanity

People who enjoy the fruits of the dominant culture always label others as lesser classes of themselves. The dominance of men, for example, leads to their identifier, 'man', becoming a global term and synonym for 'people' (or huMANity), whereas the word 'woMEN' is relegated to a sub-category of MEN. Unlike 'dis-Ability', of course, 'women' is nowadays never written as 'wo-Men'. The labels attached to classes of people, therefore, reflect the historical progress of the group along its emancipatory road.

The same argument applies to the word 'ability' (or 'able') – here the division is between the 'able' and 'non-able'. Because of the dominance of the 'able-bodied' and their culture, there is no need for them to qualify the terms they use to label the services they have created for themselves, for example, 'public railways' is understood to mean 'railway services for the able-bodied' and the word 'public' equals 'able-bodied'. When referring to disabled people, however, a qualifier (usually 'dis-') becomes necessary, for example, space on railway carriages needs to be identified as, say, space for a wheelchair (as contrasted with the unstated 'space for the shoe-bound) or 'disabled toilet' (as opposed to 'enabled' toilet).

Non-disabled people, then, see themselves as the standard of 'ableness' against which others should be measured. It is significant that non-disabled people do not apply the same standards to themselves. The history of the health sciences, fashion and sport, for example, is replete with evidence of an abstract standard to which they aspire and compare themselves.

It's a burden to us even to be human beings – men with our own real body and blood; we are ashamed of it, we think it a disgrace and try to contrive to be some sort of impossible generalized man.

Fyodor Mikhailovich Dostoevsky (1821–81). Russian writer. Notes from *Underground, 2.*

Ridiculous diets, surgical interventions, absurd clothing and endless exercises all aim at making the non-disabled body perfect. This 'abstract perfection' is located in our culture, which harbours the generalised ideal, and therein lies true 'ableness'. The 'ableness' of humanity is an abstraction: an ideal. Non-disabled people are, therefore, far from true representatives of the able-bodied or ableness but rather, in fact, a sub-group of the general, that is, they are 'people with cap-Abilities'. Seen this way 'people with dis-Abilities' (a euphemism for 'disabled people') are their equals and both groups are sub-divisions of real humanity (that is, prefixes of an abstract *able*):

In my experience even the most severely disabled people retain an ineradicable conviction that they are still fully human in all that is ultimately necessary. (Hunt, 1966)

Changing society

The shaping of humankind and the conventions of social intercourse according to an ideal favoured by people with capabilities has involved progressive ejection of personal attributes believed to diminish 'ableness'. In this process people with capabilities have increasingly turned themselves into shop window dummies (looking perfect, but lacking a human soul) whose sole purpose is displaying a commodity for sale. The purpose of life has become 'to work' instead of the purpose of work is 'to have a life'!

Human beings are by nature weak, vulnerable, physically imperfect and socially dependent and it is precisely these attributes that have been dumped onto disabled people. We are now seen as a depository of all that is physically demeaning and imperfect. Yet it is these imperfections that personify an essence of humankind. In my view, people with capabilities have lost sight of evolution's agenda and the heart and soul of humanity is *now* captured in the aspirations of disabled people. In fact, we can argue that the inferior social status of disabled people exactly mirrors where people with capabilities are going wrong. I think this interpretation can be summarised as a general hypothesis on disability:

> Disabled people have been abstracted from society and as an abstraction we embody the essence of social relationships at a particular point in historical time.

With this in mind, then, I believe the original social model of disability throws light onto the nature of both disability and humanity. The sifting out of human dependency traits and transferring these into disabled people has necessitated the creation and provision of care services by people with capabilities. Such services can never succeed precisely because they are designed as 'special' provision instead of 'natural to our species'. The historical destiny now falls on disabled people, in alliance with others who have also been marginalised by people with capabilities, to return humanity to its mission in developing a truly supportive society.

References

Campbell, J. and Oliver, M. (1996) *Disability Politics: Understanding Our Past, Changing Our Future*. London: Routledge.

Finkelstein, V. (1975) 'Phase 2: Discovering the Person in "Disability" and "Rehabilitation"', *Magic Carpet*, 27 (1): 31–8.

GLAD (2000) 'Reclaiming the Social Model of Disability Conference', London, February.

Hunt, P. (1966) 'A Critical Condition', in P. Hunt (ed.) *Stigma: The Experience of Disability*. London: Geoffrey Chapman.

Hurst, R. (2001) 'International Classification of Functioning, Disability and Health', *Disability Tribune*, September.

Leaman, R. (1981) 'Editorial', *Disability Challenge*, 1.

Oliver, M. (1981) 'A New Model of the Social Work Role in Relation to Disability', in J. Campling (ed.), *The Handicapped Person: A New Perspective for Social Workers?* London: RADAR.

Oliver, M. (1983) *Social Work With Disabled People*. London: Macmillan.

Shakespeare, T. (1993) 'Disabled people's self-organisation: a new social movement?', *Disability, Handicap and Society*, 8 (3): 256–7.

UPIAS (1976) *Fundamental Principles of Disability*. London: UPIAS.

3 Disability and Impairment
CAROL THOMAS

Disability Studies (DS) continues to grapple with the meaning of two key concepts in its lexicon: disability and impairment. Debates about what each term constitutes, and about the relationship between them, occupy many pages in DS books and journal articles. This ongoing consideration of foundational concepts should not be read, however, as a sign of academic weakness. On the contrary, it is testimony to the growing strength and richness of disability studies as it attracts writers who bring a variety of theoretical perspectives and experiential knowledge to bear.

This chapter briefly reviews the conceptual landscape associated with the categories of disability and impairment, and then presents some ideas on the direction in which DS might usefully move. Although these two concepts are allocated separate sections in what follows, I am sensitive to the argument that such a structure sustains what some see as an unhelpful disability/impairment dualism in DS thinking (Corker, 1998). Nevertheless, I find this analytical separation to be a useful device, but one to be made in the context of a discussion where the overriding interest is in the relationship between disability and impairment.

Disability

The social model of disability

In the UK, the emergent disabled people's movement of the 1970s was the force behind the reclaiming of the term 'disability' from professionals in medicine and social care (UPIAS, 1976; Campbell and Oliver, 1996). In wresting this term from the powerful grip of doctors and social workers who had long held that disability either *was* the impairment itself or resided in restrictions of activity *caused by* impairment, disabled people like Vic Finkelstein set about entirely reconstructing its meaning in the light of the social exclusions encountered in their own lived experience (UPIAS, 1976). In a radical move, they severed the presupposed causal link whereby impairment resulted in disability, asserting instead that disability was an entirely socially caused phenomenon. Disability was reformulated to mean the social disadvantages and exclusions that people with impairment faced in all areas of life: employment, housing, education, civil rights, transportation, negotiation of the built environment, and so forth. Traditional medical and welfarist models of disability, together with their culturally pervasive 'personal tragedy' counterpart, were thrown aside in favour of a social definition of disability. Mike Oliver (1990, 1996a) coined the phrase 'the social model of disability' to capture this new paradigm, and it became a touchstone in DS and the disabled people's movement in the UK.

The social model of disability unleashed a powerful drive for social and political change. Disability was exposed as a form of social oppression and exclusion that should not be tolerated, analogous to already recognised oppressions associated with gender, race, class and sexuality. Once this understanding of disability is adopted, the manifestations of disablism can be readily observed: a wheelchair user or a person with visual impairment cannot access public transport systems, or is not able to obtain a quality education that would enable them to compete for well-paid jobs in the labour market, or is represented as a person of lesser value in films and other media. The disabling 'social barriers' in the lives of people with impairments can be identified *and challenged* because socially created barriers can be dismantled. On a personal level, too, the social model of disability had a transformative effect:

> It has enabled a vision of ourselves free from constraints of disability (oppression) and provided a direction for our commitment to social change. It has played a central role in promoting disabled people's individual self worth, collective identity and political organisation. I don't think it is an exaggeration to say that the social model has saved lives. (Crow, 1996: 207)

In a relatively short period of time, the social model of disability has achieved a great deal, underpinning path-breaking empirical and theoretical work in DS (see collections in Barton and Oliver, 1997; Barnes and Mercer, 1996; Barnes et al., 2002), and serving as a battle-cry in successful, if far from completed, struggles for political change.

So, what brings disability into being?

Social modellist thinkers like Finkelstein (1980), Oliver (1990), Barnes (1991, Barnes et al., 2002) and Barton (1996) understand disability to reside principally in the socio-structural barriers that serve to disadvantage and exclude people with impairments. This perspective draws upon, and sits comfortably within, a Marxist and materialist interpretation of the world. Capitalist social relations of production, and particularly industrial capitalism, are understood to lie at the root of the social exclusion of the impaired by the non-impaired (Oliver, 1990; Gleeson, 1999; Thomas, 1999). In late eighteenth- and early nineteenth-century Britain, the imperatives of a system of generalised commodity production demanded that non-owners of the means of production sell their labour-power, to be harnessed in the service of a fast moving and exhausting industrial labour process. Those who could not sell their labour-power on 'normal' and 'average' terms faced exclusion from the opportunity to obtain independently the means of subsistence, and that independence was constructed as the basis of social standing, merit and personal identity in modern society (Oliver, 1990; Gleeson, 1999). On this economic basis, and with the assistance of an institutionalised ascendant medicine, an ideology of the 'devalued difference' represented by 'cripples', 'imbeciles', 'the disabled' took hold in all quarters of society. The rest is history: workhouses, enforced dependency, 'special' education, 'sheltered' workshops, community care, supported employment, in other words the whole paraphernalia of institutionalised care which embodies forms of philanthropic and professionalised control.

In recent years, this perspective on what brought disability into being has come to be seen as too limiting, or as downright wrong, by some writers within DS. Those informed by postmodernist and poststructuralist theoretical perspectives – Mairian Corker[1] and Tom Shakespeare to name but two – began to question the focus on socio-structural determinants (Shakespeare, 1997; Corker, 1998; Corker and French, 1999; Corker and

Shakespeare, 2002). To them, the social model appeared fundamentally flawed because of its association with a Marxian 'meta-historical narrative', positing disability as having fixed 'real' and 'essential' qualities (Shakespeare and Watson, 2001; Corker and Shakespeare, 2002). The alternative suggestions that the genesis of disability resided solely within linguistic, discursive and cultural practices entered DS debates, an application to the disability question of the influential theoretical writings of Foucault (1980) and Derrida (1978, 1993). In this perspective, being or becoming a disabled person is about being socially constructed and positioned as such by those who can exercise power through forms of knowledge. The same constructionist processes also create other identities in society as 'able-bodied', as 'normal'. Consequently, in this view, there is nothing inherent or 'essential' in an individual's body, character or behaviour that would predispose them to being a disabled person. Rather, those who wield power through the authority conferred upon them by the status and legitimacy of their knowledge – doctors, state administrators and legislators – can impose the category 'disabled' upon individuals in their purview. A person who is socially constructed as 'disabled' may often come, in turn, to construct reflexively her or his self-identity in the image of 'the disabled person'. Any hope for resistance – and it is a slim hope – lies in a 'disabled' person's ability to reject and resist the medical and associated categories imposed upon them, to break free from the discursive bonds in which they are held, by constructing an alternative positive self-narrative.

Today, the Marxist/materialist and postmodernist/structuralist perspectives are the two main theoretical axes informing conceptualisations of disability in DS. Clearly, very different ideas about the nature and genesis of disability are arrived at by travelling down one or other route. While writers may adopt other names to characterise their positions – phenomenologist, interactionist, feminist, critical realist – they tend to elaborate their concept of disability with reference to, and as variations of, these two dominant theoretical stances. The continued existence of the social model of disability is at stake in these conceptual contestations, since some in the postmodernist/structuralist camp assert that the social model has outlived its heuristic value:

> ... the British social model has been an excellent basis for a political movement, but is now an inadequate grounding for a social theory. This social model was a modernist project, built on Marxist foundations. The world, and social theory, has passed it by, and we need to learn from other social movements, and from new theoretical perspectives, particularly those of post-modernism and post-structuralism. (Shakespeare and Watson, 2001: 44).

Impairment

In severing any causal link between impairment and disability, social modellists of a Marxist/materialist hue relegated impairment to a devalued 'other' of little theoretical concern. As Oliver (1996b: 41–2) famously put it: 'disability is wholly and exclusively social … disablement has nothing to do with the body'. Indeed, to dwell on impairment in DS, and in the disabled people's movement, was thought hazardous because it was in danger of giving credence to the medical preoccupation with bodily matters, deflecting attention away from what should be at the centre: disability as a form of social oppression (Finkelstein, 1996; Oliver, 1996a).

Interestingly, critiques of the theoretical avoidance of impairment began in the materialist camp, when Paul Abberley (1987) argued that it should be recognised as something *socially* produced (by, for example, industrial accidents, environmental pollution, wars and medical practices). However, other criticisms on different grounds gathered pace in the 1990s. First, feminist writers such as Jenny Morris (1991, 1996) argued that experiences of the body should have a place in DS and disability politics, and that their exclusion was tantamount to a patriarchal rejection of 'personal' experiences:

> ... there is a tendency within the social model of disability to deny the experience of our own bodies, insisting that our physical differences and restrictions are entirely socially created. While environmental barriers and social attitudes are a crucial part of our experience of disability – and do indeed disable us – to suggest that this is all there is is to deny the personal experience of physical and intellectual restrictions, of illness, of the fear of dying. (Morris, 1991: 10)

Second, Sally French (1993) wrote about her own experiences as a person with visual impairment, noting that some restrictions on her activity *were* indeed 'caused by' her impairment; that is, they could not be explained wholly by the presence of social barriers, and would remain if all disabling social barriers in society were removed. A third set of criticisms began to be presented by writers who drew on a range of constructionist theoretical perspectives. Thus, Bill Hughes and Kevin Paterson argued that the social modellist desire to leave impairment out of account effectively colluded with medicalised ideas wherein impairment constituted a fixed, pre-social, 'biological abnormality':

> ... there is a powerful convergence between biomedicine and the social model of disability with respect to the body. Both treat it as a pre-social, inert, physical object, as discrete, palpable and separate from the self. The definitional separation of impairment and disability which is now a semantic convention for the social model follows the traditional, Cartesian, western meta-narrative of human constitution. (Hughes and Paterson, 1997: 329)

This definitional fission of the binary pair, impairment and disability, is seen as fundamentally problematic by poststructuralist writers: it is a dualism that, it is asserted, fails to understand that a process of linguistic and discursive construction and classification is at work (Corker and Shakespeare, 2002). Consequently, it fails to appreciate that these are *both* socially constructed categories which serve to divide, govern and control disabled people: 'for the materiality of the "impaired body" is precisely that which ought to be contested' (Tremain, 2002: 34).

Therefore, materialist social modellists have been both damned for leaving impairment out of account and damned for treating it as a naturalistic biological phenomenon. In the face of some of these criticisms, Oliver (1996b: 49) has suggested that those who are so-inclined could develop a 'social model of impairment', but has given no grounds for his conviction that *disability* is the overriding priority for DS and the disabled people's movement. Not only the conceptualisation of, but even the desire to engage with, the concept of 'impairment' therefore remains a subject of debate and contestation.

Ways forward?

In my view, the value of the social model of disability as a powerful tool for political struggle and as a *point of departure* in the theorisation of disability should be acknowledged and celebrated. Beyond this, DS requires the sociological conceptualisation and theorisation of both disability and impairment, and of the relationship between them. To finish, I present, in summary form, three of the suggestions that I have made for the fulfilment of these goals (see Thomas, 1999, 2002, 2003).

1   *The psycho-emotional dimensions of disability.* In the Marxist/materialist camp, my own theoretical home, the identification of the social barriers that constitute disability is too restricted. The focus is almost exclusively on material barriers that exist in the *external* social world – in employment, education, transport, housing, the built environment and so on. Of course, these barriers are crucial, but it is my contention that disablist exclusions are *also* constructed internally, operating along psychological and emotional pathways. I call these the psycho-emotional dimensions of disability (see Thomas, 1999). Of particular concern here are the impacts and effects of the social behaviours that are enacted between the relatively powerless 'impaired' and the relatively powerful 'non-impaired', for example, in familial relationships, in interactions in communities, and in encounters with health, welfare and educational services. It is about people with impairment being made to feel of lesser value, worthless, unattractive or disgusting. To accommodate these dimensions of disablism, I have suggested that the classic UPIAS (1976) definition of disability should be amended to read as follows: Disability is a form of social oppression involving the social imposition of restrictions of activity on people with impairments and the socially engendered undermining of their psycho-emotional wellbeing.

2   *Towards a materialist ontology of impairment.* The Marxist/materialist relegation of impairment to the status of devalued 'other' is singularly unhelpful. However, the postmodernist/structuralist alternatives discussed above are also of limited assistance. What is required is a materialist ontology of impairment and impairment effects – an ontology that is neither biologically reductionist nor culturally determinist (Thomas, 1999). To put it another way, we should not give the bio-medics exclusive rights over the concept of impairment, nor should we perform a 'vanishing act' by relegating what are *real bodily variations from the average* to the realms of 'purely linguistically constructed difference'. What is required is a theoretical framework that recognises the social influences in the science of biology and the irreducibly biological foundations of the social.

3   *Impairment and Impairment effects.* In Oliver's view, the social model of disability rests upon the UPIAS (1976) proposition that, in essence, disability *is social exclusion on the grounds of impairment* (Oliver, 1996a, 1996b). Oliver sees no contradiction between making a claim to the UPIAS definition of disability on the one hand, and his assertion that 'disability is wholly and exclusively social … disablement has nothing to do with the body' (1996b: 41–2) on the other hand. I do see a contradiction here, however. The UPIAS stance that disability is social exclusion on the grounds of impairment is a social relational proposition in which disability and impairment are inextricably linked and interactive. That is, while impairment is not the cause of disability, it is the raw material upon which disability works. It is the embodied socio-biological substance – socially marked as unacceptable bodily deviation – that mediates the social relationships in question. Further, the particular character of the impairment plays a critical role in shaping the forms and degrees of disablism encountered (Thomas, 2001). It follows that the theorisation of disability requires the theorisation of impairment (see Thomas, 2002, 2003). Thus, impairment should not be set aside as a category without interest or significance.

Note

1 Mairian Corker now writes, in this book and elsewhere, under the name of Mairian Scott-Hill.

References

Abberley, P. (1987) 'The concept of oppression and the development of a social theory of disability', *Disability, Handicap and Society*, 2 (1): 5–20.

Barnes, C. (1991) *Disabled People in Britain and Discrimination*. London: Hurst.

Barnes, C. and Mercer, G. (eds) (1996) *Exploring the Divide: Illness and Disability*. Leeds: The Disability Press.

Barnes, C., Oliver, M. and Barton, L. (eds) (2002) *Disability Studies Today*. Cambridge: Polity Press.

Barton, L. (ed.) (1996) *Disability and Society: Emerging Issues and Insights*. Harlow: Longman.

Barton, L. and Oliver, M. (eds) (1997) *Disability Studies: Past, Present and Future*. Leeds: The Disability Press.

Campbell, J. and Oliver, M. (1996) *Disability Politics: Understanding Our Past, Changing Our Future*. London: Routledge.

Corker, M. (1998) *Deaf and Disabled, or Deafness Disabled?* Buckingham: Open University.

Corker, M. and French, S. (eds) (1999) *Disability Discourse*. Buckingham: Open University.

Corker, M. and Shakespeare, T. (eds) (2002) *Disability/Postmodernity: Embodying Disability Theory*. London: Continuum.

Crow, L. (1996) 'Including all of our lives: renewing the social model of disability', in C. Barnes and G. Mercer (eds), *Exploring the Divide: Illness and Disability*. Leeds: The Disability Press.

Derrida, J. (1978) *Writing and Difference*. Chicago: University of Chicago Press.

Derrida, J. (1993) *Memoirs of the Blind: The Self-Portrait and other Ruins*. Chicago: University of Chicago Press.

Finkelstein, V. (1980) *Attitudes and Disabled People: Issues for Discussion*. New York, NY: World Rehabilitation Fund.

Finkelstein, V. (1996) 'Outside, "inside out"'. *Coalition*, April, 30–6.

Foucault, M. (1980) *Power/Knowledge: Selected Interviews and Other Writings, 1972–1977*. Brighton: Harvester.

French, S. (1993) 'Disability, impairment or something in between?', in J. Swain, V. Finkelstein, S. French and M. Oliver (eds), *Disabling Barriers – Enabling Environments*. London: Sage.

Gleeson, B.J. (1999) *Geographies of Disability*. London: Routledge.

Hughes, B. and Paterson, K. (1997) 'The social model of disability and the disappearing body: towards a sociology of impairment', *Disability and Society*, 12 (3): 325–40.

Morris, J. (1991) *Pride Against Prejudice: Transforming Attitudes to Disability*. London: The Women's Press.

Morris, J. (ed.) (1996) *Encounters With Strangers: Feminism and Disability*. London: The Women's Press.

Oliver, M. (1990) *The Politics of Disablement*. London: Macmillan.

Oliver, M. (1996a) *Understanding Disability*. London: Macmillan.

Oliver, M. (1996b) 'Defining impairment and disability: issues at stake', in C. Barnes and G. Mercer (eds), *Exploring the Divide: Illness and Disability*. Leeds: The Disability Press.

Shakespeare, T. (1997) 'Cultural Representation of Disabled People: dustbins of disavowal?', in L. Barton and M. Oliver (eds), *Disability Studies: Past, Present and Future*. Leeds: The Disability Press.

Shakespeare, T. and Watson, N. (2001) 'The Social Model of Disability: An Outdated Ideology?', in S.N. Barnartt and B.M. Altman (eds), *Exploring Theories and Expanding Methodologies: Where We are and Where We Need to Go. Research in Social Science and Disability*, Vol. 2. Amsterdam, London, New York: JAI.

Thomas, C. (1999) *Female Forms: Experiencing and Understanding Disability*. Buckingham: Open University Press.

Thomas, C. (2001) 'Feminism and Disability: The Theoretical and Political Significance of the Personal and the Experiential', in L. Barton (ed.) *Disability, Politics and the Struggle for Change*. London: David Fulton.

Thomas, C. (2002) 'Disability Theory: Key Ideas, Issues and Thinkers', in C. Barnes, M. Oliver and L. Barton (eds), *Disability Studies Today*. Cambridge: Polity Press.

Thomas, C. (2003) 'Developing the Social Relational in the Social Model of Disability: A Theoretical Agenda', in C. Barnes (ed.), *The Social Model of Disability: Theory and Practice*. Leeds: The Disability Press.

Tremain, S. (2002) 'On the Subject of Impairment', in M. Corker and T. Shakespeare (eds), *Disability/Postmodernity: Embodying Disability Theory*. London: Continuum.

UPIAS (1976) *Fundamental Principles of Disability*. London: UPIAS.

4 Disability, Disability Studies and the Academy
COLIN BARNES

Since the emergence of the disabled people's movement in the latter half of the twentieth century there has been a steady growth of interest in disability issues amongst social scientists in universities and colleges, referred to collectively as the 'academy', throughout the world. This has generated a radical critique of conventional thinking and research on disability related issues (see Chapter 7), a large and expanding literature from various 'social science' perspectives, and the emergence of a new interdisciplinary area of enquiry generally known as Disability Studies (Barton and Oliver, 1997; Davis, 1995: Shakespeare, 1998; Albrecht et al., 2001; Barnes et al., 2002). Hitherto, disabled activists and scholars have played a crucial role in shaping contemporary understandings of disability and this has resulted in an ongoing and sometimes uneasy relationship between the disabled people's movement and the academy. This chapter will trace the origins of these developments with particular reference to the UK and, to a lesser degree, the USA.

The re-interpretation of disability

Before the 1980s, academic interest in disability within the social sciences was confined almost exclusively to conventional individualistic explanations linked in one way or another to medicine and medical concerns. An important early example is found in the work of the American sociologist Talcott Parsons. Bowing to established wisdom, Parsons (1951) viewed short- and long-term 'sickness' as a deviation form the 'normal' state of being and, therefore, a threat to economic and social activity or functioning. For Parsons, illness, and by implication, impairment is more than a biological condition; it is a social status and those cast in what he termed the 'sick role' have certain rights and responsibilities. Thus, 'sick people' are relieved of the usual roles and responsibilities associated with non-disabled lifestyles. In return they are required to view their current status as unacceptable. To this end they are expected to seek help from those charged with the responsibility for fulfilling this task: namely, medical and rehabilitation professionals. Although Parsons' work has attracted widespread criticism from practitioners and activists alike, mainly for its deterministic tendencies, it has, nonetheless, had an enormous impact on the social sciences and professional thinking in universities and colleges throughout the world.

Following Parsons, the analysis of social responses to impairment or disability was mainly the preserve of academics concerned primarily with the reaction to and management of ascribed social deviance. A notable example is Goffman's (1968) account of the interactions between 'normal' and 'abnormal' people. However, many writers paid particular attention to the social construction of 'mental illness'. A psychoanalyst, Thomas Szasz (1961), went so far as to question the very existence of mental illness, the validity of psychiatry as a legitimate medical discipline, and the rehabilitation potential of psychiatric hospitals. He argued that the concept 'mental illness' represents little more than a mythical substitute for the various problems associated with modern living. Such ideas were given further impetus by the writings of the French philosopher Foucault who argued that mental illness, and other forms of ascribed social deviance, are social constructs generated by an increasingly dominant and moralistic social order (Foucault, 1975). Foucault's work has been particularly influential in a variety of fields including disability studies (Corker and Shakespeare, 2002).

Within sociology, interest in the general area of disability increased steadily during the late 1960s and 1970s with publications by Scott (1969), Albrecht (1976), Blaxter (1976) and Townsend (1979). Although each of these studies to varying degrees drew attention to the various economic and social consequences of the ascription of a disabled identity, the causes of disabled people's individual and collective disadvantage remained untheorised and unchallenged.

The challenge to established views came not from within universities and colleges, but from disabled people themselves (see Chapters 1 and 2). British activists were especially important as they produced a radical new interpretation of disability that generated a new approach to disability practice and theory, commonly referred to as the social model of disability. Grass roots organisations controlled and run by disabled people, such as the UPIAS and the Liberation Network of People with Disabilities, provided the fertile ground for disabled activists to explore and reconfigure the concept 'disability'. These 'organic intellectuals' (Gramsci, 1971) produced an impressive body of work, the impact of which is only now being fully appreciated. Key texts include Hunt (1966), UPIAS (1976), Finkelstein (1980), Sutherland (1981) and Oliver (1983, 1990).

Drawing on both personal experience and sociological insights, this body of work posed a direct challenge to conventional thinking and practice on disability. Moreover, although the emergence of the social model of disability provided the 'big idea' (Hasler, 1993) for the mobilisation of disabled people, it was slow to find acceptance in universities and colleges in the UK.

The coming of disability studies

Until the 1990s, studies of 'disability' in British universities were typically located within a narrow range of academic disciplines including medicine, psychology, special educational needs and social work. Sociologists, despite their traditional focus on social inequality, were content to situate the analysis of disability within medical sociology and sociologies of health and illness perspectives. These are characterised by a largely atheoretical tradition of socio-medical research driven by practical medical and health service concerns, and interactionist and phenomenological perspectives. The outcome is an extensive literature that documents the extent and nature of chronic illness, its consequences for daily living and its impact on social relationships, and the sense of self and identity (Williams, 1998).

Consequently, Britain's first disability studies course was not developed within a conventional university setting. It was conceived and developed by an interdisciplinary team at the Open University (OU) in 1975. A key figure in the production of this programme was a disability activist, Vic Finkelstein. The OU was an appropriate location for this new course as its emergence signalled a new and innovative approach to university education. In its first year the course recruited over 1,200 students, including professionals, voluntary workers and disabled people. As disabled people were increasingly involved in the production of teaching and learning materials, the course was updated twice before its abolition in 1994. The final version of the scheme was re-titled 'The Disabling Society' to reflect its wider content.

Similarly, the social dynamics of the disability experience were introduced on to the mainstream academic agenda in the USA and Canada in the 1970s. Again the link between disability activism and higher education was the key to this development. Disability rights advocates and scholars concerned with disability and related issues came together at several conferences and realised that they shared similar interests and goals. A major catalyst for bringing these two groups together was the 1977 'White House Conference on Handicapped Individuals' which attracted over 3,000 delegates. As in the UK, these early activities generated a small but significant body of work primarily within the field of medical sociology. Important early examples include Bowe (1978) and Zola (1982). These and other studies drew attention to the disabling tendencies of American rehabilitation programmes and American society generally.

However, in contrast to the British approach, this literature failed to recognise the theoretical and analytical importance of the distinction between the biological (impairment) and the social (disability). Arguments for inclusion are couched within US traditions of minority group politics and individual consumer rights. These approaches can have only a limited utility in a capitalist society characterised by vast inequalities of wealth and power such as the USA (Russell, 1998; Frances and Silvers, 2001). However, over recent years a more radical perspective has appeared, spearheaded by a small but vocal band of mainly disabled writers working in the humanities and cultural studies fields in universities in North America, Australia and New Zealand. This has resulted in the demand for a more critical interdisciplinary approach to the study of disability more in keeping with advocates of social model perspectives (Linton, 1998).

All of this has stimulated important debates about the role and development of the social model of disability within university settings and also the relations between disability activists and professional academics. This is because, historically, universities have been a predominantly reactionary rather than a truly radical political force for social change (Delanty, 2001). Furthermore, the coming of the social model and, subsequently, the development of disability studies poses a direct challenge to the kind of orthodox thinking hitherto generated in large part by scholars working in the established disciplines of medicine, sociology and psychology (Barnes et al., 2002).

The future of disability studies

When thinking about the links between universities and the disabled people's movement it is useful to consider three distinct strategies. These are the 'outside out', 'inside out' and 'outside in' approaches. The 'outside out' position is the one favoured by most professional 'experts' and academics. It is rooted in the positivist traditions of the nineteenth century and is clustered around the idea that the social world can only be properly understood through the application of the principles of rational thought, the natural sciences, and the pursuit of 'objective' knowledge (Giddens, 2001). Since this perspective is widely regarded as value free and politically neutral, it is the one that has sustained universities and colleges and those who work in them for most of their existence (Barnes et al., 2002).

However, over recent years this perspective has increasingly been called into question. This is almost certainly due to the surfeit of information generated from various sources outside universities (Castells, 1996; Delanty, 2001) and the growing use and misuse of social statistics by politicians and the media. One outcome of this situation is that some universities and subject disciplines are now striving to include lay experiences in their research. Yet in many ways this amended or 'realist' approach still situates the professional scholar as arbiter of everything that counts for acceptable and meaningful knowledge. For instance, Dyson (1999) refers to himself as a 'professional intellectual' rather than a positivist. He has recently argued that the academy has a role to play as 'instigator and sustainer of rational debate' between academic and lay communities.

Clearly then the 'outside out' perspective, largely because of its claims to value freedom and political neutrality, does not sit easily with the radical politics of oppressed groups. Moreover, by attempting to incorporate and re-interpret lay knowledge and experiences, academics and researchers are in serious danger of doing what they have always done; that is, colonising and reproducing in a less radical form the work, ideas and experience of others. Unsurprisingly, therefore there is a general concern about the role of academics amongst Britain's disabled people's movement (Finkelstein, 1996; Thomas, 2002). Consequently, attempts to build meaningful working and fruitful relationships between the academy and disabled people and their organisations based on the 'outside out' position should be treated with the utmost caution (Barnes et al., 2002).

The foundations for the 'inside out' approach can be found in the interactionist, phenomenological traditions favoured by medical sociologists mentioned above and, later, the women's movement. Proponents argue that the direct experience of a particular phenomenon is necessary not only to facilitate a thorough and meaningful analysis and understanding, but also to engender an appropriate political response. However, this can easily lead to the claim that only those with direct experience of a phenomenon are entitled to analyse and discuss it. Hence, only women can articulate about women's experiences, black people the black experience, disabled people the disability experience and so on.

Whilst there is no consensus on this particular issue amongst academics within universities, the same can also be said of the UK's disabled people's movement. In the UK's disabled people's movement some groups, including members and staff, are exclusive to disabled people. Some organisations employ non-disabled people as support workers. Others adopt a more inclusive approach and have 'non-disabled allies' in their membership and in their workforce (Morgan et al., 2001).

It is evident, therefore, that the 'inside out' approach is potentially exclusionary and reductionist. Because of the heterogeneity of the disabled population and the fact that not only people with ascribed impairments encounter oppression, exclusivity can easily lead to the marginalisation of both groups and individuals. Such a position is frequently politically and academically counter-productive. Furthermore, as noted earlier, the 'inside out' position ultimately reduces experience to the individual level and, therefore, negates the production of meaningful analyses and policy recommendations based on collective insights. Finally, studies based entirely on personal experience often read as little more than special pleading and are characteristic of what the disabled activist Hunt (1966, ix) termed 'sentimental biography'.

The alternative, the 'outside in' position, emerged from within the disabled people's movement partly in response to the ways in which experiential accounts have historically been individualised and/or medicalised by social scientists. Advocates do not deny the significance of direct experience but maintain that by itself it is not enough. Disabled people's experiences of disabling barriers (inside) must be located within a political analysis (outside) of why these barriers exist and how to eradicate them (Finkelstein, 1996). To facilitate such accounts there have to be strong working links between the disabled people's movement and the academy, since the former can provide the experience and the latter a coherent and scholarly political analysis. What is at stake, therefore, is not whether such a relationship should be constituted, but how it should be constructed and maintained (Barnes et al., 2002).

Critics have suggested, however, that this is an essentially masculine account that undermines the views of the women's movement and advocates of the 'personal is political' standpoint. Thomas (2002) suggests that the most appropriate solution to this problem is for the analysts to write themselves into the analysis; namely, to be explicit about the relationship between subjective experience (inside) and objective action in the wider world (outside). Some disabled scholars have gone further and argued that this approach is based on what they consider an outmoded ideology: namely, the social model of disability that is no longer tenable in the postmodern world of the twenty-first century and, therefore, in need of revision (Shakespeare and Watson, 2002).

Despite these reservations, each of these authors would agree that progress either within a conventional social model framework or a newer revised version is only possible through the ongoing and meaningful interaction between disabled people, their organisations, and academics and researchers working in the disability field.

Conclusion

This chapter has demonstrated how the re-interpretation of disability by disabled activists during the 1970s has had an important impact on the perceptions and analysis of disability within universities and colleges in the UK and the USA. Although slow to become established, this approach has attracted considerable attention in universities over recent years. Whilst this is to be welcomed as it signifies a growing recognition of the importance of the issues, it should also be treated with some caution. Historically, by their failure to challenge orthodox wisdom on the problems encountered by people with ascribed impairments, academics have been part of the problem rather than the solution. By its very nature academic activity has a tendency to complicate that which need not necessarily be complicated. There is little doubt, therefore, that if the links between disabled people's organisations and universities and colleges are to continue to be mutually beneficial, then academics and researchers must be actively involved with them on a continuous basis. Failure to do so will almost certainly result in the systematic dilution and inevitable neutralisation of the disability studies agenda. This is the very opposite of what is needed.

References

Albrecht, G.L. (ed.) (1976) *The Sociology of Physical Disability and Rehabilitation*. Pittsburgh, PA: The University of Pittsburgh Press.

Albrecht, G.L., Seelman, K.D. and Bury, M. (eds) (2001) *Handbook fo Disability Studies*. London: Sage.

Barnes, C., Oliver, M. and Barton, L. (eds) (2002) *Disability Studies Today*. Cambridge: Polity Press.

Barton, L. and Oliver, M. (eds) (1997) *Disability Studies: Past, Present and Future*. Leeds: The Disability Press.

Blaxter, M. (1976) *The Meaning of Disability*. London: Heinemann.

Bowe, F. (1978) *Handicapping America*. New York, NY: Harper and Row.

Castells, M. (1996) *The Information Age: Economy, Society and Culture. Volume 1: The Rise of the Network Society*. Malden, MA: Blackwell.

Corker, M. and Shakespeare, T. (eds) (2002) *Disability/Postmodernity*. London: Continuum.

Davis, L.D. (1995) *Enforcing Normalcy: Disability, Deafness and the Body*. London: Verso.

Delanty, G. (2001) *The University in the Knowledge Society*. Buckingham: Open University Press.

Dyson, A. (1999) 'Professional Intellectuals from Powerful Groups: Wrong From the Start', in P. Clough and L. Barton (eds), *Articulating with Difficulty: Research Voices in Inclusive Education*. London: Paul Chapman Publishing.

Finkelstein, V. (1980) *Attitudes and Disabled People*. New York, NY: World Rehabilitation Fund.

Finkelstein, V. (1996) 'Outside, inside out', *Coalition*, April: 30–36.

Foucault, M. (1975) *The Birth of the Clinic: An Archaeology of Medical Perception*. New York, NY: Vantage.

Frances, P. and Silvers, A. (eds) (2001) *Americans with Disabilities: Exploring Implications of the Law for Individuals and Institutions*. London: Routledge.

Giddens, A. (2001) *Sociology, fourth edition*. Cambridge: Polity Press.

Goffman, E. (1968) *Stigma: Notes on the Management of a Spoiled Identity*. Englewood Cliffs, NJ: Prentice Hall.

Gramsci, A. (1971) *Selections from the Prison Notebooks*. London: New Left.

Hasler, F. (1993) 'Developments in the Disabled People's Movement', in J. Swain, V. Finkelstein, S. French and M. Oliver (eds), *Disabling Barriers – Enabling Environments*. London: Sage in association with the Open University.

Hunt, P. (ed.) (1966) *Stigma: The Experience of Disability*. London: Geoffrey Chapman.

Linton, S. (1998) *Claiming Disability*. New York, NY: New York University Press.

Morgan, H., Barnes, C. and Mercer, G. (2001) *Creating Independent Futures: An Evaluation of Services Led by Disabled People. Stage Three Report*. Leeds: The Disability Press.

Oliver, M. (1990) *The Politics of Disablement*. Basingstoke: Macmillan.

Oliver, M. (1983) *Social Work with Disabled People*. Tavistock: Macmillan.

Parsons, T. (1951) *The Social System*. New York: Free Press.

Russell, M. (1998) *Beyond Ramps: Disability at the End of the Social Contract*. Monroe, ME: Common Courage.

Scott, R. (1969) *The Making of Blind Men*. London: Sage.

Shakespeare, T. (ed.) (1998) *The Disability Studies Reader*. London: Cassell.

Shakespeare, T. and Watson, N. (2002) 'The Social Model of Disability: An Outmoded Ideology', *Research in Social Science and Disability*, 2: 9–28.

Sutherland, A.T. (1981) *Disabled We Stand*. London: Souvenir.

Szasz, T.S. (1961) *The Myth of Mental Illness: Foundations of a Theory of Personal Conduct*. New York, NY: Dell.

Thomas, C. (2002) 'Disability Theory: Key Ideas, Issues and Thinkers', in C. Barnes, M. Oliver and L. Barton (eds), *Disability Studies Today*. Cambridge: Polity Press.

Townsend, P. (1979) *Poverty in the United Kingdom*. Harmondsworth: Penguin.

UPIAS (1976) *Fundamental Principles of Disability*. London: Union of Physically Impaired Against Segregation.

Williams, G. (1998) 'The Sociology of Disability: towards a materialist phenomenology', in T. Shakespeare (ed.), *The Disability Studies Reader*. London: Cassell.

Zola, L.K. (1982) *Missing Pieces: A Chronicle of Living with a Disability*. Philadelphia, PA: Temple University Press.

5 Whose Tragedy? Towards a Personal Non-tragedy View of Disability
SALLY FRENCH AND JOHN SWAIN

Our aim in this chapter is to address and challenge what Oliver calls the 'grand theory' of disability, that is, again in his words, 'the personal tragedy theory of disability' (1990: 1). In doing so we are building on our previous work (Swain and French, 2000; French and Swain, 2002) and on the developing politics of personal identity which reinterprets the experience of disability in positive rather than negative terms (Morris, 1991).

In the personal tragedy theory, disability, or rather impairment – which is equated with disability – is thought to strike individuals at random, causing suffering and blighting lives. This view is so dominant, so prevalent and so infused throughout media representations, language, cultural beliefs, research, policy and professional practice that we can only hope to cover a few illustrative examples. In relation to language, for instance, 'suffering/ sufferer' is perhaps the most widely used terminology in tragedy discourses to characterise the experience of disability. In the media, personal tragedy underlies representations of disability in numerous ways for different dramatic purposes, such as being bitter and twisted (for example, the character Potter in *It's a Wonderful Life*) or pathetic (for example, Tiny Tim in *A Christmas Carol*). Perhaps the most intrusive, violating and invalidating experiences, for disabled people, emanate from the policies, practices and interventions which are justified and rationalised by the personal tragedy view of disability and impairment. The tragedy is to be avoided, eradicated or 'normalised' by all possible means. Such are the negative presumptions held about impairment and disability, that the abortion of impaired foetuses is barely challenged (Parens and Asch, 2000) and compulsory sterilisation of people with learning difficulties was widely practised in many parts of the world (Park and Radford, 1999). The erroneous idea that disabled people cannot be happy, or enjoy an adequate quality of life, lies at the heart of this response. The disabled person's problems are perceived to result from impairment rather than the failure of society to meet that person's needs in terms of appropriate human help, accessibility and inclusion. There is an assumption that disabled people want to be 'normal', although this is rarely voiced by disabled people themselves who know that disability is a major part of their identity (Mason, 2000). Disabled people are subjected to many disabling expectations, for example, to be 'independent', 'normal', to 'adjust' and 'accept' their situation. It is these expectations that can cause unhappiness: rather than the impairment itself (French, 1994).

There are a number of different possible explanations of this personal tragedy theory of disability. It is sometimes thought to reflect a deep irrational fear of non-disabled people's own mortality (Shakespeare, 1994). A second form of explanation refers to dominant social values and ideologies, particularly through the association of disability with dependence and abnormality (Oliver, 1993). There is a third type of explanation, however, which suggests that the personal tragedy perspective has a rational, cognitive basis constructed through experiences in disablist social contexts. Unlike the divide between people of different genders or different races, non-disabled people daily experience the possibility of becoming impaired and thus disabled (the causal link being integral to the tragedy model). It can be argued that so-called 'irrational fears' have a rational basis in a disablist society. To become visually impaired, for instance, may be a personal tragedy for a sighted person whose life is based around being sighted, who lacks knowledge of the experiences of people with visual impairments, whose identity is founded on being sighted, and who has been subjected to a daily diet of the personal tragedy model of visual impairment. Thus, the personal tragedy view of impairment and disability is ingrained in the social identity of non-disabled people. Non-disabled identity, as other identities, has meaning in relation to and constructs the identity of others. To be non-disabled is to be 'not one of those'. The problem for disabled people is that the tragedy model of disability and impairment is not just significant for non-disabled people in understanding themselves and their own lives; it is extrapolated to assumptions about disabled people and their lives.

From this point of view, too, the adherence to a personal tragedy model by disabled people themselves also has a rational basis. For a non-disabled person whose life is constructed on the basis of being non-disabled, the onset of impairment and disability can be experienced as a tragedy, perhaps amplified if it is associated with the trauma of illness or accident. Even in affirming the social model, Oliver and Sapey state:

> Some disabled people do experience the onset of impairment as a personal tragedy which, while not invalidating the argument that they are being excluded from a range of activities by a disabling environment, does mean it would be inappropriate to deny that impairment can be experienced in this way. (1999: 26)

Furthermore, a personal tragedy view can have a rational basis for people with congenital impairments, living through the daily barrage from non-disabled people, experts, parents and the media invalidating themselves and their experiences. Indeed, within the disabling context we have outlined here, the expression of a non-tragedy view by disabled people flies in the face of dominant values and ideologies. It is likely to be denied as unrealistic or a lack of 'acceptance', distorted as an expression of bravery or compensation, or simply ignored. The tragedy model is in itself disabling. It denies disabled people's experiences of a disabling society, their enjoyment of life, and their identity and self-awareness as disabled people.

In the next section of this chapter we demonstrate, by reviewing the literature and drawing upon research, that being disabled need not be a tragedy for disabled people, but may, on the contrary, enhance life or provide a lifestyle of equal satisfaction and worth.

Who needs cure and normality?

A personal non-tragedy view of impairment and disability, similar to a tragedy view, can take many forms and be expressed in a variety of ways. Perhaps at the most basic level, impairment is simply a 'fact of life'. A participant in Watson's research typifies this:

> Tommy argued that 'I don't wake up and look at my wheelchair and think "shit, I've got to spend another day in that", I just get up and get on with it'. (2002: 519)

Furthermore, from the documented viewpoint of disabled people, far from being tragic, being disabled can have benefits. Disabled people sometimes find that they can escape class oppression, abuse or neglect by virtue of being disabled. Peter Holmes, who attended an 'open air' school in the 1950s, states:

> 'My first impression at the age of seven or eight years was its vastness. Previously all I had ever seen was factories, terraced houses and bomb sites. To a child like myself it was magnificent. The countryside and woods were overwhelming and very beautiful and the air so sweet ... We would walk through the woods and visit farms seeing animals and flowers and trees that most of us had only ever seen in books.' (Wilmott and Saul, 1998: 257)

A further way in which disability and impairment may be perceived as beneficial to some disabled people is that society's expectations and requirements are more difficult to satisfy and may, therefore, be avoided. A disabled man quoted by Shakespeare et al. said, 'I am never going to conform to society's requirements and I am thrilled because I am blissfully released from all that crap. That's the liberation of disfigurement' (1996: 81). If, for example, a person has sufficient resources, the ability to give up paid employment and pursue personal interests and hobbies following an accident, may enhance that person's life. Similarly, young people (especially women) are frequently under pressure to form heterosexual relationships, to marry and have children. These expectations are not applied so readily to disabled people who may, indeed, be viewed as asexual. Although this has the potential to cause a great deal of anxiety and pain, some disabled people can see its advantages. Vasey states:

> We are not usually snapped up in the flower of youth for our domestic and child-rearing skills, or for our decorative value, so we do not have to spend years disentangling ourselves from wearisome relationships as is the case with many non-disabled women. (1992: 74)

Though it is more difficult for disabled people to form sexual relationships because of disabling barriers, when they do any limitations imposed by impairment may, paradoxically, lead to advantages. Shakespeare et al., who interviewed disabled people about their sexuality and sexual relationships, state:

> Because disabled people were not able to make love in a straightforward manner, or in a conventional position, they were impelled to experiment and enjoyed a more interesting sexual life as a result. (1996: 106)

For some people who become disabled their lives change completely, though not necessarily for the worse. A woman quoted by Morris states:

> 'As a result of becoming paralysed life has changed completely. Before my accident it seemed as if I was set to spend the rest of my life as a religious sister, but I was not solemnly professed so was not accepted back into the order. Instead I am now very happily married with a home of my own.' (1989: 120)

The experience of disability may also give disabled people a heightened understanding of the oppressions other people endure. French (1991) found that most of the 45 visually disabled physiotherapists she interviewed could find advantages to being disabled in their work. An important advantage was their perceived ability to understand and empathise with their patients and clients. Others believed that their visual disability gave rise to a more balanced and equal relationship with their patients, that patients were less embarrassed (for example, about undressing) and that they enjoyed the extra physical contact the visually disabled physiotherapist was obliged to make. One person said:

> 'Even as students when we had the Colles fracture class all round in a circle, they used to love us treating them because we had to go round and touch them. They preferred us to the sighted physios. I'm convinced that a lot of people think we are better.' (1991: 4)

Other disabled people believe that disability has given them a different and beneficial outlook on life. Tom, whose impairment is linked to the drug thalidomide, states:

> 'Life is very good ... being born with no arms has opened up so many different things that I would never have done. My motto is 'in life try everything'. I wouldn't have that philosophy if I'd been born with arms.' (BBC Radio 4, 2002).

As for non-disabled people, the quality of life of disabled people depends on whether they can achieve a lifestyle of their choice. This in turn depends on their personal resources, the resources within society and their own unique situation. Nevertheless, the writings of disabled people demonstrate that being born with an impairment or becoming disabled in later life can give a perspective on life which is both interesting and affirmative and can be used positively. This is not generally recognised by non-disabled people, as Ian Basnett, a doctor who became disabled, explains:

> 'I was horrified by what I imagined to be the experience of disabled people, which I encountered in my practice. Now 15 years after becoming disabled, I find myself completely at home with the concept, of effectively being me! ... Now I know that my assessment of the potential quality of life of severely disabled people was clearly flawed.' (Basnett, 2001: 453)

From tragedy to identity

In recognising a positive view of disability, it is essential that this is set in the context of the social model of disability and the oppression and discrimination faced by disabled people. Our argument is that, even in a disabling society, disabled people can directly challenge the personal tragedy theory of disability. Phillipe summarises a non-tragedy view succinctly:

> I just can't imagine becoming hearing, I'd need a psychiatrist, I'd need a speech therapist, I'd need some new friends, I'd lose all my old friends, I'd lose my job. I wouldn't be here lecturing. It really hits hearing people that a deaf person doesn't want to become hearing. I am what I am! (Phillipe in Shakespeare et al., 1996: 184)

These perceptions of impairment are by no means confined to the disabled people of today. Writing in the early nineteenth century, Husson states:

> I have just reached my twenty second year, and I still don't remember ever forming a single regret concerning the loss of my eyes, a loss that seems to me to be of little importance ... people who see tell me 'You don't have the slightest understanding of treasures you have never known.' I would like to believe in the justice of this reasoning which, however, does nothing to persuade me that I am unhappy. (2001: 16)

Nor are they confined to people with physical and sensory impairments. Susan Wendell and Liane Holliday Willey state:

> ... I cannot wish that I had never contracted ME, because it has made me a different person, a person I am glad to be, would not want to have missed being, and could not relinquish even if I were 'cured'. (Wendell, 1996: 83)

> I do not wish for a cure to Asperger's Syndrome. What I wish for is a cure for the common ill that pervades too many lives, the ill that makes people compare themselves to a normal that is measured in terms of perfect and absolute standards, most of which are impossible for anyone to reach. (Holliday Willey, 1999: 96)

Nobody can predict the amount of tragedy or happiness a person will experience in life and yet people feel confident to make such predictions about disabled people. The inherent assumption is that disabled people want to be other than as they are, even though this would mean a rejection of identity. The notion of identity broadens the personal to the political, moves from the 'I' to the 'we'. Disabled people, encouraged by the Disabled People's Movement, are creating positive images of themselves and are demanding the right to be the way they are – to be equal but different. Joan Tollifson, Michlene Mason and Colin Cameron, three disabled people, explain this position:

> After a lifetime of isolating myself from other disabled people, it was an awakening to be surrounded by them. For the first time in my life, I felt like a real adult member of the human community. Finally identifying myself as a disabled person was an enormous healing. It was about recognising, allowing and acknowledging something I had been trying to deny and finding that disability does not equal ugliness, incompetence and misery. (Tollifson, 1997: 107)

> A few years later, at my special school, I remember one of the care staff loudly telling me that I should never give up hope because one day doctors would find a cure for my affliction, and I loudly told her that I did not want to be 'cured'. I remember this incident because of the utter disbelief this statement caused amongst all the non-disabled people present, and the delight this statement caused amongst my disabled friends. The school decided that I had 'The Wrong Attitude' and that I should indeed go to Lourdes so that Jesus, the Virgin Mary and St. Bernadette could sort me out.' (Mason, 2000: 8)

> We are who we are as people with impairments, and might actually feel comfortable with our lives if it wasn't for all those interfering busybodies who feel that it is

their responsibility to feel sorry for us, or to find cures for us, or to manage our lives for us, or to harry us in order to make us something we are not, i.e. 'normal.' (Tyneside Disability Arts, 1999: 35)

Whose tragedy? For many disabled people the tragedy view of disability is in itself disabling. It denies their experiences of a disabling society, their enjoyment of life, and even their identity and self-awareness as disabled people. The affirmation of positive identity is both collective and individual. Disabled identity, as non-disabled identity, has meaning in relation to and constructs the identity of others. To be disabled is to be 'not one of those'. The affirmation of positive identity challenges the tyranny of the personal tragedy theory of disability and impairment.

References

Basnett, I. (2001) 'Health Care Professionals and Their Attitudes Towards Decisions Affecting Disabled People', in G.A. Albrecht, K.D. Seelman and M. Bury (eds), *Handbook of Disability Studies*. London: Sage.

BBC Radio 4 (2002) *Archive Hour* June 2002.

French, S. (1991) 'The Advantages of Visual Impairment: Some physiotherapists' views', *New Beacon*, 75 (872): 1–6.

French, S. (1994) 'The Disabled Role', in S. French (ed.), *One Equal Terms: Working with Disabled People*. Oxford: Butterworth-Heinemann.

French, S. and Swain, J. (2002) 'Across the disability divide: whose tragedy?', in K.W.M. Fulford, D.L. Dickenson and T.H. Murray (eds), *Healthcare Ethics and Human Values: An Introductory Text with Readings and Case Studies*. Oxford: Blackwell.

Holliday Willey, L. (1999) *Pretending to be Normal: Living with Asperger's Syndrome*. London: Jessica Kingsley.

Husson, T. (2001) *Reflections: The Life and Writings of a Young Blind Woman in Post-revolutionary France*. New York, NY: New York University Press.

Mason, M. (2000) *Incurably Human*. London: Working Press.

Morris, J. (1989) *Able Lives: Women's Experience of Paralysis*. London: The Women's Press.

Morris, J. (1991) *Pride Against Prejudice*. London: The Women's Press.

Oliver, M. (1990) *The Politics of Disablement*. Basingstoke: Macmillan.

Oliver, M. (1993) 'Disability and dependency: A creation of industrial societies?', in J. Swain, V. Finkelstein, S. French and M. Oliver (eds), *Disabling Barriers – Enabling Environments*. London: Sage.

Oliver, M. and Sapey, B. (1999) *Social Work with Disabled People, second edition*. London: Macmillan.

Parens, E. and Asch, A. (eds) (2000) *Prenatal Testing and Disability Rights*. Washington, DC: Georgetown University Press.

Park, D.C. and Radford, J.P. (1999) 'From the Case Files: Reconstructing a History of Involuntary Sterilisation', *Disability and Society*, 13 (3): 317–42.

Shakespeare, T.W. (1994) 'Cultural representation of disabled people: Dustbins for disavowal?', *Disability and Society*, 9 (3): 283–99.

Shakespeare, T., Gillespie-Sells, K. and Davies, D. (1996) *The Sexual Politics of Disability*. London: Cassell.

Swain, J. and French, S. (2000) 'Towards an affirmative model of disability', *Disability and Society*, 15 (4): 569–82.

Tollifson, J. (1997) 'Imperfection is a Beautiful Thing: On disability and meditation', in K. Fries (ed.), *Staring Back: The Disability Experiences from the Inside Out*. New York, NY: Penguin Putnam.

Tyneside Disability Arts (1999) *Transgressions*. Wallsend: TDA.

Vasey, S. (1992) 'Disability Culture: It's a way of life', in R. Rieser and M. Mason (eds), *Disability Equality in the Classroom: A Human Rights Issue*. London: Disability Equality in Education.

Watson, N. (2002) 'Well, I know it is going to sound very strange to you, but I don't see myself as a disabled person: identity and disability', *Disability and Society*, 17 (5): 509–27.

Wendell, S. (1996) *The Rejected Body: Feminist Philosophical Perspectives on Disability*. London: Routledge.

Wilmott, F. and Saul, P. (1998) *A Breath of Fresh Air: Birmingham's Open Air Schools 1911–1970*. Chichester: Phillimore.

6 Dependence, Independence and Normality
COLIN GOBLE

In this chapter I will look at issues of dependence and independence, and their link with the concept of normality. After briefly discussing the historical development of these ideas in relation to disability, I will explore how they have been shaped by professional thinking and practice in services for disabled people. I will then look at alternative ideas developed by disabled people themselves. Throughout, I will make particular reference to people with intellectual impairments who, in my view, continue to face the greatest challenges in attaining their rights in this area. I will conclude with a brief outline of the challenges facing, and faced by, this group in particular.

Ideas about dependence and independence have been central to views held about disability from various perspectives, including the sociological, economic, political, medical and professional. In the first edition of this book Oliver (1993) outlined how disability as we know it was created by an interweaving of these various elements in the emergence of industrialised society. The shift from a rural, agrarian and artisanal society to an urban industrial environment, with strict new rules about time and the speed of production, created a new and often hostile working and social environment for people with physical, sensory and intellectual impairments. They often became economically and socially marginalised as, in a wage, rather than a subsistence-based economy, they became burdensome to families in which, in the previous social and economic era, they had found at least some level of integration and sustenance. The political response to this marginalisation was to 'institutionalise' provision for 'the disabled', first in the workhouse and later in more specialist institutions, such as schools for the deaf or blind, or 'colonies' for the feeble-minded and mentally defective. In these isolated, and often closed and authoritarian worlds, inmates were socialised into a view of themselves as sick, helpless, inferior and in need of help and care to survive. Thus the circle was closed, and many disabled people themselves completed the perception of disability as a 'tragic' problem, internal to the affected individual, in their internalisation of that view.

It was Oliver's argument, in that 1993 publication, that the key to understanding how and why this marginalisation happened lay in the way in which disabled people were made dependent in industrial society. This view is only partially correct, however. Whilst new forms of dependency were indeed forged in the shift from pre-industrial to industrialised society, it is important to bear in mind that few disabled people would ever have been independent in any sense in the pre-existing social and economic context. The significance of what occurred in the shift to industrialisation wasn't the loss of independence, and the creation of dependency, so much as the rise of an ideological context in which being dependent on others came to be seen as problematic in ways it had not been before. The rise of capitalism broke down pre-existing systems of solidarity and inter-dependence that had sustained many disabled people in wider society, even if it was often in devalued roles. The loss of those systems and relationships, their replacement with institutionalised and professionalised systems of 'care', steeped in a medicalised conception of disability which equated it with sickness and illness, reshaped the situation of disabled people in the social upheaval of the industrial revolution.

Such is the legacy of the historical creation of disability in modern industrial societies. It is a legacy that still bears heavily on modern day provision of services and support for disabled people in the UK, despite recent shifts from institutionalised to 'community care'. Indeed, one of the main lessons of the first decade of community care policy in my own field of services for people with learning difficulties, is that it is every bit as possible to have institutionalised regimes and practices dominant in small scale community-based settings as it was in the old mental handicap hospitals. Institutions are made as much of thoughts, beliefs and organisational practices as of bricks and mortar, despite the common use of the rhetoric of promoting independence and partnership that underpins much community care provision. I will now explore some of the reasons why this is so, before going on to look at the situation of people with learning difficulties whose quality of life is, to a greater extent perhaps than any other identifiable group of disabled people, affected by such issues.

A professional conception of independence

Professionals working in services for disabled people, doctors, nurses, social workers, teachers, therapists and so on, often use the promotion of independence as a central reference point for both theory and practice in their work. Morris (1998) illustrates how this has become the main rationale for professional interventions in disabled people's lives with the advent of community care in the UK, driven by wider health and welfare policy. Disabled people themselves have also placed issues of dependence and independence at the centre of their personal and collective political agendas, with the independent living movement being an illustration. However, as various writers have pointed out, the terms 'dependence' and 'independence' mean different things depending on what your conception of disability is (French, 1993; Oliver, 1993; Finkelstein and Stuart, 1996).

Health and welfare professionals usually work to a definition of disability, such as that of the International Classification of Impairments, Disabilities and Handicaps (ICIDH) adopted by the World Health Organisation (Wood, 1980), which focuses on functional deficits in the individual. From this perspective, which remains the dominant one in our society, disabled people are dependent because their bodies, senses or minds are somehow 'defective' and don't allow them to function independently. In short, they are 'not normal', and a return to normality, or some approximation of it, becomes the goal of rehabilitation practice. The role of professional support and services is to mitigate the effects of the functional deficits faced by disabled people in order to help them to achieve greater normality and personal functional independence.

Although there are variations, the general pattern of these professional interventions is as follows. The functional capacity, or more often incapacity, of the disabled person is assessed using scales and tools that measure their performance against 'normative' standards. Programmes are then drawn up which aim to reduce the gap between the performance of the disabled individual and the normative standard as far as possible. Success is achieved when the professional expert judges that the performance of the individual has moved significantly in the desired direction. The programme will focus on whatever the expert professional regards as the particular functional deficit that is most significant in preventing the person from achieving independent functioning. Thus, for a deaf child it might be to lip read, for a child with cerebral palsy it might focus on walking, for an elderly stroke patient it might focus on feeding himself or herself, and so on. The assumption is that the problem lies within the individual, and the response is technical intervention by skilled 'expert' professionals to help the person overcome it and return to an approximation of 'normality'.

Within this system the role of disabled people is to passively accept professional guidance and actively follow the programme, striving to achieve the highest level of functional independence and normality that they can. There is often subtle pressure placed on disabled people to be grateful for this caring attention and time devoted to them, and to conform to a passive sick role in order to be as little bother as possible to the busy, caring professionals. To step outside the parameters of this role is to risk being characterised as awkward and ungrateful, or even to invite further psycho-medical diagnosis, as in the judgement that the person is failing to adjust to his or her condition. In the learning disability field there is a particularly potent version of this psychologising of resistant and non-conformist behaviour in the classification of 'challenging behaviour'; a classification for which the response is often still institutionalisation and heavy usage of psycho-active medication.

Although it should be remembered that human service professionals often can, and do, work in alliance with disabled people to achieve emancipatory ends, it is clearly the case that many disabled people experience this professionalised approach to the issue of independence as irrelevant and oppressive (French and Swain, 2001).

Disabled people's conception of independence

Some groups of disabled people have challenged this professionalised conception of independence, and the broader socio-cultural view of disability which it reflects. They have based their approach to the dependence/independence issue on a fundamentally different definition of disability using a social model definition of disability, such as that adopted by Disabled People's International (DPI) in 1982, which redefines disability as a form of social oppression, separate and distinct from the issue of individual functional difficulty. They have argued that the dependency many people with impairments face is the creation of a disabilist society.

Brisenden (1998) has argued that the issue of the definition of disability has a direct bearing on how the issues of dependence and independence are conceived and responded to. A definition of disability such as that adopted by DPI (1982), for example, suggests that disabled people are forced into dependency on others, such as health and welfare professionals, by policies and social systems that segregate disabled people and deny them access to mainstream education, work, housing and other opportunities. To be independent, it is argued, disabled people need rights to access these things. The right to a mainstream education, for example, would help ensure that children with physical, sensory or intellectual impairments would still gain the chance to develop knowledge and skills that would help them gain access to employment, which would in turn allow them to support themselves financially. From this perspective then, independence is about rights, access and control rather than functional capacity.

Morris (1998) has argued that in our society the loss, or lack, of capacity in one or more areas of functioning often leads to the assumption that the individual is unable to exercise control over all other aspects of life as well. The independent living movement, pioneered by people with physical impairments, has, over the past two or three decades, thrown down a successful and fundamental challenge to this view by demonstrating that the presence of functional impairment need not, and should not, be used to undermine individual control and autonomy.

People with physical and sensory impairments have, however, largely shaped the social model critique of the individualised, biomedical model of disability and the dependence/independence issue. It has been difficult, but relatively straightforward for them to argue their case successfully because they are seen as able to exercise sound judgement and to speak with an articulate voice. For people with intellectual impairments the case has been much harder to make, however, partly because of the real difficulty they may have in articulating their situation, but also because, even when they do make their case, their voice is often ignored or severely devalued. Interestingly, and perhaps significantly, professionals working in alliance with people with intellectual impairments have often been at the forefront of attempts to challenge this devaluation. Usually, however, it is professions with relatively limited power in the medical and managerial dominated welfare state of the late twentieth/early twenty-first century, such as learning disability nurses, who have attempted this. Nonetheless, it does need to be remembered that professionals can and do sometimes work in alliance with, rather than in opposition to, disabled people pursuing emancipatory agendas (for example, Scott and Larcher, 2002).

Intellectual impairment and independence

For most people with intellectual impairments the issues relating to dependence and independence are no different than those outlined above for disabled people generally. They are disabled in much the same way as people with physical and sensory impairments, albeit by somewhat different disabling environments and practices. The answer to their disablement is much the same too, to establish legal rights to combat discrimination and prejudice, and to manipulate the environment to enable rather than disable. An example of environmental manipulation aimed at enabling people with intellectual impairments would be the simplification of language and use of alternative symbols and media to convey important information, such as legal information; a change that might, indeed, be welcomed by many people without intellectual impairments!

Some people with intellectual impairments face a much harder task in struggling to attain or maintain independence, in the sense of autonomous control over their lives and what happens to them, than other groups of disabled people. This is related to both the nature and site of their impairment. The reasons for this are partly cultural. The mind/brain is seen in Western culture as the seat of the autonomous self and individuality. This can be seen in conceptions of selfhood and identity promoted in much Western psychology, which both lays the foundations for the commonsense view of selfhood and identity prevalent in our society, and sets the standards against which 'aberrations from normality' are measured. In these conceptualisations the self is seen as self-contained, self-reliant, unique, separate, consistent and private. Such a view emphasises strongly the independence, autonomy and privacy of the individual (Wetherell and Maybin, 1997). To experience impairment of the mind/brain then is, in this culture at least, to be seen to lose all, or a critical part of the self, and the autonomy and independence that goes with it. The rights of people with intellectual impairments to hold, or to keep hold, of their property, money, freedom of movement, sexuality, and even their life itself, has constantly been, and continues to be, challenged through the courts and in public, political and philosophical debate. It is people with intellectual impairments who are most vulnerable, for instance, to utilitarian arguments for legalised infanticide and euthanasia. Eminent philosophers promote the argument that the likelihood that an infant will never become the self-sufficient, independent and autonomous individual so idealised in Western culture and society as reason enough to warrant killing him or her at or near birth (Kuhse and Singer, 2002).

At the same time intellectual impairment, when severe, profound and/or degenerative, does impact on individuals in ways which challenge the current thinking of us all about issues of dependence and independence. Even the disabled people's movement, not a place that people with intellectual impairments have always found very welcoming (Stevens, 2002), needs to seek ways to pursue rights, citizenship and enablement which are not necessarily built around the concept of personal independence. There is a need to develop and incorporate models which support those disabled people who are, because of the nature of their impairment as much as society's response to it, always going to be dependent on others for control and choice making, as well as physical aspects of day-to-day life.

It challenges human service professionals, workers, planners and commissioners, too, to find ways in which people with severe and profound intellectual impairments can be listened to, using behavioural and subtle communicative cues, in addition to, or instead of, conventional verbal or gestural forms of communication. Accepting and developing these modes of communication as forms of self-advocacy, and building in other sources and models of advocacy as a right, rather than an option, are potential strategies here.

Finally, it challenges society, and all concerned citizens, to seek ways and means by which the lives of people with severe or profound intellectual impairments can be valued and granted respect, even when autonomy and independence are severely limited or not possible. For this to happen we need to open ourselves to the possibility that it might be our accepted conceptions of selfhood, personhood and individuality that need to be changed or eliminated, not people with intellectual impairments. If we are to regard ourselves as truly civilised then we, as a society, surely need to look for ways of responding to our most vulnerable citizens other than by arguing for killing them at birth.

References

Brisenden, S. (1998) 'Independent living and the medical model of disability', in T. Shakespeare (ed.), *The Disability Reader: Social Science Perspectives.* London: Cassell. pp. 20–27.
DPI (1982) *Proceedings of the First World Congress.* Singapore: Disabled People's International.
Finkelstein, V. and Stuart, O. (1996) 'Developing new services', in G. Hales (ed.), *Beyond Disability: Towards an Enabling Society.* London: Sage/Open University. pp. 170–87.
French, S. (1993) 'What's so great about independence?', in J. Swain, V. Finkelstein, S. French and M. Oliver (eds), *Disabling Barriers – Enabling Environments* (1st edn). London: Sage/Open University. pp. 45–8.

French, S. and Swain, J. (2001) 'The relationship between disabled people and health and welfare professionals', in G.L. Albrecht, K.D. Seelman and M. Bury (eds), *The Handbook of Disability Studies*. London: Sage. pp. 734–53.

Kuhse, H. and Singer, P. (2002) 'Should all seriously disabled infants live?', in H. Kuhse (ed.), *Unsanctifying Human Life: Essays on Ethics*. Oxford: Blackwell. pp. 233–45.

Morris, J. (1998) 'Creating a space for absent voices: disabled women's experience of receiving assistance with daily living', in M. Allot and M. Robb (eds), *Understanding Health and Social Care: An Introductory Reader*. London: Sage/Open University. pp. 163–70.

Oliver, M. (1993) 'Disability and dependency: a creation of industrial societies?', in J. Swain, V. Finkelstein, S. French and M. Oliver (eds) *Disabling Barriers – Enabling Environments* (1st edn). London: Sage/Open University. pp. 49–60.

Scott, J. and Larcher, J. (2002) 'Advocacy with people with communication difficulties', in B. Gray and R. Jackson (eds), *Advocacy and Learning Disability*. London: Jessica Kingsley. pp. 170–87.

Stevens, S. (2002) 'Where did the disability movement go?', *Community Living*, 16 (1).

Wetherell, M. and Maybin, J. (1997) 'The distributed self: a social constructionist perspective', in R. Stevens (ed.), *Understanding the Self*. London: Sage/Open University. pp. 220–64.

Wood, P. (1980) *International Classification of Impairments, Disabilities and Handicaps*. Geneva: World Health Organisation.

7 Reflections on Doing Emancipatory Disability Research
COLIN BARNES

In 1992, Mike Oliver coined the phrase 'emancipatory disability research' to refer to a radical new approach to doing disability research. Subsequently much has been written about whether such an approach is a 'realistic goal' or an 'impossible dream' (Oliver, 1997). This chapter represents a personal reflection on some of the key issues arising from this debate. It is divided into two main sections. The first provides a brief introduction to the notion of emancipatory disability research. The second focuses on several key issues associated with this perspective. I will argue that the emancipatory research model has made an important contribution to the disability research agenda, and that in some respects it is no longer that far removed from other mainstream research agendas.

Emancipatory disability research?

Social scientists and sociologists in particular have been doing 'disability' research since at least the 1950s. There are studies dealing with 'doctor–patient' relations (Parsons, 1951), stigma (Goffman, 1968), institutional living (Miller and Gwynne, 1972) as well as large-scale surveys chronicling the numbers of disabled people in the general population (Martin et al., 1988). All of these have provided important insights into current thinking on disability and related issues.

The main problem with these and similar studies is that they are based on the orthodox view that impairments, whether physical, sensory or intellectual, are the main cause of disability and disadvantage. This began to change in the late 1960s and early 1970s with the emergence of the international disabled people's movement, the redefinition of disability by Britain's Union of the Physically Impaired Against Segregation (UPIAS), the emergence of the social model of disability, and an alternative approach to doing disability research known as 'emancipatory disability research'.

Moreover, during the 1980s, several researchers, mostly disabled, began to explore disabled people's individual and collective experiences to show how environmental and social forces disabled people with various forms of impairment (Oliver et al., 1988; Morris, 1989; Barnes, 1990). In 1989, the British Council of Disabled People (BCODP) – Britain's national umbrella for organisations controlled and run by disabled people – commissioned a large-scale study of the discrimination encountered by disabled people in Britain to support their campaign for anti-discrimination legislation (Barnes, 1991). All of this contributed to the thinking behind the emergence of the emancipatory disability research paradigm.

In 1991, the Joseph Rowntree Foundation (JRF) sponsored a series of seminars on researching disability that provided a forum for the development of this new approach. These events brought together disabled and non-disabled researchers working in the disability field and participants from research and disability organisations. One outcome of this initiative was a special issue of the international journal *Disability, Handicap and Society* (renamed *Disability and Society* in 1993) on researching disability (DHS, 1992). Inevitably, the appearance of the emancipatory disability research paradigm generated much debate within the research community, both in the UK and overseas (Albrecht et al., 2001).

This is because the emancipatory research agenda is about nothing less than the transformation of the material and social relations of research production. This means that in contrast to traditional approaches, disabled people and their organisations, rather than professional academics and researchers, should have control of the research process including project finance and the research agenda. In the early 1990s, such ideas seemed utopian to say the least. At that time the bulk of disability research was financed by large government sponsored agencies, such as the Department of Health (DoH). In many ways these bodies were dominated by traditional medical and academic interests and conventional assumptions about disability and disability related research.

As the decade drew to a close this began to change. Whilst the growing critique of traditional disability research from disabled activists and their organisations was undoubtedly a significant factor, this transformation is due to other factors too. Of note was the growing emphasis of market forces within universities and other research agencies, the increased use and misuse of research data by politicians, policy makers and the media, and the inevitable widespread disillusionment with social research amongst the general public. Today, most of the research projects dealing exclusively with disability and related issues in the UK are financed by charitable agencies and trusts, such as the JRF and National Lottery's Community Fund. Both these organisations have prioritised user-led concerns over those of the academy and professional researchers (Barnes, 2003).

Furthermore, over the last decade or so there have been several projects that, implicitly if not explicitly, conform to an emancipatory research agenda. Important early examples include: the BCODP research on discrimination and disabled people, mentioned earlier; Mike Oliver and Gerry Zarb's (1992) analysis of personal assistance schemes in Greenwich; subsequent BCODP research on media imagery (Barnes, 1992); and direct payments (Zarb and Nadash, 1994). Additionally, there is a growing emphasis on user participation, if not control, within the research programmes of the various UK research councils (see, for example, www.esrc.org.uk). Whilst these changes might not go as far as some might wish, and certainly their impact has yet to be comprehensively evaluated, they do mark something of a shift in the right direction.

Key issues in emancipatory disability research

Since 1992, there have been several attempts to identify the core characteristics of the emancipatory disability research model. These can be addressed under the following headings: accountability, the social model of disability, data collection and empowerment.

Accountability

Accountability to disabled people and their organisations is a key component of the emancipatory research model, but to be answerable to the entire disabled population is inconceivable. The label 'disabled' can be applied to almost anyone with ascribed impairment or impairments regardless of cause or severity. Hence, the potential disabled population is vast. It is also the case that for a variety of reasons, structural and interpersonal, many people with impairments do not consider themselves disabled or members of an oppressed group.

One solution to this concern is for researchers to be accountable to organisations controlled and run by disabled people themselves. The distinction between these and traditional organisations *for* disabled people run by mainly non-disabled professionals is, however, not always clear. To overcome this problem researchers must become involved with disability organisations on a long-term basis. In so doing they can become familiar with organisational structures, their goals, their controlling bodies, and procedures for accountability to members.

But this strategy poses problems for all researchers working within a market-led environment where continued employment and future career prospects are all too often determined by the ability to secure lucrative and long-term research contracts. Most of the organisations led by disabled people are local, hand-to-mouth operations with very limited resources. Inevitably, in such situations, funding for research is given a low priority, and when needed the demand is usually for small-scale locally based projects that are relatively short term in character. The problem is even more complex for researchers working within university settings. Besides the vagaries of the market, they are subject to the demands of a traditionally conservative academic community whose interests are often at odds with those of disabled people and their organisations. All this makes meaningful ongoing relations between disability researchers and disabled people's organisations difficult to sustain (Barnes et al., 2002).

The standard for accountability was set with the BCODP discrimination project cited above. It was conceived and monitored by members of the BCODP with funding from the JRF and Charity Projects. It began in 1990 and was co-ordinated throughout by a research advisory group of five people, only one of whom was a non-disabled person. The group met on a bi-monthly basis to comment on and review progress. Moreover, besides collecting data, the first five months of 1990 were spent discussing the aims and objectives of the research with key figures in Britain's disabled people's movement. Data analysis and drafts of chapters were periodically produced and circulated to the advisory group and representatives of disabled people's organisations along with requests for comments and recommendations. These were subsequently discussed at advisory group meetings before amendments were made. When the final report was completed, a protracted process of dissemination was undertaken.

Similar levels of accountability have been achieved by other BCODP research projects, including the work on direct payments (Zarb and Nadash, 1994) and the more recent 'Creating Independent Futures' project (Barnes et al., 2000).

The social model of disability

In 1983, Mike Oliver adopted the phrase 'the social model of disability' to reflect the growing demand by disabled people for a more holistic approach to the problems they encountered. Until the mid-1990s, research that adopted an overtly social model perspective was a rarity, but this is no longer the case. In some respects, the social model has become the new orthodoxy. Social model thinking underpins the work of the British government initiated Disability Rights Commission (www.drc-gb.org.drc/). Internationally, it has been incorporated into the World Health Organisation's recently developed 'International Classification of Functioning' set to replace its discredited predecessor, the 'International Classification of Impairments, Disabilities and Handicaps' (WHO, 2002).

This, of course, raises important questions about the role of experience within the context of social model research. It can be argued that including information about disabled people's experiences in research reports is empowering for some isolated disabled individuals and that the inclusion of participants' narratives is necessary to illustrate the social context in which the research was conducted. It is important to remember, however, that social scientists have been documenting the experiences of powerless people, including those who could be defined as disabled, for most of the last century. Moreover, there is always the danger that experiential accounts represent little more than 'sentimental biography' or appear 'preoccupied with the medical and practical details of a particular affliction' (Hunt, 1966: ix).

There is also the problem of selection and representativeness. Social researchers have yet to devise adequate ways of collectivising experience, and experiential research has yet to yield any meaningful political or social policy outcomes. It is important, therefore, that within an emancipatory disability research framework, any discussions of disabled people's experiences are couched firmly within an environmental and cultural setting that highlights the disabling consequences of a society organised around the needs of a mythical, affluent, non-disabled majority.

Data collection

Surprisingly, emancipatory disability research is generally associated with qualitative rather than quantitative methodologies. This is attributable to the claim that large-scale surveys and quantitative analyses are unable to capture the extent and complexity of human experience. Also, that such studies are favoured by advocates of objectivity and value freedom and therefore are easily subject to political manipulation (Abberley, 1992).

Yet the notion of objectivity is a hotly contested issue in the social sciences and science generally. Philosophers, scientists and politicians since the enlightenment have repeated the claim that 'scientists' of whatever persuasion can interpret data without reference to personal values or interests. But *all* information, whatever its source and format, can be interpreted in several different ways, and those charged with the responsibility of interpreting it are influenced by various forces: economic, political and cultural.

Within the social sciences, it is increasingly recognised that judgements are coloured by personal experience and that all propositions are limited by the meanings, implicit or explicit, in the language used in their formulation. Additionally, all theories are produced by and limited to particular social groups, and that all observations are theory laden. Traditionally, medical and academic interests have dominated disability research. Until recently these were viewed as objective and value free. Alternatives, such as social model accounts, were seen as politically biased and/or subjective. As indicated above, this is no longer the case.

There is also common ground between the emancipatory research model and other contemporary social research methodologies, including positivism and post-positivism. Early positivism is founded on a 'realist ontology': namely, the assertion that there is a 'reality out there' driven by natural laws. Social science is about uncovering the true nature of that reality in order to predict and control it. Moreover, post-positivism acknowledges important differences between the 'natural' and 'social' worlds in that the rules that govern the former are viewed as universal. Conversely, social realities are variable across time, place, culture and context. Proponents also recognise that subjective values may enter the research process at any point from conceptualisation to conclusion. They also accepted that the outcomes of social research may also influence future behaviour and attitudes (Dyson, 1998).

Researchers who adhere to a social model perspective, regardless of their theoretical leanings – whether materialist, feminist or postmodernist – all assert that there is a 'reality' out there. The social oppression of disabled people, that is historically, environmentally and culturally variable, is influenced by subjective values and interests, and is politically and socially influential. The crucial difference between advocates of post-positivism and supporters of an emancipatory research model lies in their claims to political neutrality. For the former, although recognised as sometimes unattainable, objectivity and value freedom are the stated aims; for the latter, political commitment and empowerment are the unequivocal goals.

Inevitably, this leads to accusations that politically committed researchers reveal little more than a previous allegiance to a particular version of social reality, and/or that by interpreting everyday life in a particular way they deny the significance of other perspectives, actions and beliefs (Silverman, 1998). But similar criticisms can be made of all social research. In response, researchers adopting an emancipatory framework must make their standpoint clear at the outset, and ensure that the choice of research methodology and data collection strategies are logical, rigorous and open to scrutiny, and commensurate with the goals of the sponsoring organisation and research participants (Barnes, 2003).

Finally, all data collection strategies have their strengths and weaknesses. It is not the research methods themselves that are the problem, it is the uses to which they are put. Indeed, several of the studies mentioned above employed both quantitative and qualitative research techniques when researching disability issues (see, for example, Zarb and Nadash, 1994; Barnes et al., 2000).

Empowerment

To be truly emancipatory, disability research must be empowering. It must generate data that have positively meaningful and practical outcomes for disabled people. But all research produces data. Hence, it can be argued that all research is empowering, since information generates knowledge and knowledge is power, or so the story goes.

Too much information, and in limited formats, can induce confusion, uncertainty and apathy and is, therefore, potentially disempowering. Though this is a problem for all sections of society, it is especially so for some disabled people, such as those from minority ethnic communities, people designated with learning difficulties, deaf people and older disabled people, who are routinely disadvantaged by inadequate and inaccessible education, information and communication systems. Whilst this can generate a general disenchantment with social research, it can also lead to a reliance on those who generate research findings, namely researchers. It is frequently argued that the principal beneficiaries of social research are the researchers themselves (Oliver, 1997).

But can emancipatory disability research offer anything different? I would argue that it can and has. Partly because of the reasons mentioned above, but also because empowerment is not something that can be given, empowerment is something that people must do for themselves. The important point here is ownership. Within an emancipatory framework, it is organisations controlled by disabled people that devise and control the research agenda and, equally important, to whom and with whom the research findings are disseminated. Research outcomes in themselves cannot bring about meaningful political and social transformation, but they can reinforce and stimulate the demand for change. Thus the main targets for emancipatory disability research are disabled people and their allies.

Here again, the BCODP research on discrimination provides a useful example. The data from the project were disseminated in various forms and formats. These included presentations by those involved in the research project at numerous venues and locations throughout the UK and Europe during 1992–93, and the production of various articles in journals, magazines and the popular press. Two thousand summary leaflets were produced and distributed free of charge to all BCODP groups and supporters during 1992–93. In this way the research made an important contribution to the further politicisation of disabled people, both in the UK and across Europe (Hurst, 1995). Consequently, this research played a crucial role in getting anti-discrimination legislation onto the statute books in the UK. Further, the production and dissemination of the numerous projects on direct payments and personal assistance schemes, only some of which are cited above, made a significant contribution to the argument for the introduction of the 1996 Community Care (Direct Payments) Act.

This is not to suggest that these projects in themselves are responsible for these outcomes; they are not, but they did provide some substance to the arguments for changes in policy put forward by disabled activists and their allies. In so doing they did contribute to the further mobilisation of the disabled people's movement. Whether the policy outcomes will live up to disabled people's expectations is another matter. If they do not, that may generate a demand for further research; but that is something that disabled people and their organisations must decide for themselves.

Conclusion

Much has changed over the last ten or so years in the field of disability research. There can be little doubt that the arrival of the social model of disability and the emancipatory research paradigm have had an important impact on agencies and researchers currently engaged in disability research. Where once the disability research agenda was subject almost exclusively to the interests and whims of politicians, policy makers and professional academics, now the situation is somewhat different. The argument presented here suggests that when directly linked to disabled people's ongoing struggle for change, doing emancipatory disability research can have a meaningful impact on their empowerment and on the policies that affect their lives. But whether or not there is a future for this approach depends on several factors, not least of which is the future of the UK's disabled people's movement and, of course, the support within universities available to those who choose to adopt and nurture its development.

References

Abberley, P. (1992) 'Counting us out: a discussion of the OPCS Disability Surveys', *Disability, Handiap and Society*, 7 (2): 139–55.

Albrecht, G.L., Seelman, K.D., Bury, M. (eds) (2001) *Handbook of Disability Studies*. London: Sage.

Barnes, C. (1990) *Cabbage Syndrome: The Social Construction of Dependence*. Lewes: Falmer.

Barnes, C. (1991) *Disabled People in Britain and Discrimination: A Case for Anti-discrimination Legislation*. London: Hurst.

Barnes, C. (1992) *Disabling Imagery in the Media: An Exploration of Cultural Representations of Disabled People*. Belper: Ryburn.

Barnes, C. (2003) 'Doing Emancipatory Research: what a difference a decade makes', *Disability and Society*, 18 (1): 1.

Barnes, C., Mercer, G. and Morgan, H. (2000) *Creating Independent Futures, Stage One Report*. Leeds: The Disability Press.

Barnes, C., Oliver, M. and Barton, L. (2002) 'Conclusion', in *Disability Studies Today*. Oxford: Polity.

DHS (1992) 'Special Issue: Researching Disability', *Disability, Handicap and Society*, 7 (2): 99–203.

Dyson, A. (1998) 'Professional Intellectuals From Powerful Groups: Wrong From the Start', in P. Clough and L. Barton (eds), *Articulating with Difficulty*. London: Paul Chapman.

Goffman, E. (1968) *Stigma*. Harmondsworth: Penguin.

Hunt, P. (ed.) (1966) *Stigma: The Experience of Disability*. London: Geoffrey Chapman.

Hurst, R. (1995) 'International Perspectives and Solutions', in G. Zarb (ed.), *Removing Disabling Barriers*. London: Policy Studies Institute.

Martin, J., Meltzer, H. and Elliot, D. (1988) *The Prevalence of Disability Among Adults*. London: HMSO.

Miller, E.J. and Gwynne, G.V. (1972) *A Life Apart*. London: Tavistock.

Morris, J. (1989) *Able Lives*. London: The Women's Press.

Oliver, M. (1997) '"Emancipatory" Disability Research: Realistic Goal or Impossible Dream', in C. Barnes and G. Mercer (eds), *Doing Disability Research*. Leeds: The Disability Press.

Oliver, M. and Zarb, G. (1992) *Personal Assistance Schemes in Greenwich: An Evaluation*. London: University of Greenwich.

Oliver, M., Zarb, G., Silver, J., Moore, M. and Salisbury, V. (1988) *Walking Into Darkness: The Experience of Spinal Cord Injury*. Tavistock: Macmillan.

Parsons, T. (1951) *The Social System*. London: Routledge and Kegan Paul.

Silverman, D. (1998) 'Research and Social Theory', in C. Seale (ed.), *Researching Society and Culture*. London: Sage.

WHO (2002) *International Classification of Functioning, Disability and Health*. Geneva: World Health Organisation. Available on www3.who.int/icf/icftemplate.cfm (accessed on 16 November).

Zarb, G. and Nadash, P. (1994) *Cashing in on Independence*. Derby: The British Council of Disabled People.

8 International Perspectives on Disability
JOHN SWAIN

I approach this chapter with some trepidation. As other chapters in this section have demonstrated, the arena of perspectives on disability (and impairment) is vibrant and fraught with controversy. Broadening the arena to international perspectives brings into play the meaning and experiences of disability and impairment across nations and the whole gamut of economic, political, cultural and social circumstances. The starting point is two seemingly contradictory positions. On the one hand is the social and historical construction of disability. To be impaired and disabled in China, in Afghanistan, in Zambia, in the USA – high-income (the 'developed' or minority world) and low-income (the 'developing' or majority world) – addresses widely differing experiences and encompasses different meanings, not least through differences within language. On the other hand is commonality, engendered by experiences of multi-deprivation, predominantly through common experiences of poverty. The establishment and growth of an international disabled people's movement, particularly through the Disabled People's International (DPI), is in part at least an expression and realisation of such commonality.

The social model of disability was born from the experiences of disabled people in the Western minority world. It is an expression of commonality and resistance to the dominant individual/medical/tragedy models. To look globally, however, raises a possibly more complex and controversial picture, summarised succinctly by Stone:

> For some, the social model might be right for politicised disabled people in the west, but it should not be transferred beyond the west. That would be more like imperialism than empowerment ... On the other hand, the evidence from many disabled people who live in the majority world is that the social model makes sense across cultures and countries. (1993: 3)

International experience

A starting point for an examination of international perspectives is the experiences of disabled people around the world. Perhaps not surprisingly the picture is complex, including both cultural diversity and commonalities. Anita Ghai (2001) argues that the meaning of disability has to be understood within specific cultural contexts. She begins from personal experience:

> Whereas I, who have access to the Internet and a hand driven car, can be considered a privileged disabled person, others in my country are fighting for their survival. Thus the notion of commonality raises significant questions in a country like India. (2001: 26)

This, of course, speaks to divergence in the meaning of disability realised through experience within cultures as well as between. Ghai traces subtle nuances in different discourses in Indian culture. Embedded in images and stories associated with disability are assumptions that range from a 'lack' or 'flaw' to 'deceit, mischief and evil' (2001: 27). Another theme is disability as a retribution for the past and disabled people suffering the wrath of God for misdeeds either they or their families have committed. She points out that:

> In a culture where pain and suffering are often accepted as karma (fate) and learned helplessness becomes a life trait, consideration of disability as a social issue is a difficult goal. (2001: 35)

While Charlton (1998) argues that attitudes towards disability are universally negative, he charts cultural differences under three themes. First are the ways in which the body and physical characteristics are given value and meaning. For instance:

> The facial scar in the Americas is considered a deformity, but for the Dahomey in Africa it is a badge of honor. (1998: 56)

Western bio-medical definitions of impairment are not universal and perceptions of the body/mind vary across cultures and also change over time (Stone, 2001). Charlton's second theme is religion and the messages various religious doctrines convey about disability. He quotes, for instance, Mallory:

> 'In Palau, the question of what caused a disability is of primary importance – not the medical cause, but the spiritual cause. All disabilities are believed to be caused by some failure on the part of someone to follow a tradition, fulfil a responsibility, appease an ancestor.' (1992: 14)

Charlton's third theme is language, and the notion that key concepts do not easily translate into other languages and cultures (Barnes and Mercer, 2003). He includes a quotation from an interview he conducted with Ranga Mupinda (executive director of the National Council of Disabled Persons of Zimbabwe):

> 'In Africa, in our culture, we do not even use the awful term "cripple". It's even worse. In Shona, the word is *chirma*, which means totally useless, a failure. So a person with a disability begins life as a chirma.' (Charlton, 1998: 66)

It is important in considering cultural diversity not to divorce disability from other social divisions and presumptions in Western societies. Coleridge questions presumptions about the quality of life experienced by Muslim women, which have no foundation in their expressed views:

> The discussion on gender relations in traditional societies, especially Muslim ones, is complex and is the point where indigenous values clash most obviously with 'foreign' values. It is normal in the west to portray Afghan culture as inherently oppressive of women. But most Afghan men and probably many Afghan women perceive the differential treatment as ensuring respect for women, by protecting them from harassment and from what they regard as the demeaning task of having to engage in wage-earning in the public domain. (1999: 157)

Notwithstanding the importance of cultural differences, subtle and not so subtle, it can be argued that commonality is an overriding picture. Barnes (2001) reports statements that represent the wide range of views submitted to the WHO Disability and Rehabilitation Team during the year 2000. They are drawn from over 3,500 responses to a request for testimonials, almost 80 per cent being from disabled individuals:

> 'Everything is structured in such a way that people with disability are entirely left out.' (A student with disabilities: Ghana)

> 'Over the 15 years of my disability, I have learned what it is like to be isolated, segregated, and discriminated against. I know this not only because of my own experience, but because I have joined an organisation of others who have the same condition, and who have the same experiences.' (A psychiatric system survivor: United States of America)

> 'Disabled people have been the most destitute of Africans. Government planners have tended to emphasise the majority and thus they have ignored the needs of disabled people and their families. African society already accorded women a lower status than men ... disabled women face discrimination because they are women and because they are disabled.' (A disabled woman: Zambia)

> (Barnes, 2001: 6)

The report points out that these are testimonials of multiple deprivation: economic, political and social, and the central common experience is abject poverty. This raises the complex question of what is meant by 'poverty'. Official statements and policies concentrate on standards of consumption and income-based definitions, though evidence from poor people themselves suggests inescapable association with lack of security and self-respect (Wilson and Heeks, 2000). In one of the first international reviews Coleridge states:

> Disability creates and exacerbates poverty by increasing isolation and economic strain, not just for the individual but for the family: there is little doubt that disabled people are among the poorest in poor countries. (1993: 64)

Anita Ghai writes of poverty in India and points out that it is closely associated with impairment as well as disability. She states:

> In developing countries like India, impairment is largely caused by poverty. The prevalence of impairment, particularly polio and blindness, is at least four times higher among those who are below the poverty line than those who are above it. (2001: 29)

Globalisation, and all the social change this umbrella term encompasses, has exacerbated inequality. It is on this basis that Stone argues that the social model of disability need not be solely applicable to the Western majority world:

> To my mind, separating 'disability' and 'impairment' makes sense in the majority world as well as in the minority world. ... we need to hold on to it if we are serious

about understanding how societies disable people (the struggle for social change) and why disabled people are among the poorest of the poor (the struggle for survival). (2001: 51)

In contexts of extreme deprivation and desolation, the struggle for social change is a struggle for survival and the basis of an international perspective lies in breaking down the walls of structural, environmental and attitudinal disablism.

A universal rights-based perspective?

Perspectives of disability and impairment are not just realised in understandings and experience, but also within responses across nations. Here we shall concentrate on rights-based strategies for development and social change. It has been common for some years for the universal establishment of human rights to be identified as the single most important political development (Bickenbach, 2001). The human rights approach is the main international thrust for social change emanating from the social model of disability and the global challenge to the oppression of disabled people. Writing of the DPI, Hurst states:

> DPI is unique among civil rights movements in being organised globally through a directly representative and democratic, grass-roots network. The commitment to rights by the membership has led to significant social change as national assemblies consult and work with their governments to implement a rights based approach to disability. (2003: 168)

Bickenbach (2001) argues that human rights embody the values of the respect for differences, equality of opportunity, and full participation in all aspects of social life. Nevertheless, questions have been raised about the predominant focus on the rights of citizenship. Some would argue that the minority worldview of human rights is predominantly an individual rather than a community or collective approach. Legesse writes:

> In the liberal democracies of the Western world the ultimate repository of rights is the human person. The individual is held in a virtually sacralized position. There is a perpetual, and in our view obsessive, concern with the dignity of the individual, his [sic] worth, personal autonomy and property ... If Africans were the sole authors of the Universal Declaration of Human Rights, they might have ranked the rights of communities above those of individuals, and they might have used a cultural idiom fundamentally different from the language in which the ideas are now formulated. (1980: 124, 129)

Turner has also criticised notions of citizenship as repressive rather than progressive and as excluding outsiders and preserving the rights of insiders: 'under the bland moral shield of universalism, various types of particularity must be subordinated' (1993: 14). He cites the example of various aboriginal groups in, for instance, Australia and the USA and suggests that they are faced with two alternatives. They can opt for separate development within their own 'state', but this looks like a version of apartheid. Alternatively they can attempt to assimilate into existing patterns of citizenship, but this involves the inevitable destruction of aboriginal cultures.

Though it can be claimed that the disabled people's movement is global, the evidence suggests that there are different patterns of development in different parts of the world, in different contexts; for instance, most countries of the majority world have no welfare state. Barnes and Mercer suggest:

> In the more industrialised North, campaigns have focused on the achievement of 'independent living' as well as 'full participation and equality' for disabled people. In comparison, economic conditions in the South have led disabled people to empha- sise a different strategy in their struggle for emancipation – notably, the significance of community-based initiatives for economic participation and equality. (1995: 43)

Globalisation and disability

To address international perspectives in the light of globalisation engages us in competing discourses not just about disability but also global governance, world economy, and cul- tural diversity and colonisation. Holden and Beresford (2002) suggest that there has been relatively little debate of globalisation either in relation to or by disabled people. Yet, as a reflection of the global context of disability, disabled people have organised on an inter- national scale (Priestley, 2001) and it is arguably the international political struggle that generates an international perspective.

The key features of globalisation, according to Holden and Beresford include dere- gulation of capital, the developing international labour market and employment conditions. These are associated with 'environmental pollution, unhealthy and dangerous industrial conditions and accidents, as well as poverty' (2002: 194). The notion of globalisation has been widely accepted. In general terms it is a multi-dimensional process of social change – cultural, economic and political (Cochrane and Pain, 2000). Globalisation seems evident in all aspects of social life, including what we eat, our leisure pursuits and the language we use. Indeed, Billington et al. (1998: 204) take these developments into the arena of 'iden- tity': 'where national or economically defined identities are no longer primary but exist alongside identities based on gender, ethnicity and sexuality' – and disability. This is often referred to as the emergence of 'identity politics' and is associated with the emergence of new social movements such as the Women's Movement, Gay Pride and the Disabled People's Movement (Zaretsky, 1995).

It is within this approach, too, that there are cracks for the politics of hope (Barton, 2001). The most significant development has been the growth of the DPI (see Chapter 43). The global significance of the DPI was emphasised in 1998 by Kalle Konkkola (then the chair- person of the DPI) as follows:

> 'As chairperson I have felt that DPI's meaning is more important in the Southern, Eastern and developing countries than in the Western countries especially when we look at the level of commitment. Of course the organisations in Western Europe have a commitment of working together but it appears as if the expectations on DPI are greater outside of Europe than in Europe.' (quoted in Priestley, 2001: 6)

As recognised by the DPI, the main political imperative in relation to globalisation is poverty:

> A major goal of Disabled People's International is the full participation of all disabled people in the mainstream of life, particularly those in developing countries, who form the vast majority of the world's 500 million disabled people. DPI recognizes that poverty not only leads to disability, but also allows for few concessions for the needs and aspirations of disabled people. (www.dpi.org/en/about_us/accessed 2003)

Taking the most positive view of globalisation, however, the possibilities for the politics of hope lie beyond any particular organisations. They are inherent within the democratic and participatory possibilities afforded by the Internet and other technological developments. These developments have opened up opportunities for dialogic, or participative rather than representative, democracy. The printing press opened opportunities for monologue – the few disseminate to the many. But the Internet, in particular, opens opportunities for dialogue – the many communicate with the many. Rheingold (1995) has argued that the Internet allows for greater diversity or plurality of voices to be heard and so is profoundly democratising. The Internet generates truly global electronic communities, and new forms of participation and community. Bulletin boards, websites and e-mail engender democratic possibilities and their use by disabled people's organisations testifies to their utility in democratic processes. The possibilities of an international perspective on disability, then, can be realised. An international perspective on disability challenges the global structures that lock millions of disabled people in poverty and silence.

The danger, of course, is the possibility of the further marginalisation of 'the unconnected', the disabled people who are the poorest of the poor for whom survival is the political perspective. Panos (1998) states that new communication technologies are unlikely to reach the poorest people.

There are, for instance, less Internet account holders in the whole of Africa than in London and the position of people unable to read English, the language that dominates digitalised information, is beyond available statistics. This chapter began by outlining a contradictory position and we end with what is a reflection of the same dilemma. Though the Internet holds possibilities for global participatory democracy and an international perspective on disability, such possibilities are open to few poor people, including disabled people in the majority world, thus further exacerbating inequality and heightening diversity.

References

Barnes, C. (2001) *Rethinking Care from the Perspective of Disabled People*. Copenhagen: WHO.

Barnes, C. and Mercer, G. (1995) 'Disability: emancipation, community participation and disabled people', in G. Craig and M. Mayo (eds), *Community Empowerment: A Reader in Participation and Development*. London: Zed Books.

Barnes, C. and Mercer, G. (2003) *Disability*. Cambridge: Polity.

Barton, L. (2001) 'Disability, struggle and the politics of hope', in L. Barton (ed.), *Disability Politics and the Struggle for Change*. London: David Fulton.

Bickenbach, J.E. (2001) 'Disability human rights, law, and policy', in G.L. Albrecht, K.D. Seelman and M. Bury (eds), *Handbook of Disability Studies*. Thousand Oaks, CA: Sage.

Billington, R., Hockey, J. and Strawbridge, S. (1998) *Exploring Self and Society*. Basingstoke: Macmillan.

Charlton, J.I. (1998) *Nothing About Us Without Us: Disability, Oppression and Empowerment*. Berkeley, CA: University of California Press.

Cochrane, A. and Pain, K. (2000) 'A globalizing society?', in D. Held (ed.), *A Gobalizing World? Culture, Economics, Politics*. London: Routledge.

Coleridge, P. (1993) *Disability, Liberation and Empowerment*. Oxford: Oxfam.

Coleridge, P. (1999) 'Development, cultural values and disability: the example of Afghanistan', in E. Stone (ed.), *Disability and Development: Learning from Action and Research on Disability in the Majority World*. Leeds: The Disability Press.

Ghai, A. (2001) 'Marginalisation and disability: experiences from the Third World', in M. Priestley, (ed.), *Disability and the Life Course: Global Perspectives*, Cambridge: Cambridge University Press.

Holden, C. and Beresford, P. (2002) 'Globalization and disability', in C. Barnes, M. Oliver and L. Barton (eds), *Disability Studies Today*. Cambridge: Polity.

Hurst, R. (2003) 'Conclusion: enabling or disabling globalization' in J. Swain, S. French and C. Cameron (eds), *Controversial Issues in a Disabling Society*. Buckingham: Open University Press.

Legesse, A. (1980) 'Human rights in African political culture', in K.W. Thompson (ed.), *The Moral Imperatives of Human Rights: A World Survey*. Washington, DC: University Press of America.

Mallory, B.L. (1992) *Changing Beliefs About Disability in Developing Countries: Historical Factors and Sociocultural Variables in Traditional and Changing Views about Disability and Developing Societies*. Monograph 53. Durban: University of New Hampshire.

Panos (1998) *Information, Knowledge and Development*. London: Panos.

Priestley, M. (2001) 'Introduction: the global context of disability', in M. Priestley (ed.), *Disability and the Life Course: Global Perspectives*. Cambridge: Cambridge University Press.

Rheingold, H. (1995) *The Virtual Community*. London: Mandarin Paperbacks.

Stone, E. (1999) 'Disability and development in the majority world', in E. Stone (ed.), *Disability and Development: Learning from Action and Research on Disability in the Majority World*. Leeds: The Disability Press.

Stone, E. (2001) 'A complicated struggle: disability, survival and social change in the majority world', in M. Priestley (ed.), *Disability and the Life Course: Global Perspectives*, Cambridge: Cambridge University Press.

Turner, B.S. (1993) 'Contemporary problems in the theory of citizenship', in B.S. Turner (ed.), *Citizenship and Social Theory*. London: Sage.

Wilson, G. and Heeks, R. (2000) 'Technology, poverty and development', in T. Allen and A. Thomas (eds), *Poverty and Development into the 21st Century*. Oxford: Oxford University Press.

www.dpi.org/en/about us

Zaretsky, E. (1995) 'The birth of identity politics in the 1960s: psychoanalysis and the public/ private division', in M. Featherstone, S. Lash and R. Robertson (eds), *Global Modernities*. London: Sage.

Part II
In Our Own Image

9 Disability and the Body
BILL HUGHES

When UPIAS (1976) described the principles of what was to become the social model of disability, it did so by making a clear distinction between impairment and disability. Disability became defined as social oppression and impairment became associated with bodily pathology. This distinction had the effect of removing impairment and the body from disability discourse and of undermining the credibility of the medical model. The idea that disability was a form of sickness, the outcome of which was dependency and the need for rehabilitation was contested. The new perspective suggested that disability was a problem of social organisation (Oliver, 1990). The solution to the problem of disability, therefore, did not lie in clinical tinkering with 'broken bodies' but in systematic social change.

However, during the 1990s, a critique of the social model that focused on its failure to account for impairment began to develop (Morris, 1991; Hughes and Paterson, 1997; Shakespeare and Watson, 1997; Paterson and Hughes, 2000; Hughes, 2002). The distinction between sex (nature) and gender (culture) that had inspired second-wave feminism in the 1970s became passé by the 1980s. A similar process of intellectual and political 'maturity' within the disabled people's movement underpinned the dissipation of the impairment/disability distinction. Differences within the disabled people's movement that were grounded in the different experiences of impairment promoted the view that disability identity was not a homogeneous package. The experience of oppression (say) among wheelchair users on the one hand, and those with sensory impairments on the other, was bound to be different in fairly significant ways. As the disabled people's movement began to recognise that the barriers to full participation in social life must be different for a wealthy, middle class, white, male heterosexual on the one hand, and a poor, working class, black female, lesbian on the other, then the issue of impairment as a source of differential experience became difficult to deny. If the celebration of difference was to be used as a mantra to counter the politics of exclusion, then it had to be applied to relations among disabled people as well as to relations between disabled and non-disabled people. The debate about impairment was partly a challenge to the process by which disability identity was dominated by the interests of people with mobility impairments. The fact that questions of physical access to public space had come to dominate disability politics was manifest most explicitly in the adoption of the figure of the wheelchair-user as the universal symbol for disability. These debates signified that the bodies of disabled people were the subject of political, not just biological, discourse. Impairment was social. It could not be reduced to biology or left in the hands of the medical profession. Indeed, students of the body were no longer satisfied with a body explained solely by biological data:

> Scholars have only recently discovered that the human body itself has a history. Not only has it been perceived, interpreted and represented differently in different epochs, but it has also been lived differently, brought into being within widely dissimilar material cultures, subjected to various technology and means of control and incorporated into different rhythms of production and consumption, pleasure and pain. (Gallacher and Lacqueur, 1987: vii)

The theoretical case for a social model or sociology of impairment gathered pace throughout the 1990s (Hughes and Paterson, 1997). Its practical correlate and inspiration was the growing tendency for disabled people to take pride in their lives and their bodies. Bodies that had been excluded from the labour market by the epic transformation of industrial capitalism (Oliver, 1990) and invalidated by the normalising proclivities of modern medicine (Hughes, 2000) began to discover that the physical and mental 'defects and deficits' by which they had been known for the last 150 years were a matter of social construction rather than empirical fact. The social model had to make adjustments to incorporate impairment. This may have been, in part, a response to noisy theoreticians, but it was mostly a result of the affirmative strategies of disabled people who began to trade in the stigma of shameful imperfection for the audible voice of the independent agent. The discourse that impairment is opposed to physical, cognitive and social integrity was exposed as a lie. The pathologisers had got it wrong, but the social model needed to adjust itself in order to contend with the growth of the politics of pride.

Thinking about impairment

For these practical, political reasons proponents of the social model have felt compelled to think about impairment. Originally, the social model focused on the claim that disabled people are and have been excluded from participation in social life but, until recently, has been much more reticent to examine the processes by which disabled people's bodies have been represented as inferior, blighted or in deficit. Disabled people are seen as second-class citizens and they have also had their bodies invalidated. Thinking about impairment has been inspired, mostly, by three theoretical traditions: feminism, poststructualism and phenomenology. I will briefly review the contribution that these traditions have made to the sociology of impairment.

Feminism

Feminists within the disabled people's movement were the first to argue that impairment could not be conceived in politically or socially neutral terms (Morris, 1991; Wendell, 1996; Thomas, 1999, 2001). Originally, the social model had contended that impairment was a personal problem, whilst disability was a collective issue. Yet feminists had claimed since the early 1970s that 'the personal is the political'. Logic alone suggests that if impairment is personal, then to consign it to a realm of political neutrality, in which medicine is its natural mentor, is a mistake. If one has to live with both impairment and disability, then both contribute to the experience of disability at a personal level. Indeed, feminists charged proponents of the social model with failing to take into consideration the whole realm of the 'personal and the experiential' (Thomas, 2001: 48), including what Jenny Morris (1991: 10) called 'the experience of our own bodies'.

 The danger of such claims is that they might be seen to be making some concessions to the medical model of disability and therefore to the intellectual arsenal of the oppressors. Feminists prefer to admit that some impairments involve pain and suffering and that it is politically honest and valuable to speak about such issues rather than take the *malestream* (or should it be macho) view that politics can be reduced to the elimination of barriers.

Besides, disablism or oppression is not simply something that is manifest in the discriminatory constitution of social organisation. It is also something that is felt in the form of anger, frustration or even pain.

There is also the very difficult question about whether or not impairment can be regarded as a cause of disability. The social model was unequivocal that this could not be the case and that disability could be traced, causally, to forms of social organisation. However, Sally French (1993: 17) has argued that, whilst she supports the 'basic tenets of the social model', she is compelled to argue – from her experience of visual impairment – that 'some of the most profound problems experienced by people with certain impairments are difficult, if not impossible, to solve by social manipulation'. In order to address this problem of causality, Carol Thomas (1999: 43) has proposed the concept of 'impairment effects', by which she means 'restrictions of activity which are associated with being impaired but which are not disabilities' in so far as they have nothing to do with the unequal power relations between disabled and non-disabled people. She also makes it clear that impairment effects 'should not be naturalised, or dealt with as pre-social "biological" phenomena'.

The current state of the theoretical debate about impairment and the body among feminists involved in disability studies and the disabled people's movement (who would not describe themselves as poststructuralist) is probably best illustrated by this passage from Carol Thomas's book *Female Forms*:

> I would argue that it is quite possible simultaneously to make a conceptual distinction between impairment and disability, reconceptualize the latter as a form of social oppression, understand that bodily variations classified as impairments are materially shaped by the interaction of social and biological factors and processes, and appreciate that impairment is a culturally constructed category which exists in particular times and places. (1999: 141)

Poststructuralism

Feminism is a broad church, and a number of feminists who have contributed significantly to disability studies can be described as postmodernists or poststructuralists (Price and Shildrick, 1998). Whilst they would endorse the majority of the claims that Carol Thomas makes in the passage quoted above, they would have difficulty with the way in which the passage continues to embrace a set of dualisms or binary concepts that it is, at the same time, trying to transcend. Poststructuralists are keen to deconstruct the kind of dualistic thinking that separates the world out into binaries like body and society, private and public, personal and political and impairment and disability. This is the modernist tradition of thinking, associated originally with René Descartes, and its day is done. The terms we use – like impairment and disability – are cultural constructs or linguistic signs that only have an arbitrary and conventional connection with the things to which they are supposed to give meaning. If language is to be reduced to its effects, as poststructuralists would contend, then even somatic sensations like pain and indeed the body itself are primarily cultural or discursive products. From this point of view – which is strongly influenced by the work of Michel Foucault – impairment is fully cultural and the body an outcome of social processes. Put another way: the impaired body is a historically contingent product of power and, therefore, not – as the medical profession would have it – a set of universal biological characteristics amenable to and objectively defined by diagnostic practices (Price and Shildrick, 1998).

Whilst some feminist writers, like Susan Wendell (1996), think that there are real biological differences between disabled and non-disabled bodies, poststructuralists reject such claims on the grounds that they are essentialist and argue that the body is produced by meaning and interpretation and is, therefore, best understood in terms of discourse or cultural representation. Perhaps the best way to understand this 'anti-essentialist' argument is, ironically, to think about non-disabled bodies. The non-disabled body is usually described as 'normal'. But what do we mean by 'normal'? Clearly, it is not a precise term, more of a statistical average. In other words, in reality, the normal or non-disabled body does not exist. What does exist is the linguistic convention or discourse of normality that conveys something to us about bodies and helps us to make some sense of them. If the non-disabled body does not exist in any essential sense, then the same applies to impairment. It is a metaphor, a cultural representation that, in modern times, has become located in a negative language of defect and deficit.

Phenomenology

Phenomenology starts with experience or the perception of the subject. The impaired body is not so much a biological datum as a fundamental point of reference for whosoever experiences it (Hughes and Paterson, 1997; Hughes, 1999, 2000; Paterson and Hughes, 1999, 2000). Indeed, the body is the material basis of everybody's experience. It is – as phenomenologists are keen to say – 'our point of view on the world'. It is the 'place' in which we live and by which we are recognised, but it is also an object upon which we can reflect. In all these incarnations, it is social. It is the where, why and when of our daily activities and experiences. The body is the existential foundation of self and culture. Given this social repertoire associated with our physicality, it is fair to claim that impairment is social and disability embodied. Disablism makes the world alien to impaired bodies and, therefore, simultaneously produces impairment as a particular sort of experience; one that is frequently – in a world dominated by non-impaired bodies – exclusionary, restrictive, discriminatory and oppressive.

We live in a world that is characterised by a carnal hierarchy. The non-impaired body is privileged and advantaged. The impaired body is judged as incompetent and this judgement is often carried, as a core assumption, by non-disabled persons into their everyday encounters with disabled people (Paterson and Hughes, 1999). This kind of argument tries to go beyond the social model because it locates the oppression of disabled people not in its structural origins in objective barriers but in the concrete world of lived experience and the everyday world of mundane social relationships. Impairment cannot be siphoned out from the mosaic of dimensions that regularly make everyday encounters into unsatisfactory experiences for disabled people. Indeed, such encounters compel disabled people to reflect upon their bodies and on the way in which they are perceived as 'alien'. As a disabled colleague of mine put it:

> In the context of a social environment saturated with disablist images, attitudes and behaviour and devoid of carnal information that reflects my corporeal status, I

am perpetually reminded of my body. These incidents can be major or minor – depending on how I feel or their frequency that day. They may range from being stared at or side-stepped in the street, treated as a young child, considered drunk when I am not, to being called disablist names. (Paterson and Hughes, 1999: 605)

The social and physical world has been made by and in the image and likeness of non-disabled people. It is a home for *their* bodies. Even the norms and codes of movement and timing which structure everyday communication are informed by and devised in an idiom that is based on the carnal and emotional needs of non-disabled people.

The three theoretical positions that I have described above are different in many ways, but what they all have in common is that they do not treat impairment simply as a biological or natural state. This means that the meaning of impairment and the body can be transformed from an individual medical problem into a site of social and political debate. The social model, in its infancy, did exactly this for the concept of disability and even though it did so by marginalising the debate about impairment, I would suggest that a sociological approach to impairment extends the principles of the social model beyond its original boundaries and in so doing manages to strengthen rather than compromise itself.

Conclusion

The approaches to impairment described above have tended to reduce impairment to bodies and this tends to marginalise some groups of disabled people whose impairment might be described as predominantly cognitive. For example, Dan Goodley (2001: 209) claimed, very recently, that 'a worrying omission in the "turn to impairment" is the distinct lack of focus on "learning difficulties"'. The omission arises, partly, from the reliance, in the debate about impairment, on the sociology of the body and Goodley (2001: 225) argues, convincingly, that the need for 'mutually inclusive social theories of disability and impairment that are open and inclusive to people who have been labelled as having "learning difficulties" must become a priority' (see Chapter 18). This is a real challenge for some of the ways of thinking about impairment that I have outlined in this chapter.

Finally, I would like to draw attention to a threat. My reading of the recently published *Handbook of Disability Studies* (Albrecht et al., 2001) is that it gives far too much credibility to the medical model of disability or more precisely, that it tends to restore the credibility of rehabilitation science by emphasising that disability is caused – in equal measure – by both impairment and the environment. One gets the impression, from Part I of the book, that Disability Studies – as a new species of social scientific enquiry – is the product of endless revisions of definitions, models and conceptual schemes and, in particular, owes its very existence to successive reformulations of the *International Classification of Impairments, Disabilities and Handicaps* (ICIDH). Indeed, Shakespeare and Watson (2001: 562) argue that, even within the field of disability studies, 'It is far more common, internationally, for disability to be conceived as the outcome of social and bodily processes than it is for disability to be defined … as social processes alone.' The danger here is that the term 'Disability Studies' starts to get dislodged from its radical roots in the emancipatory discourse of the social model and that impairment becomes a key tool in so doing. The debate about impairment has to remain a sociological and political debate. If it does not, then the reactionary rot might start to set in.

References

Albrecht, G.L., Seelman, K.D. and Bury, M. (eds) (2001) *Handbook of Disability Studies*. London, Sage.

French, S. (1993) 'Disability, impairment or something in between', in J. Swain, V. Finkelstein, S. French and M. Oliver (eds), *Disabling Barriers – Enabling Environments*. London, Sage.

Gallacher, C. and Lacqueur, T. (eds) (1987) *The Making of the Modern Body*. Berkeley, CA: University of California Press.

Goodley, D. (2001) 'Learning difficulties, the social model of disability and impairment: challenging epistemologies', *Disability and Society*, 16 (2): 207–31.

Hughes, B. (1999) 'The constitution of impairment: modernity and the aesthetic of oppression', *Disability and Society*, 14 (2): 155–72.

Hughes, B. (2000) 'Medicine and the aesthetic invalidation of disabled people', *Disability and Society*, 15 (3) (Special Issue 2000): 555–68.

Hughes, B. (2002) 'Disability and the body', in C. Barnes, L. Barton and M. Oliver (eds), *Disability Studies Today*. Cambridge: Polity.

Hughes, B. and Paterson, K. (1997) 'The social model of disability and the disappearing body: towards a sociology of impairment', *Disability and Society*, 12 (3): 325–40.

Morris, J. (1991) *Pride Against Prejudice: Transforming Attitudes to Disability*. London: The Women's Press.

Oliver, M. (1990) *The Politics of Disablement*. London: Macmillan.

Paterson, K. and Hughes, B. (1999) 'Disability studies and phenomenology: The carnal politics of everyday life', *Disability and Society*, 14 (5): 597–610.

Paterson, K. and Hughes, B. (2000) 'Disabled Bodies', in P. Hancock, B. Hughes, L. Jagger, K. Russell, R., Tulle-Winton, E. and Tyler, M., *The Body, Culture and Society: An Introduction*. Buckingham: Open University Press.

Price, J. and Shildrick, M. (1998) 'Uncertain thoughts on the dis/abled body', in J. Price and M. Shildrick (eds), *Vital Signs: Feminist Re-configurations of the Biological Body*. Edinburgh: Edinburgh University Press.

Shakespeare, T. and Watson, N. (1997) 'Defending the social model', *Disability and Society*, 12 (2): 293–300.

Shakespeare, T. and Watson, N. (2001) 'Making the difference: disability, politics and recognition', in G. Albrecht, K. Seelman and M. Bury (eds), *Handbook of Disability Studies*. London, Sage.

Thomas, C. (1999) *Female Forms: Experiencing and Understanding Disability*. Milton Keynes: Open University Press.

Thomas, C. (2001) 'Feminism and disability: the theoretical and political significance of the personal and the experiential', in C. Barton (ed.), *Disability Politics and the Struggle for Change*. London: David Fulton.

UPIAS (1976) *Fundamental Principles of Disability*. London: UPIAS.

Wendell, S. (1996) *The Rejected Body: Feminist Philosophical Reflections on Disability*. New York, NY: Routledge.

10 Women and Disability
ALISON SHELDON

Disability – the restriction imposed on top of our impairments by the way our society is organised – is a form of social oppression to which *all* disabled people are subject. The disabled population is not, however, a homogeneous one. It consists of people with a wide variety of impairments, and is intercut by a number of other forms of structural disadvantage. The majority of those affected by disability are women. Subject to both disablism and sexism, disabled women find themselves disadvantaged in countless aspects of their existence, yet often feel their concerns are overlooked. This chapter does not set out to create hierarchies by singling out individual disabled people as more or less oppressed than others. It recognises, though, that disablism cannot be confronted in isolation. Any consideration of disability, or indeed sexism, inevitably exposes unpalatable truths about society, the same society which disadvantages all oppressed people. It is impossible then 'to confront one type of oppression without confronting them all' (Barnes, cited Campbell and Oliver, 1996: xii). This point is crucial for our understanding of disability and gender. For disabled women to achieve collective emancipation, disability, sexism and all other dimensions of oppression must be challenged head on. In reality, however, these oppressions are generally considered in isolation one from another, thus weakening any meaningful challenge to the system and marginalising those, like disabled women, who are subject to more than one form of oppression.

Recent calls for a greater focus on 'difference' within feminist writings have been embraced by many women who experience disability, anxious that their specific experiences of oppression are neglected by the identity-based movements of which they are part – the women's movement and the disabled people's movement. The marginalisation of disabled women has thus prompted the development of a significant body of work within disability studies highlighting their plight (Fawcett, 2000; Thomas, 1999). Much of this work has borrowed heavily from feminist scholarship, in its insistence on the primacy of personal experience. How much these writings move disabled women towards what must be their ultimate goal – an end to oppression – is, however, debatable.

This chapter will consider similarities between the struggles of disabled men and women before examining the specific nature of disabled women's oppression and their lack of unity with their non-disabled sisters. Key areas of conflict arising from this lack of unity will then be discussed. Finally, a plea will be made for a more productive way forward for disabled women.

Oppression and disabled women

While having differing manifestations depending on which devalued social group or groups are involved, oppression is a unitary phenomenon of which disabled people's oppression and women's oppression are just specific examples. Disabled people and women have much in common, then, with both groups adversely affected by society's oppressive structures.

Since individuals do not fall into singular social groupings, there has been much debate about the importance of studying the interactions between different dimensions of oppression. How, for example, does disability affect women who are also subject to sexist oppression? Some regard such questions as vitally important, and are concerned about the exact nature of these interactions (Vernon, 1999). In contrast, others are concerned that:

> ... characterising people's experiences in terms of multiple jeopardies may only serve to marginalise their experiences even further and divert attention from common concerns and issues. (Zarb, 1993: 194)

This anxiety is not unfounded. There is little recognition from those who experience disability oppression and those who experience sexist oppression that their concerns are similar (Sheldon, 1999). Disabled women are said to fall between two stools – peripheral as women in the disabled people's movement, invisible as disabled people in the women's movement (Lloyd, 2001). Thus, the gendered nature of disability is not given a high priority, giving rise to some specific concerns for disabled women.

The specific concerns of disabled women

Disabled women's concerns are in many ways identical to those of disabled men and non-disabled women. They have, however, identified various areas in which they are at a unique social disadvantage, and which are peripheral issues for the movements purporting to represent their interests. For example:

> Disabled women are concerned to explore questions of sexuality and sexual identity, to challenge stereotypical images and oppressive mores relating to childbearing and motherhood, and to identify dominant imperatives around physical and social aspects of self-presentation critically. (Lloyd, 2001: 716)

It could be argued that these are, to a great extent, concerns for *all* women. Why then is mainstream feminism disinterested in these issues as they pertain to disabled women? Whilst we live in a disablist society, perhaps it is inevitable that non-disabled feminists should share society's negative attitudes towards disabled people. Alternatively, it could be argued that feminists have special reasons for wanting to distance themselves from us. A preoccupation with autonomy and independence is said to be 'one of the most pervasive feminist assumptions that undermines ... disabled women's struggle' (Thompson, 1997: 286). Hence it is proposed that:

> Perceiving disabled women as childlike, helpless, and victimized, non-disabled feminists have severed them from the sisterhood in an effort to advance more powerful, competent, and appealing female icons. (Fine and Asch, 1988: 4)

The 'personal is political' has been the rallying call of feminism for many years. Ironically, this approach can also be blamed for mainstream feminism's neglect of disability. It is often thought sufficient to examine only the personal experiences of privileged, white, non-disabled, heterosexual women. Those on the margins are overlooked. It is crucial then that mainstream feminists go beyond simply understanding their own immediate experiences, and incorporate the concerns of a more diverse group of women.

Feminism has fought long and hard to challenge society's rigid gender roles, but this struggle may not mean much to disabled women. Disabled women are perceived to be needy, dependent and passive – stereotypical feminine qualities. At the same time they are deemed incapable of aspiring to other 'feminine' roles, especially those relating to appearance, partnering and motherhood. It is posited, then, that disabled women 'have not been "trapped" by many of the social expectations feminists have challenged' (Fine and Asch, 1988: 29). This may make it difficult for disabled women to identify with the struggles of feminism. It is further suggested that the desire to be like other women may even create a tolerance of sexism in disabled women, who 'will never fight such sexism until they are enabled to discover their commonalities with non-disabled women' (1988: 29).

Whilst disabled women are oppressed in much the same way as non-disabled women, it seems that there may be little recognition of this commonality from either group. Hence there are tensions between the two groups' agendas for change. Two such areas of tension will now be briefly considered – reproductive freedom and 'care' in the community.

Disabled and non-disabled women: irreconcilable differences?

Whilst feminism insists that the right to reproductive freedom must be a cornerstone of women's liberation, the early twentieth-century movement for birth control was championed primarily by white, middle-class, non-disabled Westerners. For less privileged women, the movement advocated the eugenic strategy of population control, 'not the individual right to *birth control*' (Davis, 1982: 215). The twentieth century saw the widespread 'sterilization abuse' of thousands of disabled women, abuses that still continue today (Hubbard, 1997). Now though, disabled women are usually discouraged from becoming mothers in more subtle ways. They are persuaded that their own health might suffer as a consequence of motherhood, that their baby might inherit their 'problem', or that their own impairment(s) will make them incapable of mothering (Thomas, 1997). Reproductive freedom must not be seen, then, solely as the right *not* to bear children; it must include the right for women to *bear* children should they wish, otherwise it can become a demand which implicitly condones eugenics.

Abortion, too, is a crucial issue for both the disabled people's movement and the women's movement. Disabled people have been highly critical of prenatal screening and selective abortion, seeing them as a new strategy of eugenics (Shakespeare, 1998). Non-disabled feminists, however, have largely welcomed prenatal testing, seeing it as 'another means through which women can gain control over their own reproduction' (Bailey, 1996: 143). There seems, then, to be a conflict between this feminist perspective on abortion and the perspective of the disabled people's movement. Some argue that the two positions are irreconcilable (Sharp and Earle, 2002), but there *are* non-disabled feminists who recognise the costs of prenatal screening, both for disabled people and for women generally (Hubbard, 1997). Perhaps these women will enter into discussions with the disabled people's movement and the geneticists to forge a new way forward. Alternatively, it may be that this dilemma cannot be solved amicably without radical changes in society. I would suggest that this is where disabled people, feminists and other oppressed people should be focusing their attention.

A key concern for the emergent British disabled people's movement was the disadvantaged position of disabled residents in institutions (Campbell and Oliver, 1996). In recent years there has been a gradual move away from 'institutional care' in favour of community-based services. Whilst problems with 'community care' policies have been voiced by disabled and older people, they have largely been seen as an important step forward. These policies have, however, done little to improve the lives of younger non-disabled women. Since women are still responsible for the bulk of the 'caring' work that now takes place outside of institutions, recent changes have perpetuated their dependent role in the family by putting yet more unpaid labour their way (Finch, 1984). It is hard, then, for feminists to support 'community care' policies within today's patriarchal society. Rather than advocating changes to the social structure, many non-disabled feminists have come out in support of residential 'care', claiming, for example, that it is the only route that 'will offer us a way out of the impasse of caring' (Finch, 1984: 16). This assumption that a split exists between women who 'care' and 'dependent' people (gender irrelevant) both denies the reality that most people being 'cared for' are women, and obscures the fact that many people who need help with daily living tasks are also looking after others.

Both the debates around birth control and selective abortion, and those around community care, demonstrate how the continuing oppression of disabled people and women has created situations where it seems sides must be taken – where disabled people's best interests are seen to be at odds with those of women. It is important for all of us, and especially for disabled women, to recognise where the blame for these situations lies: not with feminism or the disabled people's movement, but with the society which both movements must seek to change.

The way forward for disabled women: personal or political?

Disabled women have been instrumental in applying feminist analyses to the understanding of disability, and an innovative body of work is growing as a result. There is, however, no one feminist means of analysis, so different writers have used different feminist approaches to support their arguments. Here I will briefly assess the merits of just two of these approaches for furthering disabled women's ultimate cause.

Much recent feminist work within disability studies has been critical of the 'malestream' focus on social barriers, claiming that it pays insufficient attention to *differences* among disabled people (Fawcett, 2000), and effectively denies our personal experience of disability and indeed impairment (Crow, 1996; French, 1993). This individualistic approach, often equated with a feminist disability politics, is not, however, without its critics (Sheldon, 1999). Whilst experience is a 'necessary starting point', it should not be viewed as 'an end in itself' (Kelly et al., 1994: 29). There are concerns from both disabled people and feminists that the limited use of 'the personal is political' as the only analytical tool can be counterproductive. As one feminist has argued, the slogan:

'... became a means of encouraging women to think that the experience of discrimination, exploitation or oppression automatically corresponded with an understanding of the ideological and institutional apparatus shaping one's social status ... When women internalized the idea that describing their own woes was synonymous with developing a political consciousness, the progress of feminist movement was stalled'. (hooks, 1984: 24–5)

Likewise, it is said that those who demand more inclusion of personal experience are hampering the development of the disabled people's movement (Finkelstein, 1996). As a solution to similar tensions within feminism, an approach is suggested that examines 'both the personal that is political, the politics of society as a whole, and global revolutionary politics' (hooks, 1984: 25). Perhaps this would be a useful way forward for the disabled people's movement.

In disability studies, though, a feminist analysis is often assumed to preclude any reference to revolutionary politics, or indeed economic structures. However, many feminists have adopted such an approach to explain their oppression. It is argued that progress for disabled people will not be achieved through a stress solely on equality of opportunity, but can best be achieved by borrowing from socialist feminists 'who call for societal transformations in addition to equality of opportunity within existing arrangements' (Fine and Asch, 1988: 27). It is not enough for women from oppressed groups to simply argue for equal rights with men, since 'knowing that men in their groups do not have social, political, and economic power, they would not deem it liberatory to share their social status' (hooks, 1984: 18). Disabled women also need to challenge the structures that create and perpetuate disability, sexism and other forms of oppression.

This materialist approach has become the dominant way of conceptualising disability in the UK. Similarly, materialist feminists argue that the current form of women's oppression has its roots in the capitalist system, and its particular division of labour (Delphy, 1984). Some kind of gender division of labour is apparent in most known societies, and where these divisions are found, women are always less valued than men. It is argued, however, that prior to the industrial revolution, women were able to contribute to the process of production. As men began to operate in the economy outside of the home, women filled the gap they left behind – the private space of the home. Excluded from productive work, they became economically dependent on male wage-earners. Hence, with industrialisation both women and disabled people became further excluded.

Such an analysis seems to provide an invaluable way of theorising the interaction between disability and sexism. It highlights the fact that disabled people and women need to fight for a new kind of society. It also shows us that there is enormous scope for coalitions between the disabled people's movement, like-minded feminists, and other oppressed groups.

Conclusion

However we experience disability and sexism as individuals, the lives of *all* disabled women are shaped by these oppressive structures. In order to eliminate all kinds of oppression, we need to transform society. Different oppressed groups may come to this realisation through the politicisation of very different personal experiences, yet in a way we are all engaged in a similar struggle. Perhaps when we all begin to challenge the same structures and institutions, significant changes will occur. We must then hold onto what we have in common. The key to all our liberation is unity among oppressed people. Rather than 'competing for "our" piece of a reduced pie ... what we need to do is demand a transformation that delivers a different pie – one big enough for all of us' (Russell, 1998: 231). Disabled women, consistently denied their piece of the pie, may be in an ideal position to forge such a collective agenda for an improved society.

References

Bailey, R. (1996) 'Prenatal testing and the prevention of impairment: A woman's right to choose?', in J. Morris (ed.), *Encounters with Strangers: Feminism and Disability*. London: The Women's Press.

Campbell, J. and Oliver, M. (1996) *Disability Politics: Understanding our Past, Changing our Future*. London: Routledge.

Crow, L. (1996) 'Including all of our lives: renewing the social model of disability', in J. Morris (ed.), *Encounters with Strangers: Feminism and Disability*. London: The Women's Press.

Davis, A. (1982) *Women, Race and Class*. London: The Women's Press.

Delphy, C. (1984) *Close to Home: A Materialist Analysis of Women's Oppression*. London: Hutchinson.

Fawcett, B. (2000) *Feminist Perspectives on Disability*. Harlow: Prentice Hall.

Finch, J. (1984) 'Community care: developing non-sexist alternatives', *Critical Social Policy*, 3 (9): 6–18.

Fine, M. and Asch, A. (eds) (1988) *Women with Disabilities: Essays in Psychology, Culture and Politics*. Philadelphia, PA: Temple University Press.

Finkelstein, V. (1996) 'Outside, "inside out"', *Coalition*, April: 30–36.

French, S. (1993) 'Disability, impairment or something in between?', in: J. Swain, V. Finkelstein, S. French and M. Oliver (eds), *Disabling Barriers – Enabling Environments*. London: Sage in association with The Open University.

hooks, B. (1984) *Feminist Theory: From Margin to Center*. Boston, MA: South End.

Hubbard, R. (1997) 'Abortion and disability: who should and should not inhabit the world?', in L. Davis (ed.), *The Disability Studies Reader*. London: Routledge.

Kelly, L., Burton, S. and Regan, L. (1994) 'Researching women's lives or studying women's oppression? Reflections on what constitutes feminist research', in M. Maynard, and J. Purvis (eds), *Researching Women's Lives from a Feminist Perspective*. London: Taylor and Francis.

Lloyd, M. (2001) 'The politics of disability and feminism: discord or synthesis', *Sociology*, 35 (3): 715–28.

Russell, M. (1998) *Beyond Ramps: Disability at the End of the Social Contract*. Monroe, ME: Common Courage.

Shakespeare, T. (1998) 'Choices and Rights: eugenics, genetics and disability equality', *Disability and Society*, 13 (5): 665–81.

Sharp, K. and Earle, S. (2002) 'Feminism, abortion and disability: irreconcilable differences?', *Disability and Society*, 17 (2): 137–45.

Sheldon, A. (1999) 'Personal and perplexing: feminist disability politics evaluated', *Disability and Society*, 14 (5): 645–59.

Thomas, C. (1997) 'The baby and the bathwater: disabled women and motherhood in social context', *Sociology of Health and Illness*, 19 (5): 622–43.

Thomas, C. (1999) *Female Forms: Experiencing and Understanding Disability*. Buckingham: Open University Press.

Thompson, R.G. (1997) 'Feminist theory, the body and the disabled figure', in L. Davis (ed.) *The Disability Studies Reader*. London: Routledge.

Vernon, A. (1999) 'The dialectics of multiple identities and the disabled people's movement', *Disability and Society*, 14 (3): 385–98.

Zarb, G. (1993) 'The dual experience of ageing with a disability', in J. Swain, V. Finkelstein, S. French and M. Oliver (eds), *Disabling Barriers – Enabling Environments*. London: Sage in association with the Open University.

11 Men and Disability
STEVE ROBERTSON

The aim of this chapter is to begin a journey of exploration regarding issues relating to disabled men. Theoretical, research and critical (auto)biographical work around gender, masculinity and disability is drawn on in order to develop a framework for understanding the relationship between men and disability where disability represents the social barriers and responses encountered by men with an impairment.

Reaching a starting point

Work by disabled feminists has done much to highlight how disability research, and disability studies in general, has historically been 'gender blind' (*sic*); that is, gender has been invisible and the experience of disabled men has been taken as representative of disabled experience in general (Morris, 1993). While recent research in disability studies has done much to correct this situation, little research exists that specifically explores the experiences of disabled men (Shakespeare, 1996, 1999). This apparent contradiction – that men's experiences are representative of all persons' experiences yet men's actual experiences are rarely researched – is paralleled in social science generally. Hearn and Morgan (1990: 7) suggest that men may frequently constitute the research subject. The research, however, is rarely 'about men in a more complex, more problematised, sociological sense'; a situation all too familiar in a medical model approach to 'disability' research where research is conducted 'on' rather than 'with' participants (Oliver, 1992).

In discussing issues of gender differences in disability studies research, Shakespeare (1996) suggests that, in general, women, working in predominantly feminist contexts, have tended to explore more personal aspects of sexuality, relationships and identity, whereas men have concentrated on employment, housing and other material social issues. This, he says, has reproduced the public (realm of the male) private (realm of the female) split and has led to an under-representation of disabled men's experiences. Yet such invisibility of men as gendered beings in research may not be accidental, rather it 'may serve men's interests, keeping their activities apart from critical scrutiny, by other men as well as by women' (Hearn and Morgan, 1990: 7) and this may also be the case in disability studies research.

Since the last edition of this book, further debate has taken place about the limitations of the social model of disability. Writers from within feminist disability studies (Corker, 1998; Morris, 1996; Thomas, 1999a) and others in disability studies (Shakespeare, 1994) whilst recognising and defending the social model (Shakespeare and Watson, 1995), have been concerned that, alone, it leaves insufficient space for exploring the socially integrated nature of the personal effects that impairment might have for an individual. Whilst not having space to fully review these debates, it is nevertheless important to recognise that the extension of the social model into questions of culture, representation and meaning, raises many questions about how these personal effects differ, both quantitatively and qualitatively, not only between disabled men and women but also between different groups of men.

This is the starting point for this journey. A recognition, in line with feminist disability research, that whilst the disability movement has been dominated by men, there 'has been an accompanying tendency to avoid confronting the personal experience of disability' (Morris, 1991: 9) by men. Yet it is through exploring the gendered nature of the experiences of disabled men (to complement ongoing work exploring the experiences of disabled women) that a richer and fuller understanding of the socially integrated nature of disability, its origins and effects can be gained. It is towards such experiences, as described in research and (auto)biography, that this journey now takes us.

Walking in the dark?

Whilst interest in 'masculinity' has soared in recent years, there remains very little qualitative research into men's actual experiences generally, and even less regarding the specific experiences of disabled men, with Shakespeare's review of such research in 1999 finding only one such article, that of Gerschick and Miller (1995). However, the last couple of years have begun to see some attention paid, mainly from those interested in the sociology of the body, to disabled men's lived experiences.

Masculinity, what it means to be male, varies in different cultures and at different times (Kimmel, 2000), but in recent Western culture has tended to be defined through notions of strength, rationality, self-reliance, potency and action. Such notions are embodied; that is, they both form and are expressed through the material body as Connell states:

> True masculinity is almost always thought to proceed from men's bodies – to be inherent in a male body or to express something about a male body. (1995: 44)

This may create dilemmas when such bodily performance cannot be sustained and negative cultural representations of disability (weakness, pity, dependence) are substituted either by the individuals themselves (leading to internally focused conflict) or by others (leading to a failure to be recognised as gendered individuals by society). Murphy (1987) suggests that this leads disabled men to experience an 'embattled identity', constantly struggling to meet society's (and their own) conflicting expectations of what it is to be male and what it is to be physically impaired. In this sense, for Murphy:

> Paralytic disability constitutes emasculation of a more direct and total nature. For the male, the weakening and atrophy of the body threaten all the cultural values of masculinity. (1987: 94)

This model sits alongside and suffers from the same inadequacies as the 'double disadvantage' model often applied to disabled women (Morris, 1993). It shifts the focus back to how individual men 'handle' the experience of impairment, rather than questioning the cultural representations of disability (and I would argue of 'masculinity') that generate any conflict experienced, and it fails to recognise the varying ways that real disabled men (re)negotiate and (re)define concepts of 'masculinity' and 'disability' in everyday life.

Oliver et al.'s (1988) early research into the experiences of 77 men following spinal cord injury (SCI) was ground-breaking in its insistence on moving away from a personal tragedy model of disability. A social adjustment model was proposed that saw the social context, including the social meanings attached to impairment, as crucial to understanding the consequences and experiences of impairment for individuals. This work developed links between the men's experience and the wider social context, (that is, it developed links between issues of agency and structure) and showed that structural, material issues were significant in shaping such experience. However, it failed to fully consider gender as part of the socially integrated meanings that impact on the experience of impairment for these men. So, for example, whilst the difficulties many of the men experienced following discharge from the hospital environment to home were highlighted, these were not considered in respect of the home being a 'feminised' space.

The work of Gerschick and Miller (1995), carrying out in-depth interviews with ten disabled men, suggests that the clash between hegemonic masculinity (the dominant form in a given place and time) and the social perception of disability as weakness generated three main coping strategies.

- *Reformulation*: where hegemonic ideals were redefined in their own terms. Thus one young man in their study, whilst requiring substantial assistance with personal care, maintained a great deal of independence in the directing of these daily activities and determining who provided which aspects of care.
- *Reliance*: where great effort is made to continue to try to fulfil hegemonic ideals. One example provided in the study is that of a man going all out to please his partner sexually – his greatest pleasure being to sexually exhaust her – in order to reduce feelings of vulnerability and reconfirm his masculine identity. Given the importance of sexual potency in hegemonic masculine identity, the construction of disabled men as asexual beings or as 'sexually safe' (Shakespeare et al., 1996; Lenney and Sercombe, 2002) can be particularly emasculating.
- *Rejection*: where hegemonic ideals are renounced and one's own ideas about what constitutes 'masculinity' are inserted, or its importance in life is downplayed. Thus when discussing fatherhood one participant could make it clear that it was not being the male 'sire' that was important (that is, the genetic fathering of a child), but taking the responsibility and emotional commitment to parenting seriously.

These three strategies are not fixed for individuals. Rather, the disabled men moved into and out of different strategies at different places and times. Gerschick and Miller, however, do suggest that those men utilising the *reliance* strategy for much of the time suffered the costs associated with never being fully able to live up to such hegemonic ideals. Such feelings of not being able to live up to hegemonic masculine ideals are far from being exclusive to disabled men. In fact, the work of Connell (1995, 2000), amongst others, suggests that such contradiction is part of the current masculine make-up.

In conducting a case study of one young man's (Paul's) experiences of shifting from a highly embodied working-class masculinity to a disabled masculinity, Valentine (1999) highlights some of the socially integrated relationships between masculinity and disability. The difficulties encountered by Paul in utilising 'public' spaces (inaccessibility, the need to plan ahead, patronising attitudes) soon led to his withdrawal to the so-called 'feminised' location of the home. He began to spend his days eating out of boredom, leading to weight gain and further increasing his dependence. For Paul, this led to a questioning of his masculinity:

'I hated myself for ages 'cause I didn't think of myself as a man. 'Cause when you'd been someone who'd been strong and 'ard working its 'ard to be stuck in on your own, sat about like a lump'. (1999: 174)

A chance meeting led Paul to become involved in wheelchair basketball, at which he soon excelled. He began to construct a new identity, that of athlete, altering his diet and beginning to work out in order to improve his performance on court. As Valentine points out, Paul's identity now involves a complex mixture of hegemonic masculine performances (those associated with sporting masculinity – McKay et al., 2000) and a re-negotiated masculinity that incorporates an improved ability to talk and listen and a willingness to undertake 'female' tasks, such as cooking for himself.

In this sense, hegemonic masculinity may be a double-edged sword in relation to disability. Certainly, some disabled men in autobiographical work consider the values attached to hegemonic masculinity as responsible for helping them survive the experience of becoming impaired:

Be a man! An old battered idea that has not fared well. Like all clichés, it embarrasses. Yet clichés spring from the cultures that give them life, and to the idea of what it meant to be a man in 1944 I owe my survival. If others can ignore such debts, I have no choice but to praise a salvation that is unfashionable if not subversive. (Kriegel, 1998: 5)

Being a man, strong, determined, not willing to show weakness or give up, Kriegel feels has helped him through to his present sense of self. Yet if Gerschick and Miller (1995) are correct in their assertion that reliance on hegemonic masculinity has great personal costs for most disabled men (this assertion is echoed in the work of Charmaz, 1995), then tapping into 'male culture', particularly sport, as a means of 'rehabilitation' following impairment is far from unproblematic. Indeed, for those men whose impairment is a result of their involvement in sport, the preservation of hegemonic masculine identities can be exceptionally difficult, but so can discarding them. As Sparkes says in an autobiographical narrative of increasing physical impairment:

I'd like to report, following Gerschick and Miller (1995), that via my experiences I have been able to wholeheartedly reject hegemonic masculinity and develop new standards of masculinity in its place ... I have and I haven't. I'd like to, I'm trying but I'm unsure. (1996: 489)

Sparkes and Smith (2002) have found in their research with men following Spinal Cord Injury (SCI) through sport, that the opportunity to create alternative masculine identities is constrained in part by powerful public narratives (Thomas, 1999b). A further example of this in recent research is the finding that the portrayal of an 'heroic masculinity' – combining aggressive action with stoic perseverance – in disability magazines can adversely affect the rehabilitation of men following SCI, as it provides only a restrictive script from which to try to (re)negotiate one's male identity promoting a reliance on hegemonic ideals (Hutchinson and Kleiber, 2000). Thus the rehabilitation process, and possibly disability in general, may be seen as gendered with 'passive acceptance' for disabled women and 'heroic effort' for disabled men being what is expected. This holding up of exemplars of heroic hegemonic ideals is also found in the wider media. Consider, for example, the representation of Christopher Reeves' stoic determination and how this is often linked to masculinity in articles such as 'Man of Steel' (*Guardian, G2*, 17 September 2002).

Pointing a way forward

This journey of understanding is certainly not nearing its end; yet in reviewing the research outlined above, I would like to suggest some pointers for future direction.

It is clear that the relationship between masculinity and disability is complex and that a single coherent identity as a 'disabled man' does not exist. Yet society's defining of men through action, doing rather than being (Morgan, 1992), provides only a limited public narrative for disabled men to draw on (or reject). Whilst identities are not fixed categories to which people belong (male, disabled and so on), neither are they so disparate as to be nothing more than free-floating, unstable discourses that can be plucked out and entered into at will (Thomas, 1999a: 112). O'Neill and Hird's (2001) work on gay, disabled men points out how the modern insistence on a 'unified' self led to the men in their study prioritising a gay over a disabled masculinity. This, they argue, results from the fact that hegemonic masculinity not only formulates marginalised masculinities (that is, any masculinities that do not aspire to, or fulfil, hegemonic ideals), but also 'decides the extent and terms of the relations between these masculinities' (2001: 221). This approach draws on Connell's (1995, 2000) work that suggests masculinity needs to be understood in terms of wider sets of gender relations that consist of power relations, production relations (division of labour), emotional relations and symbolism (the visual and linguistic practices that represent a locus of political struggle and social change). In this regard, O'Neill and Hird (2001: 207) go on to show that for the gay disabled men in their study, 'difference(s) cannot be productively analysed in social or theoretical isolation'.

What emerges, then, is a framework where disabled male identities shift, yet are formed and reformed within sets of structural and cultural relations that are relatively static. It is these relations, rather than individual 'failure to come to terms', that can limit or constrain (or alternatively provide) choices, options and social practices for disabled men. Relevant work and research into masculinity and disability should therefore give precedence to exploring and understanding the nature and impact of these structural and cultural relations and when, where and how they might need to be challenged or harnessed. This is not to return to neglecting work on understanding disabled men's lived experiences, rather it is only through such work that such relations can be more fully understood. It is hoped that this chapter has helped begin this process of understanding by drawing together research that provides accounts of disabled men's real, lived experiences.

References

Charmaz, K. (1995) 'Identity dilemmas of chronically ill men', in D. Sabo and D.F. Gordon (eds), *Men's Health and Illness: Gender, Power and the Body.* London: Sage.
Connell, R.W. (1995) *Masculinities.* Cambridge: Polity Press.
Connell, R.W. (2000) *The Men and the Boys.* Cambridge: Polity Press.
Corker, M. (1998) *Deaf and Disabled, or Deafness Disabled?* Buckingham: Open University Press.

Gerschick, T.J. and Miller, A.S. (1995) 'Coming to terms: masculinity and physical disability', in D. Sabo and D.F. Gordon (eds), *Men's Health and Illness: Gender, Power and the Body*. London: Sage.

Hearn, J. and Morgan, D.H.J. (1990) 'Men, masculinities and social theory', in J. Hearn and D.H.J. Morgan (eds), *Men, Masculinities and Social Theory*. London: Unwin Hyman.

Hutchinson, S.L. and Kleiber, D.A. (2000) 'Heroic masculinity following spinal cord injury', *Therapeutic Recreation Journal*, 34 (1): 42–54.

Kimmel, M.S. (2000) *The Gendered Society*. New York, NY: Oxford University Press.

Kriegel, L. (1998) *Flying Solo: Reimagining Manhood, Courage and Loss*. Boston, MA: Beacon.

Lenney, M. and Sercombe, H. (2002) '"Did you see that guy in the wheelchair down the pub?" Interactions across difference in a public place', *Disability and Society*, 17 (1): 5–18.

McKay, J., Messner, M. and Sabo, D. (eds) (2000) *Masculinities, Gender Relations and Sport*. London: Sage.

Morgan, D.H.J. (1992) *Discovering Men*. London: Routledge.

Morris, J. (1991) *Pride Against Prejudice: Transforming Attitudes to Disability*. London: The Women's Press.

Morris, J. (1993) 'Gender and disability', in J. Swain, V. Finkelstein, S. French and M. Oliver (eds), *Disabling Barriers – Enabling Environments*. London: Sage.

Morris, J. (1996) *Encounters with Strangers: Feminism and Disability*. London: The Women's Press.

Murphy, R. (1987) *The Body Silent*. London: Phoenix House.

Oliver, M. (1992) 'Changing the social relations of research production?', *Disability, Handicap and Society*, 7 (2): 101–114.

Oliver, M., Zarb, G., Silver, J., Moore, M. and Salisbury, V. (eds) (1988) *Walking into Darkness: The Experience of Spinal Cord Injury*. London: Macmillan.

O'Neill, T. and Hird, M.J. (2001) 'Double damnation: gay disabled men and the negotiation of masculinity', in K. Backett-Milburn and L. McKie (eds), *Constructing Gendered Bodies*. Basingstoke: Palgrave.

Shakespeare, T. (1994) 'Cultural representations of disabled people: dustbins for disavowal', *Disability and Society*, 9 (3): 283–301.

Shakespeare, T. (1996) 'Power and prejudice: issues of gender, sexuality and disability', in L. Barton (ed.), *Disability and Society: Emerging Issues and Insights*. Harlow: Longman.

Shakespeare, T. (1999) 'When is a man not a man? When he's disabled', in J. Wild (ed.), *Working with Men for Change*. London: UCL.

Shakespeare, T., Gillespie-Sells, K. and Davies, D. (1996) *The Sexual Politics of Disability: Untold Desires*. London: Cassell.

Shakespeare, T. and Watson, N. (1995) 'Defending the social model', *Disability and Society*, 12 (2): 293–300.

Sparkes, A. (1996) 'The fatal flaw: a narrative of the fragile body-self', *Qualitative Enquiry*, 2 (4): 463–94.

Sparkes, A. and Smith, B. (2002) 'Sport, spinal cord injury, embodied masculinities, and the dilemmas of narrative identity', *Men and Masculinities*, 4 (3): 258–85.

Thomas, C. (1999a) *Female Forms: Experiencing and Understanding Disability*. Milton Keynes: Open University Press.

Thomas, C. (1999b) 'Narrative identity and the disabled self', in M. Corker and S. French (eds), *Disability Discourse*. Milton Keynes: Open University Press.

Valentine, G. (1999) 'What it means to be a man: the body, masculinities, disability', in R. Butler and H. Parr (eds), *Mind and Body Spaces: Geographies of Illness, Impairment and Disability*. London: Routledge.

12 'Can you see the rainbow': The Roots of Denial
SALLY FRENCH

Childhood

Some of my earliest memories are of anxious relatives trying to get me to see things. I did not understand why it was so important that I should do so, but was acutely aware of their intense anxiety if I could not. It was aesthetic things like rainbows that bothered them most. They would position me with great precision, tilting my head to precisely the right angle, and then point to the sky saying 'Look, there it is; look, there, there … THERE!'. As far as I was concerned there was nothing there, but if I said as much their anxiety grew even more intense; they would rearrange my position and the whole scenario would be repeated.

In the end, despite a near total lack of colour vision and a complete indifference to the rainbow's whereabouts, I would say I could see it. In that way I was able to release the mounting tension and escape to pursue more interesting tasks. It did not take long to learn that in order to avert episodes like these I had to deny my impairment.

Professionals also led me along the path of denial. This was achieved by their tendency to disbelieve me and interpret my behaviour as 'playing up' when I told them I could not see. Basically they were confused and unable to cope with the ambiguities of partial sight and were not prepared to take instruction on the matter from a mere child. One example of this occurred in the tiny country primary school that I attended. On warm, sunny days we had our lessons outdoors where, because of the strong sunlight, I could not see to read, write or draw. It was only when the two teachers realised I was having similar difficulties eating my dinner that they began to doubt their interpretation that I was a malingerer. On several occasions I was told off by opticians when I failed to discriminate among the different lenses they placed before my eyes. I am not sure whether they really disbelieved me or whether their professional pride was hurt when nothing they could offer seemed to help; whatever it was, I rapidly learned to say 'better' or 'worse', even though all the lenses looked the same.

It was also very difficult to tell the adults, when they had scraped together the money and found the time to take me to the pantomime or wherever, that it was a frustrating and boring experience. I had a strong sense of spoiling other people's fun, just as a sober person among a group of drunken friends may have. This taught me from a very early age that, while the adults were working themselves up about whether or not I could see rainbows, my own anxieties must never be shared.

These anxieties were numerous and centred on getting lost, being slow and, above all, looking stupid and displaying fear. I tried very hard to be 'normal', to be anonymous and to merge with the crowd. Beaches were a nightmare; finding my way back from the sea to specific people in the absence of landmarks was almost impossible, yet giving in to panic was too shameful to contemplate. Anticipation of difficulties could cause even greater anguish than the difficulties themselves. The prospect of outings with lots of sighted children to unfamiliar places was enough to make me physically ill and, with a bewildering mix of remorse and relief, I would stay at home.

Brownie meetings were worrying if any degree of independent movement was allowed; in the summer when we left the confines and safety of our hut to play on the nearby common, the other children would immediately disperse, leaving me alone among the trees, feeling stupid and frightened and wondering what to do next. The adults were always adamant that I should join in, that I should not miss out on the fun, but how much they or the other children noticed my difficulties I do not know; I was never teased or blamed for them, they were simply never discussed, at least not with me. This lack of communication gave me a powerful unspoken message that my impairment and disability must be denied.

By denying the reality of my impairment and disability I protected myself from the anxiety, disapproval, frustration and disappointment of the adults in my life. I denied my impairment and disability in response to their denial, which was often motivated by a benign attempt to integrate me in a world which they perceived as fixed. My denial of impairment and disability was thus not a psychopathological reaction, but a sensible and rational response to the peculiar situation I was in.

Special school

Attending special school at the age of nine was, in many ways, a great relief. Despite the crocodile walks, the bells, the long separations from home, the regimentation and the physical punishment, it was an enormous joy to be with other partially-sighted children and to be in an environment where limited sight was simply not an issue. I discovered that many other children shared my world and, despite the harshness of institutional life, I thrived socially. For the first time in my life I was a standard product and it felt very good. The sighted adults who looked after us were few in number with purely custodial roles, and although they were in a permanent state of anger, provided we stayed out of trouble we were basically ignored. We lived peer-orientated, confined and unchallenging lives where lack of sight rarely as much as entered our heads.

Although the reality of our impairments was not openly denied in this situation, the only thing guaranteed to really enthuse the staff was the slightest glimmer of hope that our sight could be improved. Contact lenses were an innovation at this time, and children who had previously been virtually ignored were nurtured, encouraged and congratulated as they learned to cope with them, and were told how good they looked without their glasses on. Soon after I started at the school, I was selected as one of the guinea-pigs for the experimental 'telescopic lenses' which were designed, at least in part, to preserve our postures (with which there was obsessive concern) by enabling us to read and write from a greater distance. For most of us, the lenses did not work.

I remember being photographed wearing the lenses by an American man whom I perceived to be very important. First of all he made me knit while wearing them, with the knitting held right down on my lap. This was easy as I could in any case knit without looking. He was very excited and enthusiastic and told me how much the lenses were helping. I knew he was wrong. Then he asked me to read, but this changed his mood completely; he became tense, and before taking the photograph he pushed the book, which was a couple of inches from my face, quite roughly to my knees. Although I knew he had cheated and that what he had done was wrong, I still felt culpable for his displeasure and aware that I had failed an important test.

We were forced to use equipment like the telescopic lenses even though it did not help, and sometimes actually made things worse; the behaviour of the adults clearly conveyed the message 'You are not acceptable as you are'. If we dared to reject the equipment we were reminded of the cost, and asked to reflect on the clever and dedicated people who were tirelessly working for the benefit of ungrateful creatures like ourselves.

The only other times that lack of sight became an issue for the children at the school were during the rare and clumsy attempts to integrate us with non-disabled children. The worst possible activity, netball, was usually chosen for this. These occasions were invariably embarrassing and humiliating for all concerned and could lead to desperate manoeuvres on the part of the adults to deny the reality of our situation – namely, that we had insufficient sight to compete. I am reminded of one netball match, with the score around 20–nil, during which we overheard the games mistress of the opposing team anxiously insisting that they let us get some goals. It was a mortifying experience to see the ball fall through the net while they stood idly by! Very occasionally local Brownies would join us for activities in our extensive grounds. We would be paired off with them for a treasure hunt through the woods, searching for milk-bottle tops – the speed at which they found them was really quite amazing. They seemed to know about us, though, and would be very kind and point the 'treasure' out, and even let us pick it up ourselves sometimes, but relying on their bounty spoiled the fun and we wished we could just talk to them or play a different game.

Whether the choice of these activities was a deliberate denial of our situation or simply a lack of imagination on the part of the adults, I do not know. Certainly we played such games successfully among ourselves, and as we were never seen in any other context, perhaps it was the latter. It was only on rare occasions such as these that our lack of sight (which had all but been forgotten) and the artificiality of our world became apparent.

Such was our isolation at this school that issues of how to behave in the 'normal' world were rarely addressed, but at the next special school I attended, which offered a grammar school education and had an entirely different ethos, much attention was paid to this. The headmaster, a strong, resolute pioneer in the education of partially-sighted children, appeared to have a genuine belief not only that we were as good as everyone else, but also that we were almost certainly better, and he spent his life tirelessly battling with people who did not share his view.

He liked us to regard ourselves as sighted and steered us away from any connection with blindness; for example, although we were free to go out by ourselves to the nearby town and beyond, the use of white canes was never suggested, although many of us use them today. He delighted in people who broke new, visually challenging ground, like acceptance at art school or reading degrees in mathematics, and 'blind' occupations, like physiotherapy, were rarely encouraged. In many ways his attitudes were refreshing, yet he placed the onus to achieve and succeed entirely on ourselves; there was never any suggestion that the world could adapt, or that our needs could or should be accommodated. The underlying message was always the same: 'Be superhuman and deny your impairment and disability.'

Adulthood

In adulthood, most of these pressures to deny impairment and disability persist, though they become more subtle. If disabled adults manage to gain control of their lives, these pressures may be easier to resist. This is because situations which pose difficulties, create anxieties or cause boredom can be avoided, or alternatively adequate assistance can be sought; many of the situations I was placed in as a child I now avoid. As adults we are less vulnerable and dependent on other people, we can more easily comprehend our situation, and our adult status makes the open expression of other people's disapproval, frustration and disbelief less likely. In addition, disabled adults arouse less emotion and misplaced optimism than disabled children, which serves to dilute the insatiable drive of many professionals to cure or 'improve' us. Having said this, many of the problems experienced by disabled adults are similar to those experienced by disabled children.

Disabled adults frequently provoke anxiety and embarrassment in others simply by their presence. Although they become skilful at dealing with this, it is often achieved at great cost to themselves by denying their needs. They may, for example, sit through lectures without hearing or seeing rather than embarrass the lecturer, or endure being carried rather than demanding an accessible venue. In situations such as these reassuring phrases, such as 'I'm all right' or 'Don't worry about me' become almost automatic.

One of the reasons we react in this way, rather than being assertive, is to avoid the disapproval, rejection and adverse labelling by others, just as we did when we were children. Our reactions are viewed as resulting from our impairments rather than from the ways we have been treated; thus being 'up front' about impairment and disability can lead us to be labelled 'awkward', 'selfish' or 'warped'. Such labelling can easily undermine our courage and lead us to deny our impairments and disabilities.

Disbelief remains a common response of non-disabled people when we attempt to convey the reality of our impairments. An example of denial through disbelief occurred when I was studying a statistics component as part of a course in psychology. I could see absolutely nothing of what was going on in the lectures and yet my frequent and articulate requests for help were met with the response that all students panic about statistics and that everything would work out fine in the end. As it happens it did, but only after spending many hours with a private tutor. As people are generally not too concerned about how we 'got there', our successes serve to reinforce the erroneous assumption that we really are 'just like everyone else'. When I finally passed the examination, the lecturer concerned informed me, in a jocular and patronising way, that my worries had clearly been unfounded! When people deny our impairments and disabilities, they deny who we really are.

College

At the age of 19, after working for two years, I started my physiotherapy training at a special segregated college for blind and partially-sighted students. For the first time in my life my impairment was, at least in part, defined as blindness. Although about half the students were partially sighted, one of the criteria for entry to the college was the ability to read and write Braille (which I had never used before) and to type proficiently, as, regardless of the clarity of their handwriting, the partially-sighted students were not permitted to write their essays or examinations by hand, and the blind students were not permitted to write theirs in Braille. No visual teaching methods were used in the college and, for those of us with sight, it was no easy matter learning subjects like anatomy, physiology and biomechanics without the use of diagrams.

The institution seemed unable to accept or respond to the fact that our impairments varied in severity and type. We were taught to use special equipment which we did not need and were encouraged to 'feel' rather than 'peer' because feeling, it was thought, was aesthetically more pleasing. There was great concern about the way we looked in our professional roles; white canes were not allowed inside the hospitals where we practised clinically, even by totally blind students, and guide dogs were completely banned. It appeared that the blind students were expected to be superhuman, whereas the partially-sighted students were expected to be blind. Any attempt to defy or challenge these rules was very firmly quashed so, in the interests of 'getting through', we outwardly denied the reality of our impairments and complied.

Employment

Deciding whether or not to deny impairment and disability probably comes most clearly to the fore in adult life when we attempt to gain employment. Until very recently, it was not uncommon to be told very bluntly that, in order to be accepted, the job must be done in exactly the same way as by everyone else. In many ways, this was easier to deal with than the situation now, where 'equal opportunity' policies have simultaneously raised expectations and pushed negative attitudes underground. I am convinced that the denial of my impairment has been an important element in gaining the type of employment I have had. I have never completely denied it (it is not hidden enough for that) but rather, in response to the interviewers' sceptical and probing questions, I have minimised the difficulties I face and portrayed myself in a way that would swell my headmaster's pride.

Curiously, once in a job, people have sometimes decided that certain tasks, which I can perform quite adequately, are beyond me, while at the same time refusing to relieve me of those I cannot do. At one university where I worked it was considered impossible for me to cope with taking the minutes of meetings, but my request to be relieved of invigilating large numbers of students, on the grounds that I could not see them, was not granted. Once again, the nature of my impairment and disability was being defined by other people.

Conclusion

I believe that from earliest childhood, denial of impairment and disability is totally rational, given the situations we find ourselves in. We deny our impairments and disabilities for social, economic and emotional survival and we do so at considerable cost to ourselves; it is not something we do because of flaws in our individual psyches. For those of us disabled from birth or early childhood, denial of impairment and disability has deeply penetrating and entangled roots; we need support and encouragement to make our needs known, but this will only be achieved within the context of genuine social change.

I have drawn upon my experiences and personal reactions to elucidate the pressures placed upon disabled people to deny their experience of impairment and disability. This approach is limited inasmuch as personal experiences and responses can never be divorced from the biography of the person they concern. In addition, these pressures will vary according to the individual's impairment. But with these limitations in mind, I am confident that most disabled people will identify with what I have described and that only the examples are, strictly speaking, mine.

13 Impairment, Difference and 'Identity'
MAIRIAN SCOTT-HILL

In recent years, questions of identity have become increasingly central to the human and social sciences (Woodward, 1997; Hetherington, 1998; du Gay et al., 2000). Consequently, there is now a considerable body of literature within disability studies, drawing on a range of theoretical and conceptual frameworks, which is concerned with identity formation (Campbell and Oliver, 1996; Corker, 1996; Barnes et al., 1999; Linton, 1998; Thomas, 1999; Michalko, 2002). What these accounts share is the view that identity is concerned with the social formation of the person, the cultural interpretation of the body and the creation and use of markers of membership such as rites of passage and social categories. As such, it might be thought of as mediating between the personal, private world of everyday life and the collective space of multiple cultural forms and social relations: it is a pivot between the social and the individual.

It is clear that identity is ultimately about *both* sameness *and* difference – as Hetherington puts it, identity is 'articulated through the relationship between belonging, recognition or identification, and difference' (1998: 15). However, this chapter suggests that disability studies places a political premium on a strong, collective identity in disabled people's struggle against oppression, whilst playing down matters of difference in key areas. This approach becomes a particular problem when we consider that all disabled people, whatever definition or model is used, are people with impairments. It would seem from this that the inclusion of people with impairments in disability politics is just as important as the inclusion of disabled people in political process *per se*. Yet disability studies remains divided on the question of whether impairment constitutes *legitimate* difference and on the relationship between impairment (the individual) and identity (the social). Given that identity itself is a rather woolly concept, it is important to ask whether difference troubles may result not from impairment itself, but from the intolerance of difference coupled with a simplistic and conservative view of political process within the disabled people's movement.

Understanding identity

As suggested above, identity is social: it is constructed in and through social relations of difference. However, both 'social relations' and 'difference' can be conceptualised in various ways, with the result that 'identity' is not uniform in its meaning. It is therefore important to ask:

- What are the main units of difference?
- What underlying assumptions are made about the relationship between these units of difference?

Figure 13.1 suggests that though identity is both the *social product* of difference and a *social process* that is lived in and through social relations of difference, certain kinds of social relations place the emphasis on one or the other or both. For example, structural relations emphasise 'parts' rather than 'people' as the units of difference and so identity is more likely to be viewed as a product. Conversely, cultural relationships emphasise people and identity as process. Figure 13.1 describes four dimensions of social relations: *structural, cultural, individualist and collectivist* (see Corker, 1996: 41–5 and 2003 for a detailed explanation). A historical account of disability studies over the last three decades would probably distinguish four main models of identity on the basis of the relative weighting given to each of these dimensions: the deficit model, the dominance model, the cultural difference model and the narrative model. As the following sections show, all but the first of these models incorporate a political understanding of collective identity as an important focal point for the creation of new activities, new worlds and new ways of being. Because impairment is so central to the deficit model, all of the other models have particular implications for the inclusion of people with impairments in the collective and in disability politics.

The deficit model

In the deficit model, the main units of difference are impairment and 'normality'. The relationship between them is assumed to be one of *dependence*: impairment is a source of 'problems' and depends upon 'normality' to provide the solutions. People with impairments, or biomedical conditions, are seen to be both responsible for their individual conditions and as functionally restricted when compared to people without impairments. They are separated from each other and from people without impairments through the use of hierarchical diagnostic and administrative categories – functional difference, or 'ways of doing', is used to divide and rule. These categories are assumed to be relatively autonomous and unrelated, and are typically organised in a structural relationship based on type, degree and severity of impairment ('need') and the allocation of resources. This is a structural relationship because it emphasises 'parts' rather than 'people', and assumes that people with impairments are only connected through professional services and institutional practices. Because of the assumption of functional limitation, the effects of impairment are always adjudged as negative. Therefore people with impairments are perceived as having a negative identity that must be eradicated or normalised.

The dominance model

The dominance model of identity takes 'the individual' and 'the social' as the main units of difference, and is at the heart of approaches to disability studies that rest on the social model of disability. It is assumed that there is an inherent conflict between these units of difference: the social (disability) is the source of unity while the individual (impairment) is the source of discord and fragmentation because they are typically organised in a structural relation that emphasises inequalities of power (Finkelstein, 1993). The political challenge can only be successful when there is unity of the oppressed. But this relationship is not a

Figure 13.1   Social relations of identity

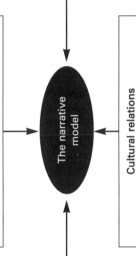

Structural relations

Emphasise the relationships between 'parts', giving priority mostly to institutions, norms and rules. They emphasise cultural systems, discourses and history. They seek underlying explanatory structures that account for social patterns and tend to view action as a mere realisation of these structures in specific circumstances. The most extreme forms of structural relations deny agency or knowledge to individual actors.

The dominance model

Collectivist relations

Emphasise 'we' consciousness, collective identity, emotional dependence, group solidarity, sharing, duties and obligations, a need for stable and predetermined friendship, group decision and particularism. They generally take an *interdependent* view of individuals, and are defined by specific and firm group boundaries which emphasis a *we* (the in-group) versus *they* (the out-group) distinction.

The cultural difference model

The narrative model

Cultural relations

Emphasise the relationships between 'people'. They give primacy to the dynamics of everyday existence, improvisation, co-ordination and interaction. They emphasise agency and intentions. They mostly address the interactive relations of people with their environment. They focus on the experience and the local construction of individual or interpersonal events such as activities and conversions. The most extreme of them ignore structure altogether.

The deficit model

Individualist relations

Emphasise 'I' consciousness, autonomy, emotional independence, individual initiative. the right to privacy, the need for specific friendship and universalism. They stress an *I* versus *you* distinction and on having an explicit and firm boundary between self and others, and take an *independent* view of the individual.

simple one because 'the social' is seen to be both a problem and a solution. It is a problem because 'normality' socially creates a negative identity. It is a solution because the social organisation of people with impairments leads to the formation of a collective disabled identity that is variously described as 'strong', 'positive', 'visible' and 'proud' (Morris, 1991; Campbell and Oliver, 1996; Barnes et al., 1999; Linton, 1998; Scott-Hill, 2002). This identity empowers and inspires disabled people, enabling them 'to challenge traditional stereotypes of passivity, pathology and weakness' (Barnes et al., 1999: 175) that are perpetrated by the deficit model through the practice of 'identity politics' (Anspach, 1979). Identity politics works to an 'outside-in' agenda (Chapter 4; Barnes et al., 2002: 253) that both polarises the individual-collective dichotomy and aims to reverse the terms of reference of the deficit model. Thus the focus is on independence, freedom and rights.

At the same time, disabled identity is built on the underlying assumption that people with impairments are only connected through their experience of and resistance to structural oppression. Impairment is both a residue of the deficit model, located in the individual, and an essence: impaired bodies are essentially different from non-impaired bodies. The emphasis on functionality, or 'ways of doing', is also retained. Further, Linton (1998: 12) suggests that 'the degree and significance of an individual's impairment is often less of an issue than the degree to which someone identifies as disabled.' This is indicative of what Thomas (1999: 113) calls a 'categorical approach to identity': identity can be 'read off' from the categories with which one identifies and belongs to. Disabled identity also tends to be regarded as the 'master identity' of the social – the category through which all other social identities are to be mediated. Difference, if sometimes reluctantly, can only be accommodated by exploring how the marked identity category disability interacts with other marked, but nevertheless discrete identity categories, such as class, race, gender, sexuality and age (Linton, 1998; Shakespeare and Watson, 1998).

The cultural difference model

The cultural difference model takes cultures as its main units of difference. With the emphasis on 'people' rather than 'parts', it assumes a cultural relation of difference between people with impairments and people without impairments. The exclusion and segregation of people with impairments from mainstream social life produces marked differences in 'ways of being' ('cultures'), which become the basis of different knowledges. These different knowledges, when claimed, mark the boundary between a 'cultural minority' and other 'cultures'. The political agenda is 'inside-out' (Chapter 4) and places a premium on the argument that the personal is political. The political goals of such a *cultural identity* tend to be mostly concerned with the pursuit of cultural autonomy and integrity. How this happens depends upon whether the version of culture deployed emphasises fixed or fluid group boundaries. For example, a fixed cultural identity is characterised by two main social-relational forms: *separatism* and *elitism*. As in the dominance model, a categorical approach to identity is assumed, but one that hinges on culture. In the first, the collective is turned completely inwards, aiming for minority rights to cultural autonomy and social co-existence sometimes to the point of nationalism. It thrives on a *we* (the in-group) versus *they* (the out-group) distinction, and there tends to be a lack of tolerance of internal differences. The most commonly cited example of this kind of identity is 'deaf identity' (Corker, 1996). In the second, some groups within the culture develop elitist and often restricted stances on culture, such as those that refer to a state of intellectual refinement associated with the arts, philosophy and learning ('high' culture). The elitist cultural identity gains power through its difference *and distance* from 'popular culture' – what ordinary disabled people do in everyday life. Within the cultural difference model, impairment is treated in two main ways: it *disappears*, because bodily differences are seen as cultural representations that are socially constructed by the normative gaze, or it is *naturalised* in such a way that it becomes the essence of cultural difference. In this way, though the model stresses interdependence of people with impairments, it also creates, rather than mitigates, inequalities of power.

The narrative model

The final social-relational form of identity emphasises the shared meanings and social and material practices that bind individuals together in society. The extent to which apparently disparate meanings and practices can be shared, and the level of interdependency that can be achieved, is embedded in the relationship between them (Corker, 2001). This is the only approach in which identity is seen as 'both socially produced in particular historical times and places, and acted upon and shaped by the individual' (Thomas, 1999: 119). It is also the only approach that dispenses with the artificial boundary between 'doing' and 'being'. The main units of difference are stories ('narratives'), but these stories are embedded in and realised through a network of social relationships between people and their environments. The act of narrating shows that words do things and actions 'speak'. Though identity does not rest on sameness or essence, it does acquire durability and permanence through the stories we tell ourselves and others about our history, our geography; about, in short, our place in the order of things. Underlying this model is a belief that generalisations and stereotypes miss the lived complexity of identity just as much as a reified, biologically based notion of individuality misses its social character. Thus, a simplistic individual–collective dichotomy is to be avoided. Similarly, because structural and cultural relations of difference penetrate each other, it is possible to acknowledge the specific tensions between them without assuming that they diverge in some fundamental way (Corker, 2003). The narrative model therefore gives equal primacy to the dynamics of everyday existence – 'popular culture' – and to social structures. Though the model understands that the particular relationship between the two will not always be the same, and is always situated or dependent on context, it does not lose sight of the fact that collective identities can come to rest on inequalities of interdependence. It is important for this reason that identity can accommodate change and respond to challenge. 'Narrative identity' (Corker, 1996; Thomas, 1999) is tolerant of difference because it deploys a version of culture that emphasises fluid boundaries, both between individuals and between the collective and the wider social system. When the political imperative is placed on relationships, people with impairments become who they are because of the way they are positioned in interaction with others in various contexts.

Impairment, difference and identity

The important point to make about the above analysis is that categorical approaches to identity tend to place restrictions on how difference – particularly difference relating to impairment – is included in political process. In both the dominance model and the cultural difference model, identity relies for its existence on its alter ego: 'negative identity'. The latter both differs from identity and provides the conditions for it to exist. Disabled identity is distinguished by what it is not – impaired. Identity is thus marked out by difference, but this marking of difference is problematic. On the one hand, the assertion of difference between disability and impairment, or the conflation of the two, involves a denial that there are any similarities between them. Difference is founded on exclusion. On the other, the claim of difference is also troubling to disabled people who acknowledge, at least at the level of private, lived experience, that they are all oppressed because they are people with impairments (Corker, 1999).

Any attempt to include impairment in the analysis of identity is seen as a threat to the unity of the disabled people's movement and its political message (Finkelstein, 1993). Put simply, if the unity of the disabled people's movement ('we') is to be preserved, there can be no qualification of exactly what 'we' means. The disjuncture between the unity of the public identity ('we are all disabled') and the private identity ('we all experience impairment') creates confusion for the disabled people's movement, which seems to contradict itself in claiming massive difference between disability and impairment *as well as* similarity. This puts a different face on the position of Barnes et al., for example, who suggest that people with accredited impairments find it:

> ... particularly hard to adopt a disabled identity, as socially oppressed. ... Unlike women and black people, their oppression has been generally submerged within the rhetoric of benevolent paternalism, professional altruism and philanthropy. ... What little evidence there is suggests that it [the disabled people's movement] has proved relatively unsuccessful in developing positive identities and group consciousness beyond specific groups; notably those with physical and sensory impairments, who are both relatively active and relatively young. (1999: 179)

If identity is articulated through the relationship between belonging, recognition or identification, and difference, both the failure to qualify 'we' and the promotion of particularistic understandings of 'we' must in themselves have direct consequences for inclusion. The political imperative of making disabled people visible and creating a unified voice against oppression (public campaigns) may seem more important than matters relating to the engagement, participation and representation of some people with impairments in the disabled people's movement (private concerns). Thus, a visible identity is both built on and excludes hidden impairments, which are said to 'pass' as normal. Presences create absences. This denies the complexity of social interaction in situations where, for example, impairment *can* only be made visible in words. It also eschews the potential of understandings of power that work in and through *in*visibility and subterfuge. Similarly, the trouble that impairment causes is exacerbated when the demand for access to work is seen as the crucial component of the struggle for equality. For, as Abberley notes, 'even in a society which did make profound and genuine attempts to integrate impaired people into the world of work, some would be excluded by their impairment' (1998: 89).

If communication is always seen to be the responsibility of the individual and/or is restricted to the examination of specific communication impairments, the collective misses the significance that communication has for political processes of representation and struggle (Corker, 2001; Scott-Hill, 2002). The division between public and private appears to absolve disability politics from the necessity of being cautious about speaking for others, assuming commonalities and creating 'new shades of universalism' (Thomas, 1999: 109). Without a relational politics, the power differential between 'inside' and 'outside' must be conceived as resulting not from difference itself, but from the lack of dialogue across difference.

References

Abberley, P. (1998) 'Disabled people and social theory', in T. Shakespeare (ed.), *The Disability Reader: Social Science Perspectives*. London: Continuum.

Anspach, R. (1979) 'From stigma to identity politics', *Social Science and Medicine*, 13A, 765–73.

Barnes, C., Mercer, G. and Shakespeare, T. (1999) *Exploring Disability: A Sociological Introduction*. Cambridge: Polity.

Barnes, C., Oliver, M. and Barton, L. (2002*) Disability Studies Today*. Cambridge: Polity.

Campbell, J. and Oliver, M. (1996) *Disability Politics: Understanding Our Past, Changing Our Future*. London: Routledge.

Corker, M. (1996) *Deaf Transitions*. London: Jessica Kingsley.

Corker, M. (1999) 'Differences, conflations and foundations: The limits to the "accurate" representation of disabled people's experience', *Disability and Society*, 14 (5): 627–42.

Corker, M. (2001) 'Sensing disability', *Hypatia*, 16 (4) (Fall): 34–52.

Corker, M. (2003) 'Deafness/Disability – problematising notions of identity, culture and structure', in S. Riddell and N. Watson (eds), *Disability, Culture and Identity*. London: Pearson.

du Gay, P., Evans, J. and Redman, P. (2000) *Identity: A Reader*. London: Sage.

Finkelstein, V. (1993) 'The commonality of disability', in J. Swain, V. Finkelstein, S. French and M. Oliver (eds), *Disabling Barriers – Enabling Environments*. London: Sage.

Hetherington, K. (1998) *Expressions of Identity: Space, Performance, Politics*. London: Sage.

Linton, S. (1998) *Claiming Disability: Knowledge and Identity*. New York, NY: New York University Press.

Michalko, R. (2002) *The Difference Disability Makes*. Philadelphia, PA: Temple University Press.

Morris, J. (1991) *Pride Against Prejudice*. London: The Women's Press.

Scott-Hill, M. (2002) 'Policy, politics and the silencing of "voice"', *Policy and Politics*, 30(3): 397–409.

Shakespeare, T. and Watson, N. (1998) 'Theoretical perspectives on research with disabled children', in C. Robinson and K. Stalker (eds), *Growing Up with Disability*. London: Jessica Kingsley.

Thomas, C. (1999) *Female Forms*. Buckingham: Open University Press.

Woodward, K. (ed.) (1997) *Identity and Difference*. London: Sage.

14 Generating Debates: Why we Need a Life Course Approach to Disability Issues
MARK PRIESTLEY

This chapter argues that we should include issues of generation and the life course when thinking about disability in modern societies. This perspective is important because it highlights how disabling societies affect people of different generations in different ways (for example, disabled children, young people, adults or older people). This perspective is important because it helps us to avoid an over-simplification of disabled people's collective experiences and redresses the marginalisation of under-represented groups (especially disabled children and older people).

Generation as difference

Disability studies has tended to emphasise the collective experiences of disabled people as an oppressed group in society, and this has been a very productive approach. There are dangers, however, in over-simplifying the collective experience when we know that disabling societies affect different people in different ways. For example, there have been increasing claims that the disability experience is markedly different for men and women, for people with different kinds of impairment, for people from different ethnic backgrounds and in different cultural contexts. In this context, a life course approach suggests that disability also carries a different significance for people of different ages and at different stages of life.

Just as gender theorists have shown how much can be gained by distinguishing between disabled women and disabled men, so a life course approach suggests that we might gain a great deal by starting to think more carefully about the generational experiences of 'disabled children', 'disabled adults' or 'disabled elders', for example. When we look at the way disability is produced and regulated within modern societies, there are some very important generational dimensions. Thinking about disability in terms of generation helps us to understand more clearly how disability and impairment are produced, how they are socially constructed, and how they are regulated in significantly different ways across the life course.

Generation, in this sense, is about more than just age. It involves thinking about the ways that important generational categories (like childhood, youth, adulthood or old age) are constructed, and how transitions between them are governed through social institutions. A good example here is the apparent lack of critical debate about disability issues in old age. The likelihood of impairment increases with age and, in Western industrialised societies, the majority of disabled people are over retirement age. Yet older people are rarely considered as 'disabled' in quite the same way that younger adults and children often are (even within more radical debates on disability rights). Understanding these anomalies is only possible if we consider the relationship between disability and generation.

To summarise, adopting a life course approach involves thinking about the way in which life course transitions are organised at a collective level within societies and about the generational significance of disability issues as they affect people of different ages. It adds a new dimension to our understanding of disability and offers new ways of thinking about a wide range of debates (in a similar way to the introduction of a gendered analysis). The following sections suggest some of these themes in relation to the body, identity, culture and structure. These arguments are developed in more detail in two recent books, Priestley (2001, 2003).

Generating bodies

The development of critical disability theory has seen a shift from historical concerns with the impaired body towards a more social and political view of disability. This shift of focus from the body to society has been critical in the development of a social model of disability. However, it has also attracted some criticism from those who take a more social view of the body (Hughes and Paterson, 1997). Thinking about the body in its social and cultural sense is less problematic for disability studies than traditional medical views of the body and has much relevance for the relationship between disability, generation and the life course.

For example, we might note that bodily impairment characteristics appear to carry a much greater social significance for disabled children and young people than they do in later life. In this sense, social concerns with bodily imperfection seem to play more heavily on disabled children and the unborn than on older people. Although social theorists have suggested an increasing tolerance towards bodily diversity in postmodern consumer societies (Featherstone, 1991), there is little evidence of such developments in relation to tolerance about the birth of disabled children. The pressures on parents and doctors to produce 'normal' children certainly appear to have less in common with celebrations of diversity than with pursuing uniformity and the normalisation of the body.

Thinking about youth and adulthood also highlights the generational significance of the body in disability debates. Idealised constructions of youthfulness play heavily on the pursuit of bodily perfection in consumer societies, while constructions of independent adulthood emphasise autonomy in physical and cognitive function. These bodily ideals contribute to disability in two ways. First, they provide cultural scripts for decoding the body's potency as an object of beauty or sexual desire – leading to the aesthetic oppression of those whose bodily characteristics are not read in this way (Hughes, 2000). Second, there is the underlying assumption that young adult bodies should be fit for production and reproduction in the interests of capital, patriarchy and the state.

The significance of a generational account of the body is also underlined in the case of old age. The impaired body has figured prominently in constructions of old age, yet rarely has this been articulated as a disability debate. Indeed, embodied experiences of impairment have been viewed as less 'disruptive' in old age than in childhood or young adulthood (Williams, 2000). It is tempting to conclude that the biographical normality of the impaired body in old age may explain why older people with impairments are rarely seen as disabled in the way that younger adults are.

Disability studies and disability activism pose some significant challenges to the normalisation of the body, such as resistance to the 'myth of bodily perfection' (Stone, 1995).

There has also been active resistance to the elimination of diversity through genetic technologies and eugenic practices. Similarly, disability culture has offered new representations of the body that place greater value on difference and diversity in constructions of physical beauty or sexual attractiveness (Shakespeare, 2000). However, it is also evident that such claims remain rooted in associations between beauty and youth, thereby failing to challenge the power relationships of a generational system that devalues bodies in later life.

Generating identities

Just as a consideration of the body throws up a number of generational issues, thinking about identity is also a useful approach. Encounters with disabling barriers and practices have a considerable impact on disabled people's identity. For example, the construction of disabled births as 'wrongful lives' and attempts to eradicate impairment characteristics devalue the perceived worth of disabled people in society. Similarly, the normalisation of child development, and the segregation of children with impairments, reinforce negative associations with 'developmental delay' and abnormality. Barriers to participation in the socially valued areas of paid employment and parenting have denied many disabled people access to the social networks and citizenship rights upon which adult identities are premised.

Institutional responses to disability have relied on definitions that tend to group disabled people together according to impairment labels or the convenience of service bureaucracies. This has been reflected in the denial of more nuanced and situated identities. For example, disabled children and young people have often been ascribed relatively static identities that privilege their impairment status above attributes of gender, class, ethnicity or sexuality. Here, age and generation are also important, since generational identities and cultures (especially youth cultures) are a significant aspect of personal biography and identity.

For example, limited access to peer networks and youth cultures may create conflicts of identity management for disabled young people, forcing them to choose between their disability identity and their youth identity. By contrast, it has been suggested that identity management in old age may be less affected by impairment or by disabling barriers. That is not to say that older people with impairments are not discriminated against as disabled people – far from it. Rather, the assertion is that impairment and disability in old age might be construed as less disruptive to normal identities of ageing than, say, impairment in younger adulthood (because disability is more widely anticipated in old age).

The development of disability culture and disability politics has been important in promoting more positive identities. However, these new identity resources are very adult-focused. Disabled children, young people and elders remain conspicuous by their absence from disability culture. For both younger and older people then, choosing positive disability identities within the movement may mean losing contact with important generational networks and identities. If disability culture is to maintain the inclusiveness of a shared disability identity, it must also resist the temptation to accept the kind of power relationships that place adult interests first.

Generating cultural representations

Cultural analyses also show how disability is constructed in different ways at different points in the life course. There is also a certain cultural similarity in the way that disability, childhood and old age have been constructed as 'non-adult' social categories (both marginal to and dependent upon adults). Such constructions have been important in the governance of disability through social institutions. For example, the cultural construction of disabled people as childlike (as innocent, asexual, or untamed) has been reproduced in the legitimation of adult power relationships based on custodial care and surveillance. Similarly, the infantilisation and social death of older people in institutional settings has much in common with that experienced by both children and disabled adults (Hockey and James, 1993).

Culturally, life course expectations in modern societies continue to be defined in relation to idealised notions of modern adulthood. Such constructions have been highly gendered, with a traditional emphasis on distinctive male and female adult roles centred on participation in productive or reproductive labour respectively (specifically, employment and parenting). By contrast, children, young people, elders and disabled people of all ages have been constructed as lacking the kind of adult attributes upon which full personhood and citizenship are premised.

However, there have been significant cultural challenges to this adult-centred construction of the life course. The recognition of generational conflict and power relationships has been mirrored in a new generational politics, in which non-adult minority groups have made new claims to adult rights and responsibilities. The emergence of movements for the rights of children and older people place an increasing strain on traditional constructions of citizenship as a uniquely adult-centred concept. Social claims from the disabled people's movement have raised similar challenges, emphasising self-determination, reflexivity and interdependence over the cultural ideals of autonomous functioning.

Generating social structures

The development of social models of disability was underpinned by a structural analysis, demonstrating how people with perceived impairments become disabled through processes of social transformation (Oliver, 1990). In particular, materialist accounts pointed to historic changes in the social relations of production and reproduction within Western capitalist economies as a driving force for the creation of disability as a social and administrative category. Here, the changing demands of industrialisation, competitive labour markets, new technologies and the patriarchal nation state have all been important.

Structural analyses also help to explain the emergence of the generational system. For example, it could equally be argued that similar processes of social change created the categories of childhood and youth. Thus, the increasing demands of industrialisation and individuation in knowledge societies have led to an extension of the training required before young people can participate effectively in productive adult labour (Irwin, 1995). In this sense, the regulation of childhood and youth as dependent non-adult states has been driven by economic developments and the changing structure of adult labour markets. At the same time, increased longevity and the exemption of older workers from those same labour markets (through retirement) created a parallel category of old age. Clearly, there are considerable parallels between these processes and those that have produced the structural dependency of disabled people in modern societies.

So, a structural analysis of disability makes little sense as a 'special case', in isolation from the production of the generational system. In particular, it is important to understand the centrality of adult work and employment in producing both disability and generational boundaries. This may help to explain why the political focus of disability debates still falls so heavily on adult-centred issues (particularly on issues of employment and parenting). While disability in youth and old age can be partially accommodated within an existing generational system of dependency, disability in adulthood stands out as a greater structural challenge. In this sense, social responses to disabled children have had much to do with structural concerns about their potential for participation in future adulthood. Conversely, the distinct lack of any institutional or policy focus on disability in old age reflects the fact that older people are already structurally exempt from productive or caring adult labour.

These structural analyses of both disability and the generational system have been premised on a particular view of the social relations of production in modern societies. As Meyer concludes:

> The life course in modern societies is itself a construct with deep cultural supports. It is not simply the aggregate product of a series of individual choices, nor is it the accidental construction of institutions organized around other cultural purposes. To a substantial extent, the life course is a conscious and purposive cultural product of the modern system. (1988: 57)

Given that much contemporary social theory is now concerned with explaining transitions from modern societies towards late modern or postmodern forms of social organisation, it is important to question how this affects our understanding of disability and the generational system for the future. Two themes seem important here. First, processes of individuation have undermined the apparent predictability of our traditional life course pathways and expectations. As a consequence, the 'normal' life course has been increasingly redefined in terms of individually negotiated 'life projects' and risks (Giddens, 1991; Rustin, 2000). As these traditional life expectations break down, it is perhaps unsurprising that the progress of disabled people's claims to full participation and equality have occurred at the same time as parallel claims from 'non-adult' generational minorities (particularly children and older people). Second, social status is becoming increasingly defined by our patterns of consumption rather than our contribution to production. Since our understanding of both disability and the generational system are premised on an analysis of the social relations of production, such changes pose an additional challenge.

Conclusion

As I hope this brief chapter shows, the concepts of generation and the life course add another dimension to our understanding of disabling barriers and disability debates.

Adopting a life course approach also raises a number of important generational questions. Why, for example, have states gone to such lengths to limit or prevent the birth of disabled children? Why have disabled children been so often excluded from mainstream education? What is the significance of youth culture and youth transitions for young disabled people? How does the expectation of an 'independent' adulthood contribute to the production of disability in modern societies? Why are older people with impairments rarely seen as disabled in quite the same way that younger adults often are? Why are different moral standards applied to the death and dying of disabled and non-disabled people? Thinking about such questions helps to explain how our understanding of disability is framed within a very particular view of normal life course progression and its social organisation in contemporary societies.

References

Featherstone, M. (1991) 'The body in consumer culture', in M. Featherstone, M. Hepworth and B. Turner (eds.), *The Body: Social Process and Cultural Theory*. London: Sage.

Giddens, A. (1991) *Modernity and Self-Identity: Self and Society in the Late Modern Age*. Cambridge: Polity Press.

Hockey, J. and James, A. (1993). *Growing Up and Growing Older: Ageing and Dependency in the Life Course*. London: Sage.

Hughes, B. (2000) 'Medicine and the aesthetic invalidation of disabled people', *Disability and Society*, 15 (4): 555–68.

Hughes, B. and Paterson, K. (1997) 'The social model of disability and the disappearing body: towards a sociology of impairment', *Disability and Society*, 12 (3): 325–40.

Irwin, S. (1995) *Rights of Passage: Social Change and the Transition from Youth to Adulthood*. London: UCL.

Meyer, J. (1988) 'Levels of analysis: the life course as a cultural construction', in M.W. Riley (ed.), *Social Structures and Human Lives*. Newbury Park, CA: Sage.

Oliver, M. (1990) *The Politics of Disablement*. Basingstoke: Macmillan.

Priestley, M. (ed.) (2001) *Disability and the Life Course: Global Perspectives*. Cambridge: Cambridge University Press.

Priestley, M. (2003) *Disability: A Life Course Approach*. Cambridge: Polity.

Rustin, M. (2000) 'Reflections on the biographical turn in social sciences', in P. Chamberlayne, J. Bornat and T. Wengraf (eds), *The Turn to Biographical Methods in Social Science: Comparative Issues and Examples*. London: Routledge.

Shakespeare, T. (2000) 'Disabled sexuality: toward rights and recognition', *Sexuality and Disability*, 18 (3): 159–66.

Stone, S.D. (1995) 'The myth of bodily perfection', *Disability and Society*, 10 (4): 413–24.

Williams, S. (2000) 'Chronic illness as biographical disruption or biographical disruption as chronic illness? Reflections on a core concept', *Sociology of Health and Illness*, 22 (1): 40–67.

15 The Changing Face of Representations of Disability in the Media
PAUL ANTHONY DARKE

The representation of disability in the media in the last ten years is pretty much the same as it has always been: clichéd, stereotyped and archetypal. Though it is not really disability imagery or representation (in any meaning of the word). It is impairment imagery; imagery where disability is understood to be the impairment almost devoid of political significance or social construction. Impairment imagery abounds on all channels and in all media forms: television, film, radio and in print. If anything, impairment imagery is on the increase. Equally, the war of words amongst disabled people themselves – academics, broadcasters, artists and lay people alike – about the nature and meaning of disability imagery/representation has grown considerably. A major new text seems to come out annually articulating some new theoretical position (decrying last year's theories as old hat and detrimental to the greater good of disability emancipation). For example, the Disability Studies postmodernists (Corker and Shakespeare, 2002) – rectifiers and revisionists – are currently, misguidedly, arguing that impairment imagery is nothing other than the Art of Art or the nature of aesthetics (if only) and not actually disempowering at all but merely a misunderstanding of art history and genre (in film, painting and literary texts).

Perhaps the most significant factor in the increase in impairment imagery is due to the fact that the mainstream broadcasters in the UK (the BBC and Channel 4 in particular), as well as many sections of the print media (the broadsheets in particular), have significantly shifted in their attitude towards disability. Whereas there used to be (within the last five years) a number of coherent disability perspective programme series on a number of UK television channels, there are now none at all. Ten years ago there was a disability television series (a politicised output made by disabled people, with a belief in the social model, themselves) on every major UK terrestrial broadcast channel. Thus, it could be argued, a significant de-politicisation of disability has taken place in favour of a fragmented impairment orientated broadcast output which is now, more than ever, linked to a charity or 'freak' philosophy: fundamentally voyeuristic and exploitative.

The move away from the domination of the number of a few terrestrial broadcasters to the addition of a plethora of competing channels from satellite, digital and cable channels has meant that the main broadcasters have started to focus more on ratings and the 'quick fix' of consumerist television. Disability, as a political issue (like many other political issues), does not seem to fit into such a schedule; except perhaps as a consumerist issue: liberal rights for the few consumer-like and normalised disabled people or the increasing business-like mentality of the large and powerful charities and their political lobby machines. For example, whereas the commercial channel ITV used to have a politicised disability programme such as *Link*, it now has *Esther*, hosted by Esther Rantzen. *Esther* is a magazine-style programme rooted in the charity consumerist/rights model of impairment and, unlike *Link*, is not made by disabled people (though it has the occasional disabled reporter). *Esther* has a number of items in each show and maybe one or two are occasionally 'disability' themed (actually impairment-specific in reality), whereas *Link* was entirely about disability and, occasionally, about impairment.

The move away from disability-specific programming – seen equally at the BBC and particularly at the 'minority' interests broadcaster Channel 4 – is, they have argued, about 'mainstreaming disability'. This is the placement of disability within the mainstream of programme production and output at those two corporations. Another pure example of mainstreaming is the cancellation of the BBC Radio 4's long-running *Does He Take Sugar* programme. It has been 'replaced' by the mainstreaming of disability stories and issues within Radio 4's lunchtime daily magazine show *You and Yours*. In fact, disability, the social process of exclusionary practices of society against disabled people, has not been 'mainstreamed': impairment has. Disability has almost entirely been lost except as a political, or even polemical, issue linked to impairment charities or particular socio-political or medical issues. For example, Channel 4 has made a big play of its disability and sexuality campaign to allow disabled people to access prostitutes, sex surrogates and be sexually active. In reality this is merely 'normalisation' under a political headline and not actually about disability. The concentration by broadcasters on impairment issues, increasingly being fed by the main wealthy charities' insidiously professional and effective (and large) Public Relations departments, is increasing as the charities opportunistically appropriate the language – not the essence – of disability social model politics and use it for their own, impairment orientated, agendas.

The seemingly paradoxical acceptance of, whilst at the same time there is a backlash against, disability political correctness can be seen as at the heart of the matter. The original intent and meaning of political correctness in relation to the social model of disability – an understanding of the genealogy of oppression through culture – is what has been negated and replaced by an acceptance of what political correctness has become: the sanitisation of past unpleasantries or objections to extreme examples of abuse against impaired individuals. By which I mean that whereas broadcasters and journalists would routinely use the term 'cripple' or 'handicapped', they now routinely use the term 'disabled', but actually have as little understanding of the politicisation of the issues as they did when they previously used the terms 'cripple' or 'handicapped'. The language has changed but not the politics behind it; for example, institutionalisation itself is not questioned, only the excesses of abuse within an institution. The media, particularly the printed press but also investigative television journalism, will highlight that a particular 'bad' 'home' is using illegal restraining practices, whilst a model of 'good practice' 'home' is just down the road and that one should learn from the other! The media will make a clear distinction, for example, between good and bad institutionalisation, whilst never actually realising (let alone understand) the politics of institutionalisation as an abuse against disabled people in itself.

Significantly, and increasingly so – and this is at the heart of the matter – a news item may well be presented by a pretty and highly normalised disabled presenter or reporter. Thus, and this is true across all forms of media representation of disability (impairment), political correctness has been a sanitising process rather than an educative or politicisation of disability (as it was originally intended to be). What one now gets (and this is especially true of television) is the clear distinction between the rights and representation of two quite distinct classes of disabled (impaired) people; the normalised and the un-normalisable disabled people; the 'good' and the 'bad' cripple (disabled people). The same could be said for race, gay and gender issues within the media and, in this sense, disabled people are being no less or better represented than other minority groups. Rights and equality are increasingly being seen as the prerogative of one group of disabled people (the 'good') over and above another (the 'bad') and this social process is being clearly reflected in representations of disabled people throughout the media; it may be subtly being carried out at the moment, but it will increasingly become less ambiguous as time goes on and other issues affect the position of both groups of disabled people within society (such as genetics and euthanasia). In addition, rights (Human Rights) is increasingly being represented as something which the bad cripple should have the right to exercise in the facilitation of their non-existence (euthanasia stories increasingly talk of disabled people's right to kill themselves as just and as an axiomatic truth).

In this context, one can see that the politicisation of disability issues that had begun within the media in the last 20 years has been rejected and replaced by the new political correctness of 'mainstreaming' or sanitising impairment. Television, in this respect, is not that different to Hollywood or the main 'serious' sections of the newsprint media. Significantly, one cannot forget the role disabled people themselves have played in this trend through their own articulation in the early days of disability imagery criticism in arguing for 'positive' images over what they saw as 'negative' imagery (which merely reinforced the dichotomy of the good and bad cripple scenario). What such an articulation has facilitated is the move towards a sanitised imagery of disability being shown: an imagery that is no more or less 'realistic' than that presumed to be 'negative' imagery. To some extent it is less realistic because it now often concentrates on an entirely non-politicised view of disability as impairment (and vice versa) that is rooted in normalised idea(l)s of white middle-classness (whereas most disabled people are poor and uneducated due to discrimination and lack of opportunities and employment). One of the problems, and what led to such a naïve call for 'positive imagery', was (and is) the misunderstanding of stereotypes and imagery itself. No image is value free or has any less or more 'reality' than any other image. Combined with this is the fact that stereotypes do indeed have a lot of value in being able to assess the reality of any given group's social position (that is, the disabled to the non-disabled).

Stereotypes are very useful in the identification of relations between social groups (the oppressed and the oppressor) and, as such, are both revealing of a wider social framework within which, in this case, disabled people are seen. Equally, stereotypes can be highly empowering and enjoyable for the oppressed in revealing the true nature and picture of their social relationships: I am right, society does see me in this way; I am not imagining it. Positive imagery, on the other hand, becomes a further threat to disabled people by making clear that to be accepted and valued by society one must be like this or that (that is, normalised and educated). Thereby an equally false/arbitrary reality is created which many disabled people either cannot or do not want to emulate. Consequently, disabled people have become more oppressed by positive imagery than they were by the apparently negative or stereotypical imagery (especially on television, but also on film and in the print media). The positive imagery, as has already been said, is fundamentally impairment imagery and a view of disability as normalised impairment: the good cripple – or those worthy of social processes such as institutionalisation, abortion or euthanasia (the tragedy model so loved by charity); or the bad cripple. Equally important is the recognition that no stereotype or archetype exists or is used in isolation: the good mother/maternal woman stereotype is often used when disability stereotypes/archetypes exist (and so on).

Many disabled critics have, and still do, call for role models in the propagation of 'positive' imagery, but, as stated above, what this actually means is the enhancement of the normalised disabled person over and above the valuation of disabled people *per se*. What disabled people, and society at large, are being fed is the image of a certain kind of valued disabled person who is physically able, educationally competent and striving to achieve a 'normal' wealthy life(style). One only has to think of the pretty Para-Olympian or the pretty disabled ex-model or dandified karate-kicking disabled television presenters, who the main charities use in their advertising, in order to see their increasing dominance as the (stereo)type used in the 'positive' representation of disabled people on television. Many disabled critics see such 'ambiguous' disabled people (seemingly political but entirely wrapped up within the mainstream oppressive structures of media and charity alike) as evil opportunists, but this is to ignore the power, prevalence and lure of the status quo which clearly shows the consequences of not 'playing along' with normality: isolation, unemployment, poverty and even persecution.

This is not to say there is not still a mass of exploitative imagery (Norden, 1994), rooted in the old style disability imagery, that is purely about exploiting disability (impairment) through the use of a range of crass and unimaginative archetypes of disability: disability as evil; disabled people as abject or atmosphere or as a quick visual fix for a poor narrative or characterisation; or disabled people triumphing (or failing) over tragedy. Such images show disability as impairment and impairment as axiomatically abject and abhorrent (this is essential to perpetuate the dominant social preference for the good cripple over the bad cripple paradigm). Drama is especially apt at still using such imagery: be that in Hollywood or the drama departments of the Western television broadcasters (in the UK, the main television networks of the BBC, ITV and Channel 4). Disabled people, the depiction of impairment, is in no less a position of purely colonialised bodies used in the service of the idea or ideal of a pure and simple 'normality' in body, morality and political ideology than, say, those of blacks or gays (and, to a lesser extent, women). Many disabled imagery critics (in visual, literary and other artistic forms) have shown clearly and repeatedly that the impaired body is the basis on which normality exists and that it is the paper upon which normality is drawn almost daily within our culture. What the more articulate critic is showing is the complex nature of image politics in relation to disability within a politicised context (as above). But, and this is becoming increasingly significant, what is interesting is the Disability Studies postmodernists who are attempting to do a number of disempowering intellectual gymnastics in order to validate their own positions as unproblematic – despite their status as ambiguous role models within society as disabled people who are actually denying disability – in favour of a normalised impairment and individualised politics of social progress that benefits the few (successful) disabled over the many disabled people who are left behind in the margins of society.

Normality, as such, is the key then to understanding both the nature of representations of disability/impairment (Mitchell and Snyder, 1997) and the criticisms of such representations from both divergent attitudes amongst disabled people and from the non-disabled critic and/or academic. Not bad for something that does not actually exist! Normality – the belief that there is an essentially correct way to have been born, look like and be – the belief in normality, has defined the nature of the representation of disability and impairment (and non-disability) by formulating it as the basis upon which otherness (abject humanity bordering on inhumanity) has been defined in all figurative representation of humanity. The recognition of the nature of representation *per se* is at the heart of Disability Art. Disability Art has been incredibly powerful in undermining the ableist (and classist) ideologies behind traditional Art Histories that validate the depiction of disability as apolitical by emphasising impairment as an individual tragedy (or entertainment through spectacle: that is, the freak). From this perspective it is easy to see and understand why (and how) some disabled people can reject one image as negative (because it fails to offer them the chance of normality), whilst another is deemed to be positive (it offers the prospect of some kind of normality). Additionally, one can see how (and why) the good and bad cripple nexus is becoming increasingly dominant: both reinforce the idea(l)s of normality, leaving no space for ambiguity on the value of one in relation to another (for example, the 'good' normal and the 'bad' abnormal). In a culture (our Western one in particular) where identity and nationhood is seen – or, to be more precise, constructed – as being increasingly under threat from unseen enemies (for example, terrorists, asylum seekers, illegal immigrants), the battles over the hegemonies of normality are increasingly less subtle and more overtly apparent (as is the case with disability representation).

Postmodernist disability image critics are starting to claim that we need to move on from the disability activists' politicised criticism (Enns and Smit, 2001) of representations, which the postmodernists see as entirely negative and anti-intellectual at worst and at best as anti-art (be that in film, literature or any other art form that has a history and tradition of representation). One cannot fail to notice that such a perspective only seems to serve the individual's progression through institutions of oppression (be they media or media studies departments within universities) allowing them to use the (or create their own) same types of oppressive or impairment-based imagery. This is not to deny that a move forward from the naïve positive/negative image dualism is necessary (as shown above), but to deny the nature of the normal/abnormal binary opposites is both intellectually wrong and politically pure folly, given the fact that disabled people, as controllers of their images, have progressed very little in the last 50 years. By which I mean that disabled people have always been making images (of themselves and of others) throughout the history of television and film and other art forms. The point is that in the past they were not revealed as disabled, or they obtained their entrance into the system through special schemes. And, more importantly, such disabled individuals never came to their art in a society that has a progressively politicised idea of what disability is – politicised by disabled people themselves in the margins of society. This has as much to do with issues of class, power and wealth as it always has done, and disabled people must not let go of the power they now have to undermine, through the analysis of the representation of images of disability, the very nature of all representations rooted in an oppressive history and tradition (and arbitrarily based on class, education, wealth and power). Few people, especially those seeking to dilute the social model of disability in various ways, seem to grasp the politics of disablement across the board of social inquiry in seeking political change; this is as true in the study of the representation of disability as it is in the demystification of the medicalisation of disablement.

The point is that no disability imagery critic worth his or her ink would argue that normality is conceived to be a unified or consolidated whole. Quite the contrary: normality (in its essential fiction) is highly unstable and fragile within the individual and society as a whole. It is the very fragility of the belief (as well as in the idea[l]) that makes representations of disability so popular, important and pervasive. Finally, it is disabled people's own ability to make and imagine images of disability that ultimately gives them a power that far exceeds those of almost any other kind of imagery – they undermine the entire value system of society: normality.

References

Corker, M. and Shakespeare, T. (eds) (2002) *Disability/Postmodernity: Embodying Disability Theory*. London: Continuum.

Enns, A. and Smit, C. (eds) (2001) *Screening Disability: Essays on Cinema and Disability*. Lanham: University of America Press.

Mitchell, D. and Snyder, S. (eds) (1997) *The Body and Physical Difference: Discourse of Disability*. Ann Arbor, MI: University of Michigan Press.

Norden, M. (1994) *The Cinema of Isolation: A History of Physical Disabilities in the Movies*. New Brunswick, NJ: Rutgers University Press.

16 Disability Culture: The Story So Far
SIAN VASEY

On one level disability culture is a given. If a disabled person needs help with eating, or crossing the road, or getting up in the morning, this is part of their cultural experience. If a person gets around in a wheelchair, reads Braille or uses sign language, this is also part of their cultural experience and their way of being. The identification of these aspects of an impaired person's life as 'disability culture' back in the late 1980s was, I think, quite a breakthrough in the struggle for the legitimacy of impairment and the impaired person's right to have a fair crack at life along with everybody else.

Viewed this way, it may be fair to say that disability culture is, in its most raw state, unique, in that it is inherently immutable. There is a purity about it, in that it is the only way of life which is not in any way manufactured. It is not fundamentally connected, for example, with fashion, the climate, geography, economics, whim, intellect, class, taste, design or etiquette. It is a culture primarily born from the experience of the unusual body and, unlike other cultures, it will never become ancient history unless there comes a time when impairment is eradicated. My culture is one of sitting all the time, a blind person's is one of experiencing the world through means other than sight and so on. We cannot change this and I think there is something quite empowering in that thought.

However, if we define our culture a bit more widely, going beyond the body, it does find a relationship with external factors, such as the engineering and technology of disability equipment. Wheelchairs, white sticks and hearing aids have their place in our cultural spectrum, but the Perkins Brailler may, in time, have antique significance and it has been a long time since the Bath chair saw useful service. So part of our culture is not immune from the effect of progress. One observation that can be made about disability culture nowadays is that blind people are forever talking about their JAWS, which has nothing whatever to do with a new impairment of the lower face (JAWS is a specialist computer package with speech output). Could it be that the truly advanced technology will toll the death-knell for disability culture? The end will surely be nigh when we have the invisible suit that when worn means we move like everyone else, and when they have come up with glasses that give 20:20 vision to all regardless of eyeball function. Watch out, it may not be the geneticists that put an end to disability, but the development of high-tech kit that truly compensates for lack of function.

The output of Disability Art practitioners is also often known as 'disability culture'. The words 'art' and 'culture' are often used interchangeably. Disability art, in the strict sense, has a relationship with the social model of disability in that it is articulating the need for change and saying how things can change for disabled people – probably with the emphasis on attitudes rather than economics. One of the things that can change for disabled people is our phenomenally low collective confidence level – which is almost a cultural characteristic in itself. The idea of 'disability pride' came from the disability arts movement and, although this did briefly get tangled up in a fairly futile debate about whether this meant we were proud of the barriers that disable (no not really!), it is something that we simply need more of. Perhaps the term 'disability pride' is a bit dated now, although 'gay pride' still seems to work for the gay movement, but disability art, and its siblings 'creativity' and 'self-expression', can make us feel good about ourselves. Disability arts is supplying us with some enjoyment, some insights into our lives, some opportunities and some role models for which we should be truly grateful.

I am not in any position to give a researched and extensive account of all the disability art that has been produced in the last ten years or of what has happened to the disability arts infrastructure, that is to say the Disability Arts Forums and specific organisations such as Graeae Theatre Company (for people with physical and sensory impairments). On the question of whether things have been happening during the decade, my perception is that they certainly have. Furthermore, if we understand by the term 'disability arts', that it is what we call the art produced by disabled artists who want to identify with other disabled people and who also want to explore the subjects of disability and impairment within their work, it is almost impossible to imagine disabled writers, poets, video-makers and visual artists, not producing this kind of work, whether anybody else knows about it or not.

I think we can safely say that, unlike other marginalised groups, we have not made much of a dent in mainstream culture. It is true to say that we do not yet have the annual disability novel in the way we have the annual ethnic novel, for example *The God of Small Things*, *White Teeth* and the current Asian literary 'must read', *Brick Lane* by Monica Ali. We may not have hit the big time yet, but you can bet your boots that all over the country disabled writers are feverishly scribbling in creative writing classes, in cafés and in their bedrooms and sooner or later a Booker winning disability novel will emerge.

Penny Pepper, who has recently published a book of short stories with disabled protagonists on the theme of sexuality entitled *Desires* (Pepper, 2003), found that when she was doing a round of local radio interviews to publicise the book she was regularly challenged as to the validity of her subject matter. The presenters, who it has to be said were often sub-Alan Partridge, seemed to see it as their duty to be astonished at the idea that anybody would ever want to read about disabled people having sex. I somehow doubt that Zadie Smith was ever challenged quite so unambiguously about whether people would want to read about two generations of Asian and West Indian people living and growing up in the London Borough of Brent. Penny got a grant from London Arts to produce this book, every penny of which, and more, was spent on just that: printing and publicising the book. She fervently believes in the idea of the disability experience being expressed through literature, but even so she found that she had to play down the idea of disability in these radio interviews in order to feel she was in any way credible to the presenters and, presumably, the listeners of local radio stations.

Lois Keith is another author taking disability as her subject matter. She now has two novels under her belt. Her first was aimed at teenagers where the major character, a teenage girl, became disabled (Keith, 1997). The most recent, *Out of Place*, is about disability in the Holocaust (Keith, 2003) which, it is extraordinary to think, is a subject that has never before been tackled in fiction. It is reasonable to speculate that both established writers and publishers suppress disability as subject matter because they feel it will not be popular.

What then is the situation now with the organisations whose job it is to nurture disability artists and their art, the Disability Arts Forums (DAFs)? And also with the variety of organisations doing similar art-specific work, such as Graeae Theatre Company and Survivors Poetry (poetry written by survivors of the mental health system). I now see that the piece I wrote 13 years ago on this subject (Vasey, 1991) was very focused on the idea of the DAFs, the central component of the disability arts infrastructure, becoming membership organisations of disabled people who supported the concept of disability arts. I think we can safely say that this has not happened, which is not very encouraging. Twelve years ago I wrote:

> Another problem with organising in the regions is that the way people often want to make a start on it, is by holding a festival or a cabaret to get people interested. This probably means importing some performers or 'The Tragic but Brave Show' a jolly time is had by all, the performers go home and people are left to get on with it – really without the wherewithal so to do. (1991: 2)

So the London Disability Arts Forum (LDAF) came to be, and through it we have a voice and a powerbase. We have a mechanism for ensuring that some portion of the resources that the government gives to the arts in general goes to disabled people. We do have to be constantly vigilant, though, that a large and growing number of disabled people are genuinely involved in it. Their involvement at the moment is probably on a more informal basis. People read *Disability Arts in London* and they go to Workhouses and perform at Workhouses, but the membership list is probably nowhere near as big as the number of people who would profess to having quite a close allegiance to the organisation. This, I hope, is a problem that can be sorted out by some diligent admin. work, but it is also a signifier that LDAF should be looking at how it involves people. It could quite easily become nothing more than the administrative mechanism by which cabarets by and for disabled people are regularly held, thus reducing the majority to our traditional role of passive recipients.

The last decade has seen some pretty profound and rapid changes to the general social/political environment. Voters have become an unprotected, rare species and people, including disabled people, are disinclined to join anything other than the AA and the National Trust. Certain political issues are very popular, the protection of foxes being one; the rights of those wishing to destroy foxes being another. Meanwhile, disabled people's along with women's issues have, it seems to me, seriously fallen out of favour and are now seen as causes espoused by only the terminally unfashionable.

There has been no wide take-up of interest in the mainstream disability movement and correspondingly no major membership take-up in the disability arts movement. However, having said that, *Etc*, the National Disability Arts Forum's e-mail bulletin, is sent to a long list of addresses on a weekly basis and *DAIL*, the monthly magazine produced by the London Disability Arts Forum, has a substantial mailing list. The DAFs certainly do not have obvious resources for the administration of membership databases. In retrospect, I do not quite remember why I thought this was so important at the time. Many people may attend a disability arts event and derive a huge amount of benefit from it, but realistically it would be very hard to engineer things, so they all, as a matter of course, joined the DAF that had produced the event. As for them being mere passive recipients of an arts event, this is just ridiculous. Everybody takes their turn at making and receiving art. Some people never make any art, possibly for reasons related to being disabled or oppressed in some other way and perhaps because they have no talent. The creation of disability arts has, at the risk of sounding like a 1950s' radio game show host, increased the chances of all those disabled people that want to, of having a go.

One thing that I just did not seem to take into account 13 years ago is that many active disabled people are active because they are utterly locked up in issues that pertain to their personal survival and freedom. Access, transport, education and the whole bag and baggage that goes with the use of personal assistance are all topics that just absorb our small army of politicos. The activists are busy with the basics and, of course, the issues they are working on are all factors that serve to keep disabled people out of participation in the arts of any kind. It is hard to get to marimba classes when the tube is inaccessible, you have no personal assistance provision in the evenings and sign language costs around £50.00 per hour.

You could liken the Disability Arts Forums to ENSA (Entertainments National Service Association) in the First World War with the role of entertaining the troops. Regardless of their membership lists, they are achieving things in different parts of the country. The North West, the North East, the West Midlands are all doing consistent work. The London Disability Arts Forum has recently held its fifth Disability Film Festival *Lifting the Lid* at a high-profile venue, the National Film Theatre. The North West Disability Arts Forum is doing a lot of cabaret work and has successfully collaborated with the Nasty Girls, a women's comedy performance group that specialises in writing comedy material to suit any disability occasion. They went down particularly well at the somewhat troubled Annual General Meeting of the British Council of Disabled People in 2002.

There is a steady take-up of disability arts by both large and small mainstream disability organisations as a way of raising morale and introducing disabled people to their culture represented within an arts event. I have recently taken up work as the director of the Ealing Centre for Independent Living. A cabaret in Ealing, the *Mega Ripple*, included: a local group of people with learning difficulties called Impact; Razz, a survivors poet; Minika Green, a superb jazz singer; and Mik Scarlet, making his debut as a cabaret compère. This actually renewed my enthusiasm for disability arts as a means of inspiring a local disability community. It really was a very successful event and, though I say so myself, well produced in that the venue: a small studio theatre, which was the right size, was made to look right and was packed with 'crips'. It was well stage-managed and finally, the talent was hot. I have been asked to organise another one in Kingston, which will make some money for my organisation and will obviously mean another night's work for the artists. This seems to me to be a good model for the future. Disability arts and disability mainstream really working together.

The work of Graeae Theatre Company I think shows how disability arts can be very difficult to achieve in ensemble work. The company has gone from strength to strength and has put on some really excellent productions. However, it had to compromise on disability arts for a while in order to achieve a truly glittering standard. Its first production, which dealt with disability head on, was *Sideshow*, a rip-roaring success back in 1981. This was followed by the slightly less successful *M3 Junction 4*. In the 1980s and the early 1990s the company continued to struggle with the concept and produced plays with disability at their centre such as: *A Cocktail Cabaret*, *A Private View*, *Hound* and *Working Hearts*. All of which were specially commissioned by the company and none of which, I think it is generally agreed, really quite cut the mustard as successful pieces of theatre. In the mid-1990s the company decided to try the existing text option and produced a wacky version of the already pretty wacky drama school favourite *Ubu*. The result was electric and a string of hits in a similar vein followed: *Fleshfly*; an adaptation of Ben Jonson's *Volpone*;

Two by Jim Cartwright; and *Usher*, an adaptation of the *House of Usher* by Edgar Allan Poe. These shows gave the company the boost it needed and without them it may well have gone belly-up. Suddenly Graeae was looking really exciting, quickly gained in confidence and was able to develop. It is now returning to the idea of disability arts and has had a major success in the form of a recent production, *Peeling*, which was visually stunning and truly entertaining. It looked, albeit in a somewhat pessimistic way, at life from a disabled woman's perspective (for further details of all their events see www.graeae.org.uk).

The National Disability Arts Forum (NDAF) has just published a brand new, high production values illustrated book of pieces by disabled people dealing with the subject of shortened life expectancy called *Shelf Life* (O'Reilly, 2003). Interestingly, it proved quite difficult to find funding for the Shelf Life Project, as potential sources were scared off by the subject matter.

Another recent NDAF project was Getting Noticed. This took the form of a collection of posters advertising disability arts events from the past decade or so. Each one has a text with the image and is laminated for robustness. Targeted at disabled young people in schools, it aimed to provide them with a sense of empowerment through discovering what has been achieved by disabled people in the arts.

Two very important groups within disability arts are Survivors Poetry and Heart 'n' Soul (a theatre and music group for young people with learning difficulties). The latter are currently running three operations at any one time: a main show, a more portable version of the main show and a disco that can be hired out. *Survivors Poetry* has been running workshops and performances consistently for the past decade and beyond. I think it is true to say that both groups have been very well managed and have discovered a loyal market, largely within their own impairment group.

Disability arts is an important part of the Disabled People's Movement where disabled people are expressing their views, ideas and experiences of disability within a vibrant collective forum. Disabled people are increasingly coming together to help each other express themselves in music, drama, poetry, forms of visual art and comedy. Disability arts is a political as well as an artistic forum that challenges and exposes negative images of disability, combats images of passivity and dependence, discrimination and oppression, and celebrates difference.

References

Keith, L. (1997) *A Different Life*. London: The Women's Press.
Keith, L. (2003) *Out of Place*. Manchester: Crocus.
O'Reilly, K. (ed.) (2003) *Shelf Life*. Newcastle-upon-Tyne: Disability Arts Forum.
Pepper, P. (2003) *Desires*. Woodford Green: Benjamo.
Vasey, S. (1991) *Disability and Culture: An Introduction to Key Issues and Questions*. Paper presented at the Disability Arts and Culture Seminar. Willesden Green Library Centre, London, 26 November.

17 'Race', Disability and Oppression
MARTIN BANTON AND GURNAM SINGH

Whilst there is now a developing body of knowledge on disability and 'race', with some notable exceptions (Begum et al., 1994; Stuart, 1993; Vernon, 1999) much of this literature tends to simply situate black disabled people as victims of oppression and/or potential and actual service users. Although an acknowledgement of the particular needs of black disabled people is clearly to be welcomed, there are many inherent dangers in what may be termed the 'service delivery' approach. Such approaches invariably fail to adequately factor in the complex interplay between 'racialisation' (Miles, 1989) and 'disablism' (Barton, 1996; Oliver, 1996) on the one hand and the mechanisms of power and powerlessness on the other. Moreover, they tend to ignore the huge diversity that exists amongst black disabled people and the differential cultural, social and economic contexts in which they live out their lives. Fawcett suggests a reflexive strategy that seeks to confront oppression in whatever guise it may appear, whilst at the same time fully acknowledging 'complexity and interrelational elements' (2000: 53).

The growing recognition of the importance of social divisions (Payne, 2000) as a means of making sense of the inequalities and hierarchies in power relations (Vernon and Swain, 2002), both within society in general and the disabled people's movement in particular, is notable. For example, specifically amongst disability activists, there has been an increasing willingness to give primacy to the differential experience of individuals and groups resulting from their social class, minority ethnic status, gender, age and sexuality. In relation to disability studies, as a consequence of the 'politics of difference' we see the emergence of new and exciting debates incorporating an analysis of disability that intersects with the experience of membership of other social divisions (Barnes et al., 2002).

Based on our shared and different experiences and insights as black activists and researchers, one disabled and one non-disabled, our central aim is to explore the complex interplay between dominant ideologies, discursive repertoires and material circumstances (Frankenberg, 1993) and how these come together to produce concrete oppressive outcomes for black disabled people.

Before proceeding, we must make a brief comment about terminology. Throughout this chapter, the term 'black' is used in a political sense to denote all visible minorities. In doing so we acknowledge that as an empirical category, for assessing need and developing service provision, the term 'black' has less utility than, for example, cultural and ethnic categories. Not all black disabled people share the same social and material conditions, nor do they all identify with the term 'black'. Despite this, we are mindful that before deciding to abandon 'black', one must not forget that it was precisely this term that formed a key ideological basis for the anti-racist movement in the 1980s and 1990s, and as a political weapon it still has some value. Therefore, we make no apology for holding onto the term.

The experience of black disabled people

The fact that most developed nations now have some kind of equality and human rights legislation provides concrete testimony to the inherent problems of modern capitalist societies and organisations, namely that of inequality. Despite the immense wealth and resources that capitalism has managed to generate, there is little evidence that inequalities, have in any way significantly diminished as a consequence. Black disabled people, in particular, have fared badly and can consistently be found to occupy the lower levels of most measures of inequality and social exclusion (Atkins, 1991; Begum, 1992; Berthoud, 1998). The complex and interactive impact of different dimensions of social inequalities on health was a key argument in the Acheson Report (Independent Inquiry, 1998). 'Race', poverty, disability and young (or old) age exemplify the factors, which combine together to produce poor health and developmental outcomes and the inefficient deployment of scarce health and social care resources. For some minority Bangladeshi and Pakistani families, the high prevalence of poverty (Modood et al., 1997) is likely to be compounded by having a disabled child. Ahmad and Atkin (1996) provide evidence that disabled children from minority ethnic groups face additional obstacles associated with structural and institutional racism (MacPherson, 1999).

In relation to service provision, whilst in some areas there is evidence of good practice, in general the bulk of data points to ongoing marginalisation of black disabled people and their carers (Beresford et al., 1996; Chamba et al., 1999). A report on the history, role and function of peer support groups for black young deaf people by Bignal et al. (2002), for example, highlights many important functions played by the groups, most notably as a place for the members to talk about their many differences in a supportive environment. They also highlight the immense barriers that are faced by such groups, namely funding, access and marginalisation. Hussain et al. (2002), in a study looking at Asian disabled young people within their own families, highlights the way racism can impact the dynamics of family life. Vernon's (2002) study of community care provision for Asian disabled people found low levels of trust between service providers and users.

Oppression and oppressed

The above findings outline some of the structured disadvantage that shapes the experiences of black disabled people. In this section, we seek to highlight some of the underlying processes and mechanisms that produce and reproduce multiple oppressions. Oppression is one of those concepts that cannot be studied from some neutral scientific perspective. It resides in two places at once, in the nooks and crannies of the culture and institutions of society, and at the same time in the deep crevices of our own existential selves. Oppression is at once a subjective feeling and an objective fact; it is both a process and an event. Prilleltensky and Gonick point out the multi-dimensional and complex nature of oppression and the centrality of power:

> For us, oppression entails a state of asymmetric power relations characterised by domination, subordination and resistance, where the dominating people exercise their power by restricting access to material resources and by implanting in the subordinated people self-deprecating views about themselves. (1996: 129–30)

Because modern society is based on a stratum of power and dominance, the experience of oppression, as Freire (1972) demonstrates, structures all our lives, both as oppressor or oppressed, powerful or powerless. In relation to the powerless, instead of challenging the ideology on which their oppression is built, oppressed groups often succumb to it. This may result in oppressed groups, at best denying their oppression or at worst they may seek to identify a position within the strata that is superior to as many other groups as possible (Lorde, 1984), thereby reinforcing the structures of oppression. This insidious infection of the ideology of oppression seeps right through to interpersonal relationships, even within the most oppressed groups (Freire, 1972) and can lead to self-destructive infighting.

There are many groups that face oppression, including poor working-class people, disabled people, black people, women, lesbians and gays, and older people. If people fit into one of these categories, they are likely to face oppression; if they fit into more than one, they are likely to face simultaneous oppression (Stuart, 1993; Mullaly, 2002; Barnes and Mercer, 2003). There is, of course, a fundamental flaw in this reasoning: it is impossible for anyone to belong to one of these categories without belonging to at least one other. Whilst each one of the categories has managed to provide an important organising framework, up to and including the building of powerful social movements, in reality, on their own, none of these categories is capable of encapsulating the true nature of human experience. No human being is reducible to one singular identity; we are indeed all 'gendered', 'raced', 'aged', 'classed', and nobody can escape the social construction of disability (Saraga, 1998).

Therefore, there is a need to recognise the oppression of others as well as our own. In our experience, groups organised around a singular overarching identity run the danger of a hierarchy of oppression, which can result in a tendency to further oppress each other rather than work together to dismantle the structures of discrimination and oppression. We believe that the individualistic ideologies, championed by the 'New Right' during the Thatcher years, have contributed to the state of affairs where people are more concerned about their own particular needs rather than the wider society.

> 'As a black woman, I can't say well I'll deal with my gender today and 'my race' tomorrow, because I have to deal with it as one person, you know. And the same can be said of disabled people and lesbians and gays, black disabled people, you know whatever combination of oppression that you might say.' (Evans and Banton, 2000: 47)

Whilst it is true to say that black disabled people face a combination of oppressions, in that they experience racism like any black person, like other disabled people they also experience disablism. As Stuart warns, the outcomes are more than the sum of the individual parts:

> The oppression black disabled people endure is, in my opinion, unique. I suggest that for these people, racism involves a process of simultaneous oppression in their day-to-day experience. It is also an experience which divides black disabled people from their black able-bodied peers. (1993: 94)

This alienation from both white disabled individuals and groups and black non-disabled communities can result in a unique sense of isolation and marginalisation, as the following testimony of a black disabled woman illustrates:

'I think black disabled people have sort of an extra burden in terms of the load that we carry. Wherein we have the prejudice within our communities to deal with on top of the prejudice ... we face as disabled people anyway irrespective, regardless of who we are.' (Evans and Banton, 2000: 46)

When it comes to service provision, black disabled people are caught in the middle, not knowing where best to go due to the lack of specific services for them. So in many cases black disabled people are put in the position where they have to go to a service that specialises in either disability or 'race'.

Institutionalised discrimination

Many 'white' organisations put the onus on the black disabled person to fit in with their services, instead of changing the way the service is delivered. This can be seen as racist, but it also causes isolation for black disabled people who may not feel able to use that service due to cultural barriers or negative experiences in the past. However, it is also important for black disabled people to feel welcome, for it is not just about the delivery of an appropriate service, but also about feeling comfortable with the overall service. Jeewa (1998, quoted in Banton and Hirsch, 2000: 34) suggests that 'it is not simply an issue of political correctness', but it is about the attitude and the way black disabled people are dealt with in the organisation by staff and the users. We are reminded of the subtle and insidious nature of institutionalised racism that the MacPherson report on the death of Stephen Lawrence inquiry highlighted:

> ... the collective failure of an organisation to provide an appropriate and professional service to people because of their colour, culture or ethnic origin. It can be seen or detected in processes, attitudes and behaviour which amount to discrimination through unwitting prejudice, ignorance, thoughtlessness and racist stereotyping which disadvantage minority ethnic people. (1999: Ch. 6.34)

Institutional discrimination is not the sole preserve of white organisations. Stigma within the black communities is also likely to contribute to isolation for black disabled people. Religious ideas about the nature and source of impairment have tended to go unchallenged. Due to the paucity of research and literature, one can only speculate what the dynamics of this can be. There appears to be a general consensus amongst most mainstream religions that impairment has 'at least some relationship to a person's "misfortune", sent by deity, fate, karma; often associated with parental sin' (Miles, 1995: 52, quoted in Barnes and Mercer, 2003: 135).

The religious model, therefore, seeks to explain disabled people's oppression as a punishment for some misdeeds in the past. Without entering a theological discussion, it seems clear that such interpretations can only result in at best the individualisation of disability and at worst providing moral and ideological justification for denying black disabled people's human rights. By implying that impairment is the fault of the parents, thereby generating guilt on the disabled person and their family, it is not surprising that disability in black communities is considered to be a taboo. The resulting stigma can lead to isolation for many black disabled people from not only their immediate family, but also the extended family and wider community. This can lead to rejection or over-protection, as is illustrated in the following quote from a black disabled woman:

'I am adopted within a Jamaican family, I was told not to tell people about Lupus, as it would affect my marriage prospect. There is a real stigma attached to disability in the black or Asian family.' (Council of Disabled People, Warwickshire and African Caribbean Project (1998), quoted in Banton and Hirsch, 2000: 6)

From victim to activist

Nobody likes to be isolated from his or her community and the need for a black disabled people's organisation reflects the reality of the multiple oppression that was highlighted earlier. The black disabled movement has sought to provide a safe space to enable black disabled people to support each other and discuss issues of concern without having to justify not only their right to speak, but also literally their right to exist.

In the last ten years there has been legislation concerning both disabled people and black people with the Disability Discrimination Act 1995, the Race Relations Amendment Act 2000, and the introduction of the Human Rights Act 1998, all of which should benefit minority groups. Of course, the changes were not voluntarily offered by the government but arose out of the action of many individuals, families, communities and groups, all fighting for social justice. Whilst the disability movement has been immensely successful in making inroads into the discourses and structures of oppression, culminating with, amongst other things, major legislative gains, it has been rather less successful in understanding and articulating the experiences of black disabled people. However, black disabled people have started to come together and claim their human right to speak and be taken seriously. They have highlighted their unique circumstances and simultaneous oppression they have faced.

Conclusion

There has been growing recognition over the past 25 years that the beliefs, understandings, objectives and priorities of service users will often not be the same as those of health and social care professionals or service providers. Ascertaining the views of service users has, as a result, increasingly come to be seen as an essential element in the provision of services, which effectively meet needs. Alongside this, a growing emphasis on human rights and social justice as underpinning approaches to service delivery has reinforced the view that listening to what service users say should become more central. In more recent times, in relation to disabled people, primarily as a result of the disability rights movement, this rebalancing of power between service provider and service user has taken on more radical and far reaching dimensions, ranging from service user involvement in policy, planning and delivery through to wholly user-led services. Notions such as advocacy, self-empowerment, peer support and social inclusion are now common currency in any discussion about disability. These gains are indeed a testimony to the contribution of black and white disabled people's struggles for equality.

In this chapter we have sought to highlight a number of key factors around the subject of multiple oppression, which includes the stigma of disability in the black communities, the ignorance about cultural issues in the disability community, and the resulting lack of appropriate service provision. There was a time when, at the level of policy making and service development, black disabled people's needs, aspirations and experiences were unacknowledged. However, over the past ten years a wealth of literature has emerged, clearly identifying what needs to be done. There have been many people looking at the needs of black disabled people and the barriers they face when needing services. Because of this and the fact that more black disabled people are getting involved in research and shaping the services that are available, things are beginning slowly to change. Black and disability organisations have started to work together to make sure that their services are available to all those who need them. However, we end on a word of caution: liberation, which after all is something we all desire, is not simply about information, but involves many strategies, not least direct action. Finally, a quote from Frederick Douglas, the black African American revolutionary who reminds us of the nature of black people's struggles:

> Those who profess to favour freedom and yet depreciate agitation, are people who want crops without ploughing the ground; they want rain without thunder and lightening; they want the ocean without the roar of its waters ... power conceded nothing without a demand; it never has and it never will. (1857)

References

Acheson, D. (1998) *Independent Inquiry into Inequalities in Health.* London: HMSO.

Ahmad, W. and Atkin, K. (eds) (1996) *'Race' and Community Care.* Buckingham: Open University Press.

Atkins, K. (1991) 'Health, illness, disability and black minorities', *Disability, Handicap and Society*, 6 (1): 37–47.

Banton, M. and Hirsch, M. (2000) *Double Invisibility: A Study into the Needs of Black Disabled People in Warwickshire.* Leamington Spa: Council of Disabled People, Warwickshire.

Barnes, C. and Mercer, G. (2003) *Disability.* Cambridge: Polity.

Barnes, C., Oliver, M. and Barton, L. (eds) (2002) *Disability Studies*, Cambridge: Polity.

Barton, L. (1996) *Disability and Society: Emerging Issues and Insights.* London: Longman.

Begum, M. (1992) *'... Something to be Proud of ...' The Lives of Asian Disabled People and Carers in Waltham Forest.* London: Waltham Forest Race Relations Unit.

Begum, N., Hill, M. and Stevens, A. (eds) (1994) *Reflections: Views of Black Disabled People on their Lives and Community Care.* London: Central Council for the Education and Training of Social Work.

Beresford, B., Sloper, P., Baldwin, S. and Newman, T. (1996) *What Works in Services for Families with a Disabled Child?* Barkingside: Barnardo's.

Berthoud, R. (1998) *Incomes of Ethnic Minorities, Secondary Analysis of the Family Resources Survey.* Colchester: University of Essex.

Bignal, T., Butt, J. and Pagarani, D. (2002) *Something to Do: The Development of Peer Support Groups for Young Black and Minority Ethnic Disabled People.* Bristol: The Policy Press.

Chamba, R., Hirst, M., Lawron, D., Ahmad, W. and Beresford, B. (1999) *Expert Voices: A National Survey of Minority Ethnic Parents Caring for a Disabled Child.* Bristol: The Policy Press.

Council of Disabled People, Warwickshire and African Caribbean Project (1998) *Disability Shameful.* Leamington Spa: CDP/ACP.

Douglas, F. (1993) *Narrative of the Life of Frederick Douglas, an American Slave, Written by Himself in 1857*. Chicago, IL: Bedford Books.

Evans, R. and Banton, M. (2000) *Learning from Experience: Involving Black Disabled People in Shaping Services*. Leamington Spa: Council of Disabled People, Warwickshire.

Fawcett, B. (2000) *Feminist Perspectives on Disability*. Harlow: Prentice-Hall.

Frankenberg, R. (1993) *White Women, Race Matters: The Social Construction of Whiteness*. London: Routledge.

Freire, P. (1972) *Pedagogy of The Oppressed*. Harmondsworth: Penguin.

Hussain, Y., Atkin, K. and Ahmad, W. (2002) *South Asian Disabled Young People and Their Families*. Bristol: The Policy Press.

Jeewa, S. (1998) *Ethnicity, Disability and SCOPE: The Case for Embracing Black Disability Issues*. Northampton: Disability Works.

Lorde, A. (1984) *Sister Outsider*. New York, NY: The Crossing Press.

Macpherson, W. (1999) *The Stephen Lawrence Inquiry: Report of the Inquiry*. London: HMSO.

Miles, M. (1995) 'Disability in an Eastern Religious Context: Historical Perspectives', *Disability and Society*, 10 (1): 49–69.

Miles, R. (1989) *Racism*. London and New York: Routledge.

Modood, T., Berthoud, R., Lakey, J., Nazroo, J., Smith, P., Virdee, S. and Beishon, P. (eds) (1997) *Ethnic Minorities in Britain*. London: Policy Studies Institute.

Mullaly, R. (2002) *Challenging Oppression – A Critical Social Work Approach*. Don Mills, Ontario: Oxford University Press.

Oliver, M. (1996) *Understanding Disability: From Theory to Practice*. Basingstoke: Macmillan.

Payne, M. (2000) *Social Divisions*. Basingstoke: Macmillan.

Prilleltensky, I. and Gonick, L. (1996). 'Polities change, oppression remains: on the psychology and politics of oppression', *Political Psychology*, 17 (1): 127–48.

Saraga, E. (1998) *Embodying the Social: Constructions of Difference*. London: Open University/Routledge.

Stuart, O. (1993) 'Double oppression: an appropriate starting point?', in J. Swain, V. Finkelstein, S. French and M. Oliver (eds), *Disabling Barriers – Enabling Environments*. London: Sage/ Open University.

Vernon, A. (1999) 'The Dialectics of Multiple Identities and the Disabled People's Movement', *Disability and Society*, 14 (3): 385–398.

Vernon, A. (2002) *User-defined Outcomes of Community Care for Asian Disabled People*. Bristol: The Policy Press.

Vernon, A. and Swain, J. (2002) 'Theorising divisions and hierarchies: towards a commonality or diversity?', in C. Barnes, M. Oliver, and L. Barton (eds), *Disability Studies*. Cambridge: Polity.

18 Who is Disabled? Exploring the Scope of the Social Model of Disability
DAN GOODLEY

Who is disabled in social model literature?

Heightened debate is a sign of a political and intellectual movement's maturity. Major points of contention occur in disability studies, within and across the areas of academia and activism. A consistent area of debate relates to the explanatory powers of the social model of disability in accounting for the disabling experiences of *all* disabled people. In this chapter I will argue that the social model of disability holds the potential for the inclusion of *all* disabled people and disabled activists. I shall consider the self-advocacy of people with learning difficulties and demonstrate how their activism and theorising contribute to social theories of disability: particularly interpretivist conceptions of 'impairment' as they are embedded in *storying the self*. I shall also introduce the activism of survivors of mental health systems, whose hegemony often lies outside of disability studies in the areas of antipsychiatry and the survivors movement, whose experiences can nonetheless increase the social model's explanatory powers in relation to poststructuralist critiques of disability professionals' knowledge, as part of a project of *discoursing the self*.

As with working-class, feminist, sexuality and critical 'race' movements, key moments can be identified in the origination of concepts and claims that gave rise to the formulation of the British disability movement's 'big idea' (Hasler, 1993): the social model of disability. By rendering disability as something outside of the impaired individual, this model has supported disabled activists and their allies in setting their sights on those elements of contemporary British life that need to be changed. Yet, questions still remain about the representative nature of this model (see chapters in this volume) and a key question is: who is disabled in the social model?

I would suggest that a number of existing 'truths' should be kept in mind when interrogating the inclusive/exclusionary nature of the social model. First, we are talking here about a social model, not a social theory (Oliver, 1996). A model has no explanatory power, but instead directs us to theorise disability and concomitant phenomena such as 'impairment', 'exclusion' and 'activism'. Second, to borrow Thomas' (1999) phrase, 'social modellists' have consistently made connections with a whole host of oppressions, including race (Stuart, 1993), gender (Morris, 1991, 1996), class (Oliver, 1990), age (Zarb and Oliver, 1993), childhood (Priestley et al., 1999) and sexuality (Shakespeare et al., 1996). The social model has engaged with diversity. I find it helpful to keep three key assumptions in mind:

- Disability studies continues theoretically to develop in ways that can and should encompass the experiences and ambitions of all disabled people.

- The social model is a philosophical and political stance from which a whole host of social theories and forms of activism can and should be developed.
- Disability studies is an arena in which social theories of disability and impairment can be developed to promote the inclusion of disabled people in mainstream life.

In the remainder of this chapter, I will suggest that the social model of disability is an all-embracing arena for disabled people. In order to demonstrate this inclusivity, it is necessary for us to widen our view of disability activism to include the personal and political actions of a whole host of disabled activists and to take seriously the experiences and views of disabled people, whose voices may not be the loudest or strongest in the field.

People with learning difficulties are disabled: storying impairment

British disability studies are increasingly engaged with the lifeworlds of people with the label of 'learning difficulties'. More importantly, people so-labelled have much to offer social theories of disability and impairment. Indeed, within the wider arena of British disability politics, we can identify contributions by representative organisations of people with learning difficulties: particularly the self-advocacy movement. Members of this movement have had representation on the British Council of Disabled People (see Campbell and Oliver, 1996), contributed to discussions and formation of recent policy (for example, the 2001 White Paper *Valuing People*) and produced a whole host of literature which demands that service providers and professionals attend to the needs and ambitions of people with learning difficulties (see, for example, www.huddersfieldpeoplefirst.com). Against this climate of activism, the movement boasts its own 'organic intellectuals' (Oliver, 1990). Members of self-advocacy groups are absorbed in debates that social modellists and disability studies can and should engage with. One example is the way in which self-advocacy groups have critically revisited notions of 'impairment' through their critiques of the label of 'learning difficulties'. In what I will term the project of *storying the self*, self-advocacy groups have contributed to an *interpretivist* model of disability and impairment (Bogdan and Taylor, 1976, 1982; Langness and Levine, 1986; Atkinson and Williams, 1990; Ferguson et al., 1992; Ferguson and Ferguson, 1995; Skrtic, 1995). Interestingly, North American formations of disability studies boast a long history of working alongside people with learning difficulties in promoting positive social change (see, for example, University of Syracuse's Center on Human Policy, www.soeweb. syr.edu/thechp/). A key aim has been in developing an interpretivist approach that conceives disability as the product of voluntaristic individuals who are engaged in the creation of identities and the negotiation of roles. Such an epistemological stance recognises the disabling aspects of the world, but approaches them through turning to the experiences, stories, interactions, scripts and social roles of non-disabled people. It is possible to view some of the activities of the British self-advocacy movement as contributing to this stance.

The self-advocacy movement has understandably been concerned with reappraising the very labels that have been foisted onto them. While physically impaired activists have celebrated 'bodily difference', self-advocacy groups have been engaged in a very different project: challenging the very label of 'learning difficulties', which constantly threatens to undermine notions of humanity. When self-advocacy groups name themselves 'People First' and promote slogans such as 'Label jars not people', they are suggesting that behind labels reside competence, humanity and voluntaristic personhood. Moreover, it is typical to see the use of oral history by members of self-advocacy groups in demonstrating their human worth. An example of this is offered by the following extract from the life story of the British self-advocate Joyce Kershaw:

> Two staff [in the Day Centre] would stand and say which row could go for dinner. But they used to eat their dinner in a little room. So I asked the boss if I could have a word with him. He said, 'Yes, what's the matter?' So I said, 'Aren't we good enough to eat with?' and he said, 'Yes why?' I said, 'Well, it doesn't seem so – the staff eat in a little room of their own.' So he said he'd see what they'd say at the meeting. Then I asked him, 'Can we call the staff by the first name?' He said, 'Why don't you ask them?' So I did. Some said yes and some said no. Those who said no I said, 'Well, call me Mrs Kershaw.' (Goodley, 2000: 93)

Kershaw's account articulates the very formations of difference between professional staff and Centre 'user'. Note, too, how the story captures Kershaw voluntarily (but also as a reaction to the cultural context) challenging the practices around her that situate people with learning difficulties as different beings. In another extract from her story, Joyce reflects upon the label of learning difficulties:

> 'Learning disabilities' – I don't like that, disability makes you believe that we are in wheelchairs and we can't do anything for ourselves, when we can. We've got jobs now, we've got paid jobs. (Goodley, 2000, 124)

This view suggests that impairment labels are open to interpretation and understood in relation to lived experiences. 'Who is disabled' in this sense depends upon how identities, roles and labels are negotiated and constructed. For Joyce, certain labels and identities do not fit with her over-arching aim to point out that learning difficulties is not an 'insurmountable pathology'. The roles she identifies as crucial to her identity as an adult human being are not adequately captured by the label of learning disabilities. Some writers of disability studies have suggested that a turn to the personal, subjective, micro-level analysis – so characteristic of interpretivism – threatens to water down the potency of the social model:

> Writers like Jenny Morris have elevated the importance of personal psychological experience in understanding disability. Such work encouraged a shift away from thinking about the real world. Finding insight in the experiences of discrimination is just a return to the old case file approach to oppression, dressed up in social model jargon. (Finkelstein, 1996: 311)

Similarly, Barnes (1998) states that most of this writing represents either 'sentimental biography' or else is preoccupied with the medical and practical details of a particular condition (Hunt, 1966). However, I would suggest that interpretivist approaches – to which self-advocacy groups contribute – illuminate the potency of *storying one's life*. Far from impairment being simply a personal experience (Oliver, 1996), stories about the construction of 'impairment' demonstrate how individuals are involved in the creation of identities and the negotiation of roles that may exclude or empower: surely a key concern for the social model of disability.

Survivors of mental health systems are disabled: deconstructing professional knowledge

Gabel (1999) and Wilson and Beresford (2002) observe that people with mental health problems – or survivors of mental health systems – have failed to gain an adequate place in disability studies writing. The reasons for this may be traced back to some of the apparent 'failings' of the social model. In addition, it could be argued that survivors have been involved in different fights to those of other disabled activists. In particular, following Chamberlin (1990) and Sayce (2000), the history of the survivors movement can be characterised by two main projects. First, survivors have been involved in rejecting the dehumanising effects of 'mental illness' labels that have been assigned through the most arbitrary, unsystematic and oppressive forms of 'scientific diagnosis'. In this sense their fight for humanity shares similarities with that enacted by comrades of the self-advocacy movement. Second, survivors have been engaged in efforts to critique professional practices and knowledges of what Rose (1989) calls the *psy-complex*: those human service and welfare institutions and assemblages of knowledge that have contributed to practices and treatments associated with 'the abnormal' (see also Parker et al., 1995). Here is one way in which the survivors movement can contribute to disability studies. Specifically, I want to focus on one theoretical development that has long been associated with the movements of anti-psychiatry and survivors, that of *discoursing the self*, contributing to poststructuralist critiques of professionalisation in the lives of disabled people.

Poststructuralist theories are concerned with troubling modernist distinctions between the natural/social, individual/society, mind/body and, for our purposes, impairment/disability. The work of Michel Foucault (1973a, 1973b, 1977) is apposite here (see Tremain, 2002, for a useful overview). Foucault's main thrust of analysis was in challenging those discourses and practices which mascarade as 'truths' emerging from the human sciences and related practices such as psychiatry and psychology. Significantly, Foucault argued that a whole host of discursive practices – technologies of normalisation and biopower – have emerged under the banner of modernist progression with the same single focus of understanding and intervention: the human subject. While commonsense may have us believe that this increased knowledge of the 'human subject' contributes to a developed society, there is a price to be paid. Foucault exposes some of the ways in which professionalised knowledges create the very objects of disciplinary intervention. 'Minds', 'bodies', 'conditions', 'depression' and so on, all become the objects of discourses through which individuals enter the psy-complex. Once in, patients are subjected to professional 'gaze', normalising assessment procedures, schooled in the methods of treating and seeing oneself. As Wilson and Beresford argue:

> We do not consider that our 'minds', or those of other psychiatric system survivors, are impaired, damaged or sick in any way. Yet it is precisely because the psychiatric system has *perceived us* in this way that we have, at times in our lives, been indoctrinated into believing that we really are 'mentally ill'. (2002: 156)

Two crucial points emerge from survivors' dealings with these systems. First, these discourses are so powerful and all-consuming that they can potentially become part of the 'consciousness' of survivors: a process Foucault termed 'subjectification'. Second, the activism of survivors with mental health problems, alongside the work of poststructuralists such as Foucault, reminds us that 'mental illness' is a phenomenon *created* via a variety of discursive practices. As Wilson and Beresford point out, this socially constructed phenomenon can therefore be rejected or at the very least resisted. The potential of such understandings for disability studies is quite groundbreaking. As Tremain argues from a Foucauldian perspective:

> Impairment has been disability all along. Disciplinary practices in which the subject [survivor with mental heath problems] is inducted and divided from others produce the illusion of impairment as their prediscursive antecedent in order to multiply, divide and expand their regulatory effects. (Tremain, 2002: 42)

Technologies of the body and mind impinge upon and direct self-regulation. Power here is elusive. *We are free but only to govern ourselves.* So people with the label of 'schizophrenia' are seduced into enacting associated patterns of behaviour associated with such a label and those close to them have expectations about the kinds of behaviour 'acceptable' to such a 'condition'. While professional knowledges 'expertly' create the very objects necessary to form clinical understandings of schizophrenia and these very knowledges are promulgated through various institutions, disciplines and treatment regimes, power is neither owned by a dominant order nor an institution but is conceived of in discourses, collections of truths about humanity. These discourses are replenished by our daily, often commonsensical usage of them in making sense of our own bodies and minds. Thankfully, they are also challenged and resisted through self-regulation of a different order. So, the mental health survivor as activist crucially subverts the available knowledges which were and are historically associated with the mental health survivor as service user or patient. The exciting possibilities opened up for disability studies are articulated by Wilson and Beresford:

> A social model of madness and distress which focused on society's failure to accommodate people with ... 'perceived impairments of the mind', we believe, further contribute to the reification of 'impairment of the mind' and run the risk of reinforcing ideas of psychiatric system survivors as Other ... In our view, any understanding of that difference should *vigorously contest* the role of the psychiatric system and, in particular, of medical/psychiatric records and discourses in the reification of 'mental illness'. (2002: 155–6, italics in original)

The social model's inclusivity would appear to further increase through adopting approaches that deconstruct the professionalisation of disabled people's lives through opening up notions of 'self' and 'impairment' for discursive analyses.

Conclusion

The social model of disability is for *all* disabled people. Often, theoretical and political debate offers a view of disability studies as a fragmented arena. But the main aim of the social model of disability is to understand and change disabling socio-political and cultural practices. Therefore, it would appear that an anti-foundationalist approach should be encouraged (Skrtic, 1995) where different social theories and forms of activism are included. While we should remain committed to the social model, we should not be precious about a particular social theory if we are to hold on to the belief that disability studies matters to all disabled people and that the world needs to be changed for the better.

References

Atkinson, D. and Williams, F. (eds) (1990) *'Know me as I am': An Anthology of Prose, Poetry and Art by People with Learning difficulties.* Sevenoaks: Hodder and Stoughton in association with the Open University and MENCAP.

Barnes, C. (1998) 'The Social Model of Disability: A sociological phenomenon ignored by sociologists?', in T. Shakespeare (ed.), *The Disability Studies Reader: Social Science Perspectives.* London: Cassell.

Bogdan, R. and Taylor, S. (1976) 'The Judged not the Judges: An insider's view of mental retardation', *American Psychologist*, 31, 47–52.

Bogdan, R. and Taylor, S. (1982) *Inside Out: The Social Meaning of Mental Retardation.* Toronto: University of Toronto Press.

Campbell, J. and Oliver, M. (1996) *Disability Politics: Understanding Our Past, Changing Our Future.* London: Routledge.

Chamberlin, J. (1990) 'The ex-patients' movement: where we've been and where we're going', *Journal of Mind and Behaviour*, 11 (2): 323–36.

Ferguson, P.M. and Ferguson, D.L. (1995) 'The interpretivist view of special education and disability: the value of telling stories', in T.M. Skrtic (ed.), *Disability and Democracy: Reconstructing (Special) Education for Postmodernity.* New York, NY: Teachers College Press.

Ferguson, P.M., Ferguson, D.L. and Taylor, S.J. (ed.) (1992) *Interpreting Disability: A Qualitative Reader.* New York, Ny: Teachers College Press.

Finkelstein, V. (1996) 'Outside, Inside Out', Greater Manchester Coalition of Disabled People *Coalition*, April, 30–36.

Foucault, M. (1973a) *The Birth of the Clinic: An Archaeology of Medical Perception*, trans. A.M. Sheridan. New York, NY: Pantheon Books.

Foucault, M. (1973b) *Madness and Civilisation: A History of Insanity in the Age of Reason*, trans. R. Howard. New York, NY: Vintage/Random House.

Foucault, M. (1977) *Discipline and Punish: The Birth of the Prison*, trans. R. Howard. New York, NY: Pantheon Books.

Gabel, S. (1999) 'Depressed and disabled: some discursive problems with mental illness', in M. Corker and S. French (eds), *Disability Discourse.* Buckingham: Open University Press.

Goodley, D. (2000) *Self-advocacy in the Lives of People with Learning Difficulties: The Politics of Resilience.* Buckingham: Open University Press.

Hasler, F. (1993) 'Developments in the disabled people's movement', in J. Swain, V. Finkelstein, S. French and M. Oliver (eds), *Disabling Barriers – Enabling Environments.* London: Sage.

Hunt, P. (1966) *Stigma: The Experience of Disability.* London: Geoffrey Chapman.

Langness, L.L. and Levine, H.G. (eds) (1986) *Culture and Retardation.* Kluwer: Reidel.

Morris, J. (1991) *Pride Against Prejudice: Transforming Attitudes to Disability.* London: The Women's Press.

Morris, J. (ed.) (1996) *Encounters with Strangers: Feminism and Disability.* London: The Women's Press.

Oliver, M. (1990) *The Politics of Disablement.* Basingstoke: Macmillan.

Oliver, M. (1996) *Understanding Disability: From Theory to Practice.* London: Macmillan.

Parker, I., Georgaca, E., Harper, D., McLaughlin, T. and Stowell-Smith, M. (1995) *Deconstructing Psychopathology.* London: Sage.

Priestley, M., Corker, M. and Watson, N. (1999) 'Unfinished business: disabled children and disability identity', *Disability Studies Quarterly*, 19 (2): 87–98.

Rose, N. (1989) *Governing the Soul.* London: Routledge.

Sayce, L. (2000) *From Psychiatric Patient to Citizen: Overcoming Discrimination and Social Exclusion.* London: Macmillan.

Shakespeare, T., Gillespie-Sells, K. and Davies, D. (1996) *The Sexual Politics of Disability.* London: Cassells.

Skrtic, T. (ed.) (1995) *Disability and Democracy: Reconstructing (Special) Education for Modernity.* New York: Teachers College Press.

Stuart, O. (1993) 'Double oppression: an appropriate starting point?' in J. Swain, V. Finkelstein, S. French and M. Oliver (eds), *Disabling Barriers – Enabling Environments.* London: Sage.

Thomas, C. (1999) *Female Forms: Experiencing and Understanding Disability.* Buckingham: The Open University Press.

Tremain, S. (2002) 'On the subject of impairment', in M. Corker and T. Shakespeare (eds), *Disability/Postmodernity.* London: Continuum.

Wilson, A. and Beresford, P. (2002) 'Madness, distress and postmodernity: putting the record straight', in M. Corker and T. Shakespeare (eds), *Disability/Postmodernity.* London: Continuum.

Zarb, G. and Oliver, M. (1993) *Ageing with a Disability: What do They Expect After All These Years?* Greenwich: University of Greenwich.

19 Disabled People, Disability and Sexuality
SELINA BONNIE

In 1992 disabled American activist and author Anne Finger said that 'Sexuality is often the source of our deepest oppression; it is also often the source of our deepest pain'. (Finger, 1992: 9). Sadly, ten years on this statement is still relevant.

Rule 9.2 of the UN Standard Rules for the Equalisation of Opportunities for Persons with Disabilities, which deals with family life and personal integrity, states:

> Persons with disabilities must not be denied the opportunity to experience their sexuality, have sexual relationships and experience parenthood. ... Persons with disabilities must have the same access as others to family-planning methods, as well as to information in accessible form on the sexual functioning of their bodies. (United Nations, 1994: 9.2)

Historically, this basic human right has been denied and disabled people's sexuality and sexual expression have been oppressed in a variety of ways. Disabled children and teenagers have been dressed in androgynous, bland or babyish clothes, denied relationships and sexuality education, and placed in segregated 'special' institutions and schools.

Disabled adults have been infantilised, sterilised, prohibited from engaging in sexual activity and marriage, and excluded from mainstream social and leisure activities.

In this chapter I have not set out to engage in an in-depth analysis of issues of disabled people, sexuality and sexual expression. I have written this chapter to provide an introduction to, and a synopsis of, the key issues facing disabled people's sexual expression.

Societal notions of disabled people's sexuality

Society at best finds the thought of a disabled person being sexual repulsive and at worst presumes we are asexual. As a disabled person this can be a very difficult reality to acknowledge; however, I would rather that someone considered the thought of me being sexually active as distasteful rather than believing me to be asexual. At least with the former they are thinking of me as a sexual being. As a disabled woman I have lost count of the amount of times that my husband has been referred to as my 'friend', 'brother' or 'carer'.

In general disabled people are rarely portrayed in the media, film, television and advertising industries. When we are it is often as the recipients of charity, evil characters in movies or tragic victims of illness or accident. We are rarely, if ever, portrayed in relationships as sexually active or as parents. How often have you seen disabled people on the catwalks of London, Milan or Paris Fashion Week or on the pages of Cosmo, Vogue or FHM?

There is an unspoken taboo about relationships and disabled people. Disabled people's sexual and emotional needs are rarely included in any discussion or representation in everyday life, whether this is in the papers and magazines we read, or the movies we watch. This reinforces the public's attitudes and expectations towards disabled people as seeing them as 'sick and sexless' rather than participating in full sexual and family relationships. (Lamb and Layzell, 1994: 21, cited in Shakespeare et al., 1996: 11)

Disabled people are guilty of this denial of disabled sexuality too. We all know that there is more to disabled people's lives than just employment, health care or education. So why is it only now that some disabled people's organisations are just starting to address and discuss the issue?

Historically, access to transport, housing, personal assistance, employment, education, and getting our rights enshrined in legislation have been the priority for the disabled people's movement. Social, leisure, relationships and sexual expression have been pushed way down the list of priorities, while disabled people have fought to achieve a better quality of life and independent living. This can also be related to the distinction between fighting for public rights and private rights, an issue which has been much debated in the women's movement.

Identity and belonging

I believe that any discussion of disabled people, disability and sexuality would not be complete without addressing issues of identity and belonging.

Identity

There are many events in life that influence how we identify with the world around us (Chapter 13). A variety of elements fuse to form our identity, and our sexuality is an important part of that. People express their sexuality in many ways. How we dress, if we wear makeup, if we flirt, how confident we are in life and the relationships we form are all influenced by, and in turn influence, the development and expression of our sexuality. Having the opportunity to express our sexuality in turn enables us to define our identity.

Gender and gender roles are an important facet of our identity. Some people refer to disabled people as 'the third gender'; for example, when it comes to public toilets one usually finds the Ladies, Gents and then the accessible toilet. The reason that is often mooted to justify this is that the separate accessible toilet facilitates disabled people whose assistants are not of the same sex. However, I find having to use the 'gender neutral' toilet quite insulting and I believe that the French have the correct idea by just having unisex toilets for everyone!

Belonging

People gain a sense of belonging from having the opportunity to express their sexuality. However, forming and maintaining non-sexual relationships with family, friends, work colleagues or relevant communities of interest can also provide this comfort.

Sexual expression is just one part of the overall communication of our self. For many people it is a very important part of their life and of how they express their identity. To travel throughout life constantly being denied this type of expression has had a detrimental effect on many disabled people's confidence and sense of self-worth.

It can be very difficult for many disabled people to gain a sense of belonging to a community or a movement if they have multiple identities or experience multiple oppression, for example, a gay disabled person or a disabled woman. A gay disabled person may face homophobia in the disabled people's movement, but they may also find it difficult to gain a sense of belonging in the gay movement due to inaccessible bars and clubs and a preoccupation with aesthetics and the body beautiful. Many disabled women have also experienced exclusion by the women's movement because of the desire of the women's movement to shift away from the traditional notion of women as carers, and by the disabled people's movement because the movement is still very patriarchal.

Experiences

Traditionally, there has been a taboo around discussing sexuality, sexual expression and related matters in public. Sex was for marriage and procreation, and disabled people were not expected or encouraged to experience either.

Expressing one's sexuality is not just about sex. Sexuality is about relationships, confidence, self-image and choice making. It is about how we as human beings see and express our personalities and ourselves. Morris states:

> ... many people assume we are asexual, often in order to hide embarrassment about the seemingly incongruous idea that such 'abnormal' people can have 'normal' feelings and relationships. (1989: 80)

Disabled people encounter many barriers with regard to expressing our sexualities. I believe, however, that the most significant of these barriers can be listed under the headings of: attitudinal, environmental and informational, interpersonal, and educational barriers.

Attitudinal barriers

Shakespeare et al. (1996) equated admitting that one is a disabled person with coming out as a gay, lesbian or bisexual person. I believe that even disabled people who are heterosexual go through a process of 'coming out' when they start to assert their sexuality.

'Parental overprotection is often cited as a hindrance to social experiences' (Baker and Donelly, 2001: 74). Parents tend to overprotect their disabled offspring, treating them as unable and childlike. Children do not have sexualities and so parents find it difficult to see their disabled offspring as sexual beings, and not as vulnerable and impressionable people at risk. Therefore it is often a source of great concern for parents when their disabled offspring start to assert and express their sexuality.

When I had my first serious relationship at age 19, my parents genuinely believed that I was vulnerable and 'being led astray' purely because I was a disabled person. I watch them now with my three siblings who are in their teens, and non-disabled, and my parents are a lot more lenient with them than they were with me.

Traditionally, disabled people have had to endure medical intervention to 'correct deformed bodies' or to 'cure' us and make us 'normal'. A prevailing attitude in today's society is the overwhelming preoccupation with aesthetics and body image. The combination of intrusive medical intervention, society's obsession with the perfect body, and our denial as sexual beings has led to many disabled people having very low self-esteem, confidence and poor body image.

Environmental and informational barriers

There are numerous studies and articles that document that many non-disabled people genuinely believe that disabled people are incapable of sexual expression or sexual pleasure (Morris, 1989; Owens and Child, 1999; Shakespeare, 2000). Many never consider that disabled people also require access to services related to sexual expression, such as adult shops, family planning clinics, adult websites, pubs and clubs and other places where social relationships are formed, or services are provided.

Traditionally, key issues usually pursued for service provision or rights are: education, training, housing and health. It is really only in the past decade, particularly with the growth of the disabled people's and independent living movements, that disabled people are starting to question why social, leisure, relationships and sexual expression have not been addressed with regards to access and support services.

Informational barriers can be as disempowering as environmental barriers. Access to information is absolutely vital, particularly in today's information-driven world, and the area of sexual expression should be no exception. In a truly inclusive society, adult literature would be available in accessible formats, adult websites would be built using the principles of universal design and family planning services would have information both in accessible formats and appropriate to the needs of disabled people. Unfortunately we do not live in a truly inclusive society and so disabled people's informational needs, and wants, are often unmet.

In Ireland, the best example I have seen thus far of information written to suit the needs of disabled people is the *Safe Sex* booklet that was written specifically for gay learning disabled men, by the Gay Men's Health Project. For disabled women, a key example of positive and useful information provision is a chart on 'Reproductive and contraceptive considerations for women with physical disabilities' in *The Baby Challenge* by Mukti Jain Campion (Campion, 1990: 8–9).

Interpersonal barriers

In general, society does not view disabled people as sexual beings, and this denial of sexual expression greatly impacts on disabled people's confidence and quality of life. Social interactions, such as flirting, can be very difficult for some disabled people. Body language and eye contact are important aspects of flirting or chatting someone up, but this can be very difficult if the disabled person is blind or if their body experiences spasms. People who are deaf, hearing or speech impaired also find it very difficult to interact and flirt in regular social places, such as pubs and clubs, as the noise levels make it very difficult to be understood.

Educational barriers

Although I have already discussed informational barriers, I think it is important to also highlight the key educational barriers particularly faced by disabled children and young people. Disabled people are not equipped by society to be sexually responsible. Relationships and sexuality education in mainstream schools does not include information specifically relevant to disabled people. I believe that it is very dangerous to try to deny that the disabled child or young person has a sexuality. There have been numerous cases where young disabled people have been raped or sexually abused and they did not know that what was happening was wrong, or what they should do, because sexuality had not been discussed with them and they had not received any 'stay safe' education. Disabled people who are born with an impairment or who become disabled in childhood become accustomed to numerous adults, such as parents or the medical profession, examining them. This can make it very difficult for the young person to then distinguish between appropriate and abusive behaviour from adults. By educating these young disabled people, I believe that they would have been more empowered to protect themselves.

The bigger picture – current debates and issues

Thus far in this chapter I have explored the issue of identity and belonging and I have outlined the key barriers facing disabled people's sexual expression and sexuality. At this point I think it is important to highlight that it is not all bad news. Over the past decade a number of key disabled activists and academics have researched and written about issues of disabled people, disability and sexuality (Morris, 1989, 1991; Shakespeare et al., 1996; Davies, 2000; Shakespeare, 2000, 2001; Tepper, 2000). Disabled actors Mik Scarlet, Mat Fraser and Lara Masters, who all project quite a strong sexuality, have broken into mainstream television. Organisations such as SPOD (which aids the personal and sexual relationships of people with disabilities) in the UK have continued to develop, and the growth of the worldwide independent living movement has led to a greater number of disabled people living their lives as they choose.

Various notable advances around the globe include: some brothels in Australia have been made wheelchair accessible; a Dutch Council is paying for a disabled man to access a prostitute once a month; and people with significant impairments are travelling to The Netherlands and Denmark to access sex services, which have been established by the state specifically for disabled people.

There are a number of key debates raging at the moment that are worth addressing. When considering these debates it is important to remember that today, in the twenty-first century, these options for sexual expression are still only empowering a very minimal percentage of disabled people to explore their sexuality and realise their sexual desires.

Devotees are non-disabled men who are specifically sexually attracted to women who are amputees or who have other physical impairments. The devotee community is particularly big in the USA, with numerous websites and magazines devoted to the issue. This has also been referred to as 'disability fetishism' (Kafer, 2000) and has been the subject of much debate both in non-disabled society and the disabled people's movement.

There are many facets to this debate. Two key strands have been that many people find devotees and their organisations distasteful and believe them to be exploitative of disabled women. However, many disabled women who are active in this community find the experience of being desired and considered more beautiful than non-disabled women extremely empowering. They believe that society should not judge the devotees as deviant just because they explicitly desire disabled women.

Sex surrogates are trained professionals who engage in sexual activity with people who experience difficulties with the sexual expression or performance. The surrogate works at the direction of the therapist who prescribes this form of treatment/therapy for the client. This system operates in many countries and is regulated by the Code of Ethics (2002) and Code of Practice from the World Association for Sexology (WAS) and the International Professional Surrogates Association (IPSA). These services are not specifically designed for disabled people, but do provide a supported opportunity for disabled people to explore sexual expression. I would not advocate for disabled people to use this type of service because I believe it medicalises disabled people's sexual needs. However, if a disabled person is sexually oppressed and frustrated and has the opportunity to access such a service, I consider surrogacy a far healthier option than remaining frustrated!

I have recently conducted research into the area of facilitated sexual expression in the independent living movement. This aspect of personal assistance was first brought to my attention in 1996 (Shakespeare et al., 1996) and it has intrigued me ever since. If a disabled person (leader) who uses the services of a personal assistant (PA) has a significant impairment and needs their PA to assist them with tasks such as eating or washing and so on, isn't it likely that they may also need assistance with sexual activity?

This form of assistance has many implications attached, particularly legal, ethical and moral. For example, a PA who facilitates their leader by soliciting a prostitute, or assisting with masturbation, could find himself or herself in a very difficult legal situation. Equally the leader, as an employer, could be breaching employment law and public policy by bringing facilitated sexual expression into the working relationship.

The key recommendations emanating from my research were that the existing content of PA training needs to be developed to include sexuality and that a Code of Practice for Facilitated Sexual Expression should be developed. Leaders should be supported to develop individual grades of facilitation, which can then be negotiated with their PA as this will help to protect both the leader and the PA. Model employment contracts, which include ethical guidelines, should also be developed.

Disabled people experience many barriers in relation to becoming parents. Historically, there has been a worldwide practice of forcibly sterilising disabled people (particularly women) and administering contraceptives without consent. Although women with learning difficulties have been particularly targeted by these eugenic practices, many people with physical, mental or sensory impairments have also had to endure these abuses.

Many mothers with significant impairments have had their children taken from them by social services because they have been 'unable to look after the children'. For the majority of these mothers the provision of adequate personal assistance provision and support services would have enabled them to care for their children, thus negating the need for the children to be removed.

Conclusion

Disabled people are, and have a basic human right to be, sexual beings. A lot of disabled people lack the level of support they need to achieve the level of sexual expression to which they aspire.

The barriers which disabled people face must be broken down and there are a number of key ways in which this should happen. Physical access and access to information in its broadest sense must be addressed. In today's modern age there is no excuse for poor, inaccessible design and service provision. Staff in day centres and rehabilitation settings should be trained to appropriately respond to disabled people's sexual expression. Peer support services for disabled people and support services for parents and guardians specifically in the area of sexuality and sexual expression should be adequately resourced, and appropriate relationships and sexuality education should be available to disabled people in schools and centres.

Liz Crow says:

> I've always assumed that the most urgent Disability civil rights campaigns are the ones we're currently fighting for – employment, education, housing, transport etc., etc., and that next to them a subject such as sexuality is almost dispensable. For the first time now I'm beginning to believe that sexuality, the one area above all others to have been ignored, is at the absolute core of what we're working for … It's not that one area can ever be achieved alone – they're all interwoven, but you can't get closer to the essence of self or more 'people-living-alongside-people' than sexuality, can you? (Cited in Shakespeare, 2000: 165)

Despite the difficulties, issues and implications which I have explored in this chapter, it is important to remember that a lot of disabled people do have fulfilling and fun sex lives, we are getting into long-term relationships, becoming parents and so on.

Tepper stated that:

> Pleasure is an affirmation of life. … Pleasure adds meaning to our lives. Sexual pleasure is particularly powerful in making one feel alive. It is an antidote to pain, both physical and emotional. … Sexual pleasure can enhance an intimate relationship. It can add a sense of connectedness to the world or to each other. (Tepper, 2000: 288)

I agree with Mitch Tepper. Sexual pleasure and freedom are truly powerful and, in this new millennium, not one disabled person should have to endure enforced celibacy. Ultimately, my vision for the future is that society will accept us as sexual beings. This must start by disabled people taking ownership of the issue, debating it, and engaging in a personal and collective growth and development around our sexual expression and sexuality.

References

Baker, K. and Donelly, M. (2001) 'The social experiences of children with disability and the influence of environment: a framework for intervention', *Disability and Society*, 16 (1): 71–85.

Campion, M.J. (1990) *The Baby Challenge*, London: Routledge.

Davies, D. (2000) 'Facilitating sex and relationships for people with disabilities', *The Right to Be Sexual – A Radical Proposal*. http://www.bentvoices.org/culturecrash/daviessarfp.htm accessed 25 March 2002.

Finger, A. (1992) 'Introduction', in T. Shakespeare, K. Gillespie-Sells and D. Davies (eds) (1996) *The Sexual Politics of Disability*, London, Cassell.

Kafer, A. (2000) 'Amputated desire, resistant desire: female amputees in the devotee community', *Disability World*. http://www.disabilityworld.org/June-July2000/Women/SDS.htm accessed 26 March 2002.

Lamb, B. and Layzell, S. (1994) cited in T. Shakespeare, K. Gillespie-Sells and D. Davies (eds) (1996) *The Sexual Politics of Disability*. London: Cassell.

Morris, J. (1989) *Able Lives: Women's Experiences of Paralysis*. London: The Women's Press.

Morris, J. (1991) *Pride Against Prejudice: Transforming Attitudes To Disability*. London: The Women's Press.

Owens, T. and Child, L. (1999) 'Outsiders still out', *Disability Now*, http://www.disabilitynow.org.uk/search/99_02_Fe/p29out.htm accessed 23 March 2002.

Shakespeare, T. (2000) 'Disabled sexuality towards rights and recognition', *Disability and Society*, 18 (3): 159–66.

Shakespeare, T. (2001) 'Coming out and coming home', in *Equality News*, Equality Authority of Ireland, Autumn Issue, 17–18.

Shakespeare, T., Gillespie-Sells, K., Davies, D. (1996) *The Sexual Politics of Disability*. London: Cassell.

Tepper, M. (2000) 'Sexuality and disability: the missing discourse of pleasure', *Sexuality and Disability*, 18 (4): 283–90.

United Nations (1994) Rule 9 of '*UN Standard Rules for the Equalisation of Opportunities for Persons with Disabilities*', gopher://gopher.un.org/00/sec/dpcsd/dspd/disabled/ar48-96.en accessed 2 April 2001.

World Association for Sexology (WAS) and The International Professional Surrogates Association (IPSA), *Code of Ethics and Code of Practice*, http://www.sexresearch.sotcom.ru/coe.html accessed 01 April 2002.

Part III
Controlling Lifestyles

20 Righting the Picture: Disability and Family Life
MICHELE WATES

Family and disability: misleading stereotypes

Charity posters portraying disabled people as socially isolated, passive recipients of caring attention make it easy to overlook the fact that disabled people are members of families in which, naturally, they give as well as take. Many disabled adults have an active role in caring for children whether as birth, step, adoptive or foster parents, as aunts, uncles or grandparents. Disabled children also enjoy reciprocal friendships and may be involved in looking after siblings or other relatives.

The aim of charity advertising, however, is to invite pity and loosen purse strings by emphasising the need for charitable intervention. In order to do this the vulnerability of disabled people is stressed. The social context of family life is either hidden or else tends to be problematised. Pictures of disabled people as parents are rarely used and, when they are, the message is mixed.

The Multiple Sclerosis (MS) society, whose membership includes a great many women and men who successfully carry out parenting responsibilities, does not choose to show parents integrated within the family context in its poster campaigns, but rather uses images of parenting to heighten a sense of vulnerability and loss. A poster in the 'MS tears lives' campaign, for example, incorporates a photograph of a naked toddler reaching up his hand to his naked father (shown from the back and from the shoulders down only). The man has no identity but a strip of paper has been torn from his leg to represent the effects of the disease. It is purely the father's, and to an even greater extent his *child's,* vulnerability that we are being invited to pick up on.

A fund-raising advert for a charity specific to motor neurone disease shows a photograph of a man who has the illness smiling as he cuddles his infant son on his lap. However, the father's natural and evident delight is belied by the tragic note sounded in the caption, 'Soon I won't be able to hold my son'.

Attempting to counter the criticism that charities have dealt in negative stereotypes of disabled people by including notions of resilience and personal strength and using colour pictures of actual disabled people doing 'positive' things does not, as David Hevey showed in his fascinating analysis of photography and disability imagery (Hevey, 1992), alter the basic premise that the problem is primarily located in the disabled individual; in what they can and cannot do and in society's *perceptions* of what they can and cannot do.

Disabled people point out that barriers to their participation in everyday life, such as inaccessible buildings, transport, information and so on; discriminatory and inappropriate service structures; restricted access to employment and consequent poverty, all have a huge impact upon the lives of people with impairments and their families. This is what in reality constitutes disability. A recent government-sponsored poster campaign with the slogan 'See the Person, not the Disability', was felt by many to be seriously missing the point. Disability *should* be seen; because only in this way can it be recognised for what it is and the barriers dismantled.

Such approaches are seen by many as attempts to move away from the medical model whilst unfortunately holding to its central tenet; that the personal characteristics of the disabled person are at the heart of the matter.

Research perspectives on disability and family life

Much of the research with a bearing on the family lives of disabled people also begins from the assumption that disability is a personal characteristic – whether physical, intellectual, emotional or sensory – that to a greater or lesser extent causes problems for the disabled person and *for those who live with them*. In so far as this research has a social dimension, it is concerned with evaluating the psycho-social adjustment and 'resilience' of the family unit in the presence of impairment (Olsen and Wates, 2003).

From this perspective, the presence or absence of external supports is not seen as determining outcomes, but becomes merely an indicator of the extent to which families have or have not come to terms with difficulties related to the presence of the disabled child or adult (Ferguson et al., 2000).

In line with this body of research, the development of services in the statutory and voluntary sectors has largely focused upon evaluating the family life of disabled people in terms of its internal strengths and/or its pathologies, with a view to determining the viability of the family unit and the 'capacity' of the disabled adult to parent successfully. The effect has been to deflect the attention of both researchers and policy makers away from vital social, economic and organisational issues that determine a family's access to resources and support.

Researchers and policy makers have their own version of the 'positive thinking' of recent advertising campaigns. The introduction of concepts such as 'the strengths model' or 'the empowerment model' are intended to indicate that, given sufficient personal resilience and the right professional intervention, the disabled person and family may be viable.

Writers and researchers committed to the rights of disabled children have argued that far more attention is needed to the wider social, economic and environmental factors that restrict the lives of disabled people and their families (Oldman and Beresford, 1998; Joseph Rowntree Foundation, 1999; Shakespeare et al., 2000). Whilst there have been significant shifts towards accepting these arguments in relation to the families of disabled children, the situation regarding disabled parents has received far less attention and remains less well understood.

Service providers focus on questioning capacity rather than providing support

The assumption made in research and fostered by charity advertising that children's interests are inherently threatened by the vulnerabilities of disabled people is reflected in the way that statutory service providers and the voluntary sector respond to families in which one or both parents are disabled. Rather than identifying and accommodating any specific support requirements that disabled adults may have in relation to their parenting role, the professionals' role is seen as being to 'hold the ring' so to speak, arbitrating and making judgement calls between potentially conflicting perspectives and interests.

In the government-issued guidance *The Framework for the Assessment of Children in Need and their Families* (Department of Health, 2000), there is extensive and welcome discussion of the impact of wider socio-economic and environmental factors, such as housing, family social integration, employment, income and so on, in relation to families that include disabled children. Yet neither the policy nor the practice guidance issued as part of the *Framework* directs the attention of those making assessments to family and environmental factors affecting families in which a disabled adult is present. This is a serious omission, given that unresolved difficulties in these areas will have an equal, and in some cases an even greater, impact on children's welfare where it is the *parent* rather than the *child* who is directly affected.

Rather than considering how best to tackle barriers to social inclusion and address parental support needs, discussion of disabled parents in the *Framework* is limited to discussion of the potential impact upon the disabled adult's parenting capacity and responses (Jones et al., 2002; Wates, 2002a).

In consequence, the (mainly non-disabled) children of disabled parents come to be seen as the primary 'clients' and the potential recipients of services, rather than the disabled adults with parenting responsibility for those children. All too frequently disabled parents report that they cannot access resources and receive no attention from service providers unless and until the difficulties experienced within their families, sometimes as a direct result of the lack of timely support, attract potentially stigmatising labels such as 'child in need', 'child at risk', 'young carer' or yet more seriously (and by no means always appropriately in the opinion of the Social Services Inspectorate) trigger child protection procedures (Goodinge, 2000; Wates, 2002a).

Australian researchers based at the University of Sydney carried out a major study in relation to child custody decisions taken by the courts in New South Wales and came to the conclusion that disabled parents and their families are treated unfairly by the courts. They argue that there is considerable anecdotal evidence that a similar thing is happening in other parts of the world, including the UK (McConnell and Llwellyn, 2000; Booth, 2000).

In this country family rights supporters find that the presence of impairment is not infrequently cited in custody disputes as a reason why a child 'will have a better life chance' with the non-disabled parent or even in the care of a local authority. In the case of parents with learning difficulties, such challenges are particularly likely to go unquestioned.

Upholding children's welfare by supporting parents

There has for a long time been a clear and explicit understanding in the child support sector that children's needs and rights are most appropriately met wherever possible within the context of their own families, and that the best way to ensure this is by supporting parents to fulfil their responsibilities. This principle is enshrined in the Children Act 1989.

Government regulations and guidance accompanying the Act make it clear that this should apply to disabled parents and their children as to other families.

Given that the voluntary sector has always played a substantial role in upholding the welfare of children by supporting parents, it is a matter of concern that in the family support sector the relevance of so-called 'special needs' has only been considered in relation to disabled children. It is encouraging that a number of national organisations and local projects (including many that have up until now addressed this area mainly through projects directed at supporting 'young carers') are showing a willingness to re-examine practices and review the accessibility of their information and support in relation to disabled parents. (Wates, 2002b; Aldridge and Becker, 2003; Newman and Wates, forthcoming 2004).

Just as the problem/action of disabled parents is felt to have 'outlined' them for undue scrutiny, it appears at the same time to have 'sidelined' them as a group of disabled adults with entitlement to financial and practical support in carrying out their social roles and responsibilities. *A Jigsaw of Services,* the report of an inspection carried out by the Social Services Inspectorate (Goodinge, 2000), found that parenting tasks and roles were not generally included in local authority eligibility criteria determining which adults receive health and social services. This was borne out in a study of social services departments protocols and policies in respect of disabled parents commissioned by the Joseph Rowntree Foundation (Wates, 2002a).

Parenting responsibilities are not taken into account when assessing levels for either the severe disability allowance or the disability living allowance. There is no benefit that takes into account the additional costs of being a disabled parent, even though the carers allowance contributes to the cost of parenting a disabled child, whilst parenting needs are specifically excluded from assessment for the Independent Living Fund.

Disabled parents: rights and entitlements

Service providers, as the SSI inspectors pointed out (Department of Health, 2000), must note the requirement of the 1995 Disability Discrimination Act 'to take reasonable steps to change policies, practices or procedures which make it impossible or unreasonably difficult for disabled people to use a service.' They encourage service providers to adopt a self-critical approach to elements in their own practice that might either create or exacerbate difficulties experienced by families in which one or both parents are disabled.

The inspectors noted, for example, the disproportionate number of parents with learning difficulties whose children become involved in child protection procedures. This did not appear to be justified by the inspectors' analysis of the casework records relating to those families. Their report suggests that the high incidence appeared to result in part from the way services respond to certain groups of parents; the omission of parenting tasks and responsibilities from eligibility criteria for community care services and reluctance in some areas to recognise disabled adults' additional needs as parents (Goodinge, 2000: 5.6 and 5.12).

A Jigsaw of Services identified that the particular support needs of disabled parents are more likely to be met when their existence as a group of service users with distinct requirements is recognised and promoted by written policies (Goodinge, 2000).

Involvement of disabled parents in bringing about change

The Joseph Rowntree Foundation (JRF) study of social services departments' policies and protocols (Wates, 2002a) showed that the involvement of local groups of disabled parents, with representation in some cases from disabled parents' national organisations, made an appreciable difference in terms of developing service designs that were more effectively linked in with the appropriate specialist adult services as well as children's services, less likely to be experienced as stigmatising, and better able to respond flexibly to family situations.

The fact that research studies by paid academics are often regarded as more important evidence than user feedback, personal accounts and service provider concerns, has had the effect of marginalising much useful information and feedback from disabled parents themselves and from those who are seeking to support them more effectively.

A widespread consultation with disabled parents (Disabled Parents Network, 2003) was carried out to inform preparation of a rights and information handbook. This highlighted a number of issues that disabled parents consider critical.

Consultation with disabled parents on access to information and services

It is very difficult indeed for disabled parents to find information and access support when needs change unexpectedly within a family. This may be because of a change in a parent's health, as a result of something that happens to a child, or because of a change in family circumstances. Since it is in the nature of family life that both foreseen and unforeseen changes occur, services must have flexibility and responsiveness inbuilt to have any chance of responding quickly and in a supportive manner.

A striking number of parents reported that they had found direct payments very helpful. Direct payments mean that parents are given money to use in the way that they think best to meet their own and their family's support needs, rather than having to fit in with services provided by the local authority.

At the same time as expressing their enthusiasm, parents involved in a user group for people receiving direct payments stressed the need for proper supports, both for parents but also for social workers, many of whom are currently hesitant to recommend direct payments for fear that they may be setting people up to fail.

Parents who have a sense of what they are entitled to and know about things like how to get hold of and use direct payments are clearly in a stronger position. This underlines how important it is that information is made directly available to disabled parents in accessible formats. Disabled parents' access to information and support will only become widespread when the subject is routinely addressed, both in the manuals, handbooks and information sheets concerned with parenting and also in those that relate to disability.

Service providers and voluntary organisations have a duty to accommodate the support and information requirements of disabled adults with parenting responsibilities. As one parent said, 'It shouldn't be down to informal conversations with other parents and the luck of the draw with professionals as to whether you get information or not.'

Making the links between disabled children and disabled parents

'We had sex education at "special" school but no one ever talked about the possibility of us becoming parents.' (Wates, 1997: 29)

The links between disabled parents and disabled children have been insufficiently recognised. Both face an issue around whether the world accepts their existence, welcomes the resource that they represent and accommodates their requirements. And naturally – although often overlooked – the disabled children of today will be amongst the disabled parents of tomorrow.

These issues have been thoughtfully and powerfully explored in a collection of writing by women who, whether raised disabled since childhood or having acquired impairments in adulthood, have gone on to make the links between parenthood and disability. The book contains work by women from a number of countries who have publicly and/or privately pursued the rights of disabled people in relation to parenting and challenged both internalised limitations and externally imposed constraints (Wates and Jade, 1999).

As O'Toole (1999) points out, today's disabled parents are the first whose right to found families and live as other families has been in any way upheld in law, whilst the current generation of disabled children are the first to be raised largely outside the shadow of enforced institionalisation. At the same time we live with the scientific myth that with the right technological interventions and pre-birth selections disability might be eradicated, and with the social myth that such an outcome would be desirable. It has never been more important to explore the realities of disability in relation to family life.

References

Aldridge, J. and Becker, S. (2003) *Children Caring for Parents with Mental Illness: Perspectives of Young Carers, Parents and Professionals.* Bristol: The Policy Press.

Booth, T. (2000) 'Parents with learning difficulties, child protection and the courts', *Representing Children*, 13 (3): 175–88.

Department of Health (2000) *The Framework for the Assessment of Children in Need and their Families.* London: The Stationery Office.

Disabled Parents Network (2003) *'It shouldn't be down to luck ...'* Results of a consultation with disabled parents on access to information and services to support parenting. London: National Centre for Disabled Parents.

Ferguson, P.M., Gartner, A. and Lipsky, D.K. (2000) 'The Experience of Disability in Families', in E. Parens and A. Asch (eds), *Prenatal Testing and Disability Rights.* Washington, D.C.: Georgetown University Press.

Goodinge, S. (2000) *A Jigsaw of Services: Report of an SSI Inspection of services to support disabled adults in their parenting role.* London:DH Publications.

Hevey, D. (1992) *The Creatures Time Forgot: Photography and Disability Imagery.* London: Routledge.

Jones, A., Jeyasingham, D. and Rajasooriya, S. (2002) *Invisible Families: The strengths and needs of black families in which young people have caring responsibilities.* York: Joseph Rowntree Foundation.

Joseph Rowntree Foundation (1999) *Foundations.* Report of research by Jenny Morris 'Supporting disabled children and their families'. York: JRF.

McConnell, D. and Llwellyn, G. (2000) 'Disability and discrimination in statutory child protection proceedings', *Disability and Society*, 15 (6): 883–895.

Newman, T. and Wates, M. (eds) (2004 forthcoming) *Disabled Parents and their Children: Building a Better Future* (provisional title). Barking: Barnardo's.

Oldman, C. and Beresford, B. (1998) 'Homes unfit for children: Housing, disabled children and their families'. Bristol: The Policy Press.

Olsen, R. and Wates, M. (2003) *Disabled Parents: Examining Research Assumptions*. Dartington: Research in Practice.

O'Toole, C.J. (1999) 'A Child of Both Countries', in M. Wates and R. Jade (eds), *Bigger than the Sky: Disabled Women on Parenting*. London: The Women's Press.

Shakespeare, T., Priestley, M. and Barnes, C. (2000) *Life as a Disabled Child: A qualitative study of young disabled people's perspectives and experiences.* Leeds: Centre for Disability Studies.

Wates, M. (1997) *Disabled Parents: Dispelling the Myths*. Oxford: NCT and Radcliffe Medical Press.

Wates, M. (2002a) *Supporting Disabled Adults in their Parenting Role*. York: Joseph Rowntree Foundation.

Wates, M. (2002b) 'Disabled parents: good practice for mainstream parent support projects and organizations', *DPPi Journal*, 39 (July): 10–12.

Wates, M. and Jade, R. (1999) *Bigger than the Sky: Disabled Women on Parenting*. London: The Women's Press.

21 Disability and Childhood: Deconstructing The Stereotypes
JOHN M. DAVIS

During the 1990s academics argued that we did not know what disabled children/young people thought about education, health and social services (Baldwin and Carlisle, 1994; Priestley, 1998). It was suggested that this lack of understanding fostered stereotypes that depicted disabled children as passive asexual victims who were incapable of making life choices and unlikely to progress to independent adulthood (Shakespeare and Watson, 1998; Alderson, 1993, 2000; Middleton, 1999). There is considerable evidence that for decades disabled children have experienced discrimination in education, health and social service settings. Middleton (1999) argues that disabled children fail to fulfil their potential and exhibit low self-esteem because: they lack positive role models; they are undervalued by their peer group and adults; they encounter unhelpful professionals who ignore their wishes; and they experience physical and emotional abuse in home, school and residential settings. This chapter draws from academic literature and disabled children's/young people's own accounts to highlight disabled children's experiences. Initially, it paints a very negative picture of isolation, disempowerment and mistreatment. However, it concludes that disabled children/young people are a diverse group; not all their life experiences are negative; and that many disabled young people act in powerful ways.

Education

It was argued that negative images of disabled children permeated the education system where they were employed to justify segregation between and within mainstream and special schools, and to restrict disabled children's opportunities, for example, by streaming and/or the use of special units (Davis and Watson, 2001):

> 'I don't know my character or whatever I dunno. Or maybe it's my visual impairment, but everyone seemed really protective ... It's like they don't make you feel independent. Like they want to do stuff for you. It's like you want help, but you don't want like charity ...' (Davis et al., 1999: 8)

> 'I wanted to go to my local school but when we went to see it ma mum realised it wasn't accessible, then we had to go to other schools until we found one. When I got there I didn't know anyone at all.' (Davis and Hogan, 2002: 12)

Despite developments linked to the Warnock report, many disabled children still experienced segregated schooling or mainstream education that was not fully inclusive (Clark et al., 1997). For example, many teachers employed 'petty regulations' to restrict the choices of disabled children (Kenworthy and Whittaker, 2000):

'The people here are too protected. I can do a lot more things than they give me credit for.' (Davis and Watson, 2001: 683)

A process of labelling also occurred, and still occurs, where disabled children's abilities go unrecognised, and their inabilities to attain developmental norms are constantly reinforced by daily interaction with teachers, psychologists and a variety of health professionals:

> Academic streaming, professional values, issues of safety, fear of litigation, concepts of normality, social class values and ideas concerning a variety of criteria relating to physical and social skills can be employed by professionals to label children ... some adults labelled the children to suit their own interests. They allowed the requirements of their structural role within the education process to govern their perceptions of the children. This process is combined with and reinforced by the tensions created by market place educational policy ... (Davis and Watson, 2001: 684)

Processes of educational segregation have a strong bearing on disabled children's social and cultural experiences, such as the ability to develop friends at home, play in local spaces and mix with a variety of children in school (Davis et al., unpublished; Corker and Davis, 2000; Priestley, 1998):

> Many children did not attend their local school, either because they went to segregated schools some distance from their homes, or because the only accessible mainstream school also involved travelling. They therefore had few friends at home. In these cases, friendships outside the school day tended to be confined to family members. The way provision was delivered shaped the peer groups of disabled children. For example, some schools had a 'base' for children with particular impairments; in other schools, disabled children had to sit at a particular table in open plan classrooms or even had separate spaces in the dining hall and the school playground; often children associated with others as a result of shared transport facilities. This outcome was sometimes used by staff to reinforce their belief that disabled children preferred to associate with other disabled children, irrespective of the children's own preferences. (Corker and Davis, 2000)

In the main, studies that have asked disabled children about their educational experiences paint a bleak picture of segregation, bullying and inequality.

Health

Very often parents and disabled children are initiated by medical professionals into a medical culture that does not allow space for them to challenge traditional orthodoxy and that fails to recognise conflicts of interest between children, parents and professionals (Avery, 1999; Mayall, 1998; Shakespeare and Watson, 1998). Adults are deemed 'experts' and children are assumed to be unable to put forward their own solutions to their own life problems. This very often leads adults to make decisions about children's lives without consulting them, or assuming that they know what is best for children. Children's problems are identified and resolved by parents and/or professionals and ownership of their own choices is taken away from children (Davis and Watson, 2000). For example, in the health field too much emphasis is placed on adult/parents' views at the expense of understanding the things that disabled children and teenagers want to change about the services that they encounter. In the most part, this has occurred because a perception exists that disabled children are unable to put forward their own views and that they lack competency and agency (Bricher, 2001; Robinson, 1997; Shakespeare and Watson, 1998; Davis and Watson, 2000; Corker and Davis, 2000). This perception has come about because much of the health-based literature concentrates on illustrating the things disabled children cannot do (for example, how they fail to achieve developmental 'norms'), rather than understanding their skills and abilities (Bricher, 2001; Priestley, 1998; Woodhead and Faulkner, 2000; Alderson, 2000).

In contrast, it has been argued that disabled children are very capable of making their views known when adults make the effort to learn the different ways in which they communicate (Davis et al., 2000). For example, a number of writers have demonstrated that children are capable of making complex medical decisions (Alderson, 1993; Bricher, 2001). Others have urged us to recognise children's knowledge concerning health matters (Mayall, 1994, 1996). But this can depend on the way medical staff interact with children and parents (Bricher, 2001):

> 'There is one consultant who should be the perfect role model of how to treat the parents and children, he always talks to my son and to me and he can always find the words at the level you need.' (Davis, 2003: 9)

> 'My consultant always talks to me and he is really funny like he makes jokes – the last time I was in he said, 'Aren't you married yet?' and he just makes you feel that you are being treated like a grown up.' (Davis, 2003: 8)

Alderson (2000, 1993) highlights children and teenagers' ability to make decisions about their lives. She stresses that it is important for those that work with children to reflect on the language they use and the processes by which they engage with children. It would appear that more time should be invested in explaining treatments in an appropriate manner and more time should be given to children to consider whether they wish to go through specific medical interventions (Bricher, 2001; Middleton, 1999). Some studies have argued that disabled children are sometimes subjected to experimental procedures where there is no evidence that the procedures are necessary or are going to be successful (Bricher, 2001). When we relate this finding to the fact that many children experience a lot of pain as a result of medical intervention, it reinforces the argument that medical professionals should have to justify the appropriateness of interventions (Middleton, 1999). Medical intervention should also be balanced with the fact that long stays in hospitals reinforce the social isolation of disabled children.

Social Services and transition

Traditionally, social and health professionals have promoted a perspective that families of disabled children are heroic. This stereotype overlooks that fact that not all disabled children are service users (Priestley, 1998). Jenny Morris (1999) uses a Barnardo's (1996) definition of transition as: transition from school to training, employment or unemployment; moving out of the parents'/carers' home, transition to adult sexuality, coupledom, marriage and possibly parenthood; financial independence from parents (or carers). She suggests that generally young people aged 16 to 20 are in transition from school to adulthood and that local authority service providers have a duty to provide a transition plan. Some 30–40 per cent of disabled people have great difficulty in establishing independence:

> 'I went to an interview for a computer post but the guy just asked me if I could tell the time I told him where he could stuff his job – he thought I was thick.'

> 'I went to the careers people and all they wanted to do was talk about what benefits I would get. I don't wanna talk about benefits a want to talk about a job.'

> 'I wanted to do computers, the careers guy tried to put me off and he said computers was "very competitive, are you sure you want to do that?"'

> 'The careers advisers think you don't have the brain. I wanted to work for youth service, which a now do. But they didn't help.'

(Davis and Hogan, 2002: 25–26)

Morris (1999) found that most local authorities did not collect information on disabled young people's health and support aspirations, rather they focused on establishing the number of young people that might fall into already defined service categories. This suggests that services are not user-led. It is similar to the situation in education where a statement or record of SEN (Special Educational Needs) often leads to children receiving the support the local authority or school can afford, rather than the services they have been assessed as requiring (Fairbairn and Fairbairn, 1992).

Many of the young people in Morris's (1999) study found it difficult to move away from their parents, either because of parental pressures or because the services were not available to facilitate such a move and develop feelings of safety in the young people. This situation was exacerbated by the fact that young people and their parents often find it difficult to access information on available services. This is particularly the case for young disabled people from ethnic groups. A number of studies suggest that Black and Asian disabled people have to contend with individual racism and institutional racism, particularly in service provision in school and later in the working environment (Ali et al., 2001).

Of particular concern were the high costs of moving away from home (which contrasted with the low incomes that were available to young disabled people) and a lack of accessible accommodation:

> 'I tried to do the independent living thing but it takes about a year to go through whole process and they are still deciding what I will get. In the end it all comes down to money.' (Davis and Hogan, 2002: 27)

> 'I got this new flat but I didn't get a pa so ma mum comes round everyday – that's not independent living.' (Davis and Hogan, 2002: 27)

Hirst and Baldwin (1994) found that disabled young people were half as likely to be in paid employment than their peers, often relied on benefits, were less likely to have active social lives/intimate relationship, and were more dependent on their parents to access leisure facilities. In relation to developing independence, Morris (1999) suggests that transition is restricted because there is a lack of well-trained specialist support staff and supported living projects available to young people. She promotes the concept of independent living as a solution. The Independent Living Movement promotes disabled people's rights to form personal and sexual relationships (Shakespeare et al., 1996), to be a parent and to choose how they want to organise services to support their full participation in society (Morris, 1993). There is very little recognition of the ability of disabled children and young people to plan their own services (Davis et al., 2002). This may be one of the reasons why young disabled people are more socially isolated than are other young people. Morris argues that transition is also made difficult because, very often, young disabled people do not have contact with other young people who experience the same impairment and, therefore, do not have access to knowledgeable peer support.

Disabled children in the new millennium

The above characterisation of disabled children's experiences in education, health and social services, though accurate, does not tell the whole story of disabled children's/young people's lives. There is a danger that by concentrating too much on the social problems that they encounter, we will reproduce the passive stereotypes associated with medical model images of disabled children/young people (Davis and Watson, 2002). What is lacking is an understanding that disabled children/young people do not always have negative experiences of services, and that they are human beings first before they are service users:

> 'Our school is better than my old school. At my old school children who used wheelchairs wasn't allowed to do PE. Here is better, we play indoor cricket, and smack it and go and the teachers are very good at including everyone. The teachers don't believe I'm disabled, they always encourage me to do PE.' (Davis and Hogan, 2002: 19)

Some disabled children encounter supportive professionals and organisations, some are resilient (overcoming their 'learned dependency' when given the opportunity: Alderson, 1993; Swain, 1993), and others are very capable of confronting negative stereotypes, oppressive structures and entrenched attitudes with overt and silent resistance (Davis and Watson, 2002; Davis et al., 2000). In the educational, health and social service setting they can be adept at promoting their own rights and at gaining support from adults and other children/young people to confront oppressive practices:

> 'I kick off'n then I they ignore me and say, 'IM HERE'. For years they wouldn't even talk to my mum properly let alone me.'

> 'When I was little I went to a mainstream play scheme during the summer holidays. They treated me the same as all the other kids. The only problem was when we went to the park we had to walk and all the kids battled over me and who could push my chair. I wasn't supposed to go to the mainstream scheme but when I was

little me and me brother were dead close and he wouldn't let go. He just cried and cried until they let me stay.' (Davis and Hogan, 2002: 19–20)

In social services, Morris (1999) indicates that there are examples of good peer support networks, such as the organisation Young Arthritis Care, and that Muslim young men have suggested that they draw strength from their religious and spiritual affiliations (Ahmad and Atkin, 1996). She also suggests that more creative approaches are required by local authorities to respond to young disabled people's wishes. She cites the example of Sunderland Social Services where day centres were closed and revenues channelled to set up, amongst other things, theatre arts workshops, individualised support and a horticultural service. In Liverpool, the Children's Fund has directed a significant part of its budget to fund new projects that will enable disabled young people and adults to organise art projects that promote change in local services, create apprenticeships for young disabled people in Access Audit, and be involved in developing accessible play and leisure opportunities. Other studies have demonstrated that, when time is given to asking disabled children/young people how they want to organise their own lives, they are fully capable of taking charge of organising a multitude of leisure activities and accounting for different disabled children's/ young people's tastes (Davis and Watson, 2000). So the message for the new millennium is that we have to identify from their own perspectives the problems that disabled children encounter, but we must also recognise that they can provide their own local-based solutions to these problems (Davis et al., 2003). This requires us to address the material inequalities in our society and channel resources directly to young disabled people to enable them to organise their own services that take account of their diversity of hopes and aspirations.

References

Ahmad, W. and Atkin, K. (1996) *Race and Community Care*. Buckingham: Open University Press.

Alderson, P. (1993) *Children's Consent to Surgery*. Buckingham: Open University Press.

Alderson, P. (2000) *Young Children's Rights: Exploring Beliefs, Principle and Practice.* London: Jessica Kingsley.

Ali, Z., Fazil, A., Bywaters, P., Wallace, L. and Singh, G. (2001) 'Disability, ethnicity and childhood: a critical review of research', *Disability and Society*, 16 (7): 949–67.

Avery, D. (1999) 'Talking "Tragedy": identity issues in the parental story of disability', in M. Corker and S. French (eds), *Disability Discourse*. Buckingham: Open University Press.

Baldwin, S. and Carlisle, J. (1994) *Social Support for Disabled Children and Their Families: A Review of The Literature*. Edinburgh: HMSO.

Barnardo's Policy Development Unit (1996) *Transition to Adulthood*. Ilford: Barnardo's.

Bricher, G. (2001) 'If you want to know about it just ask. Exploring disabled teenagers' experiences of health and health care'. PhD Thesis, unpublished, University of South Australia.

Clark, C., Dyson, A., Millward, A. and Skidmore, D. (1997) *New Directions in Special Needs Schooling: Innovations in Mainstream Schools.* London: Cassell.

Corker, M. and Davis, J.M. (2000) 'Disabled children – (still) invisible under the law', in J. Cooper (ed.), *Law, Rights and Disability* London: Jessica Kingsley.

Corker, M. and Davis, J.M. (2002) 'Portrait of Callum: The disabling of a childhood?', in R. Edwards (ed.), *Children, Home and School: Autonomy, Connection or Regulation*. London: Falmer.

Davis, J.M. (2003) *Alder Hey Consultation of Children and Teenagers Who Experience Complex Impairments and Their Parents*. Liverpool: Royal Liverpool Children's NHS Trust and The Liverpool Bureau for Children and Young People.

Davis, J.M. and Hogan, J. (2002) *Diversity and Difference: Consultation and Involvement of Disabled Children and Young People in Policy Planning and Development in Liverpool.* Liverpool: Liverpool Social Services (Quality Projects)/Liverpool Children's Fund/Liverpool Bureau for Children and Young People.

Davis, J.M., Priestley, M. and Watson, N. (unpublished) 'Play away: social exclusion, disabled children and anti-social play spaces'. (Submitted to *Urban Geography*.)

Davis, J.M. and Watson, N. (2000) 'Disabled children's rights in every day life: problematising notions of competency and promoting self-empowerment', *International Journal Of Children's Rights*, 8 (3): 211–28.

Davis, J.M. and Watson N. (2001) 'Where are the children's experiences? Analysing social and cultural exclusion in "special" and "mainstream" schools', *Disability and Society*, 16 (5): 671–87.

Davis, J.M. and Watson, N. (2002) 'Countering Stereotypes of Disability: Disabled Children and Resistance', in M. Corker and T. Shakespeare (eds), *Disability and Postmodernity*. London: Continuum.

Davis, J.M., Watson, N., Corker, M. and Shakespeare, T. (2003) 'Reconstructing disabled childhoods and social policy in the UK', in A. Prout and C. Hallet (eds), *Hearing the Voices of Children*. London: Falmer.

Davis, J.M., Watson, N., Cunningham-Burley, S. (2000) 'Learning the lives of disabled children: developing a reflexive approach', in P. Christiansen and A. James (eds), *Conducting Research With Children*. London: Falmer.

Davis, J., Watson, N. and Priestley, M. (1999) 'Dilemmas of the Field: What Can the Study of Disabled Childhoods Tell Us About Contemporary Sociology?'. Paper presented at the 1999 BSA conference *For Sociology*. University of Glasgow, 6–9 April 1999.

Fairbairn, G. and Fairbairn, S. (1992) 'Integration: An ethical issue?', in G. Fairbairn and S. Fairbairn (eds), *Integrating Special Children: Some Ethical Issues*. Aldershot: Avebury.

Hirst, M. and Baldwin, S. (1994) *Unequal Opportunities: Growing Up Disabled*. London: HMSO.

Kenworthy, J. and Whittaker, J. (2000) 'Anything to declare? The struggle for inclusive education and children's rights', *Disability and Society*, 15 (2): 219–32.

Mayall, B. (1994) *Negotiating Health: Primary School Children at Home and School*. London: Cassell.

Mayall, B. (1996) *Children, Health and the Social Order*. Buckingham: Open University Press.

Mayall, B. (1998) 'Towards a sociology of child health', *Sociology of Health and Illness*, 20 (3): 269–88.

Middleton, L. (1999) *Disabled Children: Challenging Social Exclusion*. Oxford: Blackwell Science.

Morris, J. (1993) *Independent Lives*. London: Macmillan.

Morris, J. (1999) *Hurtling into a Void. Transition to Adulthood for Young Disabled People*. York: Joseph Rowntree Foundation.

Priestley, M. (1998) 'Childhood disability and disabled childhoods: agendas for research', *Childhood*, 5 (2): 207–223.

Robinson, J. (1997) 'Listening to disabled youth', *Child Right*, 140, 546–7.

Shakespeare, T., Gillespie-Sells, K. and Davies, D. (1996) *The Sexual Politics of Disability*. London: Cassell.

Shakespeare, T. and Watson, N. (1998) 'Theoretical perspectives on disabled childhood', in K. Stalker and L. Ward (eds), *Growing Up With Disability*. London: Jessica Kingsley.

Swain, J. (1993) 'Taught helplessness? Or a say for disabled students in schools', in J. Swain, V. Finkelstein, S. French and M. Oliver (eds), *Disabling Barriers – Enabling Environments*. London: Sage.

Thomas, D. (1978) *The Social Psychology of Childhood Disability*. London: Methuen.

Wates, M. (1997) *Disabled Parents: Dispelling the Myths: Voices of Disabled Parents*. Abingdon: Radcliffe Medical Press in association with the National Childbirth Trust.

Woodhead, M. and Faulkner, D. (2000) 'Subjects, Objects or Participants? Dilemmas of Psychological Research with Children', in P. Christiansen and A. James (eds), *Conducting Research with Children*. London: Falmer.

22 Housing and Independent Living
JOHN STEWART

A place to live is a basic need for everyone, be that a house, flat, maisonette or some other type of residential dwelling. For disabled people, however, this dwelling place, one's *home*, may be difficult to get into and out of, and difficult to get around inside. It is part of the built environment that disability studies identifies as a site of struggle over what constructs disability and being disabled. Access and use of their homes are of immediate concern to disabled people. Barriers to either access or use which are, literally, built into the way the dwelling works, directly and necessarily compromise independence. Resolving those problems may become both serious and expensive because resolution can involve moving or major adaptation of the dwelling. Before we examine the housing circumstances in which today's disabled people live, and the initiatives that are being developed to improve access and reduce dependency in this intimate part of the built environment, let us set the issue within the explanatory framework which disability studies affords.

Independent living

It is obvious that living in one's own home relates unequivocally to the notion of *independent living* as understood within disability studies. From that perspective there are two relevant lines of debate: first, independent living is commonly understood in *functional* terms and second, it has been redefined as a *civil rights* issue concerned with personal autonomy. At first sight the functional perspective appears practical and focused on the needs of disabled people to use their residential dwelling in the manner they can and wish to do. The functional perspective on independently living in one's dwelling will be concerned with step heights, ramped access, door widths and furniture height, corridor widths and level floors for manoeuvre, electrical and plumbing appliance height and location, work surface height and location, window opening, ease of use of all fixtures and fittings particularly for heating and lighting (and that is far from a definitive list). The perspective fits comfortably into the British welfare tradition of utilitarian Fabianism, but it does not begin to explain why this issue should be addressed at all as a matter of public policy, except in terms of the help which should be offered to 'deserving cases'. Hence disabled people are in danger of being constructed into a deadweight cost on welfare which, whatever the fine phrases of policy documents or law might be, are actually viewed as charitable objects where the real issues are who should pay for it and under what terms.

Morris (1993) contrasts the more functional ideology of independence, that has dominated health and welfare services since the poor law, with the civil rights approach which is now informing debates in disability studies. She argues that the functional approach teaches disabled people that:

> ... unless we can do everything for ourselves we cannot take our place in society. We must be able to cook, wash, dress ourselves, make the bed, write, speak and so forth, before we can become proper people, before we are 'independent'. (Brisenden, cited in Morris, 1993: 8)

She contrasts this with the philosophy in which disabled people base their notion of independence as a civil rights issue:

> ... that all human life is of value; that anyone, whatever their impairment, is capable of exerting choices; that people who are disabled by society's reaction to physical, intellectual and sensory impairment and to emotional distress have the right to assert control over their lives; that disabled people have the right to fully participate in society. (Morris, 1993: 7)

To use an image from ecclesiastical art and architecture, Morris opens a diptych showing us on the left-hand panel an illustration of disabled people trying to do things in the non-disabled world in order to establish that they are independent; on the right-hand panel disabled people are claiming that their citizenship entitles them to full social participation. Extending that idea, imagine a central panel making a triptych showing a built environment providing functional independence leading to the *social inclusion* of all citizens, which Morris so nobly asserts, whatever their condition or impairment. The residential dwellings we occupy should allow us functional independence to make a reality out of the 'independent living' at the core of current community care policy. At present, most dwellings will not give a high level of independence to most disabled people. These perspectives set the scene for how, in the UK, we have attempted to meet the *functional* needs and the *inclusive citizenship* rights of disabled people.

Residential dwellings and functional independence

Since 1974 the United Nations has recommended the building of homes to an adaptable standard, but in Europe most countries, including the UK, failed to implement it. The Chronically Sick and Disabled Persons Act 1970 sought to ensure that a range of public buildings were accessible, though in reality this has never been widespread, with many people still being denied access. Following a long campaign by disabled people's organisations and research by the Joseph Rowntree Foundation (Cobbold, 1997), however, pressure was put on government to amend some arcane red-tape called Part M of the Building Regulations. If enacted it would ensure adaptable standards to new-build private dwelling houses. The last Conservative government had circulated to the construction industry its draft amendments, but conducted no negotiations to implement these proposals. Once in office, the new Labour administration lost no time in persuading irascible and sceptical building industry chiefs to give the new regulations a chance: the policy came into effect in autumn 1999. As the Construction Minister, Nick Raynsford, stated:

> 'The extension of Part M [of the Building Regulations] is an important measure that complements this government's commitment to implement the remaining duties of Part III of the Disability Discrimination Act. Part III will improve disabled people's

access to goods and services and Part M will ensure better access to new domestic dwellings. This is, therefore, a key obligation for this Government, which is committed to social inclusion'. (DETR, 1998a)

This is clearly the type of structural change which has been needed to ensure that in the long run disabled people have the opportunity of independent living. But physically accessible dwellings are only part of the story. Disabled people have to be able to pay for such dwellings. One of the key problems is the basic division in tenure between owner occupation and social rented housing. The former is subject to open market forces (and adaptations are largely the responsibility of the owner); the latter is allocated according to housing need, and subject to government social and economic policy, but does offer fully adapted properties within its stock, at affordable rents.

The government's policy of subsidising the *rents* of social rented housing rather than their *building costs* is increasing disabled people's dependency on state benefits. Over the 18 years of Conservative government in the UK, there was a general shift from a policy of subsidising the capital costs of dwellings (the bricks and mortar subsidy) to a reliance on individual tenants paying the subsidy through their rents, which would be compensated through their individual claims for means-tested housing benefit. The levels of this payment have been restricted for groups of people considered 'non-deserving', while those considered 'deserving', including disabled people, have found their rents – and hence their levels of housing benefit – increasing.

All would be fine if one is prepared to accept continued reliance upon this benefit in order to finance living somewhere, but latterly this has been constructed by politicians into a 'dependency culture'. Furthermore, escape from such dependency becomes ever more problematic. The effect of higher benefits as a transfer payment for higher rents is to strengthen the benefits-trap where any increase in income *through employment* leads automatically to a reduction in income through state benefits, making employment financially unattractive (Stewart et al., 1999).

Social rented housing – satisfying need without rights

Social rented housing is of significance to disabled people. It is the only sector that provides dwellings which are meant for, or 'specially provided for' or adapted to the needs of disabled people. As an echo of our welfarist past, they are still referred to as 'mobility homes' or 'wheelchair' housing – generically it is 'special needs' housing. It may not be where it is needed, but it is a matter of housing policy that there should be some. Disabled people have access to it on grounds of their housing needs, rather than income. There is an issue about what proportion of disabled people would not be able to afford owner-occupied property adapted to those standards.

Today's special needs housing derives from an individualised dependency model, providing either customised 'wheelchair dwellings' or 'mobility housing'. The needs of disabled people were viewed as special – and hence separate. The dwellings were to be of a different standard from dwellings for non-disabled people. It certainly attempted to meet physical needs for functional independence within the dwelling, and the fact that a

Ministry of Housing and Local Government manual of 1949 (*Housing for Special Purposes*) lists all the now commonplace necessary adaptations concerning access is testament to the fact that much more could have been done sooner because building technology was not a barrier to access. The alternative approach would have been to build all homes to an accessible standard. Half a century later we have at last embarked on this more fruitful line of provision, underpinned, if not actually inspired, by the social model of disability: we are going to build lifetime homes.

It is encouraging that the government now support the provision of lifetime homes, but it should be borne in mind that we are starting from almost a nil base. It will take a generation or more before there are appreciable numbers of such residential properties available. Although in the future finding housing already built to accessible standards should be easier, in the meantime we have to rely on the mobility standard homes and wheelchair standard dwellings that currently exist. It is that story which is outlined next.

During the 1980s, public sector house building declined. However, 'special needs' housing increased from one-fifth to one-third of that declining number of completed public sector dwellings. Dwellings for disabled people became an ever larger proportion of the public sector homes actually built. Concurrently housing associations grew in importance as social landlords, by new building (20,000 per annum), adaptations and the transfer to them of some 277,000 local authority dwellings by the end of 1997. Hence housing associations now take the lead in the provision of wheelchair dwellings and other housing for disabled people.

Using the Housing Investment Programme returns it can be shown that about 30,000 wheelchair homes had been built and adapted by 1995, whilst in addition there are 57,000 'other dwellings for disabled people' that were not wheelchair housing. Whether that figure is sufficient depends on normative notions of need, over which there is considerable disagreement (Stewart et al., 1999). It has been 'estimated' that the need for wheelchair dwellings is in the order of 40,600, whilst that for mobility housing is about 69,000. The basis of such estimates is highly problematic (Harris et al., 1997).

The expression of need even at the level of functional independence has some curious implications. One could be forgiven for thinking that if there are only 30,000 wheelchair dwellings in the country, they would actually be occupied by wheelchair users. A large proportion of wheelchair dwellings are, however, occupied by households with no wheelchair users. Examining data for housing associations in the social rented sector, it can be shown that in new allocations of tenancies for 1997–98, only 23 per cent of wheelchair-user households who became tenants were, in fact, allocated wheelchair properties. In 1997–98 a total of 6,405 tenancies to wheelchair dwellings were allocated. Of these, 4,750, or 74.2 per cent, did not have a wheelchair user in the household. The gross disparity between the intended and actual use of these newly available dwellings demands some explanation. On the face of it there appears to be a mismatch, but whether this is because of management issues or the applicants' preferences in conjunction with location, size, type or cost of the wheelchair dwellings is not known.

One explanation offered for the mismatch of wheelchair users to wheelchair dwellings has been the preponderance of one-bedroomed dwellings as wheelchair homes. Sixty per cent of newly allocated wheelchair dwelling-tenancies are one-bedroomed, and if one-bedroomed dwellings are not acceptable to most wheelchair users, obviously they will not be found in such tenancies. Another has been that many disabled people reject the concentration of specialist facilities on one site. A third explanation could be connected with the painfully slow development of co-operation between the housing agencies and social services departments. The government's initiative '*Supporting People*' has still to show its capabilities in this area. Of course, what we do not know is whether these wheelchair-accessible dwellings were allocated to people with *some* mobility condition or impairment.

The proportion of social rented-sector tenants who identify themselves as 'permanently sick or disabled' has been increasing steadily. It is now about 9 per cent of all tenants, whilst the other sectors have stayed the same. If social rented housing offers the only real opportunity for disabled people to live in appropriately adapted housing, and if supply met demand, what is the problem? Financing is the problem. The housing association grant has been lowered (as part of the move away from 'bricks and mortar' subsidies to individualised means-tests). In order to meet their costs, housing associations can increase rents. As the vast majority of social rented tenants were already on housing benefit, the burden of increased rents falls on that part of the social security budget. To improve their housing position, disabled people must seek social rented housing and, it might be argued, in order to pay for it, have to be on housing benefit.

Dwellings adapted for disabled people are more expensive than 'ordinary' housing: that was the orthodoxy. The costs of such adaptations were, it was claimed by lifetime home campaigners, exaggerated. In addition, some types of 'adaptation', whilst expensive, were deemed acceptable by the industry and the state (inside lavatories, for example), whilst others are still considered to be 'special' (level access and/or ramps, for example). Indeed, housing associations had a 'multiplier' applied to their total building cost indicator for the area when providing dwellings for disabled people. That subsidy has been reduced, but in order to stay solvent what housing associations are not supposed to do is charge tenants in costly wheelchair housing higher rents than other tenants. At the moment, disabled tenants claiming housing benefit are protected from regulations about maximum rent levels, entitlement and pressure to move and share accommodation if single.

The question of housing need as expressed by the 'experts' versus demand from the users, and the problems of either higher bricks-and-mortar subsidies or higher rents (with ever-higher housing benefit entitlement) is most elegantly solved by lifetime homes. The costings are comparable with general needs housing. New domestic dwellings are going to have to conform to basic accessibility standards anyway, but are also built with the possibility of being easy to adapt to a much higher level of mobility should the need arise at a later date. Lifetime homes can be thought of as universalist – anyone can occupy them. They neither stigmatise nor create dependency. The decision to adapt fully can still be related to individual needs.

A very significant set of changes in the relationship between social care and social rented housing provision on needs grounds started in 2003. Housing benefit will exclude all aspects of housing support costs (DETR, 1998b). Prior to 2003, all kinds of support could be charged against housing benefit and the housing revenue account including 'assistance' of various kinds, from arranging plumbers to budgeting advice; settling disputes, resettlement, life skills training; negotiating access to professionals; shopping; counselling; monitoring alarms; cleaning tenants' rooms; providing and running restaurants and so on. In future, central government will allocate money to local authorities who will corporately decide how it should be spent locally on support services for *vulnerable people*, identified as: older people; people with learning disabilities; 'people with mental health problems or some disabilities'; victims of domestic violence; vulnerable young people; people with an alcohol or drug addiction and ex-offenders (DETR, 2001). Hence, disabled people are on the list of service user groups who 'Supporting People services provide housing related support to ... who live in specialist supported housing and in their own homes' (DETR, 2002). In reality, it seems likely that support costs will be the responsibility of social services departments, presumably operationalised by their purchasing officers on an individual needs basis.

On the face of it, this should not significantly affect disabled people in terms of their *housing* needs because those costs ought to be wholly covered by housing benefit. The contested area will be on-site provisions, such as most of those listed above, and here disabled people will have to compete with those other service user groups. My point here could well be, why should disabled people pursuing the social model bother to engage with this further extension of professionalised need determination, and do so in competition with other vulnerable groups? The answer will turn on how far the administration of this measure erodes the cover to the total rent which housing benefit affords.

In terms of new build or adaptation schemes in line with the lifetime homes principle, there should be no disincentive to new initiatives as the whole idea rests on built features, not services. The difficult issues reside in the purchase and provision of supportive services. It could be argued that the uncertainty is a disincentive to *schemes* of housing for disabled people as the costings for services of support would, in future, have a less certain funding. Disability rights activists should not, on the face of, it be too concerned, as they tend to reject such specialist provision. The list of 'experts' who know what disabled people should have, however, lengthens and widens from the individualised needs assessment by housing professionals, social security adjudication officers, to social services purchasing managers – over the one issue, living independently in one's own (socially rented) home.

References

Cobbold, C. (1997) *A Cost–Benefit Analysis of Lifetime Homes*. York: Joseph Rowntree Foundation.

Department of the Environment, Transport and the Regions (1998a) 'Better Access Planned for New Homes'. Press Release 178/ENV. London: DETR.

Department of the Environment, Transport and the Regions (1998b) *Supporting People: A New Policy and Funding Framework for Support Services*. London: The Stationery Office.

Department of the Environment, Transport and the Regions (2001) *Supporting People: Policy into Practice*. London: DETR.

Department of the Environment, Transport and the Regions (2002) *Overview: The Supporting People Programme*. London: DETR. Note 1 of 10.

Harris, J., Sapey, B. and Stewart, J. (1997) *Wheelchair Housing and the Estimation of Need*. Preston: UCLAN/NATWHAG. http://www.leeds.ac.uk/disability-studies/archiveuk/archframe.htm

Ministry of Housing and Local Government (1949) *Housing for Special Purposes*. London: HMSO.

Morris, J. (1993) *Community Care or Independent Living*. York: Joseph Rowntree Foundation.

Stewart J., Harris J. and Sapey, B. (1999) 'Disability and dependency: origins and futures of "special needs" housing for disabled people', *Disability and Society*, 14 (1): 5–20.

23 Changing Technology
ALISON SHELDON

Technology is constantly changing. Society as we know it depends on this fact. That which we take for granted today would have been the stuff of science fiction as little as 50 years ago. In 50 years' time, we will doubtless be excited, perturbed and baffled by yet more new developments. In the early years of the twenty-first century, it is computers and the Internet that have captured the public imagination and found their way into not just our working environments, but also increasingly into our domestic spaces. This technology is arguably changing the society in which we live, and with it, the social category of people we consider 'disabled'.

Some disabled people are finding ways to use Internet technology to their advantage – to access information and services, to affiliate with others, and to find new means of self-expression and dissent. It seems, though, that recent developments are disempowering others yet further. Many are unable to gain access to the technology, whilst others find that its usage results in increased dependency and further isolation from mainstream society. Current trends are likely to present particular problems for certain segments of the disabled population, such as those with learning difficulties, those outside the world of paid employ-ment, the growing number of older disabled people, and others who simply 'don't get on with computers' – a group including many who are not currently deemed disabled. Hence we may see increasing polarisation between the technological 'haves' and 'have-nots' in the disabled population. We may also witness shifts in the 'disabled' category itself.

Many extravagant claims are made about technology's potential role in the lives of dis-abled people. However, the area is lamentably under-researched. In the last throes of the twentieth century, I talked to disabled people about their experiences and opinions of this rapidly changing technology and about their hopes and fears for the future (Sheldon, 2001). These were 'ordinary' disabled people – largely unwaged, and many in older age groups. This chapter is rooted in their knowledge, and thus focuses on the use of comput-ers and the Internet in non-work settings.

Disabled people's complicated relationship with technology will be briefly considered, before the crucial issue of access to technology is examined. The liberatory potential of Internet technology will then be evaluated in relation to two key areas – information and communication.

Changing technology and disabled people: emancipation or oppression?

Technology is not neutral. It is created by the same oppressive society that turns those with impairments into disabled people. Whilst 'stamped with the desires and needs of the ruling class' it is, at the same time, 'produced amidst conflicting social relations, and thus holds the possibility of being a tool for liberation as well as for social control'

(Davis et al., 1997: 6). It is no surprise, then, that disabled people have a complicated relationship with technology. We are often excluded from mainstream technology, a factor said to have contributed to our current labour force exclusion and indeed, to the creation of the modern 'disability' category (Finkelstein, 1980; Oliver, 1990). At the same time, we have become the recipients of an ever-growing business involved in developing and marketing technologies specifically for our ascribed needs. Many of us have been impaired as a direct result of modern technology. Others would not be alive today without it. *All* of us are now dependent upon it to satisfy even our most basic needs (Illich, 1973).

Every new technological breakthrough is invariably hailed as a saviour for disabled people, as a way of minimising their 'deficits' and thus making them less dependent on other people. This despite the fact that dependency on others is a part of life for *everyone*, and may well be preferable to dependency on unreliable technology. Internet technology is capable of delivering a myriad of services directly into disabled people's homes, thus reducing the need to travel or rely on others for assistance. It is here that its main benefits are often assumed to lie. Disabled people, however, want *choice* in how they make contact with the world. Access to the latest technology, though regarded as increasingly necessary, was not considered the highest priority for the disabled research participants. Most considered the removal of more traditional disabling barriers to have greater urgency. This created concern amongst many that technology might be provided as a cost-cutting exercise, reducing the need to make more meaningful social changes, and effectively segregating them in their own homes. There is a very real danger that disabled people could be further disadvantaged through such 'technical fixes', since with the increasing power of technological tools one has a 'barring of alternatives' (Illich, 1973: 23). Many may find themselves more isolated than before, and less capable of satisfying their needs in other ways. As one commentator suggests, this uncritical faith in technology, underpinned by an individual model of disability:

> ... is often reflected in laws, policies, institutional arrangements and social attitudes which privilege technological solutions to the problems faced by disabled people. (Gleeson, 1999: 99)

It is clear, then, that technological systems must never be pushed onto people as a sticking-plaster solution to deeper social problems. It is also clear that this could easily happen in the current political climate.

It is suggested that a less over-optimistic analysis of technology's implications for disabled people would come from the disabled people's movement, which may be 'central to ensuring that technology is used to liberate rather than further oppress disabled people' (Oliver, 1990: 126). Many of those who embrace a social model of disability are equally enthusiastic about our future prospects, however, claiming for example that with the appropriate technology we can become part of the 'main-stream of life' and 'contribute fully in society' (UPIAS, 1981: 1). Others voice concerns that technology can be used in oppressive ways (Corker and French, 1999). There is a small but growing body of work within disability studies that emphasises technology's 'double-edged nature' (Oliver, 1990) and stresses that it can be 'both oppressive and emancipatory, depending on the social uses to which it is put' (Gleeson, 1999: 104). Similarly, the disabled people who participated in the research project identified a number of potential pitfalls and promises for disabled people which they associated with the increasing reliance on technology in today's world.

Access all areas?

Disabled people have long been denied access to the technology that others take for granted, and there is little evidence that this exclusion is dissipating. Despite this, the issue of access to technology is often obscured because of the undue emphasis placed on its *potential* for improving disabled people's lot (Roulstone, 1993). This is a particular concern, since a new form of social segmentation is predicted between those with and without access to the new systems (Jouet and Coudray, 1991). The disabled people participating in the study were deeply concerned about access, revealing a number of barriers that stand in the way of disabled people's beneficial use of computers and the Internet.

Of these barriers, finance looms largest. Assistance to purchase computer equipment is currently limited to those disabled people in work or education, a situation that must be challenged. The pace of change itself presents a huge barrier to those with limited means. As one research participant explained: 'I want to have me own [computer], but you know … they're so expensive … And then you've got to keep up with it … they always say if you were to buy your computer you can always guarantee the next day it's out of date, so it's just costly updating it …'

Disabled people want systems which they can use physically, they can understand, and are affordable. For many, these systems simply do not exist. Despite organisational rhetoric to the contrary, disabled people are not 'designed in' to products from the outset, making expensive add-ons necessary. Whilst it is true that certain gains have been made by the corporations that develop and market the new systems, it is unlikely that the free market will ever guarantee access for a relatively small social grouping with little disposable income. At present there is no effective regulation to ensure that corporations attend to the accessibility of the equipment they develop. This situation must be remedied as a matter of urgency.

We must not be distracted, however, into denying the socio-structural origins of the problem. Access to technology is *not* simply a technical issue with technical solutions. The inaccessibility of technology is just one more symptom of disabled people's continuing oppression. In Britain, the disabled people's movement has organised around the premise that no one aspect of the disablement of people with impairments should be treated in isolation (UPIAS, 1976). This approach suggests that as well as considering access to technology as a purely *technological* problem, other aspects of disabled people's exclusion must also be considered – access to the wider world of employment, education, housing, transport, the built environment and so on. Equal access to the beneficial use of technology can only be secured alongside the removal of these more traditional disabling barriers (Roulstone, 1998).

The fieldwork demonstrated that whilst a consideration of access is vital, it is not sufficient. We must not assume that all people want to use technology or, indeed, see any utility in doing so. The potential value of Internet technology for disabled people will now be considered in relation to just two crucial areas – information and communication. Here too, however, the issue of access still looms large.

Hitching a ride on the information superhighway

'I think [the Internet's] great – especially for disabled people. Look for information and you can get it no matter where it is.'

(author's unpublished research)

There was a lot of enthusiasm for the Internet's role in information provision. Surfing the net was a form of leisure activity for many, relieving the boredom of the resource centre, or their enforced isolation in the home. Those research participants able to use the Internet at a resource centre for disabled people were particularly struck by the savings in travel, money and time that accessing information in this way could allow. Open access to information is considered vital for *all* in today's society. It is, however, a particular concern for disabled people, who are isolated by a variety of other barriers. Computers and the Internet can provide new ways for disabled people to obtain the information they need, in formats which are accessible to them. They also allow us to become our own experts, and take control of the information that we lack.

There is a growing body of information produced by and for disabled people available on the Internet, and for those with the technology this is enabling access to hitherto undreamed of information. Without substantial changes, though, 'easy access to the information that can really empower and liberate people still looks likely to be the preserve of an affluent minority' (Haywood, 1998: 26). Furthermore, in the current political climate, the increased use of Internet technology as a means of disseminating information may have an adverse effect on other means of information provision. The unconnected majority of disabled people may find that accessing information (and indeed other consumer goods) in traditional ways becomes even more problematic as these facilities become more available online. Thus, the Internet is not the panacea that many suggest. There is still a need for appropriate and accessible information to be disseminated to disabled people in other ways, or the disabled community may simply become yet more polarised.

Even those *with* Internet access complained of difficulties in finding the right information: 'It's overwhelming sometimes'. Discriminatory web design also creates major barriers which prevent disabled Internet users from accessing information. At present, the Internet is relatively unregulated, and policing it at a national level is problematic because of its global nature. For disabled people's unmet informational needs to be fully respected there must, at the very least, be appropriate legislation and regulation. As one research participant told me, laughing at the soundbite: 'Information is a right, not a privilege'.

It's good to talk ...

When you think of how many disabled people use electronic or whatever devices to communicate now, who it would have been assumed even 50 years ago or less than that, that those people had no capacity for communication ... It's so important.'
(author's unpublished research)

The potential for otherwise isolated 'housebound people' to maintain and initiate friendships from their homes is one of the main advantages said to be gained from use of the Internet (Haywood, 1998). It is further suggested that disabled people, excluded from their geographic communities, might find themselves included in online communities – communities untainted by 'the contaminating effects of physicality, prejudgement, or prejudice' (Avery, 1998: 2). Many disabled people have little contact with others and live very isolated lives. In the absence of more meaningful social transformation, the Internet can provide another means of communicating and connecting with others, a means that circumvents many of the barriers to disabled people's mobility.

For some of the research participants, the Internet provided an essential link to the world, often giving a sense of community membership that they would have otherwise lacked. Several people were particularly enthusiastic about the possibilities for 'passing' as non-disabled that the Internet offers. Others, however, pointed out that since we all exist in a real world where such deception is not necessarily an option, the liberatory potential of passing in cyberspace may be somewhat limited. Furthermore, the potential still exists for Internet technology to be used as a 'technical fix'. One participant, for example, felt that the Internet actually exacerbated his isolation, providing a poor second-best to actually *being* with people: 'Communication with another human being is summat that a machine ain't gonna compete with, and it can't compete with it no matter 'ow good that machine is.'

Communication encompasses more than just interpersonal interaction, however. Computers and the Internet offer the potential for disabled people to gain a political 'voice' and to organise collectively to improve their world. Another of the Internet's potentials is said to lie in its ability to advance 'the interests of politically and socially disadvantaged groups' (Fitzpatrick, 2000: 386). Some even suggest that the growth of a worldwide disabled people's movement is 'evidence of the part which new technologies can play in facilitating the empowerment of disabled people' (Johnson and Moxon, 1998: 255). However, the proof for such claims remains elusive.

It is easy to find examples of disabled people coming together on the Internet to discuss, for example, disability research (disability-research@jiscmail.ac.uk), or disability politics and direct action (danmail@yahoogroups.com). Whilst it is likely that such participation has an empowering effect on certain individuals who might otherwise be starved of such interaction, many disabled activists seem to 'have disappeared into the phone lines to discuss issues and share support' (Cunningham, 2000: 11). The implications of this for the disabled community as a whole are debatable. How far any of this networking will translate into material gains in the real world is also unclear. The Internet's success as a political tool cannot be measured by the number of websites or discussion lists. Instead, we must look to the effects produced outside cyberspace. If and how these effects will be manifested remains to be seen. It is vital, however, for activists within the disabled people's movement to use any means at their disposal to make a better world, and perhaps the Internet will become an important tool in this process.

Conclusion

Being part of the mainstream of society currently entails keeping up with that society's changing technology, something that is not possible for many disabled people, or indeed for many of their non-disabled peers. The disabled community risks becoming more polarised as the technological 'haves' leave their less fortunate contemporaries behind. The boundaries of the 'disabled' category may even be redrawn in the future. Whilst this might be liberating for some currently disabled people, those disabled by the society of the future will not be so enthusiastic. We cannot then assume that the 'problem' of disability will be solved with each new technological innovation. Instead, we need to transform society – the society that created the Internet, the society that oppresses. Nonetheless, the latest Internet technology also offers great potential for disabled people's self-emancipation, enabling access to essential information, and providing new means to affiliate and express dissatisfaction with the world. It remains to be seen whether the increasing use of such technology by a disabled elite will facilitate the emergence of effective new strategies for improving that world for everyone.

References

Avery, D. (1998) 'Electronic parenting or, it takes a (listserv) village to raise families with disabilities', *CMC Magazine*, January: 1–11. http://www.december.com/cmc/mag/1998/jan/avery.html

Corker, M. and French, S. (1999) 'Reclaiming discourse in disability studies', in M. Corker and S. French (eds), *Disability Discourse*. Buckingham: Open University Press.

Cunningham, A. (2000) 'Where have all the activists gone?', *Coalition*, October: 8–12.

Davis, J., Hirschl, T.A. and Stack, M. (1997) 'Introduction: Integrated circuits, circuits of capital, and revolutionary change', in J. Davis, T.A. Hirschl and M. Stack (eds), *Cutting Edge: Technology, Information, Capitalism and Social Revolution*. London: Verso.

Finkelstein, V. (1980) *Attitudes and Disabled People*. New York, NY: World Rehabilitation Fund.

Fitzpatrick, T. (2000) 'Critical cyberpolicy: network technologies, massless citizens, virtual rights', *Critical Social Policy*, 20 (3): 375–407.

Gleeson, B. (1999) 'Can technology overcome the disabling city?', in R. Butler and H. Parr (eds), *Mind and Body Spaces: Geographies of Illness, Impairment and Disability*. London: Routledge.

Haywood, T. (1998) 'Global networks and the myth of equality: Trickle down or trickle away?', in B.D. Loader (ed.), *Cyberspace Divide: Equality, Agency and Policy in the Information Society*. London: Routledge.

Illich, I.D. (1973) *Tools for Conviviality*. London: Calder and Boyars.

Johnson, L. and Moxon, E. (1998) 'In whose service? Technology, care and disabled people: the case for a disability politics perspective', *Disability and Society*, 13 (2): 241–58.

Jouet, J. and Coudray, S. (1991) *New Communications Technologies: Research Trends. Reports and Papers on Mass Communication. No. 105*. Paris: UNESCO.

Oliver, M. (1990) *The Politics of Disablement*. London: Macmillan.

Roulstone, A. (1993) 'Access to new technology in the employment of disabled people', in J. Swain, V. Finkelstein, S. French and M. Oliver (eds), *Disabling Barriers – Enabling Environments*. London: Sage in association with the Open University.

Roulstone, A. (1998) *Enabling Technology: Disabled People, Work and New Technology*. Buckingham: Open University Press.

Sheldon, A. (2001) 'Disabled People and Communication Systems in the Twenty-First Century'. PhD thesis. Leeds: University of Leeds.

UPIAS (1976) *Fundamental Principles of Disability*. London: UPIAS.

UPIAS (1981) *Policy Statement*. London: UPIAS.

24 Communication Barriers: Building Access and Identity
CAROLE POUND AND ALAN HEWITT

'Language is centrally involved in power, and struggles for power.' (Fairclough, 1989: 18)

'The hardest thing to bear is not to be able to get it across ... this means others have the power, it means always being the underdog, no, underneath the underdog.' (Hewitt, personal communication)

These statements remind us of the central importance of language both in having a voice and gaining access to social and political debate. The experience of living with language disability poses challenges to identity and inclusion, like many hidden disabilities, pushing the social model of disability to grapple with alternative discussions of access, inclusion, identity and impairment.

This chapter draws on the experience of individuals living with aphasia, a communication disability affecting the ability to use and understand words. Aphasia is a common consequence of stroke, itself the major cause of long-term disability in the UK. Yet people with aphasia and many other communication disabilities have had little voice or impact within disability discourses. This is not surprising, given that the very nature of their impairment – language – is the primary tool by which people gain access to ideas, discussion and different stories of disability.

In this chapter we will illustrate some of the internal and external barriers faced by people living with impairments of language and communication and offer suggestions for developing the concept and practice of communication access for all.

The media of communication

It is easy to take for granted the power of language. Language is not just the means of communicating with each other. It is the means of forming and refining ideas. It is the medium for understanding, questioning and developing thoughts and discussion. It is the means of being included, having a voice and exercising influence.

Spoken and written language in discussions, meetings, telephone calls, letters, books, articles, e-mails and Internet information are just some of the ways to debate ideas and issues with others. Being permitted to enter and be included within the debate is a critical means of understanding, negotiating and influencing. But authentic interaction depends not just on people who are prepared to engage with each other, but also on mutually intelligible and accessible forms of communication. Given the centrality of language to power and the ability to engage with power, it is interesting to note the invisibility of language within discussions of disabling practices and environments. Within health and disability forums exclusion begins with invitations and agendas that are inaccessible to people with reading impairments and follows with unintelligible fast-paced meetings where rapid access to ideas and questions provides the basis for inclusion. The few people with language impairment who manage to penetrate this secret world of debate talk of their frustration and exhaustion at trying to change the communication practices of others within these disability forums. People who focus on discussion of barriers and access within the physical environment can seem oblivious to the barriers and exclusionary practice they themselves are operating within the communication environment.

Barriers and communication disability

'Living with aphasia is facing daily struggle – pain, confusions, isolating, anxiety – and learning and understanding within the social world.' (Ireland, 1997)

These aphasic words from Chris Ireland paint a vivid picture of the confusing range of internal and external barriers identified by people who live with aphasia. Reporting on interviews with 50 people with aphasia, Parr et al. (1997) identified four overarching types of barrier faced by individuals living with language impairment:

- *Environmental barriers*: people with aphasia talked of being sidelined by the pace of life and language and the noisy blare of social environments. 'People talking all at once … the noise … I can't cope with that' (1997: 128).

  Other barriers are imposed by the language environment itself – the way people cloud and clutter language with the complex, the abstract and the unclear, preventing engagement with everyday discussion and debate.

- *Structural barriers*: resources, services, opportunities so often depend on understanding the letters, the forms, the telephone calls that allow access to those resources. Lack of flexibility in teaching methods and lack of creativity in including people in office-based communications, for example, routinely and invisibly exclude people with aphasia from education and work:

  'Obviously the meetings for me to express myself is pretty difficult.' (1997: 128)

- *Attitudinal barriers*: the equation of communication disability with 'having nothing to say' and being stupid clearly illustrates the 'Does he take sugar' syndrome:

  'Some of them actually thought I think you are an imbecile.' (1997: 128)

- *Informational barriers*: written and spoken information is a vital commodity in negotiating services and support, but can be useless when presented in a style or format which cannot be understood:

  'Why, what, how'; 'You cannot always ask'. (Parr et al., 1997: 129)

Basic adaptations involving use of technology, such as e-mail and voice-activated computer systems, sign language interpreters and minicoms, information in large print or on audio cassette, may support the inclusion of some people with communication disabilities. But key to their success is that the adaptations themselves rely on skilful access to language in the form of reading, writing and understanding spoken language, the very core of the impairment. Furthermore, these solutions do not take account of a key barrier to participation – time.

Time barriers

For people with communication disabilities the issue of time may far outweigh the relatively straightforward challenge to adapt to physical or spatial environments. The rapid rhythm and tempo of everyday life make few allowances for a calmer, slower, more deliberate form of interpersonal communication. For people with communication disabilities this slower tempo is not a choice, but the only accessible pace.

Experience of involving people with aphasia in recruitment, research, meetings and working parties at Connect highlights a range of temporal barriers to participation. (Connect is the communication disability network promoting innovative therapy and support services for people living with stroke and aphasia.) The barriers include:

For the person without aphasia:

- time to listen;
- time to develop skills as conversation partners and communication supporters;
- time to negotiate and inform oneself about communication preferences;
- time to negotiate communication breakdowns, for example, when words or ideas suddenly go missing;
- time to record discussion and decisions in an accessible way, for example, 'aphasia friendly' minutes emphasising key points and supported by pictures; and
- time to research and prepare useful communication props, for example, papers written in a clear and accessible style with key concepts highlighted, and clear one-page summaries of ten-page documents.

For the person with aphasia, additional time may be needed:

- to find words;
- to formulate and express ideas;
- to process ideas and respond to questions; and
- to negotiate choices and decisions.

Slippery access to words and ideas will additionally require time to pin down thoughts and convey them to oneself and others:

> 'With aphasia I get a sense of an idea and it remains opaque, like seeing through a frosted glass, without precise definition. Or a concept wrapped in cellophane seen from afar.' (Khosa, 2004: 19)

Subtle changes in the tempo of a conversation place new demands on both communication partners. These include how to manage lengthy silences and word struggles, how to support people with few words to have equal access to the conversational floor, how to support everyone in holding on to ideas and decisions when the pace of the conversation puts additional strain on memory.

These changes place an onus on those in the communication environment to reflect on and develop their skills substantially. (Kagan and LeBlanc, 2002)

Reactions to communication disability

'Please, I've had a stroke. I'm aphasic and have problems. Can you speak very very slow? And they end up me and them practically arguing on the phone to slow down and I go: 'I am aphasic' and that confuses them because they haven't got a clue what aphasic is.' (Alf, in Parr et al., 1997)

A particularly striking feature of communication disability is the ignorance of others in knowing how to react to it. Many disabled people are subject to the disabling assumptions and attitudes of other people. But somehow the greater visibility of certain disabilities will give clues or suggestions as to possible reactions. People with aphasia may not have the luxury of using speech to direct more common-sense reactions from their communication partners. One person with severe aphasia tells how she was given tuna every day of her seven-month hospital stay. She had been able to indicate that she was a vegetarian, but no-one on the ward had the skills or confidence to spend time translating the written hospital menu, negotiating likes and preferences, involving the person with aphasia in true choice about what she might like and be able to eat. A recent ethnographic study (Parr, 2004) yields a crop of examples of well-intentioned family members, friends, health workers and volunteers marking out the person with the communication disability as a 'special case' with changes in vocabulary, volume and tone of voice. Within nursing home and health-care settings the bustle of activity revolves around, but not with, the anonymous resident/ 'patient', known by name only to the busy staff who lack the time or skills to probe a person's story and identity.

Stories are an important means of expressing and affirming who we are, inevitably influencing how others interact with us. Telling, constructing, revisiting and developing stories are also an important way of understanding changes to life's biography and incorporating disability into evolving identities. But how does one shape and share stories of identity without language?

Language and identity

It is extremely dangerous to try to break the maternal cord connecting a man to his own language. When it is ruptured or seriously damaged his whole personality may suffer disastrous repercussions. (Maalouf, 2000: 110)

Maalouf's interest in the way language, as perhaps the strongest attribute of identity, divides and separates individuals from themselves and their communities in a profound way is echoed by Sue Boazman: 'My identity had been snatched away and in its place was a person I no longer recognised' (Boazman, 1999: 17). In describing the impact of stroke and aphasia on her sense of self, Boazman refers not just to the isolating personal experience of losing language, but also the way it placed her at the mercy of nursing and medical staff, well-wishers and others who wielded the power of words.

Sudden loss of language and the experience of stroke share many features with other individuals' experiences of sudden acquired disability. The shift from life as a non-disabled person to the opaque 'borderlands' of otherhood (Thomas, 1999) is not exclusive to people who have a stroke. However, an interesting additional challenge is that if language is the core of what makes us human, and the primary means of exploring new narratives of illness and disability, how do individuals negotiate personhood or the development of changed identities following sudden loss of speech, understanding, reading and writing? How does your own and others' difficulty with understanding and using words impact on your ability to talk about and question fragile new forming identities with others who are also grappling with a concept at the edge of words? Given these difficulties, how much greater is the risk, as a language-impaired person, that your personal disability narrative will be hijacked by outsider stories constructed by families, professionals, researchers and the media?

Many people explore concepts of disability and identity by being exposed to and engaging with discussion of alternative representations of disability. New stories of disability can challenge internalised stereotypes offering a precious escape route away from the set 'tragic stroke victim' or 'courageous little fighter' paths purveyed by mainstream media and disability charities. The means of accessing new narratives is not obvious when academic texts, articles and website stories are hidden behind the veil of language.

For those who can get there, self-help groups provide invaluable opportunities to explore old and new identities. Meeting, supporting and just 'being' together are powerful experiences which, in many respects, transcend words. Meetings between people who share a common communication disability, but who each individually require different levels and types of communication support, are not without challenge. Negotiating communication support from non-language-impaired people, such as relatives, volunteers or health professionals, is an option but one which runs the risk of meetings being dominated and controlled by those who can speak and write. Notwithstanding these challenges, self-help groups remain a rare bastion of power and identity for many people with aphasia.

Access to a sense of personal and social confidence, to a more certain identity, is for many people a pre-requisite to asserting one's voice, to feeling you have a possibility and a starting point to interact with power. So language, identity and power become crucially interwoven. Without language, it is very hard to grasp the core of identity, and without language and identity it is virtually impossible to hold and interact with power. How, then, can those who possess intact language and power develop skills, environments and structural supports which acknowledge this imbalance and model more equal power relations?

Creating communication access

Perhaps the greatest challenge to supporting and developing communication access for all is the current lack of clarity about what communication access is. Most people with and without communication disability may recognise communication difficulty and breakdown, but few can identify and articulate cornerstones of communication access in the way that most people can attempt some first principles of physical access.

In our opinion, communication access is about developing communication that is clear, comfortable and easy to understand and interact with, regardless of your preferred style of communication. It will cover communication in spoken and written form, communication that is face to face or remote, communication about everyday happenings or complex, theoretical debates. The benefits of enhanced communication access are better, faster, clearer communication between everyone, not just between those with and without a communication disability.

Revisiting the media of communication that are the common currency of everyday life: talking, discussion, meetings, books, papers, articles, e-mail, the Internet, television, radio, newspapers and so on, the multi-faceted nature of any approach to communication access is clear. A world where everyone with communication disability has (more) equal access to opportunities and engagement in life would look, feel and sound qualitatively different to the traditional look and structure of language environments. Those charged with implementing communication access need to think creatively about ways of engaging people, processes, environments and infrastructures with new communication practices, practices that attend, non-tokenistically, to the diversity of communication.

What, then, would a world where all individuals have access to opportunity and connections really look like? First, there would be a range of communication skills training and induction programmes for those without communication disability. These would cover listening skills, 'interpreting' skills enabling non-communication disabled people to adapt their spoken and written language to make it accessible, and training in monitoring language for clarity and flexibility. Such training should be statutory in the way that basic health and safety legislation requires knowledge of 'lifting and handling'. Whilst not requiring the technical training of, say, sign language interpreters, these basic communication skills would enable everyone to share responsibility for respecting and involving people with communication disability. Specialist training might aim to develop communication supporters who offer the one-to-one interface between people with and without language impairment.

At Connect, for example, trained communication supporters facilitate inclusion in meetings by going through papers at pre-meetings, supporting the person with aphasia to follow conversational exchange and ask questions, by taking notes on line and by spending time after the meeting to review ideas, concepts and decisions. Communication access training focusing on written documents is a further aspect of developing communication skills, supporting everyone in an organisation to reword complex, abstract documents and information into clear and concrete language. Training also supports people to consider format, layout and use of pictures that most readily support communication access. The situation where everyone in the organisation, from therapist to receptionist to researchers to finance director, takes responsibility for monitoring and changing their use and presentation of language is a healthy first step towards inclusive communication.

Beyond changes to people are changes to structures and processes. Markers of good communication access in meetings, for example, will include attention to the length and timing of meetings. Critically, meetings should be timed to coincide with best times, avoiding, for example, lengthy evening meetings. Breaks need to be frequent and agendas structured carefully to give the additional time required to clarify and debate issues where understanding and questioning will inevitably take longer. Clearly these requirements also necessitate skilled listening, checking and planning on the part of the chairperson. Additional communication support within meetings may be 'on-line drawing' and key word writing for explanation and clarification on a flipchart. If a discussion and decision cannot be concisely drawn and written, it is unlikely that the members share a clear and unambiguous understanding of the discussion. Furthermore, the art of translating discussion in this way will, by its nature, require the cut and thrust of debate to go at a slower, more accessible rate and be punctuated by clarifications. Whilst this change in style and tempo may pose new challenges to accommodating diversity, these features are often at the nub of the communicative exclusion faced daily by people with aphasia.

A final aspect of communication access is attention to environments. Accessible buildings will be those where thought has been given to signage and information design as well as physical layout. Easy access to pen and paper for on-line drawing and writing support will feature heavily, as will well positioned and ample flipcharts or overhead projection so that the spoken word is not the only means of entering or following debate. Easy access to quiet, pressure-free spaces will support people who require quiet and calm to develop thoughts and conversations.

Physically accessible buildings frequently aim to enable people with physical disabilities to negotiate an environment as independently as possible. A misguided notion of communication independence has for too long focused on changing the skills of the impaired individual, failing to push communication partners to take responsibility for enhancing their own communication skills and promoting communication interdependence. The time is ripe for change.

Towards inclusionary practice – losses and gains

Communication access is a poorly understood concept that offers intriguing challenges to all concerned with inclusionary practice. Moving beyond tokenism places significant resource and training demands on people, processes and environments. Truly exploring communication difference and diversity will enable people with communication disabilities to move out of the ghetto constructed by their impairment and the disabling practices of those around them. It will support people with and without language impairment to enrich communication practice, share power and celebrate the creativity and challenge of communication difference. In the words of Chris Ireland, poet in residence at Connect:

> Language is a gift
> Language is flowing
> Language is so powerful
> More powerful than before
> More scared – more fearful
> More demanding – more exhausting
> More screamful – more scheming
> Not so available and not so understand
> (in Pound et al., 2000: 238)

References

Boazman, S. (1999) 'Inside Aphasia', in M. Corker and S. French (eds), *Disability Discourse*. Buckingham: Open University Press.

Fairclough, N. (1989) *Language and Power*. London: Longman.

Ireland, C. (1997) 'Foreword', in S. Parr, S. Byng and S. Gilpin with C. Ireland (1997), *Talking About Aphasia*. Buckingham: Open University Press.

Kagan, A. and LeBlanc, K. (2002) 'Motivating for infrastructure change: toward a communicating accessible, participation-based stroke care system for all those affected by aphasia', *Journal of Communication Disorders*, 35: 153–70.

Khosa, J. (2003) 'Still life of a chameleon: Aphasia and its impact on identity', in S. Parr, C. Pound and J. Duchan (eds), *Aphasia Inside Out*. Buckingham: Open University Press.

Maalouf, A. (2000) *On identity*. London: Harvill.

Parr, S., Byng, S. and Gilpin, S. with Ireland, C. (1997) *Talking About Aphasia*. Buckingham: Open University Press.

Parr, S. (2004) *Living with Severe Aphasia: Communication Impairment*. York: Joseph Rowntree Foundation.

Pound, C., Parr, S., Lindsay, J. and Woolf, C. (2000) *Beyond Aphasia: Therapies for Living with Communication Disability*. Bicester: Speechmark.

Thomas, C (1999) 'Narrative identity and the disabled self', in M. Corker and S. French (eds), *Disability Discourse*. Buckingham: Open University Press.

25 Controlling Inclusion in Education: Young Disabled People's Perspectives
SALLY FRENCH AND JOHN SWAIN

Many volumes have been written on inclusive and special education, mostly by non-disabled people working in the field. Although the voice of disabled people is generally absent from these debates, it is slowly becoming more prominent as disabled adults recount their schooldays and young disabled people talk of their experiences of school today (Cook et al., 2001). The perspective of disabled people is vital, as Oliver explains:

> ... there is an enormous wealth of experience and pain out there which special education has not yet acknowledged ... getting into and opening up some of that is one of the priorities in beginning to move special education from the way it is going at the moment ... Current discourses around integration or inclusion are still professionally led ... while the words have changed the reality hasn't. (2000: 115)

As well as specific accounts of disabled people's experiences, the issue of education has been theoretically analysed within Disability Studies (see Armstrong and Barton, 1999; Moore, 2000) and organisations of disabled people, such as Disability Equality in Education, Parents for Inclusion and the Alliance for Inclusive Education, are active in promoting and implementing inclusive policy and practice for all disabled children.

In this chapter we will examine the meaning of inclusive education, taking particular account of the perspective of young disabled people. We will argue that inclusive education is unlikely to succeed unless young disabled people and disabled adults are fully involved. Before we can do this, however, it is necessary to consider the meaning of 'inclusion' and its differentiation from the related concept of 'integration'.

Rieser defines integration as:

> ... a matter of location, placing a disabled child in a mainstream setting, usually with some additional support to access what was being offered in the school, changing the child to fit in with the social and academic life of the school. (2002: 132)

He defines inclusion, in contrast, as:

> ... valuing all children irrespective of their type or degree of impairment, or reconstructing the institution to remove barriers so teaching and learning take place so all children can be valued for who they are, participate, interact and develop their potential. (2002: 132)

Inclusive education, therefore, means more than simply placing a disabled young person in a mainstream school and providing extra support. Inclusion demands major changes within society itself and should not be viewed in a vacuum.

Because of the broad social and political content and ramifications of the concept of inclusion its precise meaning, not surprisingly, differs among countries and cultures (Armstrong and Barton, 1999). Inclusion can best be regarded as a process that is slowly evolving and unfolding (Ballard, 1999). Dyson and Millward (1999) believe that most of what passes as inclusive education today is simply reproducing 'special' education in mainstream settings.

When considering the inclusion of disabled children into mainstream school, an understanding of childhood culture is very important. The majority of children, including disabled children, report that friendships are the most important aspect of their lives at school (Vlachou, 1997). Cook et al. (2001) note the strength of young people's friendships in a special school and their strong sense of belonging and inclusion. There are also many accounts by disabled adults who testify to the importance of the friendships they made with other young disabled people within special schools (French and Swain, 2000). Sullivan, speaking of her experience in a hospital school, recalls:

> ... for the first time I began to make friends with other children, to have fun ... Every weekend when my mother, brother and sister came to visit me I had so much to tell them about school, about my friends, the teachers and the nurses that I lived with. (1992: 173)

A prominent theme when talking to young disabled people about their experiences at mainstream school is the embarrassment they feel at being 'different' and how this can impact on their relationships with other children. Stephanie spoke about her experience of receiving mobility training.

> 'She came to my school. She was saying that I had to use a symbol cane and I said yes because I thought all you had to do was put it up when you were crossing a road, but I was taught all this stuff about using it along the pavement and to hold it in a certain way. I didn't like it at all. I refused to go ... It made me feel embarrassed. I don't want to offend anyone but it made me feel really old, like a granny.' (French et al., 1997: 29)

Adam, a visually-impaired young man we interviewed, found that the special treatment he received as a disabled person interfered with his friendships and peer relationships:

> 'I got bullied because I was taken away from my friends, all my friends used to sit at the back of the class and I had to sit at the front, and I had to have a massive lamp and they wouldn't let me write on normal paper – I had to have thick lined paper and it made me feel really stupid. People would take it out on me and I was always behind because they worked too fast and I couldn't see anything.' (authors' unpublished research)

Franklin et al. (2001) found that 26 per cent of the visually-impaired secondary school pupils they surveyed disliked using low-vision aids. The main reason they gave was 'feeling different', but they also mentioned that the aids were difficult to use and that using them could lead to bullying. Franklin et al. state:

> Adolescence is a time when pressures to conform to group norms are particularly intense and anything which singles out young people as being different from their peers is likely to be resisted by many of this age. (2001: 112)

Some young disabled people dislike having a designated helper in the classroom. A young disabled woman interviewed by Priestley said 'I prefer it when I haven't got support because it's more … interesting. You can talk to your mates' (1999: 94). Shaw (1998) found, however, that young disabled people had mixed feelings about helpers. One young person said '… I don't really like having the supporter to work because other kids go "Look, you've got a supporter. You can't work by yourself." ' Another young person did, however, value working with his helper:

'I've improved a lot since I had my helper. She was my friend … She helped me to understand why I shouldn't be doing this, or I should be doing that. She understands what I was going through so she knew how to stop it.' (1998: 78)

Allan (1999) found that the behaviour of disabled children was officially labelled as 'difficult' with little attempt to interpret or understand it. In one pupil's record it stated:

'Raschida is being extremely difficult about accepting that she requires help and is trying to pretend to be able to read print which we are aware is too small or too obscure.' (1999: 74)

Another young person was criticised for accepting help from her peers, although this may have been a strategy for maintaining contact with them. Her record stated that:

Participation in the wider activities of the school is important and a reasonable degree of firmness will be required to discourage Susan from being too dependent on others. (1999: 75)

This quotation highlights the pre-eminence of 'independence' in Western culture and the subsequent antipathy to any show of dependency.

As well as having problems with adult assistants, Ballard and McDonald (1999) found that the young disabled people they interviewed did not like young non-disabled people being forced to help them by, for example, being on a roster. One young person explained:

Some students complained that they were not getting their work done as much as they should as they were having to read stuff to me. They tried to put in place a buddy system where everyone in the class had to take turns sitting with me and I hated that. (1999: 110)

Young disabled people want to be 'one of the crowd' and do not like to be singled out from their peers, which frequently occurs when 'help' is given to them at school. Stephanie recounted such an incident:

'I wanted to go and see this dance show and needed to sit near the front and my mum said I had to go and ask someone so the seat could be reserved. I ended up sitting next to the headmaster. I hated it. I was sitting there thinking "I can't do anything, I can't clap or anything because he'll be watching me."' (authors' unpublished research)

James, a young man with cystic fibrosis interviewed by Bailey and Barton (1999), was annoyed if teachers asked him how he was feeling because it drew attention to him. Similar feelings were recounted by Adam, though he admitted 'using' his impairment to advantage on occasions:

> 'I'm always being asked if I'm OK. Can I see this? Can I see that? Do I need help? It's over-protection, it's really annoying ... I must say though that if I need something, or if I want something, I will use my eyes to get attention to myself ... I do it if I want some money.' (authors' unpublished research)

Priestley (1999), in a study of young disabled people in mainstream schools, found that they used disability for the benefit of themselves and their friends. One young person, for example, told staff that she needed a helper in an attempt to relieve her friend of a maths lesson and Craig, who is a wheelchair user, said, 'Sometimes I do muck about on me way to lessons, but then I just say me chair's slow, you know.' (Priestley, 1999: 100).

A young disabled woman interviewed by Ballard and McDonald (1999) constantly felt under scrutiny:

> 'Because people were going to so much trouble for it to be a success I felt that I had to try all the time, I could never be a bit invisible. If I did not do well in a subject there would be a meeting about why this was happening ... I felt I had to perform.' (1999: 110)

Vlachou-Balafouti (2002) comments that disabled children are often treated as 'cases' or are subject to an intense 'professional gaze'.

Research with non-disabled young people indicates that their disabled peers are being completely rational in their attempts to minimise their difference. Vlachou (1997) found that young non-disabled people tended to view their disabled peers as inferior, dependent and less competent. Their perceptions were influenced by the arrangements made for young disabled people in school. The young people said:

> 'They've got special equipment and some special teachers that could help them to understand things and special computers so they know what they're doing.' (1997: 125)

> 'They need help because they don't know what to do.' (1997: 153)

Being with disabled peers can also tarnish a young non-disabled person's image. As a young person said, 'Some people think they're tough and disabled people are weak so they don't want to be seen with them.' (Vlachou 1997: 162). This process was articulated by Goffman (1968) in his concept of a 'courtesy stigma'.

Young disabled people have to counter these perceptions of themselves in order to enter the culture of their peers. Lewis, a young visually-impaired man we interviewed, said:

> You have to prove yourself. You have to be the first to do the dares and stuff. You have to be the one with the most bottle to keep in with them. (authors' unpublished research)

Research has shown that young disabled people are twice as likely to be bullied as their non-disabled peers (Nabuzoka and Smith, 1993). Dawkins (1996) identified four factors that make bullying likely in children whose appearance is different: being alone at break, being male, having fewer than two good friends in the class and receiving extra help in school. Shaw reports one young person as saying:

> 'They would say I was a baby and I was in a pram and things because I was in a wheelchair ... They were not used to seeing people in wheelchairs in the school and they didn't really think about what they were saying.' (1998: 79)

Similarly, a visually-impaired young person said:

> 'I'm getting bullied at school because of my eyes. They often call me 'cockeye' and I'm scared of it because it's not fair on all the people who are like me with disabilities.' (Franklin et al., 2001: 134)

People with learning difficulties can also be the targets of bullying in mainstream school. A woman with learning difficulties recalled, 'Roman Hill was difficult for me, very much, because I used to be tormented there.' (Rolph, 2002: 66), and the mother of a woman with learning difficulties said 'She just had to muddle along in a class where everybody used to take the mickey out of her. She had an awful time in that school.' (Rolph, 2002: 64). Franklin et al. (2001) make the point, however, that young disabled people are just as likely to be bullied in a special school as a mainstream school.

Some young disabled people value the experience of being with disabled friends. Stephanie recounted her experience of a holiday with other visually impaired young people:

> I thought it was brilliant ... I did things that I wouldn't normally do, like archery. I did dry-slope ski-ing, bowling, trampolining, I liked that, I did athletics and swimming. It showed me that I was not the only person who couldn't do things the way fully sighted people do them. It made me realise that all I can do is my best and not to give up. (French et al., 1997: 27)

Disabled young people do not deny the struggles they experience in coping with the practicalities of accessing the curriculum and negotiating a disabling physical environment. Two young people with chronic illness interviewed by Bailey and Banton (1999), for example, reported that they lacked energy and felt weary when walking from class to class. The overriding impression from accounts given by young disabled people, however, is that inclusion into the social aspects of school – fitting into childhood culture, making and maintaining friendships – is even more important and is often disrupted by the help which is given to circumvent more obvious barriers.

Conclusion

Young disabled people and adults have reported a wide range of experiences in both 'special' and mainstream schools. Their views about what they need to feel included have not, however, been explored or addressed. It is clear from their accounts, however, that inclusion means far more than accessing the curriculum or moving around the building. As Cook et al. state:

> Inclusion has a powerful psychological dimension of belonging. Whilst being included in educational policy terms is about having access to ostensible standards of education, the confidence that comes from social inclusion is the context for such access. (2001: 309)

The move towards inclusive education is complex and requires changes at all levels of the education system and society.

References

Allan, J. (1999) 'I don't need this: Acts of transgression by students with special educational needs', in K. Ballard (ed.), *Inclusive Education: International Voices on Disability and Justice*. London: Falmer.

Armstrong, F. and Barton, L. (eds) (1999) *Disability, Human Rights and Education: Cross-cultural Perspectives*. Buckingham: Open University Press.

Bailey, J. and Banton, B. (1999) 'The impact of hospitalisation on school inclusion: the experiences of two students with chronic illness', in K. Ballard (ed.), *Inclusive Education: International Voices on Disability and Justice*. London: Falmer.

Ballard, K. (1999) 'Concluding thoughts', in K. Ballard (ed.), *Inclusive Education: International Voices on Disability and Justice*. London: Falmer.

Ballard, K. and McDonald, T. (1999) 'Disability, inclusion and exclusion: some insider accounts and interpretations', in K. Ballard (ed.), *Inclusive Education: International Voices on Disability and Justice*. London: Falmer.

Cook, T., Swain, J. and French, S. (2001) 'Voices from segregated schooling: towards an inclusive education system', *Disability and Society*, 16 (2): 293–310.

Dawkins, J.L. (1996) 'Bullying, physical disability and the paediatric patient', *Developmental Medicine and Child Neurology*, 38 (7): 603–612.

Dyson, A. and Millward, A. (1999) 'Falling down the interfaces: from inclusive school to an exclusive society', in K. Ballard (ed.), *Inclusive Education: International Voices on Disability and Justice*. London: Falmer.

Franklin, A., Keil, S., Crofts, K. and Cole-Hamilton, I. (2001) *Shaping the Future: The Educational Experiences of 5 to 16 year old Blind and Partially Sighted Children and Young People*. London: Royal National Institute for the Blind.

French, S., Gillman, M. and Swain, J. (1997) *Working with Visually Disabled People: Bridging Theory and Practice*. Birmingham: Venture.

French, S. and Swain, J. (2000) 'Personal perspectives on the experience of exclusion', in M. Moore (ed.), *Insider Perspectives on Inclusion: Raising Voices, Raising Issues*. Sheffield: Philip Armstrong.

Goffman, E. (1968) *Stigma*. Harmondsworth: Penguin.

Moore, M. (ed.) (2000) *Insider Perspectives on Inclusion: Raising Voices, Raising Issues*. Sheffield: Philip Armstrong.

Nabuzoka, D. and Smith, P.K. (1993) 'Sociometric status and social behaviour in children with and without learning difficulties', *Journal of Child Psychology and Psychiatry*, 34 (8): 1345–1448.

Oliver, M. (2000) 'Profile', in P. Clough and J. Corbett (eds), *Theories of Inclusive Education: A Students' Guide*. London: Paul Chapman.

Priestley, M. (1999) 'Discourse and identity: disabled children in mainstream high schools', in M. Corker and S. French (eds), *Disability Discourse*. Buckingham: Open University Press.

Rieser, R. (2002) 'The struggle for inclusion: the growth of a movement', in L. Barton (ed.), *Disability Politics and the Struggle for Change.* London: David Fulton.

Rolph, S. (2002) *Reclaiming the Past: The Role of Local Mencap Societies in the Development of Community Care in East Anglia, 1946–1980.* Milton Keynes: The Open University.

Shaw, L. (1998) 'Children's experiences of school', in C. Robinson and K. Stalker (eds), *Growing Up with Disability.* London: Jessica Kingsley.

Sullivan, S. (1992) 'My school experience', in R. Rieser and M. Mason (eds), *Disability Equality in the Classroom: A Human Rights Issue.* London: Disability Equality in Education.

Vlachou, A.D. (1997) *Struggles for Inclusive Education.* Buckingham: Open University Press.

Vlachou-Balafouti, A. (2002) 'The process of change and the politics of resistance in educational contexts: the case of disability', in L. Barton (ed.), *Disability Politics and the Struggle for Change.* London: David Fulton.

26 User-led Organisations: Facilitating Independent Living
GEOFFREY MERCER

Over recent decades the goal of 'independent living' has been central to disabled people's campaigns around the world. This chapter explores its introduction in Britain and, more specifically, the contribution made by organisations controlled by disabled people in the design and delivery of service support.

The discussion starts by outlining the emergence of direct action to overturn mainstream, producer-dominated welfare services by user-led organisations, such as Centres for Independent Living (CILs), in the late 1970s and 1980s. These ambitions are associated with a radical critique of the 'social barriers' that create disability and of the assumption that disabled people have suffered a 'personal tragedy' and must accept a passive role in their 'social care' and rehabilitation. The discussion then considers the impact of a 'New Right' influence on government policy that promised a retrenchment in the welfare state, but also promoted 'consumer' or 'user' involvement in public services and increased opportunities for user-led organisations to supply services. Finally, new data from a national survey of user-led organisations are presented to illustrate their experiences in attempting to implement service support for independent living (Barnes, Mercer and Morgan, 2000).

The road to independent living

The Independent Living Movement (ILM) in America epitomised the change to rights-based, user-led direct action. It originated when disabled students persuaded several universities to fund personal assistants. Their experience spawned innovative ways to overcome the lack of welfare programmes, including the first CIL at Berkeley, California in 1972. This emphasised advocacy of disabled people's rights and service support in such areas as attendant referral (personal assistance), peer counselling and general 'independent living' skills, as well as accessible housing, transport and built environment. With legislative encouragement and federal funding, the number of CILs quickly expanded to over 200 (Crewe and Zola, 1983).

By contrast, in the UK the first inclination was to explore opportunities to reform public welfare services rather than inaugurate separate provision. High hopes were invested in the Chronically Sick and Disabled Persons Act 1970, heralded by some as a 'Charter for the Disabled', but inadequate funding and opposition from established social care interests blocked the desired improvements. Institutional living was securely entrenched, backed up by local authority domiciliary 'personal care' and considerable, unpaid 'informal care' from family and friends. The rehabilitation and social integration of disabled people were equated with the professional determination of their 'special needs'.

By this time, the disabled people's movement was taking shape and attention turned from lobbying for the enhancement and extension of existing services to taking the initiative in demonstrating the merits of independent living. This was interpreted as leading ordinary lives in the community with appropriate service assistance:

> We do not use the term 'independent' to mean someone who can do everything for themself, but to indicate someone who has taken control of their life and is choosing how that life is led. (Brisenden, 1986: 178)

A key break with mainstream provision occurred in 1979 when disabled residents at Le Court Cheshire Home in Hampshire persuaded the local authority to allow cash payments (equivalent to the costs of residential 'care') to inmates through a third party, in this case the residential home. Disabled people used these funds to make accommodation accessible for their use and to employ their own personal assistant (PA). Despite their dubious legality, such schemes attracted widening interest precisely because they enabled disabled people to assume more choice and control over their community living support – in stark contrast to Social Services Departments (SSDs) who relied on regimented 'care' regimes typified by day centres.

The growing politicisation of disabled people underpinned the appearance of many organisations controlled by users, such as People First and Survivors Speak Out, which focused on breaking down the hierarchical character of service relationships and provider dominance. Disabled people now looked beyond self-help towards self-determination, where they made the decisions about their lifestyle. User-led aspirations were exemplified by the setting up of Hampshire Centre for Independent Living (HCIL) and Derbyshire Centre for Integrated Living (DCIL) in 1985. Each demonstrated its own priorities: HCIL concentrated on supplying information, advice and peer support for those employing personal assistants, while DCIL stressed seven basic support needs for information, counselling, housing, technical aids, personal assistance, transport and access. Its focus on 'integrated' living signalled the importance of working in 'partnership' with health and local authorities. Nevertheless, both held that the long-term aim was not simply alternative service provision, but to transform the bases of social exclusion (Davis and Mullender, 1993).

Involving consumers

Criticism of state involvement with social welfare was at the heart of 'New Right' thinking that emerged in the late 1970s. Its targets ranged from the 'excessive' size and growth of state expenditure to welfare dependency among client groups. One favoured solution entailed the construction of quasi-markets in health and social care. From this perspective, competition enhanced service efficiency and effectiveness because providers had to respond to consumer priorities or risk their 'exit' (shopping elsewhere for goods and services). To advance this strategy, the NHS and Community Care Act 1990 required that consumers be fully informed and consulted about services backed up by a complaints procedure and redress. The Act also sponsored welfare pluralism by allowing SSDs to purchase services from the non-statutory sector, including user-led organisations. The New Labour government elected in 1997 re-iterated the importance of these initiatives and located users 'at the heart of social care' in its modernisation agenda for public services.

Yet this form of consumer involvement has done little to trigger the anticipated empowerment of disabled people. Too often, user participation in public service provision has turned out to be little more than 'cosmetic'. Statutory and voluntary agencies have claimed that suitable individuals are hard to recruit and/or unrepresentative of the wider community, but they often prefer to consult with organisations *for* rather than *of* disabled people, and exclude some groups, such as people with learning difficulties, because of their presumed 'incapacity'. Besides, effective involvement presumes training, receiving information in accessible formats, provision of accessible transport, plus payment for user's time and expenses to enable attendance at meetings (Beresford and Croft, 1993).

In addition, disabled people's organisations have called for democratic involvement in decision-making from the assessment of individual needs through to strategic issues (Morris, 1993). They have argued that market competition between providers does not necessarily improve consumer choice, given that disabled people are mostly on low incomes and the range of available services is largely decided for them by SSDs, who are in turn subject to firm budgetary constraints. Moreover, the traditional focus on home-based and individual physical and personal care criteria has been resistant to change (Priestley, 1999). While monitoring and evaluation demands have multiplied, this means very little unless users are already involved in determining service standards. Overall, the injection of private sector values and practices has encouraged a 'new managerialism' that has privileged demands for economic efficiency rather than consumer power/social engineering (Braye and Preston-Shoot, 1995).

Direct payments

The basic uncertainty surrounding the status of direct (including third party) cash payments (whereby SSDs deliver welfare services as well as financial benefits) was finally settled by the Community Care (Direct Payments) Act 1996, although local authorities retained discretion over its implementation. Since then more groups of disabled people have become entitled to receive direct payments (see Chapter 33). This reflects their rising popularity with both user and local authority interests. For users, direct payments offer more reliable service delivery, greater flexibility in support provision, and enhanced control over how personal assistance is provided and by whom. They attracted attention at the local authority and national government levels because they were rated as both cost effective and in line with recent community care reforms (Zarb and Nadash, 1994).

Nonetheless, there is general agreement that it is a daunting undertaking for an individual to become a PA employer (Glasby and Littlechild, 2002). This has presented increasing opportunities for organisations (voluntary and private) to offer administrative training and backing for those disabled people wanting to employ their own PA or pay for their own support services. That said, direct payments constitute a consumerist approach and are no guarantee of independent living, at least until wider social and environmental barriers have been addressed.

User-led organisations: from theory to practice

The next stage is to seek answers to the central question: how far and in what ways have user-led organisations progressed in translating hopes for independent living support into practice? A recent survey in 2000 identified 85 organisations fitting this description across England, Scotland and Wales. Sixty-nine (84 per cent) completed a questionnaire asking about their aims, resources, service and campaigning activities, and future ambitions. Their experience confirms the relatively late development of user-led organisations, particularly those identifying as CILs, at least compared with the USA. Thus, over 80 per cent were established after 1986, mostly in the 1990s.

There is a broad consensus that user-led organisations offer a distinctive approach to service provision. This encompasses: adherence to a social model; democratic accountability; promoting independent/integrated living through widening user choices and control; and including all disabled people. Notwithstanding the general agreement, user-organisations resist being forced into a single mould. For example, acceptance of a radical, social (barriers) model approach to disability is widely regarded as the litmus test of organisations of disabled people. The conversion from political philosophy into day-to-day practice is, however, sometimes problematic and contentious, particularly because organisations must operate within a policy environment geared to a medical/individual approach to disability (Priestley, 1999).

The overwhelming majority stresses its accountability to members and/or service users, mostly through a management committee, with almost three-quarters requiring at least 50 per cent user representation. One-third have representatives of their funders, while 17 per cent include carers. There is an obvious determination to maintain disabled people's control through a user-dominated management committee: four out of five organisations require that at least 51 per cent are disabled people, while half restrict representation to disabled people. All organisations have a written constitution and/or a mission/policy statement setting out key aims and objectives. Even so, this survey confirms earlier unease that not enough users/members rank as active participants (Davis and Mullender, 1993).

Organisations offer contrasting service portfolios that generally reflect local user priorities and resources. Information provision is the predominant activity (82 per cent), followed by peer support (67 per cent), Disability Equality Training (58 per cent), and personal assistance support (54 per cent). The other main areas covered are employment advice/training (38 per cent), housing advice (32 per cent) and education advice/support (30 per cent). Survey respondents broadly agree on their desire to expand on their current activities, with a significant minority hoping to take on the mantle of a fully-fledged CIL.

At present only half of responding organisations record their average weekly service usage. These indicate very considerable variation, with one-quarter supporting 25 or fewer users, while another quarter give backing to between 80 and 300 users. Most organisations accept that more should be done to recruit users, but criticise 'mainstream' providers for routinely obstructing attempts to deliver the level and range of services valued by disabled people. Additionally, many claim that they have insufficient time or resources to identify potential users from hitherto marginalised groups, such as minority ethnic communities, gays and lesbians, younger and older cohorts, mental health system survivors, and people with learning difficulties or with communication needs. A further complaint is that mainstream providers seem unaware of, or are reluctant to publicise, user-led services.

However, the main limitation on organisational aims and objectives is attributed to the lack of adequate or appropriate resources (funding, staffing and premises). There is a general dependence on local authorities (83 per cent) for core funding, grants and service level agreements. Typically, these are insufficient to sustain the desired level and range of independent living services. Furthermore, most funding is short-term, for three years or less, although over 85 per cent of organisations manage to avoid the obvious drawbacks in relying on only one funder. Community Fund/Lottery grants are also widely favoured (55 per cent), followed by income from services and membership fees (33 per cent). Opinions divide over the merits of receiving monies from other sources, particularly charities, or where it is linked to specific impairment groupings. An extra irritant is that funding is increasingly conditional on implementing monitoring and evaluation procedures that place excessive demands on scarce resources.

Inadequate staffing levels are another crucial issue. As many as 13 per cent of responding organisations do not have any paid employees, and 12 per cent have only one. In comparison, there are a handful of much larger examples with over 30 full- or part-time employees. Most hold to a policy of only hiring disabled staff unless no suitable disabled applicant is available. An associated issue is whether to make up for the lack of full- and part-time staff by taking on volunteers. Around 20 per cent do not employ any, while 36 per cent have 10 or more volunteers. Some respondents questioned their potential exploitation as unpaid labour, although many disabled volunteers appreciated the opportunity to acquire work training and experience. At the same time, organisations welcomed the idea of formal training for all staff, including accredited programmes for independent/integrated living and direct payments advisors.

Accessible and affordable office accommodation is an added potential constraint, as when an unfavourable location restricts the range of potential users and activities. Less than half of organisations enjoy exclusive use of their premises, with the majority sharing with other voluntary agencies, sometimes in uneasy proximity to impairment specific organisations.

The concentration on service provision sometimes clashes with the pursuit of other objectives. Most notably, a majority of organisations feels that a campaigning role compromises its charitable status or attracts a negative reaction from funding agencies. While there are long-established examples of CILs being separated from a local campaigning coalition of disabled people, a contrary trend is illustrated by their merger into the Derbyshire Coalition for Inclusive Living in 2000. In this sample, 70 per cent of organisations campaign on disability issues, such as service cuts, access and charging for services, particularly at the local or regional levels, with some national mobilisation around disability rights.

Survey respondents are very critical of the way in which the independent living label has been taken over by mainstream service providers and organisations *for* disabled people. They refer to the 'colonisation' of personal assistance schemes by private agencies and the growth of Independent Living Centres and advisors geared to traditional rehabilitation thinking. These are charged with diluting the philosophy of independent living, and perhaps some re-medicalisation of disability. One suggestion is to introduce a 'kitemark' to differentiate those organisations adhering to a social barriers approach, although others express misgivings that this will stifle local innovation and diversity.

Interviews with 72 users re-iterate the significant contrasts between traditional and user-led services (Barnes et al., 2001). The former are criticised for their assessment procedures (provider-led, focus on financial considerations rather than user priorities), lack of reliability and flexibility, and poor helper/helped relations (high turnover, little credence given to user views). Making complaints is widely regarded as a waste of time. In comparison, user-led organisations are rated as more responsive to disabled people's needs and valued for their peer support, while the participation of disabled people at all levels is regarded as empowering.

Notwithstanding this broad consensus that user-led organisations are the preferred suppliers of independent living services, survey respondents also note areas where improvement is required. These centre on: better publicity, automatic referral at point of diagnosis by health professionals, more involvement in the assessment, design and evaluation of services, improved/more accessible premises, comprehensive coverage of the disabled population, enhanced and secure funding, and a well-trained and better paid workforce.

Conclusion

User-led organisations have been significant instigators of service support for independent living, yet despite suggestions that these services are the 'shape of things to come' (Morris, 1993), their general impact and expansion remain relatively slow. Most often, local authorities are unable or disinclined to secure their adequate funding, and there are few alternatives. This has obvious implications for the type and range of service provision so that organisations demonstrate considerable contrasts in their scale of operations. Overall, this makes for a tense relationship with funding agencies. This is further exacerbated because user organisations are often constrained by the demands for more 'efficient' provision within a system still attached to a medical approach to disability. Additionally, competition from non-user-led agencies has intensified over recent years, while vigorous campaigning by service organisations for disability rights may antagonise funding agencies.

Nevertheless, there are notable exceptions where user-led organisations, such as CILs, have made an extraordinary mark on disability politics. They have confirmed the potential of disabled people's collective organisation and capacity to realise user-friendly and enabling services. The enduring impression is of progress in facilitating 'ordinary lives', although much work still needs to be done in reaching all disabled people and maintaining the challenge to their social oppression.

References

Barnes, C., Mercer, G. and Morgan, H. (2000) *Creating Independent Futures: An Evaluation of Services Led by Disabled People. Stage One Report*. Leeds: The Disability Press.

Barnes, C., Morgan, H. and Mercer, G. (2001) *Creating Independent Futures: An Evaluation of Services Led by Disabled People. Stage Three Report*. Leeds: The Disability Press.

Beresford, P. and Croft, S. (1993) *Citizen Involvement: A Practical Guide for Change*. Basingstoke: Macmillan.

Braye, S. and Preston-Shoot, M. (1995) *Empowering Practice in Social Care*. Buckingham: Open University Press.

Brisenden, S. (1986) 'Independent living and the medical model of disability', *Disability, Handicap and Society*, 1 (2): 173–8.

Crewe, N.M., Zola, I.K. and Associates (1983) *Independent Living for Physically Disabled People*. San Francisco, CA: Jossey-Bass.

Davis, K. and Mullender, A. (1993) *Ten Turbulent Years: A Review of the Work of the Derbyshire Coalition of Disabled People*. Nottingham: Centre for Social Action.

Glasby, J. and Littlechild, R. (2002) *Social Work and Direct Payments*. Bristol: The Policy Press.

Morris, J. (1993) *The Shape of Things to Come? User Led Services*. London: National Institute for Social Work.

Priestley, M. (1999) *Disability Politics and Community Care*. London: Jessica Kingsley.

Zarb, G. and Nadash, P. (1994) *Cashing in on Independence: Comparing the Costs and Benefits of Cash and Services*. London: BCODP.

27 Leisure and Disabled People
LIZ CARR

Perhaps the easiest way to characterise 'leisure' is in terms of 'free time'. This is the amount of time we have available outside the world of work or paid employment. Sociologists generally agree that there was less of a division between work and leisure in pre-industrial Western societies. But industrialisation brought with it long working hours away from home or the community. Consequently the distinction between work and free time was forged. At the same time gradual but significant increases in material wealth amongst the general population gave many people the opportunity to spend their 'disposable income' on recreational activities. So, especially in the latter half of the twentieth century, leisure-specific industries became significant (Tomlinson, 1990). In late capitalist society, therefore, leisure plays an increasingly important part in the lives of everyone, whether disabled or otherwise.

Though work is still regarded as the main source of an individual's social identity, patterns of consumption and lifestyle choices are now considered equally important in shaping our individual and collective identities. In this chapter I will briefly explore the significance of leisure in the lives of disabled people with regard to mainstream leisure-type actives, and alternatives specifically for disabled people. It will be suggested that, as in work, disabled people's opportunities to enjoy leisure are limited. This raises important questions about disabled individuals' ability to formulate a positive sense of self.

Leisure and disabled people

Although many disabled people are unemployed, it is now generally agreed that they have relatively less free time than non-disabled contemporaries, and that their opportunities to participate in recreational pursuits are greatly reduced if they are not in work. For disabled people, leisure is often reduced as the necessities of life are more time consuming due to impairment-related considerations and disabling barriers. For example, essential personal and domestic tasks, such as getting out of bed, going to the toilet, getting dressed, preparing meals and cleaning the house, often take longer to complete as impairment increases.

Also, if disabled people use personal and domestic assistance for routine daily functions, then this may have an impact on free time. This is particularly so if someone does not have complete control over these services. Support services are often controlled by someone else who is employed by agencies, such as local authority social services departments. Negotiating with support or 'care' managers to organise appropriate personal and domestic support is both time consuming and emotionally demanding.

People's ability to enjoy leisure is closely related to their employment status. We are, in the main, socialised into the belief that work is good and idleness reprehensible. Consequently, people excluded from the workplace, including women at home, retired, disabled and unemployed people, often find it difficult to organise their leisure time. As well as money, status and a social identity, paid employment provides an important source of social activity. Many people, especially as they grow older, often spend their free time with workmates or colleagues. This is also the case for disabled people. For example, research on the experiences of disabled men with acquired spinal cord injury showed that those in work expressed greater levels of satisfaction with their social lives than those who were unemployed. Indeed, the majority of the men not working felt that they had too much free time and insufficient resources to fill it (Oliver et al., 1988).

A major source of dissatisfaction amongst disabled people with regard to leisure is directly linked to their limited disposable incomes. This is attributable to either unemployment and/or underemployment: low status, insecure jobs with low pay and poor working conditions, and higher impairment and disability related living costs (see Chapter 29). The majority of disabled people do not have sufficient incomes to cover the full costs of impairment-related expenditure, let alone leisure activities. In general, their standard of living is judged to be substantially lower than that of non-disabled peers (Burchardt, 2000).

The situation is made worse by the fact that while people can access essential technical aids and support, such as electric wheelchairs, reading aids, accessible computing equipment and personal assistants through Government employment schemes while they are seeking or in work, the same is not true for those excluded from the workplace. Therefore, unemployed disabled people are often denied access to appropriate technical aids to enhance their free time and leisure experiences, unless they buy them themselves or go 'cap in hand' to voluntary agencies and charities.

Types of mainstream leisure activities

Despite the enormous variety of leisure activities available in the twenty-first century, the most popular in the UK are those that are situated in the home. These include watching television, visiting or entertaining friends, listening to the radio, listening to music and reading (HMSO, 2002). At first glance this may seem to have obvious advantages for people whose activities may be restricted due to impairment and or inaccessible environments. It is important to recognise, however, that most home-based leisure pursuits are geared to the needs of the majority and therefore are inaccessible to certain sections of the disabled community.

For many people, for example, watching television is more than simply a pastime; it is also an important topic of conversation. Yet accessing popular television programmes poses particular problems for people with sight-related or hearing impairments. Equally important is the fact that many programmes contain deeply disturbing and depressing media messages about impairment and disability that are offensive to many sections of the disabled community (Pointon and Davies, 1997).

Socialising with friends at home is the UK's second most popular leisure activity. But it is important to remember that many disabled people do not have a home of their own; many live in various types of residential institutions, 'therapeutic' communities or 'group homes'. Others continue to live with their parents long into adulthood, due to the continuing lack of accessible housing and/or community based services. Many are simply homeless. People labelled with 'learning difficulties' or 'mental health' problems are particularly vulnerable to this type of deprivation (Barnes and Mercer, 2003).

Research shows that disabled people generally have fewer friends than non-disabled peers. This is especially so for young disabled people who, unlike their non-disabled contemporaries, are disproportionately reliant on their immediate family for social activities, and people with newly acquired impairments. Many young disabled people attend segregated special schools and colleges that often separate them from non-disabled peers living in the local community. Peer group relationships are especially important for both disabled and non-disabled people during the adolescent or formative years when they are struggling to develop an appropriate adult identity (Hirst and Baldwin, 1994). Many studies have reported that disabled people's circle of friends often diminishes following the onset of impairment. The chronic shortage of suitably accessible housing also means that social interaction between disabled and non-disabled people is extremely difficult (Barnes and Mercer, 2003).

Reading is one of the most popular home-based leisure activities, yet many newspapers and magazines are rarely, if ever, published initially in an accessible form for people with sight-related impairments. The selection of talking books may be limited and costly. Newspapers are not produced in Braille and only a few magazines are available in this particular medium. Whilst there are voluntary agencies, such as the Talking Newspaper Association, which will provide taped versions of these publications, they are usually a summary or digest of the original and are delivered on a weekly basis. To many disabled people this represents a form of censorship.

Increasingly, free time is being spent on computer and internet based pastimes. The growth of the World Wide Web means that we now have the opportunity to access information and services in seconds from all over the world in the comfort of our own homes. In many ways the Internet offers us the opportunity to transform the way we spend our free time. Besides accessing useful information, users can go shopping, go on virtual tours of museums, visit other countries, play games, listen to movies, contribute to news groups and discussion lists on topics of interest, and chat to people from all over the world.

Whilst all of this has obvious positive implications for people, who for various reasons lead particularly isolated and solitary lives, there are very real dangers stemming from these developments that have yet to be fully explored.

In many ways, this brave new world of cyberspace created by the Internet allows anyone, whether disabled or otherwise, with a computer, to throw off the shackles of daily living and re-invent themselves in any way they choose. For disabled people, the everyday realities of living with impairment and disability in a disabling society can be forgotten. In such a world the consequences of impairment can be ignored and no-one need be disabled. Though this may provide some momentary and much needed respite from the daily routine of living as a disabled person in an overtly hostile physical and cultural environment, the long-term psychological effects of such a 'Walter Mitty' type existence for the individuals concerned cannot be overlooked. Both sociologists and psychologists have long since documented the negative emotional implications of similar withdrawal strategies (Heatherton et al., 2000; Wilson, 2003).

Also, as the physical world has been organised around the needs of non-disabled people, so too has the Internet. For example, over the last decade or so various British governments have routinely trumpeted the benefits of the Internet for all sections of society. This has led to the claim that all the Government Departments' data will be online by the year 2005. Yet their own Gateway website: www.gateway.gov.uk., has come under fire for being inaccessible to many sections of the disabled community (http://www. tomw.net.au/media/20010601.html.). (See Chapter 23.)

Of course, privatised leisure activities such as those mentioned above are especially important for disabled people, if only because of the environmental and cultural difficulties which disabled people encounter outside the home. As in all areas of social life, and well documented elsewhere, transport and access difficulties severely restrict disabled people's ability to enjoy popular mainstream leisure activities, such as going to the cinema, theatre, pub, clubs and restaurants (Heiser, 1995; Shelley, 2002).

Indeed, leisure and social activities are heavily weighted in favour of car owners and those with ready access to the car of a family member or friend. Yet households with a disabled member are only half as likely to own a car as those without a disabled member. Whilst those entitled to higher rate DLA (Disability Living Allowance) mobility component may be eligible to hire or buy a car through the Motability scheme, red-tape, inflexibility, mileage restrictions, and the high cost of adapting vehicles all mean this may not be a viable option for everyone (Barnes and Mercer, 2003).

Furthermore, public transport is still difficult, if not impossible, for many disabled people to use. It is also very expensive for disabled individuals to use taxis or pay a driver every time they want to go anywhere. Hence, those who wish to go out but have no car, either because of the cost involved or because they are unable to drive, are forced to rely on others, usually family or friends, to drive them about. This can be emotionally draining for all concerned, but is especially so for the disabled person as it is a constant reminder of their dependent status and enforced functional inadequacy.

As with transport, spontaneity and choice in where one goes and who one goes with are limited further by the general inaccessibility of most of our public buildings. This impacts on every aspect of disabled people's lives and means that they are often either excluded from these places altogether or else they have to compromise their requirements, control and dignity to be included. For example, wheelchair users are often barred from theatres, cinemas, clubs and concerts by steps, narrow corridors and doorways, and inaccessible toilets. Consequently, many disabled people tend not to venture into 'unknown territory', but instead stick to tried and tested places (Shakespeare et al., 1996).

People who may not normally need help at home will often require assistance outside to negotiate a hostile physical and social environment. For instance, Deaf people need interpreters to communicate with those unable to use British Sign Language (BSL) – the language of the deaf community. Also, people with physical or sensory impairments may need personal assistants to open doors or read inaccessible information, such as menus in restaurants. While such assistance is in many ways necessary and enabling, it is also often a demanding and frustrating experience as the disabled person must maintain a sense of control that may inhibit their ability for enjoyment. There are also financial implications for the disabled person when employing interpreters or personal assistants for leisure activities. Besides the helpers' wages, the disabled person also has to cover the cost of any expenses they might incur during the leisure experience. When visiting a theatre or a cinema, for example they will need to buy two tickets, one for themselves and one for the personal assistant.

Transport and physical access are not the only considerations that disabled people must confront before they can enjoy mainstream leisure pursuits outside the home. There is a definite ignorance, and even apprehension, surrounding disability amongst many people working in mainstream leisure industries that cannot be explained simply with reference to access. Institutional discrimination is so prevalent in leisure facilities that disabled people are routinely shunned because they are viewed as 'bad for business'. Where access is available it is often via a separate entrance or situated in a segregated area (Shelley, 2002). Such practices do not represent or promote inclusion, and do little to enhance the disabled person's self-esteem. Furthermore, for many disabled people, a doctor's signature is a necessary but unwanted passport to non-medical resources or activities, including leisure pursuits. For example, medical certification may be needed when disabled people wish to use particular facilities, travel by air, or visit other countries (Begum, 1996).

Alternatives to mainstream leisure activities

One outcome of the above is the steady growth of segregated leisure activities for disabled people. Often within the context of such facilities, professionals and 'carers' present leisure pursuits as 'therapy' or 'rehabilitation'. Besides re-enforcing the widespread view that all aspects of disabled people's lives are legitimate areas for professional intervention and control, such practices serve, whether intentionally or otherwise, to introduce an element of obligation to such activity. This effectively undermines the notion of choice and pleasure usually associated with leisure pastimes and pursuits. This tradition can be traced back to the growth of charities for disabled people in the nineteenth century, but became institutionalised in the state sector with the National Assistance Act 1948 and the Chronically Sick and the Disabled Persons' Act 1970. Both laid a duty on local authorities to establish suitable facilities, such as day centres, adult training centres (ATCs) and social clubs, to provide lectures, games, outings and other recreational activities for disabled people (Drake, 1999).

Many disabled people are introduced to the idea of using these services by professionals as part of a rehabilitation process. Staff and careers officers at special schools and colleges sometimes present them to young disabled adults as an acceptable alternative to unemployment. Research shows that most users, across all age groups, view day centres and similar organisations as simply 'somewhere to go' (Carter, 1981). They are often the only alternative to the debilitating social isolation that can so easily characterise the reality of living with impairment in contemporary British society. No surprise, then, that it is often disabled users who are the staunchest supporters of such facilities.

There is little doubt that such units provide a range of activities and services, both social and educative, which give users a level of autonomy and independence unavailable elsewhere in the community. In the majority of cases, however, these facilities are unable to give disabled people the confidence and skills to achieve these goals beyond their boundaries. Further, recent changes including the adoption of currently more fashionable names such as 'Disability Resource Centres' and the co-opting of users into management structures, cannot conceal the fact that these organisations are invariably controlled by non-disabled people and represent nothing more than a conventional segregative solution to the 'problem' of disability. They run counter to the idea and development of an inclusive society.

Other alternatives include the various charities and voluntary agencies providing particular leisure opportunities for disabled people. Many were set up as a specific response to the barriers mentioned above. Examples include Sports for Young Disabled Women, which organises climbing and other outdoor activities, and Riding for the Disabled. There is also a national network of social clubs known as PHAB (Physically Handicapped and Able Bodied) Clubs. This was set up explicitly to bring disabled and non-disabled people together, but integration is often limited and there is an ethos of 'doing for' rather than 'doing with' disabled users. Again, the problem with many of these organisations is that they are not run by disabled people themselves and therefore are implicitly, if not explicitly, segregative and do little to challenge inaccessible mainstream facilities (Barnes and Mercer, 2003). All of which has major implications for a disabled individual's ability to develop a positive sense of self and identity. However, as is well documented elsewhere in this book, this unfortunate and ongoing situation has helped to generate the development of a nationwide self-help movement and an alternative 'disability' culture that offers hope for the future.

Conclusion

For most people, free time is when they can exercise choice over what they do. Indeed, it is through the exercising of choice that we explore, express and define our identity. This chapter has suggested that disabled people's opportunities to exercise choice with reference to popular leisure activities is limited by a variety of factors, economic, environmental and cultural. It has also been suggested that as a result of this exclusion a host of segregated facilities have emerged which, although they offer some alternative opportunities for recreational-type pursuits, fail to address the problem of discrimination in the mainstream leisure industry.

References

Barnes, C. and Mercer, G. (2003) *Disability*. Cambridge: Polity.

Begum, N. (1996) 'General practitioners' role in shaping disabled women's lives', in C. Barnes and G. Mercer (eds), *Exploring the Divide*. Leeds: The Disability Press.

Burchardt, T. (2000) *Enduring Economic Development: Disabled People, Income and Work*. York: The Joseph Rowntree Foundation.

Carter, J. (1981) *Day Centres for Adults: Somewhere to Go*. London: Allen and Unwin.

Drake, R. (1999) *Understanding Disability Policy*. Tavistock: Macmillan.

Heatherton, T.H., Kiek, R.E., Hebl, M.R. and Hull, J.C. (eds) (2000) *The Social Psychology of Stigma*. London: Guilford Press.

Hirst, M. and Baldwin, S. (1994) *Unequal Opportunities: Growing Up Disabled*. York: Social Policy Research Unit.

HMSO (2002) *Social Trends*. London: HMSO, Office of National Statistics.

Heiser, B. (1995) 'The nature and causes of transport disability in Britain and how to overcome it', in G. Zarb (ed.), *Removing Disabling Barriers*. London: Policy Studies Institute.

Oliver, M., Zarb, G., Silver, S., Moore, M. and Salisbury, V. (1988) *Walking Into Darkness: The Experience of Spinal Cord Injury*. Tavistock: Macmillan.

Pointon, A. and Davies, C. (1997) *Framed: Interrogating Disability in the Media*. London: British Film Institute.

Shakespeare, T., Gilespie-Sells, K. and Davies, D. (1996) *The Sexual Politics of Disability*. London: Cassell.

Shelley, P. (2002) *Everybody Here: Play and Leisure for Disabled Children and Young People*. London: Contact a Family.

Tomlinson, A. (1990) *Consumption, Identity and Style*. London: Routledge.

Wilson, S. (2003) *Disability, Counselling and Psychotherapy*. London: Palgrave.

28 Disability and Ageing
ANN MACFARLANE

'Grow old along with me, the best is yet to be.'

R. Browning, *Rabbi Ben Ezra*

Robert Browning's poetic words do not fit comfortably in the lives of older people, the more so if you are an older disabled person. One image of older people is that which reflects an older population who enjoy going on cruises and taking holidays three months out of every twelve. Another view is one that highlights the downside of becoming an older person and portrays poverty, ill-health and isolation. A plethora of new legislation and changing policies focus on health care, social inclusion and social justice and draw together many priorities for supporting older people. The reality for many older people, particularly for those who have an impairment and experience disabled barriers, is that daily life is still mainly a struggle and is plagued with concerns.

These basic areas of concern include money, particularly pensions and investments, access to and the cost of transport, housing, personal care, employment, leisure and relationships; in fact, all the issues that have been a priority and of concern for disabled people, the Disabled People's Movement and Centres for Independent Living, particularly over the last 25 years. This has been the period in which disabled people have managed to mobilise, come together and organise themselves in order to debate the issues that affect their lives, and this mobilisation has included a small element of older people. A major outcome of these debates is the term 'independent living'. This term has enabled and supported many disabled people and the Disabled People's Movement to campaign on human and civil rights and has focused on the importance of independent living in relation to the planning, delivery and monitoring of services in the lives of disabled people.

The Disabled People's Movement defines 'independent living' as 'being in control of one's life'. In practice, this means having choice over how assistance is provided, who provides it and when. People who provide this service are called 'personal assistants'. Independent living may change over time as disabled people make changes to their lives, as they grow up, grow older and have different experiences. As an older person ages there is the very real possibility of becoming a disabled person, with one person in two acquiring an impairment. The experiences of impaired mobility, sight and hearing are the most common in older people. Personal assistants may be pivotal to supporting an older person to achieve independent living. A personal assistant is someone who works with the person on his or her terms. A personal assistant does not *look after* or *care* for the person. Oliver summarises the independent living philosophy as follows:

> Central to this philosophy is the issue of personal assistance which is necessary for disabled people to participate in all of the activities of everyday life and includes work, leisure pursuits, education and personal relationships. Choice and control are key factors in this participation and disabled people must exercise both of these in making decisions both about their personal assistance and in the activities in which they wish to participate. (2000: 3)

Many older people would reply 'And so say all of us.'

For all older people, and this includes older people irrespective of race and culture, much of what has been said about disabled people and independent living may apply. Older people have traditionally been excluded from the debate. It is, however, possible to catch some glimpses of what independent living means to older people. Research undertaken by Clark et al. (1998) reveals that older people view remaining in their own home as marking the final boundary of their independence. Older people make a clear distinction between being 'at home' and being 'in a home' and they define assistance as *help* not *care*. They want services to support them to care for themselves. The most common services open to older people who qualify, following a community care assessment, are home care and meals on wheels. These traditional services have often fallen short of expectations and have placed older people within a dependency model, which disempowers them. In 1996 the NHS and Community Care (Direct Payments) Act was available to people between the ages of 18 and 65 and gave local authorities the power to give cash for care for those who met the criteria of being 'willing and able' to manage a community care package. Disabled and older people lobbied government to extend the legislation to include older people and in February 2000 this expansion was achieved. A direct payment is one way to achieve independent living that provides choice and control. Now, following a community care assessment, an older person may choose to have money in the form of a direct payment rather than traditional service provision.

Government policy has, until recently, determined entitlements to older people by chonological age. The attendance allowance can be applied for when a person reaches 65, while the mobility allowance, unless applied for prior to 65, is not available and yet impaired mobility causes huge difficulties in terms of accessing community activities. Voluntary sector organisations may determine the age of 50 as being 'older'. Many insurance companies who offer policies to older people may decide on several different age brackets and premiums to determine when older people can expect to receive a retirement pension, money for health requirements or for compensation claims following an accident.

Perhaps one way older people can be defined is through the concept of 'life changes'. Getting older is a time when children have left home, when a career or paid work has ended or when leisure of sporting pursuits has become too demanding and something less fatiguing is required. It is a time when older people may leave their home and move to a smaller dwelling or sheltered accommodation. It might relate to losing a partner and friends and when financial circumstances change. Life changes relating to the older generation can come within a wide timeframe and may determine when a person feels 'older'. Acquiring an impairment and experiencing disabling barriers occur irrespective of age and can certainly add to the image and feeling of becoming 'older'.

Older people themselves are slowly beginning to come together to determine their own agenda and, as with the Disabled People's Movement, they are finding it hard to acquire adequate funding to further their own issues. In the late 1990s Better Government for

Older People was established to ensure that older people have a consultative role and are involved in the planning, delivery and monitoring of services that affect their lives. The process is beginning to influence changes in health and social care and other crucial aspects of daily living, such as accessible transport, and has significantly raised the profile of older people at local level. Other national organisations, such as the Joseph Rowntree Foundation, Help the Aged and Age Concern have begun the process of consultation with older people and finding ways to include older people in research and in decision-making processes. However, these organisations are not controlled and managed by disabled people and there is still a long way to go in terms of older people taking control of their own agenda and obtaining the funding to ensure positive outcomes. It is only now that voluntary sector organisations and statutory bodies are beginning to recognise the 'added value' of including older people in the debate on these issues. A further challenge for the policy and the decision-making bodies is to ensure that their consultation and planning processes include and enable older people to input their views. The emphasis in deciding policies and strategies that relate to older people should be one of social inclusion and fair access. These policies and strategies require the development of integrated objectives between organisations, departments and community initiatives and should demonstrate best value in planning, provision and monitoring of services.

Many of the policies and practices that discriminate against younger disabled people impact on older people. There are differences and similarities, and for disabled people and older people to work together on the common issues could reap significant changes and benefits. The ability to go out, participate in community, employment and leisure activities, and enjoy accessible housing and transport are issues where discrimination and oppression may occur for both groups and these must be challenged and changed.

Older people have the right to represent their own interests, and access issues must be addressed in order that older people can be included in debates that affect them. Harding summarises the overall situation for older people as follows:

> If all older people are being offered are the high cost, high dependency services then that, eventually, is what they will be forced to use. A national strategy is needed to turn this situation around and to support the independence and inclusion of older people. Such a strategy needs to be comprehensive, not piecemeal, and to address the needs of older people in the round. (1997: 2)

She concludes:

> Older people have a key role in formulating such strategies, since they know better than anyone else what it takes to retain health, autonomy and inclusion in society in older age. (1997: 2)

For older people who become ill and may acquire an impairment, to gain health, autonomy and inclusion is equally important. There are pockets of good practice where older people are coming together and this good practice needs emulating across the country. Considerable thought and energy needs to be focused on older people who live in rural areas, those isolated in their own homes and to include older people in minority ethnic communities. Many older people acquire mobility and sensory impairments and experience mental health difficulties brought about by being excluded.

Voluntary sector organisations have a dynamic role in contributing to the development and delivery of services with older people. Small, locally-based services make a big difference, for example, befriending ethnic minority communities and ensuring that services are culturally sensitive. It is vital to harness the energy and expertise of older people who can provide advocacy and information.

The development of expertise on the use of legislation can play a vital part in ensuring that older disabled people know about and receive entitlements. Entitlements come in the form of money, equipment, personal assistance and services, some or all of which can make a significant difference in a person's quality of life. There is still a great deal of ignorance and misinformation as a result of professional people not making themselves aware or keeping themselves up to date on new and changing legislation that has the potential to enhance the lives of older people. It is true that there is a great deal of new legislation and, when pressures mount, there is limited time to exercise good practice. However, knowing and interpreting legislation for older people can bring many benefits and change lives. A brief overview of this legislation will highlight its relevance for older people.

In 2001, the government's *National Service Framework for Older People* (DoH, 2001) focused upon:

- rooting out age discrimination;
- person-centred care with older people treated as individuals with respect and dignity; and
- promoting older people's health and independence.

Rooting out age discrimination in the provision of health and community care services could make an impact on the lives of older people. Much of the inequality and discrimination that currently exist in these areas of provision could significantly improve with the input of the coherent voice of older people.

Social care services are debarred from the use of age in their eligibility criteria and policies and the use of age to restrict available services. Commissioning strategies must be flexible enough to take account of individual needs and eligibility criteria are not to be more stringent for older people than for other groups. An area of concern is that for some older people, who require non-residential community care services, it may mean demonstrating a higher level of need in order to qualify for a service. As past research has shown, older people often require 'a little bit of help', especially at the appropriate time, in order to continue managing their lives in their own environment. A little focused assistance can prevent a fall, an admission to hospital, or several re-admissions to hospital. Another area of age discrimination has been cost ceilings for support that have often been set far lower for older people than for those under the age of 65. Many local authorities spend less on services for older people. Costs will now be levelled up to comply with the *Fair Access to Care Services* (DoH, 2002) guidance issued in April 2002. This guidance provides a national framework for councils to use when determining their eligibility criteria for supporting adults of any age. They will be expected to adopt a consistent approach to defining priorities for meeting needs in order to promote independence and quality of life. This includes a common understanding of risk assessment and the focus for reviews.

The National Service Framework for Older People focuses on person-centred care and states that NHS and social care services are to treat older people as individuals and enable them to make choices about their own care. This is to be achieved through the single assessment process, integrated commissioning arrangements, and integrated provision of services, including community equipment and continence services. Older people will also be entitled to appropriate and accessible information so that they can make informed choices and decisions that will make a difference to their quality of life, whether that is their health requirements, domestic, social or personal care needs.

The Health Act of 1999 focuses on joint commissioning and pooled budgets and considers the importance of a lead commissioner with the idea that this will provide an integrated approach to service provision, rather than working to organisational boundaries. Section 31 of the Health Act details partnership arrangements. It is possible for money to be given to a local authority that can then translate this into a direct payment for the health care required by the older person. Where it is not possible for direct payments to be made in lieu of health care, the arrangements for the delivery of health care should be compatible with the increased independence that the direct payments are facilitating.

Older people should have input into their lives that is responsive to gender, personal appearance, communication, diet, race, culture, religious and spiritual beliefs. This holistic and person-centred approach is demanding a fresh appraisal of training for care managers, social workers, doctors and nurses and other paramedical professionals who have been greatly in control of service provision. It will take a huge shift in the mindsets of many professional people and highlights the need for older people to be in control of the services they require. Critical issues arising from legislation and policies around older people's needs are:

- The importance of agencies agreeing arrangements assessments, whether single or separate, placing the old person at the centre of the process, ensuring that the person understands this process and what his or her rights are in determining outcomes. The older person will also need to know timescales around the assessment process, their right to question and complain, and the review and monitoring processes.
- Information gathering and sharing among the different agencies, thus avoiding older people, and those who support them, having to provide the same information to different people.
- Recognition of greater prevalence of some illnesses among specific groups. Provision must be culturally appropriate and serve the needs of those for whom their first language is not English. Direct payments can be helpful in providing the flexibility that personal assistants can offer when people have fluctuating impairments.

Conclusion

As younger disabled people are reaping the benefits of the achievements of the Disabled People's Movement over the past 25 years, so older disabled people will begin to see improvements as they continue to come together to debate the way forward. Other disabled people are slowly beginning to benefit from technology and the next ten years will see advances and create higher expectations. Expectations in other areas will increase and older people, particularly those with an impairment, will want and have a right to access inclusive mainstream services, good quality information, personal assistance and direct payments, accessible and affordable public and private transport and high-quality health care. This list is not exhaustive and indicates the pressure that will be placed on a variety of commissioners and providers responsible for effecting change.

Keeping these key independent living principles at the forefront of development and planning, older people may engage with Robert Browning's philosophical approach:

"Grow old along with me, the best is yet to be."

References

Clark, H., Dyer, S. and Horwood, J. (1998) *That Bit of Help: The High Value of Low Level Services for Older People*. Bristol: The Policy Press and Joseph Rowntree Foundation.

Department of Health (2001) *National Service Framework for Older People*. London: Department of Health.

Department of Health (2002) *Fair Access to Care Services*. Policy Guidance. London: Department of Health.

Harding, T. (1997) *Lives Worth Living: The Independence and Inclusion of Older People*. London: Help the Aged.

Oliver, M. (2000) *Three Year Review*. London: National Centre for Independent Living.

29 Employment Barriers and Inclusive Futures?
ALAN ROULSTONE

Paid work has been widely acknowledged to be the source of positive identity, financial stability, to enhance wider life opportunities and is seen as a key indicator of social inclusion (Department for Education and Employment, 2001). With the election of the New Labour government in 1997 the emphasis on paid employment has increased apace. New Labour have increasingly emphasised welfare-through-work and attempted to reduce disability benefit claims through work-based tax credits. There appears to be a strong and abiding commitment to getting many disabled people into employment. New Labour's welfare reforms and the introduction of the New Deal for Disabled People (NDDP) were captured in the phrase 'Work for those who can and security for those who cannot' (Department of Social Security, 1998).

Recent developments in job retention pilots, job brokerage and Workstep (see www.dwp.gov.uk) all reaffirm the commitment to employment-based welfare for vulnerable social groups. The advent of the Disability Discrimination Act in 1995 was seen as responding to the major barrier of employer attitudes towards employing disabled people. Perhaps most notably the UK government placed employment at the heart of its recent strategy for learning disability (Department of Health, 2001). This is symbolic, given the barriers traditionally faced by people with learning difficulties accessing and keeping employment.

The evidence, however, clearly points to long-standing and continued barriers to disabled people obtaining employment. A recent survey by the Royal National Institute for the Blind (RNIB) noted that blind and partially sighted people are just as likely to be unemployed in 2002 as they were before the Disability Discrimination Act was introduced in 1995 (RNIB, 2002). Government figures suggest that many disabled people are not employed but want to work (Labour Market Trends, 2001). Disabled people are more likely when in work to be in poorly paid and lower status work than their non-disabled counterparts. Disabled people are more likely to leave the labour market before the official retirement age. However, some optimism attaches to disabled people's working futures – why?

The promise of employment

The period 1944 to date has seen diverse attempts to link disabled people with employment. This is significant; since the rise of the industrial revolution to 1944 there were few and limited attempts to connect disabled people with employment. The assumption had long held that disability equalled non-employability. The nature of heavy industrial work more effectively excluded disabled people. According to radical disability writers, the industrial system had designed out those whose bodies and intellects were not 'suitable' for an industrial system based around the 'average' worker (Finkelstein, 1980; Ryan and Thomas, 1987).

The Tomlinson Committee report (1943) and the Disabled Persons Employment Act of 1944 that followed – a product of the labour shortages of the Second World War – highlighted the employment potential of many disabled people. For the first time, the connecting of disabled people's skills with labour market opportunities was seen as an important policy goal. The Act provided for a quota scheme, which required employers with 20 plus employees to employ 3 per cent of its workforce from a population of registered disabled people. It was made an offence to recruit a non-disabled person if the company was below quota. The Act also introduced a register of disabled people, a Special Aids to Employment scheme, designated employment which could only be undertaken by disabled people and sheltered (section 2) employment for those deemed to have between 30 per cent and 80 per cent productivity (for a detailed account, see Thornton and Lunt, 1995). Whilst medically focused, the 1944 Act brought to public consciousness the notion that disabled people were employable, given suitable 'rehabilitation' and workplace accommodations.

Wider promise is seen to attach to the changing nature of work itself. The restrictive assumptions of the factory and factory system are seen by some writers to have been erased with the more open and flexible nature of white-collar workplace. For example, new computer-based technologies offer greater scope for workplace integration as they allow, in principle, more creative use of working time, data manipulation and information control (Cornes, in Oliver, 1991; Roulstone, 1998). Changing attitudes and the impact of the disabled people's movement can also be seen as positive developments, making employment more likely for disabled people (Campbell and Oliver, 1996).

The development of Disability Working Allowance and more recently the Disabled Person's Tax Credit reward work financially, and have begun to make risk-taking more likely in leaving disability benefits (linking rule relaxation), whilst less punitive regulations allow disabled people to earn more without their benefits being affected (earnings disregard).

The Disability Discrimination Act 1995, legislation closely modelled on the Sex Discrimination and Race Relations Acts (Doyle, 1994), is seen as a having a key role in reducing discrimination in employment (Disability Rights Commission, 2002). The Act makes it unlawful for an employer or their employees to treat someone 'less favourably' in interviews, offers of employment, terms and conditions of employment and requires employers to look at making 'reasonable adjustments' to avoid less favourable treatment where possible (Gooding, 1995). The Act is also seen by its advocates to have a powerful educational role. The fines and orders it imposes are seen to educate other employers to the dangers of failing to adhere to the Act's provisions.

Disabling barriers remain

The above then might strongly suggest that unemployment, under-employment and relatively poor labour market status are likely to be consigned to history. Whilst some clear advances have been made, this judgement lacks credibility at this time. The weight and engrained nature of attitudes and discrimination ensure that government employment schemes, legislation and initiatives are weakened. The benefit traps noted above have not been erased completely and the benefits system continues to hold internal contradictions and conflicts. The number of recipients of disability and incapacity benefits has increased between 1998 and 2001 (Social Trends, 2002: 144).

The complex mixture of programmes and initiatives makes it difficult to predict the extent to which disabled people's employment will be increased and enhanced. The exact relationship between New Deal personal advisors, job brokers, Workstep contractors, Jobcentre Plus and Disability Support Teams is very difficult to predict. Whilst some limited advances have been made, many barriers remain. We can begin to understand these barriers as:

- personal (social capital);
- attitudinal;
- environmental; and
- governmental (law, benefits and schemes).

The most recent Labour Force Survey evidence suggests that disabled people of working age are significantly less likely to be economically active, that is, in work or looking for work. In the summer of 2000, 52 per cent of disabled people were economically active, against 86 per cent of non-disabled people (Labour Market Trends, 2001). Of the economically inactive disabled people, 33 per cent said they would like to work if they had the opportunity. If we compare the employment rate of disabled and non-disabled people, the figures are even more stark: 47 per cent of disabled working-age people are in employment, compared to 87 per cent of non-disabled people. Disabled people are more likely to work part-time, be in the lower three social class groupings and to be self-employed.

There are a number of explanations for the above differences in employment and economic activity. A personal explanation, more widely known as human capital theory, suggests that disabled people are less likely to be in employment than non-disabled people of the same age as they have less educational and employment 'capital' to offer. There is evidence that due to 'special schooling' and historically low expectations, disabled people are less likely to have undertaken formally valued education and training (Barnes et al., 1999). Conversely having educational qualifications does enhance disabled people's employment chances (Burchardt, 2000). There are, however, wider barriers that need to be understood.

Evidence suggests that even similarly qualified disabled people earn less than their non-disabled peers (Burchardt, 2000). More evidence is required on the interaction of education, disability and employment; however, many of the arguments about educational deficits are a product of the medical model of disability, which emphasises and measures what people with impairments cannot do. The evidence from the Policy Consortium for Supported Employment recently suggested that many people with learning difficulties, traditionally a group facing the greatest employment barriers, can do some form of work either in open or subsidised mainstream employment (O'Bryan et al., 2000).

There is now a well-established literature on the negative attitudes that attach to disability in the employment sphere. Graham et al. (1990) established that disabled people are twice as likely to receive a negative response to a job application compared to a non-disabled applicant. French's (1997) work explored the negative attitudes of non-disabled health professionals to their disabled colleagues, whilst Roulstone (1998) explored a range of negative attitudes to disabled colleagues which included resentment, perceptions of dependence, pity and disbelief at the ability of disabled colleagues.

Even with good employer intentions, many older buildings are physically inaccessible, that is, environmentally inaccessible (Roulstone, 1998). Although the Disability

Discrimination Act 1995 is likely to lead to some welcome access improvements, the Act establishes that environmental improvements need only occur where it is 'reasonable'. The exact interpretation of 'reasonable' is made by lawyers, but for sure the Act will not erase some of the most engrained barriers which will continue to be seen as too costly for employers (Gooding, 1995). The cost of lost employment opportunities is rarely weighed up against this evaluation of financial costs.

It seems odd to state that the very policies, initiatives, schemes and benefits designed to aid disabled people to get and keep employment may act as barriers to employment. The most significant policy changes aimed at employment of disabled people were embodied in the 1944 Disabled Persons Employment Act. The quota scheme, Disabled Persons register, Designated Jobs, Special Aids to Employment scheme, grants for upgrading premises and later Fares to Work, personal assistance and reader services all stem from the detail or spirit of the Act.

Key problems with the Act's provisions were its concern with labour market rather than the barriers to employment *per se*. That is, when labour market shortages reduced, key parts of the Act's provisions lapsed into disuse. For example the quota system, originally designed to sanction non-compliance was rarely enforced, whilst exemptions from the quota were frequently given to employers. This is a severe limitation of the quota scheme and one that is very disappointing when compared to the French and German quota schemes (Thornton and Lunt, 1995).

Designated or reserved employment gave registered disabled people first choice of taking up a job. Sadly these were very stereotypical and took the form of lift and car park attendants. Registration proved stigmatising and the number registering declined dramatically throughout the period 1960–93 (Thornton and Lunt, 1995).

Recent shifts to in-work benefits, such as Disability Working Allowance and Disabled Person's Tax Credit, are to be welcomed, but as means-tested benefits and allowances they place disabled workers' finances under close scrutiny. This has limited take-up of in-work benefits and has been claimed mainly by those already in work (Burchardt, 2000). The wider problem of loss of housing and council tax benefits on receipt of tax credits is a continuing problem.

The above benefits and income conflicts have led some commentators to argue for a disability income for all disabled people, whether in work or not (RNIB, 2002). This would enhance a personal sense of security, but may be seen as a disincentive to employment. A modest disabled person's income guarantee has been introduced by the New Labour government. This is seen, however, as institutionalising low pay for this employment group, the opposite of what many disabled people want.

The recent shift towards welfare-in-work seems, on the surface, to be laudable, given the recorded benefits of work. However, the New Deal for Disabled People (NDDP) as the flagship policy development for many disabled job seekers can be viewed in two very different ways. The official view (DfEE and DSS, 2000) is that NDDP is unique in providing carefully tailored advice, support and job matching for disabled people. The NDDP interview has, until recently, been voluntary and is filtered through the newly-formed Jobcentre Plus, a hybrid of the former Benefits Agency and Employment Service. Personal Advisors help disabled people find the best option for them, given their 'disability' experience and education, whilst Job Brokers will play an increasing part in matching jobs with disabled job seekers. The idea here is that benefit claiming and work are increasingly connected and aim, wherever possible, to encourage paid work as the first option for disabled people entering the labour market after education or who may have just lost their current job.

A very different view (Roulstone, 2000) is that NDDP is simply the last in a long line of schemes that place the onus on vulnerable employment groups to access and remain in the labour market. That is, the focus is upon how disabled people overcome their problems in getting employment, rather than looking at why too few opportunities exist and the quality of those jobs. There is, it is argued, a real risk that as a society we might simply be institutionalising poor work for many disabled people. In wider policy terms, disabled individuals' failure to gain employment after using NDDP support may lead to victim blaming, as has happened with previous employment-related schemes (Burchardt, 2000).

The evidence to date on the New Deal for Disabled People is provisional (Arthur et al., 2000; Disability Now, 2002; Sainsbury et al., 2002), and much employment growth seems to be due to economic growth more generally (Institute for Fiscal Studies, 2000). The pilot nature of the NDDP and the patchy employer response have meant that few of the NDDP opportunity providers have achieved the modest targets they were set.

Conclusion

Many debates are still to be had, not least the question of whether disabled people are better off in employment in a globally competitive capitalism. If we assume that the future of employment is one of managing risks and the state taking the worst edges off a highly impersonal exchange of commodities, this has serious implications for some people with impairments. It is perhaps no coincidence that recent commentaries point to the 'business case' of employing disabled people. This 'case' emphasises that many disabled people could work with suitable employment environments.

A pressing question that needs to be addressed is what do we mean by enabling employment? Recent research points to the importance of acceptance of difference, managerial openness, flexible working practices, awareness of legislation and available service support as important indicators of more enabling employment (Roulstone et al., 2003). However, much more needs to be done to tease out what we mean by enabling employment in the twenty-first century.

As with many questions, the answers may already be available. Marx's assertion 'from each according to their ability and to each according to their needs' will continue to hover over any critical debates about the future of work for some disabled people. Clearly, UK disability employment policy needs: to join up in such a way that abilities are realised to the full, to enhance employer incentives to employ, and to provide a decent disability income for all regardless of work status.

References

Arthur, S., Corden, A., Green, A., Lewis, J., Loumidis, J., Sainsbury, R., Stafford, B., Thornton, P. and Walker, R. (2000) *New Deal For Disabled People: Early Implementation*. Department of Social Security, Research Report No.106. London: DSS.

Barnes, C., Mercer, G. and Shakespeare, T. (1999) *Exploring Disability: A Sociological Introduction*. Cambridge: Polity.

Burchardt, T. (2000) *Enduring Economic Exclusion: Disabled People, Income and Work.* York: Joseph Rowntree Foundation.

Campbell, J. and Oliver, M. (1996) *Disability Politics: Understanding Our Past, Challenging Our Future.* London: Routledge.

Department for Education and Employment and Department of Social Security (2000) *New Deal for Disabled People to Be Extended Nationally.* www.dfee.gov.uk accessed 2003.

Department for Education and Employment (2001) *Towards Full Employment in Modern Society.* London: TSO.

Department of Health (2001) *Valuing People: A New Strategy for Learning Disability for the 21st Century.* London: TSO.

Department of Social Security (1998) *A New Contract for Welfare: Support for Disabled People.* London: TSO.

Disability Now (2002) *New Deal Probe.* September 2002.

Disability Rights Commission (2002*) Strategic Plan 2001–2004.* London: DRC.

Doyle, B. (1994) *New Directions Towards Disabled Workers Rights.* London: IER.

Finkelstein, V. (1980) *Attitudes and Disabled People.* New York, NY: World Rehabilitation Fund Monograph.

French, S. (1997) 'The attitudes of health professionals towards disabled people', in S. French (ed.), *Physiotherapy: A Psycho-Social Approach.* Oxford: Butterworth-Heinemann.

Gooding, C. (1995) *Blackstone's Guide to the Disability Discrimination Act 1995.* Oxford: Blackstone.

Graham, O., Jordan, P. and Lamb, B. (1990*) An Equal Chance or No Chance?* London: The Spastics Society.

Institute for Fiscal Studies (2000) *New Deal Evaluation Working Paper.* London: IFS.

Labour Market Trends (2001) *Disability and the Labour Market*: *Results from the Summer 2000 Labour Force Survey.* London: National Office for Statistics.

O'Bryan, A., Simons, K., Beyer, S. and Grove, B. (2000) *A Framework for Supported Employment.* York: Joseph Rowntree Foundation.

Oliver, M. (1991) *Social Work, Disabled People and Disabling Environments.* London: Jessica Kingsley.

Roulstone, A. (1998) *Enabling Technology: Disabled People, Work and New Technology.* Buckingham: Open University Press.

Roulstone, A. (2000) 'Disability, dependency and the new deal for disabled people', *Disability and Society*, 15 (3): 427–443.

Roulstone, A., Gradwell, L., Price, J. and Child, L. (2003) *Surviving and Thriving at Work: Disabled People's Employment Strategies.* York: Joseph Rowntree Foundation.

Royal National Institute for the Blind (2002) *Work Matters.* London: RNIB.

Ryan, J. and Thomas, F. (1987) *The Politics of Mental Handicap.* London: Free Association Books.

Sainsbury, R., Corden, A. and Thornton, P. (2002) *Evaluation of New Deal for Disabled People.* www.spru.ac.uk accessed 2003.

Social Trends (2002) *Social Trends 2002 Edition.* No.32. London: ONS.

Thornton, P. and Lunt, N. (1995) *Employment for Disabled People: Social Obligation or Individual Responsibility?* York: Social Policy Research Unit.

Tomlinson Report (1943) *Report of the Inter-Departmental Committee on the Rehabilitation and Resettlement of Disabled Persons.* London: HMSO.

Part IV
In Charge of Support and Help

30 The Crafting of Good Clients[1]
KEN DAVIS

Becoming disabled brings us into some odd relationships with people. One that most of us are familiar with is the doctor–patient relationship. When we're in it, we play a role, the sick role. We're expected to play it whether we're sick or not. Most of us know that it is in our best interests to play it – we've never been taught the lines, but we soon catch on to what we're supposed to say.

Soon enough, we're bumping into the disability 'professionals'. There are lots of them, they have different titles and work for different agencies, and often we get a bit confused as to who they are. They learn about disability by doing courses and reading books. Some of them are given diplomas for doing this, so they can then prove how expert they are in disability matters. These paper qualifications help them get jobs and make careers out of our needs.

Sometimes these 'professionals', such as occupational therapists and social workers, call us their 'clients'. Even people who help us to keep our homes clean, or people who work in day centres, also call us their 'clients'. This confuses us even more.

Most of us probably thought that becoming a client was a matter of personal choice. Like going to a solicitor, if we can afford it – or if we can't afford not to. Solicitors, accountants, consultants of all kinds, they too are regarded as professional people – but should we use their services, we have the choice, we decide. If they don't come up to scratch, we can complain to their professional body and seek redress. Or we take our custom elsewhere.

But the situation with disability 'professionals' is different. Well, yes, we can complain about their performance and we may or may not get redress via their employers. But if we decide to take our custom elsewhere – well, unless we're very well-heeled, it's best to forget it. To all intents and purposes, these denizens of the disability industry are the gatekeepers to the services we need. We either go through them, or do without. Take it or leave it.

No wonder many of us get confused. We grow up to expect that, if we become a client of some professional service or other, that it is a voluntary thing, something we do as a matter of choice. But, in terms of disability services, the choice available to us amounts to little more than Hobson's choice. The law gives local authorities the power to decide, and they, in turn, define the kind of workers they want. Various schools, universities and other training establishments churn out the 'professionals'. Together they decide what we get.

Whether we're happy or unhappy about this situation is merely academic. Going over the top of our heads is well-rooted and par for the course. Despite the growth of the disabled people's movement, these paper professionals still think it quite normal to sit down round the table and decide what's best for us. So it is quite natural that, along with all their other decisions, they should define the nature of their relationship to us.

Given that this is the case, it is interesting and instructive to reflect on why it is that these people have decided to call us their 'clients'. I mean, they know just as well as disabled people what is usually understood in terms of the professional–client relationship. So why have these workers been so keen to graft their ambitions on to terminology, the Latin root of which lies in patrician–plebian; master–slave; patron–dependant subservience?

One possibility is that they do actually see themselves as superior – as opposed to seeing us as inferior or helpless. Maybe they do think of themselves as being professional in the same, or similar, sense to that which is commonly understood. Or maybe they have forgotten that they are involved in a relationship, and that the consequence of setting themselves up as 'professionals' automatically casts us in the role of 'client'.

Hearing some of these people explaining the terminology can be equally interesting. For example, they may say that 'client' is a nice easy word, which avoids the anonymity of 'person' or 'disabled person'. Or that you can't use 'person with a physical impairment' all the time because the phrase is too long! Or that 'client' gives a disabled person some dignity, some status. That one is particularly pleasing, as it conveys the idea of equality wrapped up in more recent connotations which assign customer status to both patron and client. A very neat bit of professional sleight of speech, suggesting equivalence in choice and control, even though they and we know that the reality is very different.

When you look more closely at this apparently innocent use of words, it is easy to see that it is all part of a very carefully engineered process. Just how consistent it is with the prevailing relationship of disabled people to our able-bodied society comes clear when you look at some of the many questions which can be raised. For example, how did these so-called professionals come to get involved with us – and what is at stake for them in the way they define their relationship to us?

The first question begs many others – but those of us who are familiar with some of the history of the disabled people's movement will recognise that today's 'disability professionals' are on a career path which has been carefully and painstakingly carved out by generations of their predecessors. Our movement's long campaign to redefine disability has left little room for doubt that society has been constructed by able-bodied people in ways which serve and perpetuate their own interests. Yet these people have used our consequential marginalisation and dependence not as a starting point for developing with us a struggle for social change and equal opportunities, but as a handy and convenient fact to justify the development of all the inappropriate disability services with which we are now so familiar.

This disingenuous acceptance of the status quo, pregnant with career opportunities, is basic to those who feed on the effects of social problems, rather than engage in the struggle to deal with causes. It is a well-established form of parasitism, resting on bits of biblical dogma such as 'the poor always ye have with you' (John, xii.8). The updated version of the old Poor Law, which sustains most of today's welfare professionals, depends for its continuity on such counsels of despair. It has become, let's face it, a nice little earner.

Nowadays, these people have got it made. As a body, they have influenced government and secured their future so effectively that they and their agencies are written by name into the Statute Book. Their barrier-ridden, able-bodied world of inaccessible streets, buildings, transport and information – coupled with limited services of personal assistance – severely inhibited the extent of disabled people's own influence. Nevertheless, our movement grew rapidly, as a reaction against these oppressive social conditions. We have made some advances, but we have yet to eclipse the influence of these professional disability parasites. Although the day will inevitably come, we have yet to secure legislation appropriate to our real needs – as the limitations of the grudgingly conceded Disability Discrimination Act (1995) make abundantly clear.

At this juncture, our lives are still substantially in their hands. They still determine most decisions and their practical outcomes. The Community Care (Direct Payments) Act

(1996), again conceded only after years of hard campaigning by the disabled people's movement, offers some of us the bitter-sweet taste of professionally restricted freedom. The control that our professional guardians and gatekeepers hold over our access to it reflects the way in which the decision-making process has been carefully reinforced by ensuring that the climate of ideas that surrounds the making of disability policy is also under their influence. Which brings us back once more to the web of words they have spun to entrap us.

Effective control of the climate of ideas requires a thoughtful approach to the choice of words. This is why the selection of 'professional' and 'client' can never be dismissed by disabled people as irrelevant or innocuous. There is, to address the second question, much at stake for the disability industry, in terms of jobs and status, pay and conditions, and career opportunities, if they begin to lose their grip.

To obviate this, they need to contain the idea of their dominance and our dependence within a coherent philosophical framework designed to encapsulate, reinforce and sustain the interests of the industry. Such a framework needs to be flexible enough to move with the times, keep abreast of public sympathy, but ensure that their control over our lives remains essentially untouched. Thus, it has come to be that the disability 'professionals' and us, their 'clients', live within the carefully crafted, mechanical embrace of 'care'.

Today's generation of 'professionals' have packed this artificial ethos with endearing little catchphrases such as 'community care' 'caring professionals' and 'care managers'. The idea of 'care' has been carefully nurtured until it has become the hallmark of solid social acceptability, the key to political creditworthiness, and the disability industry's 'son of Star Wars' project, designed to shield their programmes of social control from criticism by rogue 'clients' and our supporters.

It is an increasing obligation on our movement to challenge both the mythology of care and the reality of their manipulation of disability policy and decision-making. Part of the process of gaining control over our lives involves us in resisting their attempts to box us in the pigeonhole of 'client' – and to expose their self-styled, self-seeking efforts to elevate their second-hand knowledge about disability into a 'profession'.

The disabled people's movement has already done much solid work in redefining disability and in creating the basis of a new hegemony of ideas which rests on direct experience of the problems we face in our daily lives. We have carried some workers in the disability industry along with us. In supporting our own active participation in, and control over, our own affairs, such people are giving us the right kind of help. However, for the majority of the 'professionals', despite their need to cling to power, their careful crafting of our dependence is disintegrating before their very eyes.

Note

1 This paper was first published in *Coalition*, September 1990, 5–9, and has been revised.

31 Modernising Services?[1]
VIC FINKELSTEIN

'Doctors are increasingly being demotivated by protocols, guidelines
and government targets that undermine their professional autonomy
and ability to deliver the right care to patients, BMA chairman Ian Bogle is
warning.'

Press Release (17.10.02). BMA News (19.10.02),
British Medical Association.

For my sins I have been afflicted with the challenge of living with the consequence of a
broken neck, being a refugee from apartheid South Africa, cancer of the throat and surviving as a single parent following my wife's terminal cancer. I have suffered the vagaries
of fashionable government policies whilst working as a clinical psychologist in the NHS,
made wide use of health and social services concerning disabled people and witnessed the
stultifying effect of the 'market' on disability studies in higher education where for over
20 years I taught practitioners working in the field. I have also been an active player in the
growth of the contemporary disabled people's movement in the UK.

I can claim, therefore, some familiarity with a variety of issues and services for disabled
people!

Meeting a 'need'

A few months ago I added to this list of qualifications by graduating from hospital following a stroke. Returning home set the scene for my latest experience of the modernised
social services approach to 'community care'.

The issue was: who should pay for a rail fitted adjacent to the toilet prior to my discharge from hospital? This was a dilemma because I was suddenly confronted with a
choice – discharge from hospital without delay provided I made arrangements for a rail to
be fitted immediately, or remain in hospital until social services could arrange the fitting.
I could not return home safely without the rail.

Enquiries revealed that the earliest the hospital could arrange a home visit with me to
assess the need for the rail, make a referral to the local social services, co-ordinate fitting
the rail and enable my hospital discharge, involved a delay of at least a week. This meant
staying in hospital longer than necessary. Alternatively, a friend and a relative could per-
sonally obtain the rail and a private builder could do the fitting immediately. I would need
to pay for the rail and a small amount to a builder. Despite the depressing prospect of trying to reclaim costs from social services, the advantage of immediate return to my family
really gave me no healthy alternative. I say 'healthy alternative' because, quite apart from

saving the health authority a week's hospital bill and the local authority costs of non-essential occupational therapy (OT) time, the inaccessible bed and toilet on the ward meant I was rapidly deteriorating into an unhealthy state of absolute dependency.

The rail was fitted and I returned home.

Correct procedures

The rail proved completely satisfactory and no 'care' professional ever raised any concerns about the fitting. Naturally it took a little while to begin the process of resuming an independent life. As soon as I was able, I contacted the pertinent social services OT to request payment for the rail. She was absolutely adamant that *no* payment could be made because I had the rail fitted without going through the *right* procedures. Bewildered by this apathetic response to an initiative, that undoubtedly saved the 'caring' professions time and money, I asked if I should now have the rail removed so that social services could fit a new one according to correct procedures? Any independent spirit I might have audaciously expressed was swiftly crushed. With the confidence of a modernised professional I was told in no uncertain terms that if I did that I would go on a waiting list for the replacement!

If I understand the rules correctly: I should have acted the total 'fool' and slavishly accepted a subservient patient role of dependency in order to obtain a service that everyone agrees I needed from the 'caring services', or be punished for taking an initiative in regaining *my own* independence. In practice, then, modernising social services appears to mean inhibiting intelligent patient self-management.

Being professional

As a former employee of the NHS, I was taught that being a 'professional' entails flexible decision making about the level of 'intervention' and appropriate allocation of resources. 'Professionals' used to have responsibility for their own actions; within guidelines but not entrapped by them. Sadly, in this, my most recent experience of 'care', such professional judgements were not allowed or attempted. Does the provision of 'care' have to be a technical process that is merely managed by an anonymous functionary? Technicians, of course, can exercise *some* judgement but, more importantly, this role does not preclude compassion, courtesy, sympathy or concern about one's state of health and so on – that is, an expression of 'care' in the most positive sense of the word. Regretfully, I have to say that in all my contact with social services on *this* matter I was never asked: 'How are you feeling?'; 'Was there anything else that I needed?'; 'How else may we help?'; and so on. This was definitely not a 'caring' experience!

In my need for a bathroom rail I cannot help but conclude that OT is not about being 'occupational', it is not about providing 'therapy', and it is also not about being a 'profession'. So what *is* OT for disabled people living in the community? In practice, a coherent philosophy for the 'profession' within the framework of 'community care' has proved elusive. This appears to have little to do with poor pay and conditions of work. Perhaps, then, it is no surprise that within the Professions Allied to Medicine (PAMs), OTs consistently bemoan their insufficient numbers and lack of status.

Professional autonomy

Is de-professionalising the statutory education, health and welfare services, while maintaining worker illusions about who and what they are, the hidden agenda behind modernising public services? Transforming professionals into rule-following technicians who rigidly follow a covert cost-cutting agenda appears to be an extraordinarily effective way of making changes that otherwise would be instinctively resisted.

My recent sample of the 'modernised' chiropody service seemed to capture the very essence of this de-professionalisation process.

Perhaps not surprisingly, having a cervical spinal injury resulting in tetraraplegia followed by a stroke, rendered toe and fingernail maintenance a little beyond even my ingenuity. My GP (General Practitioner) referred me to the chiropody service and a home visit was duly arranged. On the chiropodist's arrival I was obliged to feed information into one of the longest forms I have yet encountered. I, of course, complied by adopting the usual 'fool' role expected from a subservient disabled patient and answered all the questions without even joking that all the information was available in the referring GP's file. I even raised no objection when a sample of blood was taken from my finger *without any explanation*!

My toenails were expertly cut and filed and the chiropodist then began packing away her kit. I was surprised by this because it was obvious that attention to my fingernails was long overdue and it was clear that these were going to be neglected without a word of explanation. I was forced to change demeanour and asked whether she would cut my fingernails (thinking maybe their condition hadn't been noticed)? Somewhat flabbergasted by the fleeting reply – that she was not insured for attending to fingers – I then naïvely expected to be informed who *would* provide this service: perhaps in the 'modernised' services one technician dealt with toes and another with fingers? But she volunteered no further information.

I tried to regain my composure after this worrying problem was impassively dumped on me by the chiropodist. She proceeded to examine the blood sample test taken earlier. Adopting an all too obvious demeanour of sincerity, that she must have been taught to use in these situations, she announced that there was no indication of diabetes! This information was imparted as if she was giving an anxious patient good news. Now I was totally bewildered – the chiropodist could not provide necessary fingernail attention but she could give an unsolicited medical opinion (the mind boggles at the legality of this)! I was trying to make sense of this farcical situation as she closed up her equipment box and informed me that as I did not have diabetes she would not be coming again. She proceeded to fold some leaflets which she then tried to pass on to me without further ado, except to indicate that the leaflets contained information which I might like to have.

Sadly, I must confess that at this juncture I exploded. Why had she bothered coming at all – what was the point of handing me leaflets when the reason for obtaining a GP referral was because I could not manage on my own and I had no one to assist me; why insult my integrity by conducting a test, the result of which I (or my GP if disabled people cannot be trusted) could have informed her over the telephone; why service half my nails and then leave me with the urgent need intact? I calmed down and asked her where I might obtain the professional expertise that actually was needed, but in a terse response I gathered that even this information was not forthcoming.

I exploded again, declaring that she was behaving like an automated technician with no freedom to decide what was appropriate for me on the basis of her own professional assessment. This seemed to hit a raw spot and for the first time she seemed genuinely animated. She was a 'professional', she asserted, and had fully qualified.

So, sadly, this is what matters have come to; it is a fancy piece of paper that makes one into a professional. It's not *what you do* but *what certification you have* that is the defining feature of the modern health and social welfare worker.

As she left, I felt my long finger nails and wondered where other than in the health and social welfare service could workers actually maintain so many illusions about the quality of the work they were providing – can anyone imagine half a car service because the technician is insured for the front and not the back of a car … ?

The disabled professional

In all my contact with the community-based professions, following my stroke, extensive forms were completed, but in the end the factor that determined whether or not I was to receive a service was dependent upon predetermined criteria embedded in an assessment form. No personal clinical judgements were ever required.

Not that long ago literature aimed at the 'caring' professions was awash with concern about assessing the 'needs' of disabled people as a requirement for providing better services. Now this seems to have vanished. Then we were inundated with discussion about 'empowering' clients. This concern, too, seems to have disappeared. Now interventions appear to be unashamedly determined by bureaucratic rules. My access to physiotherapy was ruled 'out of court' because I do not have contractures and the rehabilitation team (occupational therapist, physiotherapist and social worker) could not provide any assistance because I did not require more than one service (the knock-on effect of obtaining my own rail in the bathroom).

'Able to make you able' was adopted as the slogan for the 1999 OT Day. As far as disabled people are concerned, I cannot think of a more apt expression of the way 'assessment of needs' and 'empowerment' have been abandoned in favour of verbiage. The point about 'disability', of course, is that the individual has a permanent impairment and consequently the central issue is *social and environmental restriction*: making the physical and social world accessible to us. Making people 'able' is a medical goal that, outside advances in medical science, not even that profession would so grandly prescribe for us. While we might understand why professionals with capabilities see the world in their own image, there must surely be some awareness that after such fundamental twentieth-century advances in *disability studies* it is meaningless, if not actually offensive, to confront disabled people with the phrase 'able to make you able'? This is one thing OTs *cannot* do.

But then unreal aims, confused objectives, increasingly restrictive practice and widespread illusion about what a 'professional' is, appear to be the hallmark of the modernised health and community care services. I cannot help feeling, when I contemplate the rigid restrictions imposed on 'caring' practice, that in this respect PAMs are very 'disabled'. External barriers imposed on the ability to control one's own decision-making touches the very essence of 'disability'. In my view, there is absolutely no chance of improving the quality of health and social service provision as long as the hidden agenda is to disable professional decision making.

New model services

Perhaps I can be so bold as to suggest that it might only be disabled people who could be 'able to make the Professions Allied to Medicine able'. The long history of inappropriate provision has convinced many disabled people that a change in service paradigm is needed. In brief, 'deliverer determined' community-based services need to become 'recipient requested'. This means developing support systems that are responsive to self-defined aspirations in the community.

There can be no permanent vacuum in the provision of services that disabled people really want and need. If these services are flawed or do not exist, there will be an inevitable drive for their creation. This process started some time ago when, for example, Ken and Maggie Davis, using their experience of alternatives to institutional 'care', went on with other disabled people in Derbyshire to found the first Centre for Integrated Living (CIL).

CILs are facilities created by disabled people to service such self-defined aspirations and, in my view, workers in these centres have the potential to become the foundation for an embryonic Profession Allied to the Community (PAC). Such a professionalisation process would replicate the steps taken by women when they spontaneously created a midwifery service. In my view, the most appropriate service provision is user initiated. User generated support services create opportunities for harmonising user and provider needs and at the very least avoid falling into the trap of seeing disabled people as incapable of defining their own support needs, especially within the community.

Allying service development with community-based aspirations requires substantially different worker attitudes and guidelines for providing professional assistance. Setting up CIL services has already involved a transformation in the way disabled people think about themselves and the public identity they wish to cultivate. In my view this has been the beginning of a journey in which a whole new cultural matrix of human relationships is waiting to be discovered. If PAMs do not wish to become increasingly alienated from the communities they are supposed to serve, I can only suggest they join disabled people in their instinctive opposition to 'care' and make their own unique contribution to the new PAC service structures that, one way or another, *will* emerge over a period of time. Growing health and welfare service user self-confidence inevitably means there is less and less willingness to participate in training and academic courses that feed the 'care' débâcle.

Conclusion

In the 'modernised' public services, health and welfare practitioners increasingly seem to equate professional decision making with technical duties reliant upon rule-following consistency. The decline in 'professionalism', while maintaining an illusion of expertise in decision making in the health and community care services, is surely one of the wonders of our era. 'How have the Professions Allied to Medicine allowed this to happen?' was a question that repeatedly troubled me when I had to come to terms with a range of sympathetic and apathetic professionals on returning home from hospital after my stroke.

One answer seems to be that academic and training courses have been very effective in diverting practitioner skills onto the identification of an itinerary of criteria for intervention (expertise in form-filling), rather than the art of handling the complexities of flexible clinical decision making. Cultivating worker satisfaction in 'correct' form-filling appears to have become an essential qualification for the professional 'care' worker, and academic institutions are unashamedly competing in this lucrative market. It seems curious, however, that there is so little discussion about form-filling skills being merely a rehearsal for technical proficiency in feeding computer compliant data into computers, *which will then decide resource allocation*. Far from enhancing the status of the 'caring' professions, compliance with the de-skilling practice inherent in 'Modernising Social Services', will eventually completely destroy any vestige of 'professionalism', in the very best sense of this word.

While PAMs and 'community care' academic courses for practitioners in the health and social services continue to flounder in an intellectually bankrupt 'care' philosophy, developing a PAC could bring into production a virgin field for fertilising, cultivating and reaping user *and* service provider aspirations. Such an alliance has the potential to reintroduce innovation, initiative, excitement and personal reward in delivering the community based support that disabled people want.

Community care services for disabled people based on the assessment of need and managed by PAMs demean both workers and users. I believe they will have to be replaced by services based on the identification of aspirations managed by PACs in an alliance of workers and users.

The de-skilling of doctors who are 'increasingly ... demotivated by protocols, guidelines and government targets that undermine ... professional autonomy ...' (Press Release, BMA News) is only the last stage in a long process of disabling the health and welfare professions. It is in this respect that professional service providers and disabled service users should find they are increasingly using the same language to address the problems that they face!

Note

1 This paper is an edited version of 'Professions Allied to the Community', *Coalition*, March 2000, Greater Manchester Coalition of Disabled People.

32

Disabled Health and Caring Professionals: The Experiences of Visually Impaired Physiotherapists
SALLY FRENCH

Disabled people are widely discriminated against in most types of employment (Burchardt, 2000), which makes it likely that they will find entry to employment of professional status, such as the health and caring professions, particularly difficult. Although it might be considered that health and caring professionals would be knowledgeable and understanding regarding disabled people, there is considerable evidence to suggest that this is not the case (Abberley, 1995). Baron et al., talking of social workers, state:

> Most of the practice teachers admitted they had given little forethought on the suitability of their working environment to disabled colleagues and only did so when asked to take on a disabled student. (1996: 367)

Most of the overt justification for the exclusion of disabled people from the health and caring professions is in terms of the disabled people themselves: their presumed inability to cope, the adverse effect they may have on patients and clients, and the assumption of proneness to accidents (French, 2001). Allen and Birse state that:

> Health care professionals share the values and expectations of their society and show the same reactions that unstigmatised individuals have towards those with differences. (1991: 150)

Negative attitudes are sometimes rationalised and disguised as concern, emphasising that disabled people may damage themselves, or others, by undertaking such demanding work. Alan Dudley, a blind social worker, states:

> 'There were concerns about situations they were putting me in, whether there were dangers to me and whether I was at risk. There were concerns about how I perceive situations when I have no sight ... Practical things like would I be able to get to the houses ... Situations like, how would I deal with it if I got threatened or even attacked, and would they somehow be to blame for that?' (French et al., 1997)

Gething (1993) believes that the views of health and caring professionals may be even more negative than those of the general public, due to the unequal relationship they have with disabled people and the fact that they come into contact only when disabled people are deemed to need their help. It also seems likely that the acceptance of more than a few disabled professionals would seriously challenge the traditional professional/client relationship where the professional is considered to be the expert and occupies a dominant position over the client. Carole Pound, a disabled speech and language therapist, talks of the 'divided identity' involved in being a disabled health professional:

I am struggling to interact with you simultaneously as Carole the Speechie and Carole the 'patient' ... This divided identity is a fascinating issue. Two selves so clearly related and yet so carefully circumscribed and kept distinct. It puzzles me now how little I reflected on the unnatural disengagement of these two protagonists. (2004)

The rest of this chapter will examine a study that I undertook of the working lives of 45 visually impaired physiotherapists which was based on semi-structured interviews (French, 2001). The aim of the study was to discover their experiences of employment, particularly within the NHS.

Visually impaired people have been trained as physiotherapists in sizeable numbers over the course of the twentieth century. There are currently about 250 visually impaired physiotherapists practicing in Britain, including many who are totally blind. Physiotherapy is not a profession that would immediately spring to mind as being suitable for visually impaired people. This is because it requires competent mobility around busy wards, considerable paperwork and the use of sophisticated electro-medical equipment. In recent years, other potential difficulties have arisen, including an increase in community work which involves travel and varying environments.

Visually impaired people are trained as physiotherapists because of an historical accident. Physiotherapy evolved from massage which blind people traditionally practised. Up until 1916 they were trained in small numbers in ordinary schools of massage, but with the First World War, and the large number of blinded servicemen, a special school of massage was opened by the Royal National Institute for the Blind (RNIB) in London. This segregated arrangement lasted until 1995. Visually impaired people are now integrated into mainstream physiotherapy courses within universities.

The acceptance of visually impaired people in the physiotherapy profession has not been straightforward and various crises have arisen. There was, for example, much prejudice against visually impaired physiotherapists when the NHS was introduced, as the ex-principal of the RNIB college explained:

'I had to do a lot of reassuring that the chap wasn't going to fall over as soon as he got into the department and that he wouldn't be a liability and knock everything off the trolleys – all those sorts of daft things'. (French, 2001: 62)

New electrical treatments also posed a threat to the existence of visually impaired physiotherapists unless 'special' adaptations were devised. Treatment with ultraviolet light, for example, was made possible by the invention of the erythemameter, which indicates the redness of the skin by means of audible signals. Jenkins (1957) describes how a group of blind students were made to demonstrate the use of this device to a panel of experts appointed by the Chartered Society of Physiotherapy.

In June 1954, a group of blind students gave a demonstration using the erythemameter, to a panel of experts appointed by the Chartered Society of Physiotherapy. The results obtained by the instrument were found to be parallel with visual impression. In 1955 a further demonstration was given; this time with the technique of application of ultra-violet irradiation. The standard of work was considered very satisfactory. (1957: 79)

A further crisis arose in 1971 following an inspection of the RNIB college by the Chartered Society of Physiotherapy. In the inspection report it states:

> A high proportion of the students appear to be studying physiotherapy from Hobson's choice rather than a burning desire to do so. A number of the students commented that they wanted a job working with people and that this seemed to be the only one available. The normal interest of physiotherapy students in the broader medical field was not apparent ... the visitors felt most strongly that the whole question of training blind persons as physiotherapists should be reconsidered. (CSP, 1971)

It appears that the visually impaired students were devalued and barely tolerated by the professional body because of their lack of employment opportunities.

The visually impaired physiotherapists I interviewed had encountered many barriers. Many people found the environment of hospital wards difficult. Alice explained:

> 'Definitely it's easier to work in the out-patient department than struggle round the wards trying to find the patients ... I haven't got enough sight to recognise a patient by any sort of facial feature unless I've seen them for a great many days ... And I suppose the next difficult aspect was the anxiety about how many bottles, tubes and drips were likely to be attached to the patient. I would go very slowly and cautiously so as never to knock anything over, and luckily I never did, but that was an anxiety. And of course if the lighting wasn't very good then that added to all the problems.' (French, 2001: 129–30)

Some of the physiotherapists, however, mentioned the help provided by patients on the ward. Julia said:

> 'Well, I didn't need to ask for help in the wards I worked on every day because once the patients knew who you were they couldn't wait to shout "Stop, there's a table!" You'd say "Where's Mr Brown?" and they'd say "Hang on, I'll go and look for him." The patients were my first ally.' (2001: 135)

This type of help has dwindled in recent years as there is now a far higher turnover of patients, and people with minor illnesses are less likely to be admitted to hospital than they were in the past.

Another barrier, which was highlighted by Malcolm, related to modern electro-therapy equipment:

> 'There's some stuff around nowadays that is not easy to use. I bung bits of "high-mark" [a tactile marking substance] on, which does work on the whole. One interferential machine we've got is not easy to use. In fact as a totally blind person, or a non-display reading person, you wouldn't be able to use it. But there is an older one that I can use ... You can still find stuff but you have to look around.' (2001: 120)

However, by virtue of their professional autonomy, some of the physiotherapists successfully side-stepped the issue of inaccessible equipment. John explained:

'I'm not an electrotherapy person ... There's an ultra-sound/interferential combined unit which I can't use ... I don't know whether it's impossible to use it as a blind person but because I'm very disenchanted with ultra-sound I've no great desire to learn how to use it. And with lasers, well reading all the research, it's very doubtful whether it's of any benefit whatsoever ... Equipment hasn't really been an issue.' (2001: 121)

Paperwork created a barrier for the majority of the physiotherapists. Pam said:

'I do the minimum ... I have to get so close to the paper really. The older you get the more tension and back ache and neck ache you get leaning forward in awkward positions ... I don't always record what I'm doing. If I've just taken someone for a little walk down the ward I might not log that ... We have to record what we do though or they might think 'You're not working enough, we don't need you.' (2001: 122)

Others had found modern technology extremely helpful with regard to paperwork. Terry, who uses print enhancement software, said:

'My world changed the day I got a computer ... I used to use a typewriter and then I applied to get a computer from the *Access to Work* scheme and I got given some training and, believe me, it's the best thing that ever happened to me ... I flash it all up on the screen, all my patients' notes ... large as I want. I can also print things out in large print so I can read it back.' (2001: 124–5)

A further barrier that many of the physiotherapists mentioned was meetings. Sharron said:

'I've worked in some very difficult situations with some very autocratic doctors and at team meetings it's a problem of picking up their non-verbal communication, when they're getting angry and things. To a certain extent it affected my ability to handle difficult situations, you know, knowing when it might be best to say nothing.' (2001: 137)

Transport posed another barrier, especially with the increase in community work. Terry explained:

'It means I have to go everywhere by bus. The problem is I have to deliver frames, so I sometimes have to get on a bus with a walking frame ... I try and avoid it when the kids are going to school ... or in the rush hour ... I've managed it so far.' (2001: 118)

Most of the physiotherapists found that work-related education was inaccessible to them. Sarah felt that this adversely affected the way colleagues perceived her:

'One course I went on recently, the chap went through it at such a rate of knots that I did miss out quite a bit. As a senior you are expected to do your part in the teaching and if you say, "I don't feel happy to teach that because I didn't grasp it all" it reflects back on you. You're the one that looks inadequate. People have never understood.' (2001: 96)

The attitudes and behaviour of colleagues were mixed and could either create barriers or help to dismantle them. Pam spoke of a lack of understanding of visual impairment among her colleagues:

> 'I'm a registered blind person but they haven't got a clue ... If I stay in one building I'm fine, it's only when I go over to G ... that I get really lost ... and one of the physios says, "So you're not talking to me today!" because I've walked right past them ... and I've worked with them for years; oh dear! ... I just say "I didn't see you" but they don't seem to learn.' (2001: 140)

John, on the other hand, had found colleagues very helpful:

> 'I'm lucky that the helpers, and all the staff generally, help with all the extra bits of paper that are around. The truth of the matter is that, as a blind person, you could get involved in form filling by putting it on the computer, but what the hell's the point because it's going to take an awful lot of time.' (2001: 128)

The different experiences of Pam and John may reflect the ambiguity of partial sight when compared with total blindness.

The way that visually impaired physiotherapists are treated by different hospital trusts was also apparent. This is illustrated in the quotations below from two physiotherapy managers:

> 'I was relocated to another hospital which was extremely difficult for me to get to from home. It required catching three buses. So I actually had to take out a grievance with the Trust about it.' (Hilary)

(2001: 118)

> 'The Trust has put at my disposal a car which I use for business mileage ... it does mean that if I have to go to say ... well, I had to go to Leeds to sit on the NHS Equal Opportunities Working Party and because it is such a nightmare to get to Leeds on the train ... the assistant actually drives me there.' (Stephen)

(2001: 120)

A wide variety of strategies were used by the physiotherapists to cope with their work, some of which were damaging to themselves. Sarah spoke of the need to work long hours:

> 'The whole job is pressurised, you never go home at night forgetting about it ... There's always something and I just find that it takes over my whole life and I do nothing else but physio and of course things take longer because you can't see ... I work considerably more hours, just to do a reasonable job.' (2001: 127)

Other physiotherapists spoke of the need to develop cognitive strategies:

> 'I didn't like the weekends because you had to go on to wards that you weren't familiar with and you had to rely so much on your echo location [the detection of objects through sound] for getting around ... The mental exhaustion of concentration in unfamiliar surroundings is quite tiresome.' (John)

(2001: 129)

'I use my memory much, much more ... people are always saying "How can you remember all the telephone numbers?" Well, it's obvious why you do that when you are visually impaired, because it takes you such a long time to look them up.' (Hilary)

(2001: 161)

Most of the physiotherapists used strategies of openness and assertion to get the help they needed:

'I tell anybody, even if somebody comes for an informal visit and I'm showing them the hospital, I tell them because I find it so much easier. ... Sometimes people say "Have you forgotten your glasses today?" and I find it simpler to say "Well actually I'm registered blind and I use a white stick to walk about outside." I put it as bluntly as that.' (Charlotte)

(2001: 142–143)

'I tend to ask more and defend myself a bit more than I used to. I'm more open than I used to be. Older and more experienced is probably the reason. You tend to say "Hey look, can this be adapted, can this be adjusted?" ... Before I might have "put up" and "shut up".' (Malcolm)

(2001: 143)

For a few of the physiotherapists, attempts to minimise disability and compensate for it were prominent coping strategies. Sarah explained:

'I try to cover it up [disability] as much as possible. I ask to work in the same cubicle so that I'm not stumbling over things all the time ... I try to put on as normal a front as possible ... and that's a tremendous strain. My sick record is super but, you know, it's partly because you never want to give people cause to say "Oh dear, we've got problems with her in more ways than one." ... I'm determined that nobody will ever say "You're not doing that adequately."' (2001: 141)

Overall, the physiotherapists felt that work had become more difficult despite the introduction of equal opportunity policies and the Disability Discrimination Act.

Although there was considerable agreement among the physiotherapists with regard to barriers and coping strategies, it was also clear from the research that barriers are perceived, appraised, experienced and acted upon differently. Both contextual factors (for example, position in the hierarchy) and individual factors (confidence and assertion) can modify barriers and how they are dealt with.

The study indicates that barrier removal is very complex. Despite sophisticated computer equipment, for example, most of the physiotherapists felt that it took them considerably more time to successfully hold down their jobs. Reliance on cognitive strategies was said to be exhausting and most people were motivated to change the environment rather than attempt to change themselves.

The physiotherapists were prepared to cope with difficult barriers in order to satisfy their own goals and aspirations. People did not necessarily work in areas where lack of sight was less of a problem, although some people did go into private practice in order to create their own environment. Reasons such as 'believing in the NHS', 'not being a businessperson' and 'needing the stimulation of colleagues' dissuaded many of the physiotherapists from private practice. Julia, a totally blind physiotherapist, for example, spoke enthusiastically of community work since the institution for people with learning difficulties where she worked had closed.

Conclusion

This research provided a detailed exploration of the ways in which visually impaired physiotherapists cope with their work, entirely from their own perspective. Although the sample was very specific, most of the findings can be related to other visually impaired employees and disabled employees generally. It highlights the complexity of barrier removal and the creativity of disabled people who contend with barriers at work on a daily basis.

References

Abberley, P. (1995) 'Disabling ideology in health and welfare – the case of occupational therapy', *Disability and Society*, 10 (2): 221–32.

Allen, M. and Birse, E. (1991) 'Stigma and blindness', *Journal of Ophthalmic Nursing and Technology*, 10 (4): 147–51.

Baron, S., Phillips, R. and Stalker, K. (1996) 'Barriers to training for disabled social work students', *Disability and Society*, 11 (3): 361–77.

Burchardt, T. (2000) *Enduring Economic Exclusion: Disabled People, Income and Work*. York: Joseph Rowntree Foundation.

Chartered Society of Physiotherapy (1971) *Inspectors' Report on the Royal National Institute for the Blind School of Physiotherapy*. 13 January. London.

French, S. (2001) *Disabled People and Employment: A Study of the Working Lives of Visually Impaired Physiotherapists*. Aldershot: Ashgate.

French S., Gillman, M. and Swain, J. (1997) *Working with Visually Disabled People: Bridging Theory and Practice*. Birmingham: Venture.

Gething, L. (1993) 'Attitudes towards people with disabilities of physiotherapists and members of the general public', *Australian Journal of Physiotherapy*, 39 (4): 291–96.

Jenkins, J. (1957) 'Physiotherapy: the biggest professional outlet for the blind in Britain', *New Beacon*, 51 (482): 76–9.

Pound, C. (2004) 'Dare to be different: the person and the practice', in S. Byng and J. Duchan (eds), *Challenging Therapies*. London: Taylor and Francis.

33 Direct Payments
FRANCES HASLER

There is little doubt that direct payments are a revolutionary new way of providing the type of health and social support traditionally provided by family, friends and/or professionals to disabled people. They are revolutionary because unlike other forms of support, which are generally controlled by someone else, they give the disabled person an opportunity to control the services used. This is because direct payments are, quite simply, cash payments made directly to an individual by local authority social service departments as an alternative to, or in addition to, other services provided by that department. They mean that people who use, or could use, social services support have the option of receiving funding to organise their own support instead of using 'traditional' social services, such as home care or day centres.

Background – history of direct payments

The first 'direct payments' in the UK were made to a small group of disabled people in Hampshire in the early 1980s. At the time, the options available to disabled people with high support needs were either unpaid care by family or residential care. Some volunteer helper schemes were being developed, but these were not widespread. The group, who met while living in a Cheshire Home, wanted an alternative to institutional care; they wanted the opportunity for 'independent living'. They persuaded the local authorities that were sponsoring them to live in the institution to pay an equivalent amount direct to them, to enable them to employ people to assist them in flats or houses in the community (HCIL, 1985; see also Chapter 26).

Throughout the 1980s direct payments schemes, often referred to as 'independent living' schemes, developed slowly and only operated in a limited number of areas in the country. Most local authorities were not keen to take on independent living schemes because they either considered them too risky or were wary of handing over all the control to disabled people. Direct payments schemes represented for the first time a shift of power to disabled people. A feature of the early direct payments options was that they were usually paid via a third party – a voluntary organisation – so that the authority was not giving cash direct to individuals. Social services for disabled people were based on legislation dating back to the 1940s; this stipulated that authorities were not allowed to make payments in lieu of services (Glasby and Littlechild, 2002). Although these third-party schemes were mainly a response to legal concerns about direct payments, they proved to be a useful resource for disabled people, providing advice about recruiting and managing assistants.

Direct payments in the UK mirrored the system of paying for residential care; namely, they combined money from social services authorities with whatever social security benefits were due to that person. A little known but crucial social security benefit at that time was the domestic care allowance, which was being used by many of the independent living pioneers. When the benefits system was changed in 1986, the Government decided to withdraw the domestic care allowance. The disabled people's movement organised a successful campaign to challenge this change of policy. The Government announced in 1987 that it would bring about the introduction of a new Independent Living Fund (ILF) that would replace the previous allowance. The ILF swiftly grew in popularity, gaining many thousands of users (Kestenbaum, 1995). But one element of the ILF system was problematic; namely, as a payment system originating in the social security system, it was means tested. Users could neither work nor save without losing most or all of their ILF.

Moreover, the concept of direct payments was not confined to the UK. Across Europe, disabled people were developing similar schemes. In 1989, a European Network for Independent Living (ENIL) was set up at a conference in Strasbourg. This conference resolved to fight for a legal right to direct payments for independent living (ENIL, 1989).

In the UK, given the piecemeal and slow development of local authority direct payments schemes and the financial limits of the ILF, getting new legislation to underpin a right to direct payments became a key goal. The campaign was led by the British Council of Disabled People's (BCODP) Independent Living Committee. They backed up their campaign with research commissioned from the Policy Studies Institute (Zarb and Nadash, 1994) that demonstrated that payments were both more cost efficient than equivalent services and provided more user satisfaction. They gained good support from MPs and professional bodies, notably the Association of Directors of Social Services, and in 1996 the Community Care (Direct Payments) Act became law.

Why Direct Payments matter

Direct payments were conceived as a way of achieving equality for disabled people. As one early user put it:

> 'Our dream was that disabled people would be enabled to fulfil their roles in terms of taking the opportunities society offers and meeting the responsibilities society requires.' (Mason, 1998: unpaged)

The inspiration for direct payments in the UK had come from the USA – one of the BCODP Committee had met people from the Berkeley Center for Independent Living, which pioneered the use of paid support workers or personal assistants (PAs) in the USA. But although the UK's disability movement drew inspiration from the USA, it had developed a home-grown philosophical and political framework known as the 'social model of disability'. As we have seen in Chapter 26, the social model underpinned the development of all organisations of disabled people, including the UK's network of Centres for Independent Living (CILs), during the 1980s and 1990s. The use of PAs was identified as a 'basic need' in order to enable disabled people to achieve independent living. Direct payments were seen as the best way of paying for PAs because they give the maximum amount of choice and control to the disabled individual.

Wherever in the world direct payments were being discussed, it was always within the context of disabled people's struggles for rights. The ENIL conference, mentioned above, was explicit about this. The Strasbourg Resolution states:

> We firmly uphold our basic human right to full and equal participation in society as enshrined in the UN Universal Declaration of Human Rights (extended to include disabled people in 1985) and consider that a key prerequisite to this civil right is through Independent Living and the provision of support services such as personal assistance services for those who need them. (ENIL, 1989: unpaged)

For individual users, direct payments matter because they give them choice and control. They can arrange services from a person they choose, at times they choose, for assistance delivered in a way they control. Disabled people interviewed about the benefits of direct payments say things like, 'Its given me my life back' or 'I've got my freedom' (see Zarb and Nadash, 1994). By clear implication, using conventional services takes over your life and restricts your freedom. Direct payments users get more than a choice of bedtimes. The flexibility offered by the system allows people to work, to travel, to be active parents, in short to do the range of things that non-disabled people expect to do. The denial of opportunity to do these things is a denial of basic freedoms.

How direct payments work

Although direct payments arose from a disability rights perspective, in legislative terms they fit within community care law. This has been a constraint on how they have developed.

The Community Care (Direct Payments) Act came into force in 1997. It covered disabled people aged 18 to 65, across the UK. In England, it was amended two years later to allow payments to older people. It was supplemented in 2000 by the Carers and Disabled Children Act, which enabled payments to carers and to 16 and 17-year-olds. Then in 2002, the Health and Social Care Act extended the scope yet further and made it mandatory for local authorities to offer a direct payments scheme. Similar changes have taken place in the other countries of the UK, but devolution means that some details of the law are different, particularly in Scotland (Glasby and Littlechild, 2002).

At present, most adults eligible for community care services can choose to take all or part of the service in the form of payment. There are some exceptions, covering people receiving compulsory care under mental health or criminal justice measures. In addition, parents of disabled children eligible for support under the Children Act can be offered payments instead of services. Carers can also opt for direct payments in lieu of a service if they so choose. However, few carers get services in their own right so, hitherto, take-up among this group has been limited.

Direct payments should not be imposed on a person – they must be 'willing' to have them. And because they are aimed at enabling independent living, users must be able to 'manage' the payment, either alone or with assistance. These criteria, which are written into the legislation, have caused some difficulties in implementation.

The amount paid varies from one person to another, and from one local authority to another, but is always based on an individual assessment of need. The usual method is to set an hourly rate which will cover the full cost of employing an assistant, including holiday pay, training and so on. But this is not the only way of calculating a payment and authorities are using diverse ways of costing a direct payments 'package'. Once agreed, the money can be used to organise support from people or services chosen by the user.

Direct Payments are intended to support independent living, so they cannot be used to pay for permanent residential accommodation. Nor are they intended to replace existing support networks within families or communities and, therefore, cannot usually be used to pay close relatives or anyone living in the same household as the user.

Users are expected to open a separate bank account to hold their direct payments, and to account for their use. Payments are not taken into account when assessing income for social security benefits and are not liable to income tax. The following fictitious example shows how direct payments are used.

Example

Gilly is a single parent, a wheelchair user. She is assessed as needing four hours help each day. To cover this she gets £210 per week. She employs a personal assistant to visit every morning for two hours and every evening for one hour. The remaining hours she uses to buy longer periods of help as and when she needs them; for example, when she was ill, or to take her daughter to a theme park. She has to budget the money involved, to allow for replacement workers when her regular assistants go on holiday, and to cover other costs such as advertising for new staff. So although she gets £7.50 per hour, the amount she can pay her workers is much less than this. Gilly's assistants are vetted by the Criminal Records Bureau, as they will be helping her look after her child.

Support services

As noted above, early 'third-party' direct payments schemes offered support and advice to disabled people in addition to processing their payments. When direct payments became established, disabled people worked to set up support organisations in every locality, so that users would have a ready source of information and advice on getting and using direct payments. The National Centre for Independent Living (NCIL) was set up with funds from the Department of Health (DoH) to assist the implementation of direct payments. In fact, the spread of support organisations was patchy, with users in the South having a far greater chance of finding a local scheme. Support schemes offer a range of services, covering information on using direct payments, advice and training on recruitment and management of workers, and peer support from other users. Many offer a payroll scheme, to calculate wages and tax due. Some offer a referral system for potential assistants or basic training for assistants (Hasler et al., 1998).

Inclusion

Direct payments were initially developed around the needs of people with a physical impairment. Their translation to a wider disability community has necessitated some rethinking about how they can or should be used. Probably the most debated issue has been the idea of 'able to manage'. Some early direct payments schemes specified that users must take responsibility for every aspect of managing their payments. They were anxious to break a culture of dependency, where other people made choices on behalf of disabled people. But this approach contains inherent contradictions. Most problematically, it creates indirect discrimination against some disabled people. Independent living organisations were quick to recognise that they needed flexible models of independent living:

> Another challenge is ensuring that enabling choice and control, through direct payment schemes, cannot be exclusively for one impairment group or age group in our society. What is good for one must be available to all. We need to develop our organisations and systems to enable *all* disabled people to have the opportunity of independence. (Mason, 1999: unpaged)

This flexibility has not been adopted by all local authorities. Stereotyped ideas about the capacity of mental health service users or people with learning difficulties to manage their own support have limited the spread of direct payments to these user groups. At the end of 2001, DoH monitoring showed that over 5,000 people in England were using direct payments, but that fewer than 500 of them were people with learning difficulties and an even smaller number were mental health service users.

The picture was very varied across the country, with some authorities using innovative support schemes to enable all sorts of users to take up direct payments, and other authorities still limiting their payments schemes to a tiny handful of users. The government's response was to make direct payments mandatory, and in 2003 new guidance was issued, with the aim of making payments available to all:

> The presumption should be that a person will (with assistance if necessary) be able to manage direct payments unless the council has compelling reasons to conclude that they are not. (Department of Health, 2003)

Black users have been under-represented in many direct payments schemes. The reasons for this are complex, relating to lack of appropriate information and barriers to accessing community care services in general. In addition, research has identified doubts about the concept of 'independent living' in some communities where interdependency in the family is the cultural norm. The prohibition on employing relatives has been a barrier to some people taking up payments. In 2002, the DoH funded research into the take-up of direct payments by black people.

Older people were initially excluded from direct payments but, although they have been eligible since 1999, take-up has been small. Part of the reason is a greater concern about the safety of employing people directly. A bigger part is probably the rationing of services to older people, meaning that the packages of care they are offered are often very small. Employing people to visit for half an hour at a time is not easy. In addition, the current regime for charging for services in England is a deterrent, as users may end up contributing the bulk of the cost themselves. In Scotland, where personal care is now free, the numbers of older people using direct payments has risen.

Workers

One of the persistent criticisms of direct payments has been that they are unfair to workers. Claire Ungerson asserted that they exploit low paid women workers, describing the employment market for personal assistants as a 'flea market' (Ungerson, 1999). Others have pointed out that low pay is directly linked to low rates of direct payments. Few studies have looked directly at the experience of personal assistants, although Glendinning et al. (2000) did ask them about doing health-related tasks.

Developments

Direct payments initially developed slowly. The 1996 Act was a cautious one, and local authorities were often sceptical or nervous about implementing it. However, since 1999 they have had strong support from government, and have been extended to more and more user groups. Government has also recognised that support schemes need to be developed if direct payments are to become a mainstream option. Governments in England and Scotland have invested large sums in the voluntary sector to support the development of direct payments support schemes.

Newer user groups present a new set of questions about how payments could or should work.

New models of support

The new guidance on direct payments suggests that assistance with managing the payments can be extensive:

> Direct payments may also be provided through someone with power of attorney for the user or a user-controlled trust, for example in certain cases where the user has a cognitive impairment or mental health problem. (Department of Health, 2003)

This is a long way from the early days when some schemes insisted that users manage every aspect of employment, to guard against perpetuating dependency.

Now most users opt for specialised help with some aspects of management, such as payroll. Increasingly, users are asking support schemes to provide training for their PAs, in order to achieve the quality of service they require. But it remains important to these users that they specify the nature of the training received, and that CILs, controlled by disabled people, are delivering the training.

In two decades, direct payments have moved from being a small-scale, user-led solution to unmet support needs, to being a central part of community care policy. As they continue to develop, they both require and allow creativity in the way that support is organised. They offer all service users what those earlier pioneers sought:

> ... the freedom to make decisions about your own life and to participate fully in your community. (Evans, 1996: unpaged)

References

Department of Health (2003) *Direct Payment Guidance*. London: Department of Health.

ENIL (1989) 'Strasbourg Resolution', European Conference on Personal Assistance Services for Disabled People, 12–14 April, Strasbourg. (Available on www.leeds.ac.uk/disability-studies/archiveuk/index.)

Evans, J. (1996) 'Direct payments in the UK'. Paper presented at European Network on Independent Living Conference, Stockholm: National Institute for Independent Living, June.

Glasby, J. and Littlechild, R. (2002) *Social Work and Direct Payments*. Bristol: The Policy Press.

Glendinning, K., Rummery, S., Halliwell, S. and Jacobs, S. (2000) *Buying Independence: Using direct payments to purchase integrated health and social services*. Bristol: The Policy Press.

Hasler, F., Campbell, J. and Zarb, J. (1998) *Direct Routes to Independence*. London: Policy Studies Institute.

HCIL (1985) *Project 81: One Step On, Hampshire*. Hampshire Centre for Independent Living. (Available on www.leeds.ac.uk/disability-studies/archiveuk/index.)

Kestenbaum, A. (1995) *Independent Living: A Review of Findings and Experience*. York: Joseph Rowntree Foundation.

Mason, P. (1999) 'Facing our own futures'. Paper presented at Facing Our Futures Conference, Southampton: National Centre for Independent Living, July.

Ungerson, C. (1999) 'Personal assistants and disabled people: an examination of a hybrid form of work and care', *Work, Employment and Society*, 13 (4).

Zarb, G. and Nadash, P. (1994) *Cashing in on Independence*. Derby: The British Council of Organisations of Disabled People. (Available on www.leeds.ac.uk/disability-studies/archiveuk/index.)

34 Disability, Care and Controlling Services
FRANCES HASLER

Naming the problem

Disabled people have long grappled with the contradiction of their desire to lead independent, autonomous lives and their reliance on a state system of welfare that is based on their perceived lack of autonomy, their dependence.

As long ago as 1966, Paul Hunt was pointing out the gap between social responses to disability and disabled people's own sense of self.

> I think the distinguishing mark of disabled people's special position is that they tend to 'challenge' in their relations with ordinary society. This challenge takes five main forms: as unfortunate, useless, different, oppressed and sick.
>
> Severely disabled people are generally considered to have been unlucky, to be deprived and poor, to lead cramped lives. We do not enjoy many of the 'goods' that people in our society are accustomed to ...
>
> But set over against this common-sense attitude is another fact, a strange one. In my experience even the most severely disabled people retain an ineradicable conviction that they are still fully human in all that is ultimately necessary.
>
> (Hunt, 1966:)

Numerous commentators since have explored this problem:

> One of the most important causes of our second class citizenship is the way society looks at persons with disabilities. There is a tendency to label people who are different as 'sick'. Sick people do not have to work and are exempted from the normal duties of life. As long as we are considered sick by the general public, there will be little understanding, for example, why we need to use regular public transportation, why we demand real jobs and not just therapy. (Ratzka, 1992:)

Brisenden described 'an ideology of independence', the idea that disabled people who need assistance from another person are 'dependent'. The idea is based on a view of independence being indissoluble from bodily autonomy and mental competence:

> It teaches that unless we can do everything for ourselves, we cannot take our place in society. We must be able to cook, wash, dress ourselves, make the bed, write, speak and so forth before we can become proper people, before we are independent. (Brisenden, 1989:)

Framing the debate

The 1980s saw a number of parallel developments in social care. From the disabled people's movement came the idea of independent living. At the same time, the concept of rights for 'carers' was growing. The official policy of care in the community, which meant closing long-stay mental hospitals, was accepted as the future for most people with learning disability or long-term mental health problems.

The interests of disabled people, carers and former hospital residents should have been overlapping. All three groups have an interest in state sponsorship of community-based support. Differences in the way each group framed their own needs, however, and in the ways care professionals conceptualised these needs meant that a coalescence of aims was rare.

Caring

Brisenden wrote one of the most memorable criticisms of being forced to rely on a family member for assistance:

> It exploits both the carer and the person receiving care. It ruins relationships between people and results in thwarted life opportunities on both sides of the caring equation. (Brisenden, 1989:)

This view sees the interests of both carer and disabled person as being served by an independent living approach. But the burgeoning carers' movement, representing female family carers, was based on the construction of disabled people as 'dependent'. The theories of the movement were concerned with 'the dilemmas which caring causes for women, the tension between paid work and unpaid caring (which can be hard work)' (Finch and Groves, 1983). The problem in this approach, in which disabled people are seen as a 'burden' shouldered by female caregivers, is that it relies on excluding the voice of disabled people.

Morris has dissected this approach. She writes of feminist academics who, in discussing what was meant by the term 'caring':

> ... emphasised that it involved not just feeling concern but also taking charge of others ... The terms in which feminist academics wrote about older disabled people the way that they were given no voice and were constructed as dependent people flowed naturally from the ... general assumption that older and disabled people are 'other', not normal, not 'one of us'. (Morris, 1993: 47)

She notes the ability of some academics to 'feel that a denial of a home and family life were appropriate social reactions to growing older or experiencing physical, sensory or intellectual impairment' (1993: 48). The notion that caring is a burden runs through the literature of the time. This notion was neatly inverted by Nasa Begum in the title of her study of disabled women: *The Burden of Gratitude* (Begum, 1989).

Nationally, the idea that families are the primary source of 'care' has been eagerly embraced by government. The carers' movement was initiated by women who were questioning the assumption that they should provide unpaid assistance to disabled and older relatives. But their quest for recognition and reward has resulted in an institutionalisation of their role. There are acts of parliament setting out what is due to carers, and a government website devoted to carers (www.carers.gov.uk). This approach defines them by their functional usefulness to government (saving the treasury money), rather than their relationships (wife, brother, parent).

Independent living

Disabled people's solution to the problem of other people defining them as 'dependent' has been to re-define 'independent' in ways that liberate rather than oppress (see Chapters 6 and 26). In particular, independent living is defined as having choice and control, rather than being able to do things for yourself:

> Independent living is the emancipatory philosophy and practice which empowers disabled people and enables them to exert influence, choice and control in every aspect of their life. (Campbell, 1996)

> Independent living for disabled people means being able to live in the way you choose, with people you choose. It means having choices about who helps you and the ways they help. It is not necessarily about doing things for yourself, it is about having control over your day to day life. (National Centre for Independent Living, leaflet)

The idea of a Center for Independent Living (CIL) originated in California. When CILs were set up in the UK, they were founded on similar lines to those in the USA, incorporating the basic 'independent living principles'. This meant that the services provided would be available for all disabled people regardless of their impairment, gender and background, and that the organisation should be run and controlled by disabled people. It is always intended to be a challenge to the status quo:

> Independent Living is also an ideology and a social and political movement. Inspired by the example of the struggle for equal rights by racial and ethnic minorities and the women's movement during the last decades, the Independent Living movement sees itself as a civil rights movement of disabled people and as a political force. (Berkeley archives)

Although independent living covers the full range of activities of a disabled person's life, CILs in the UK have tended to focus on a few core subjects, such as accessible housing and the use of personal assistants.

Independent living is a radically simple idea. It has taken a long time to spread because it is so challenging to the status quo of welfare provision. Following over a decade of 'pilot' schemes, in 1996 disabled people won the right to direct payments for personal assistance. This means that they can arrange their own services, buying the help they want, in the way they want it. It takes away the professional oversight of disabled people's lives.

The construction of disabled people as 'not normal', not 'one of us', is challenged by disabled people who say they can do their own assessments, arrange their own care packages, manage their own budgets.

Fault lines

As Brisenden and Morris indicate, it is not just physical autonomy that is required in order for disabled people to qualify as 'independent'. People with intellectual impairments, or those experiencing mental or emotional distress, also suffer from inappropriate responses to their support needs. In particular, they are seen as a risk to themselves or others, in need of control as well as care. This results in their access to independent living being more circumscribed than that of people with physical impairment.

Almost as soon as the Community Care (Direct Payments) Act came into force, service professionals in some areas began to look for reasons not to implement it. The arguments against fell into three categories: that disabled people would not be responsible managers of public money; that as direct payments give users what they want, this is unfair to other users who have to take what they are given; and that direct payments are only suitable for the elite few, and certainly not suitable for people with learning difficulties.

By contrast, some professionals have worked as allies of disabled people, becoming champions of direct payments. To date, they remain a minority.

Opponents of direct payments started to define people who were unable to use them by reason of their vulnerability or incapacity to choose. The 'test' for independence moved from being able to clean your own teeth or make your own tea, into how well you could manage a bank account or write a contract of employment.

Disabled people's organisations (which were predominantly led by people with physical impairments) gradually realised that in stressing the competence of independent living pioneers as managers, they were colluding in applying a non-disabled set of norms. It might be argued that this was a necessary step in getting the idea of direct payments accepted and put into statute. Whatever the reason for the original approach, people with learning difficulties and, more latterly, mental health service users have been steadily challenging these functional tests.

The contest of models of independence has limited the extent to which people with learning difficulties and mental health service users have identified with the independent living movement. The bridges are currently being built, but the fact they are needed at all reflects how difficult it has been to gain acceptance for user-designed services.

Vulnerability

Part of the argument against direct payments was the supposed vulnerability of service users. It is a concept that owes nothing to disabled people and everything to professional concerns. The conceptualising of some people as 'vulnerable' is used to justify over-protective and custodial care where other people make the decisions. The word started to appear in the social care lexicon as the new Labour government attempted to marry commitments to fiscal prudence with commitments to social justice. So they focused on services to 'vulnerable' people; this both put disabled people in the category of the deserving poor (as opposed to undeserving dole scroungers, for example) and also put them firmly in the 'not like us' category. At the same time, the government was full of modernising zeal, which meant services that focused on independence, on self-determination:

> ... the guiding principle of adult social services should be that they provide the support needed by someone to make most use of their own capacity and potential. (Department of Health, 1999)

The two concepts come together in the Care Standards Act 2000. This defines someone to whom personal care is provided in their own home under arrangements made by a domiciliary care agency as a 'vulnerable adult'. Guidance to the Act states that:

> ... the needs of the service user lie at the heart of the provision of personal care. Service users need to be kept informed and enabled to make choices concerning their care, and participate in the process, thereby maintaining their independence.

The concept of vulnerability constantly undercuts the ideal of independence. Vulnerable people are seen as weak, open to attack or damage. Allowing a vulnerable person to control her or his own destiny is seen as risky. And, by state approved definition, anyone who is using a home care agency is 'vulnerable'. Their choices and participation are limited by other people's assessment of their capacity.

Risk

The professional tendency to control is not only expressed in arguments about direct payments or vulnerability: another weapon used to achieve compliance in disabled service users is 'health and safety'. The management of risk has become an imperative, almost an obsession, in provision of care services. The outcome for disabled people has been a major restriction on their lives. One manifestation of this is 'no lifting' policies, where people have been literally confined to bed because they are deemed too difficult to lift. The human costs have been huge:

> She also suffers from pressure sores as a result of sitting in her wheelchair all the time, and the *nursing staff will not treat these* because it would necessarily involve lifting her. (Private communication, emphasis added.)

Risk management imperatives are set out in legislation. The current Mental Health Act allows both compulsory detention and treatment on the grounds of protection of others. The Act also allows a person's consent to be overridden regardless of capacity. The only safeguard, after medication has continued for three months, is a second opinion from a doctor appointed by the Mental Health Act Commission.

Government justifies the continuance of coercive mental health legislation on grounds of public safety. According to the mental health charity, Mind, this concern is overblown. They say that statistics show that:

... there has actually been a steady 3 per cent annual decline in the proportion of homicides committed by people with mental disorders. (Mind, 2002)

The readiness with which professionals and politicians limit the lives of disabled people, on the grounds of safety to others, is quite breathtaking. The soul-destroying effect of being controlled by others is one of the reasons why so many disabled people shun institutional care:

> I remember the countless times I have seen disabled people hurt, treated as less than people, told what to do and how to behave by those whose only claim to do this came from prejudice and their power over them. (Hunt, 1966)

For many years, disabled people have identified their desire for an autonomous life as a human rights issue. The implementation of the Human Rights Act in the UK has given campaigners a new focus for linking struggles for independent living to the human rights agenda. Not surprisingly, they view the sort of lack of care when professionals refuse to lift a person from her bed to deliver vital health treatment as a breach of human rights.

A landmark case in 2002 (*ABX&Y* v. *East Sussex*) gave encouragement to this view. It was judged that:

> Any risk assessment needs to take into account the needs of the disabled person, their Convention (and Charter) rights.

This judgement brings an important dimension into the debates around care and control. It says that the disabled person's dignity and human rights are central to how services must be delivered. This goes further than mere rhetoric about respecting user views or promoting independence. It gives people rights.

Citizenship

Disabled and older people who use social care services face a contradiction. Policy aims for the services are supposed to be about independence, choice, dignity. But the underlying values informing service provision are about vulnerability, risk, disability being viewed as a burden to the individual, their carers and the state.

> At present social services perceive older people as a tiresome bundle of needs. (OPAG, 2000)

As a way of challenging these values, older and disabled people are promoting the concept of citizenship. Services should aim to enable people to fulfil their rights and responsibilities as citizens. Older and disabled people do not just want to be involved in developments in social services or health. They are interested in the environment, in the justice system, in art.

Achieving the shift in attitude and resource allocation that a citizenship approach requires may take some time. Services are rationed and allocated on the basis of perceived vulnerability and risk:

There is little understanding (outside of the independent living movement itself) that independence could, or should be, established as a basic and universal human or civil right. ... Removal of all of the barriers to disabled people's full social and economic participation requires practical action across a variety of social and economic sectors such as education, transport and employment. ... Public support systems typically have great difficulty linking all of these actions together and, instead, tend to have different administrative functions to deal with them separately. (Zarb, 2003: 3)

Zarb attributes the continuance of the problem to economics:

Put crudely, removing all of the barriers to disabled people's full social and economic participation is considered to be simply too expensive when compared to meeting the costs of other social and economic priorities. (2003: 4)

Disabled people are viewed as 'less than' other citizens. Even a measure supposedly about disabled people's rights, the Disability Discrimination Act, includes the assumption that services are not about rights. Access to social care services is not covered by the Act.

The Disability Rights Commission is now campaigning to change this omission. They are seeking to establish a right to independent living. If they succeed, services will have to stop being about care or control, and start being about support, partnership and citizenship:

We need to question why, in the 21st century, it is still seen as acceptable for disabled people to be living in institutions against their wishes, to be denied access to basic support to enable them to enjoy a family or social life, and to be guaranteed no more than the bare minimum services necessary for day to day survival. (Zarb, 2003: 15)

References

ABX&Y v. *East Sussex*, notes on judgement available from Disability Rights Commission.

Begum, N. (1989) *The Burden of Gratitude*. Warwick: University of Warwick Social Care Practice Centre.

Berkeley archives at www.cilberkeley.org/archives, accessed 2003.

Brisenden, S. (1989) 'A charter for personal care', in J. Morris (1993) *Independent Lives? – Community Care and Disabled People*. Basingstoke: Macmillan. p. 27.

Campbell, J. (1996) *Back to a Vision of the Future*. London: NCIL. (www.ncil.org.uk)

Department of Health (1999) *Modernising Social Services*. London: HMSO. (www.doh.gov.uk)

Finch, J. and Groves, D. (eds) (1983) *A Labour of Love: Women, Work and Caring*. London: Routledge & Kegan Paul.

Hunt, P. (1966) 'A critical condition', in P. Hunt (ed.) *Stigma: The Experience of Disability*. London: Geoffrey Chapman.

Mind's evidence to the health committee inquiry on provision of NHS mental health services, 2002 (www.mind.org.uk/policy).

Morris, J. (1993) *Independent Lives? – Community Care and Disabled People*. Basingstoke: Macmillan.

National Centre for Independent Living (undated) NCIL Leaflet. Available from NCIL, 250 Kennington Lane, London, SE11 5RD or www.ncil.org.uk/publications

OPAG (2000) *Our Present for the Future, The Older People's Advisory Group's Perspective on the Better Government for Older People Programme 2000*. (www.bgop.org.uk)

Ratzka, A. (1992) *Tools for Power: A Resource Kit for Independent Living*. London: Institute for Independent Living. (www.independentliving.org//toolsforpower)

The Care Standards Act 2000. Guidance Notes. London: HMSO.

Zarb, G. (2003) 'Why We Need a Legal Right to Independent Living'. Paper presented at the European Congress on Independent Living. 24–26 April, Arona, Tenerife.

35 Counselling and Disabled People: Help or Hindrance?
DONNA REEVE

In recent years, more and more people have been turning to counselling to help resolve personal difficulties in their lives. Disabled people also want access to counselling which meets their perceived needs (McKenzie, 1992), whether they want to look at marriage problems, childhood traumas, stress or bereavement, or issues associated with disability or impairment. Some writers have acknowledged, however, that disabled people have been generally avoided as a client group by psychotherapists and counsellors and that there is a legacy of prejudicial attitudes, with an associated dire need to undertake more conscious-ness-raising, training and research (McLeod, 1998). Consequently, whilst many disabled people do manage to find counselling services that are helpful, others are faced with inaccessible counselling agencies or counsellors who do not understand the lived experience of disability.

In this chapter I discuss some of the particular problems that can undermine the counselling experience of disabled clients, showing how and why the counselling relationship can end up being more of a hindrance to personal growth and self-fulfilment than a help. As well as identifying some of the potential pitfalls, I suggest changes which could remove some of the barriers that can cause disabled people to give up on counselling as having anything useful to offer them.

Counselling theory: the loss models

Within the counselling literature, theories which attempt to understand personal responses to disability assume that there will be a process of psychological adjustment as the individual comes to terms with their impairment. In order to overcome their perceived loss, disabled people are expected to grieve and go through a process of mourning akin to that of bereavement, expressing feelings of anger and denial before they can become psychologically whole again (Lenny, 1993). These 'loss models' arise from the imagination of non-disabled people about what it must be like to experience impairment, assuming that becoming disabled must be psychologically devastating (Oliver, 1996). This contradicts reports of disabled people themselves, who instead locate the source of emotional distress in the failure of the environment to take account of their needs (Oliver, 1995). These loss models have been criticised for failing to take into account the socially constructed nature of disability, although they may have some limited use for understanding individual responses to impairment (Reeve, 2000).

Despite the contradiction between theory and reality, these loss models are commonly presented in the counselling literature as the only way that disabled people respond to disability. Not only do these models suggest that disabled people *need* counselling to help them adjust to their disability, but if they also fail to show the predicted symptoms of the mourning process, then they are in denial – a classic catch-22 situation (Lenny, 1993). A psychologist at Stoke Mandeville described how one of his patients with spinal cord injury came to him requesting help so that he could become depressed – his counsellor had told him that his lack of depression meant that he had not come to terms with his disability (Kennedy, 1998).

The crude application of these models to understand the emotional issues affecting disabled people can be oppressive. For example, a wheelchair user who is angry and frustrated at being unable to access restaurants and other public places is unlikely to be helped by a counsellor who interprets this anger as a sign that he or she has not yet adjusted to disability, instead of as a very reasonable response to the experience of discrimination and exclusion. Counselling responses to disability based on the loss models are disempowering because they reinforce the notion that disability is an individual problem caused by impairment, rather than recognising the role that society plays in creating and maintaining disability.

As well as using models which predict the way that people are expected to adjust to disability, counsellors also work within different theoretical frameworks, such as psychodynamic, cognitive-behavioural and person-centred approaches. Whilst all of these focus on the individual rather than society, person-centred counselling would appear to offer the least intrusive approach with its lack of assumptions about how people respond to disability (Lenny, 1993). Irrespective of the approach used by a counsellor, it is important that emotional reactions of a disabled client to the experiences of exclusion and discrimination are not pathologised:

> We are so used to pushing and shoving our way in, being our own advocates, being on the outskirts, being the exception, being different, that we start to think we are the exception in ways and situations other than those related to the disability. Clinicians must understand this process and not label it as a personality disorder. (Olkin, 1999: 85)

Despite the suggestion by the loss models that disabled people need counselling to deal with disability, and that disability is going to be the only issue they want to talk about, there is relatively little literature about working with this particular client group. Whilst there are some counselling books that provide practical information about working with disabled people (such as Brearley and Birchley, 1994), there are fewer books which treat disability as a form of social oppression rather than an individual problem (Corker, 1995; Olkin, 1999). This dearth has ramifications for counselling training and practice, which I will now discuss in more detail.

Disability: a missing element in counselling training

Although there has been a substantial rise in the number of counsellors being trained, the number of disabled counsellors and counselling students remains low (Withers, 1996). The high cost of training courses coupled with inaccessible teaching rooms and course materials results in the exclusion of many disabled people who have the potential and interest to train as counsellors. The increasing need for such courses to become accredited and recognised academically is leading to more counselling courses being offered within university settings, which potentially excludes even more disabled students if entry requirements stipulate a first degree. Courses require students to undertake skills practice within counselling agencies and many also expect students to have received counselling themselves. The inaccessibility of many counselling venues, together with the high cost of receiving personal counselling, further compounds the barriers faced by disabled people who want to become counsellors.

The scarcity of disabled students on counselling courses means that disability is not present 'in the room' in the same way that gender, sexuality and ethnicity are. Many disabled people who train as counsellors have to deal with reactions of pity, anger and embarrassment from prejudiced tutors and fellow students (Withers, 1996), a situation made more difficult if they are the only disabled person on that course. When I undertook a counselling diploma, the denial of my identity as a disabled person was a very disabling experience. The insistence by the rest of my group that I was 'just like them' invalidated my experiences of exclusion and oppression that I faced as a disabled person in society. It would be unthinkable for a group to deny the identity of a member of any other minority social group in this way.

A major difficulty for many counselling courses is that they are expected to cover a lot of counselling theory and practice within a relatively short time. Consequently, there is little teaching time devoted to issues around equal opportunities – maybe two days in a two-year part-time Diploma course – and Disability Equality Training is generally absent from these courses. The general lack of social model approaches within the counselling literature, coupled with little or no teaching of disability as an equal opportunities issue alongside gender, ethnicity and sexuality, mean that the prejudices and stereotypes which abound in society about disability are not exposed and challenged within counselling courses (Reeve, 2000). This can have adverse effects on future counselling relationships if counsellors are unaware of their own prejudicial attitudes towards disabled clients.

Counselling services: inaccessible or 'elsewhere'

It can be very difficult for disabled people to find accessible counselling services. Voluntary sector counselling agencies operate on a shoestring budget and are often sited in old buildings with poor access. Consequently, disabled clients who cannot access the available counselling rooms may be offered counselling by telephone or in a different place; one agency counselled clients with mobility impairments in a local church because their usual counselling rooms were located up a flight of stairs with no available lift. Private counsellors do not provide a viable alternative because they are expensive and very few homes in the UK are wheelchair accessible. This experience of exclusion from services that non-disabled people take for granted can have an emotional effect on disabled clients because it serves to remind them that they are different and that they are 'out of place'. This psycho-emotional dimension of disability (Thomas, 1999) can be further compounded by counsellors who fail to treat their disabled clients with forethought and respect; for example, by failing to move furniture out of the way before a client who is a wheelchair user arrives for their counselling session.

The low number of disabled counsellors within counselling practice contributes to the failure of counselling agencies to bear in mind the access needs of potential disabled clients. Some agencies believe that disabled people do not want counselling because they never see disabled clients – failing to recognise that being situated in an inaccessible build-ing or failing to produce information about the counselling service in accessible formats may contribute to this misconception! Another myth is that disabled people are counselled 'somewhere else' by experts who have the perceived specialist counselling skills needed to work with this client group. In reality, while there are a few counselling agencies that specialise in working with disabled clients, these are not available to the vast majority of disabled people. As anyone in society can become disabled at any time, through an acci-dent or illness, this myth defends a counsellor against having to look at their own fears and vulnerabilities about illness, disability or death. Other counsellors feel de-skilled and out of their depth when working with disabled clients because counselling cannot 'fix' disability or impairment.

The way forward

Although much of the counselling literature suggests that disabled people need counselling to help them 'accept their disability' and to 'mourn their losses', it is paradoxical that counsellors and counselling agencies appear ill-equipped to work with disabled clients. I now want to suggest four changes that would improve the counselling experience of disabled clients.

It is vital that Disability Equality Training becomes a mandatory part of all counselling courses so that students (and tutors) learn about the social model of disability and understand how disability is socially constructed rather than being caused by a person's impairment. The training also needs to include a discussion about the psycho-emotional dimensions of dis-ability, social practices and processes which undermine the emotional wellbeing of people with impairments (Thomas, 1999). Counsellors need to be more aware of the emotional con-sequences of living with prejudice, exclusion and discrimination and how this can impact on the self-esteem and self-worth of their disabled client. Not only would this training enable students to realise the extent of disablism within all aspects of social life, but it would directly challenge many of their own prejudices and stereotypes about disabled people. Unfortunately some students (and counsellors) are reluctant to look at their own prejudices around disability because they already claim to 'unconditionally accept all people' and believe that they do not need Disability Equality Training (Reeve, 2000).

Secondly, it is important that disabled people are not viewed as a client group to be counselled 'somewhere else' and instead that all counsellors are trained to be able to work with disability-related issues if and when they arise. Disabled people are not just people with impairments, they are also parents, siblings, children, workers and friends; as such they are subject to the same range of emotions and difficulties as non-disabled people and should have access to the same choice of counselling services if they want them. More importantly, as anyone can become disabled or be affected by disability in the family, dis-ability issues are likely to be present in some form or other in much of the work done by mainstream agencies. For example, counsellors working within alcohol and drug agencies may see clients who have become disabled through substance misuse or who are drinking because of the stresses of caring for a disabled member of the family. Disability may or may not be the presenting issue, but counsellors need to be aware of the effects that disablism can have on the lives of their clients and their families. In my view, it is not necessary for disabled clients to be counselled by disabled counsellors – who can be just as prejudiced as non-disabled counsellors – although it would improve the degree of client choice if more trained disabled counsellors were available within the counselling profession.

Thirdly, counselling agencies must conform to the Disability Discrimination Act 1995 and make their services accessible to both disabled and non-disabled people. This includes supplying information in accessible formats and providing access to a British Sign Language (BSL) interpreter; where premises cannot be made accessible, alternative counselling provision through telephone counselling or home visits must be made. Counsellors can be trained to counsel effectively over a telephone or minicom, but the counselling experience is different for both parties to that of face-to-face counselling. There are issues about safety, neutrality and privacy when seeing a client in their own home, but these should not be used as an excuse to refuse counselling services to disabled clients. Counsellors who are not fluent in BSL will need to adapt to the particular challenges of working with a third person in the room when counselling a deaf client. Counsellors need to be flexible about the parameters of counselling sessions when working with disabled clients because impairment effects may impact on the frequency, timing and length of counselling sessions (Olkin, 1999). External factors, such as the availability of community transport, may influence when a disabled client can attend, as well as their punctuality.

Finally, working with disabled clients not only challenges where and for how long counselling sessions take place, it also questions the usefulness of traditional counselling approaches which pay little attention to issues of power both within the counselling relationship and outside the counselling room (McLeod, 1998). A counsellor working within a person-centred approach, offering the core conditions of empathic understanding, unconditional acceptance and genuineness, can help someone make sense of the relationship between themselves and society, impairment and disability (Lenny, 1993). However, like other oppressed groups in society, disabled people may have fewer choices open to them because of prejudice and discrimination, and this fact cannot be ignored by the counsellor. I agree with Olkin, who states that counselling with disabled people must 'incorporate the socio-political into the therapeutic' (Olkin, 1999: 300). Consequently, counsellors must be aware of the rights of disabled people and be prepared to help their clients achieve them, otherwise they risk being part of the problem faced by disabled people in society (Reeve, 2000).

Conclusion

Whilst some disabled people do experience counselling that is supportive and empowering, others face inaccessible counselling rooms, inappropriate counselling models and prejudiced counsellors, which can result in counselling which instead is an oppressive, disabling experience. Although the counselling world has started to realise that disabled people have been avoided as a client group, urgent improvements are needed within counsellor training, practice and theory if counselling is to be more of a help than a hindrance for disabled clients.

Current counselling theory is based on the experiences of non-disabled people which has led to the proliferation of the loss models that claim to describe the psychological effects of disability, in addition to counselling approaches which fail to acknowledge the effects of living with discrimination and oppression. As well as recognising the many different ways that disabled people deal emotionally with the experience of disability, it would be beneficial to move towards more socially aware forms of counselling that recognise the impact of the world 'out there' on the counselling room 'in here'. Counsellor training must include a social model approach to disability, teaching students about the structural and psycho-emotional dimensions of disability and their effects on the emotional wellbeing of disabled clients. Counsellors also need to consider their own prejudices and assumptions about disabled people if they themselves are not to become part of an oppressive culture (Corker, 1995). Disabled people have a right to the same range and quality of counselling services as other client groups in society, and the Disability Discrimination Act 1995 must be implemented by counselling agencies in order to make their services available to disabled people. Counsellors need to develop more flexible and imaginative ways of working with their disabled clients.

References

Brearley, G. and Birchley, P. (1994) *Counselling in Disability and Illness* (2nd edn). London: Mosby.

Corker, M. (1995) *Counselling – The Deaf Challenge*. London: Jessica Kingsley.

Kennedy, P. (1998) 'Spinal cord injuries', in A.S. Bellack and M. Hersen (eds), *Comprehensive Clinical Psychology, Vol. 8*. Oxford: Pergamon. pp. 445–62.

Lenny, J. (1993) 'Do disabled people need counselling?', in J. Swain, V. Finkelstein, S. French and M. Oliver (eds), *Disabling Barriers – Enabling Environments*. London: Sage and Open University Press. pp. 233–40.

McKenzie, A. (1992) 'Counselling for people disabled through injury', *Social Care Research Findings (No. 19)*. York: Joseph Rowntree Foundation.

McLeod, J. (1998) *An Introduction to Counselling* (2nd edn). Buckingham: Open University Press.

Oliver, J. (1995) 'Counselling disabled people: a counsellor's perspective', *Disability and Society*, 10 (3): 261–79.

Oliver, M. (1996) 'A sociology of disability or a disablist sociology', in L. Barton (ed.), *Disability and Society: Emerging Issues and Insights*. Harlow: Longman. pp. 18–42.

Olkin, R. (1999) *What Psychotherapists Should Know About Disability*. New York: The Guilford Press.

Reeve, D. (2000) 'Oppression within the counselling room', *Disability and Society*, 15 (4): 669–82.

Thomas, C. (1999) *Female Forms: Experiencing and Understanding Disability*. Buckingham: Open University Press.

Withers, S. (1996) 'The experience of counselling', in G. Hales (ed.), *Beyond Disability: Towards an Enabling Society*. London: Sage and Open University Press. pp. 96–104.

36

A Critique of Professional Support and Intervention
PAUL ABBERLEY

In a wide-ranging think-tank report aimed at developing a vision for social care in the year 2020, it is asserted that,

> Our public services have often failed because they have been built around the needs of agencies and professions, rather than service users. (Hughes, L. 2002: 70).

Elsewhere in the same volume, another author offers evidence that 'fundamental difficulties' in 'achieving the outcome of integrated or seamless care at the level of individuals and their carers' were 'associated with professional values, socialisation experiences and boundary maintainance' (Wistow, 2002: 63). In this chapter I use the example of how occupational therapists (OTs) see their work to explore some of the ways in which we might understand how the situation outlined above comes about.

The Open University's current introductory course in social science, DD100, explores in its third unit (Hughes and Ferguson, 2000) the ways in which the exercise of power structures people's everyday lives. To do this it examines how two different kinds of theory, that of the German sociologist Max Weber (1864–1920) and the analysis put forward by Michel Foucault (1926–84), might help us understand the ordering of lives in and through social institutions:

> Is power, as Weber suggests, something that certain people 'hold' and 'exercise' over others, or, following Foucault, is it more valuable to see power as something that 'works through' institutions and agents? (Hughes and Ferguson, 2000: 4)

When, in this chapter, I refer to Weberian or Foucauldian approaches, I am not usually talking about things either of them said, but about the kind of things we could say using their respective approaches. I am trying to show how 'high-level' theory can help us understand and comment on the things that rank-and-file health and welfare professionals think and say about their work, and how what they do as a result of this has effects on the lives of disabled people.

For both thinkers, an encounter with representatives of a state welfare institution always involves an exercise of power because it has the potential to make welfare users 'act in ways which they would not otherwise have chosen' (Hughes and Ferguson, 2000: 125). This is brought about by the 'professional' using coercion, domination, persuasion and manipulation to structure the lives of those to whom they provide 'services'. For Weber the State exercises bureaucratically organised, impartial, top-down power, based on authority and delegated through a myriad of institutions and agencies. Foucault's emphasis is upon internalisation; the way in which power works within the human mind, shaping through habituation what it is possible to think and what it is not, constructing familiar chains of language and observations:

> Agents acting on behalf of the institution are not so much 'following orders' as reproducing for others, as truth and common sense, a set of values and norms they have internalized from their own exposure to the culture and structures of the institution. (Hughes and Ferguson, 2000: 127)

Whilst superficially Weber's analysis would seem to fit the 'golden age' of the Keynesian Welfare State (1945–75) and Foucault's the consumer-oriented managerialism of more recent years, a Foucauldian approach would contend that even in the 'golden age' the bureaucratic structure was only partially successful in imposing its rules, procedures, expertise and so on. Some people, some of the time, escape 'the system'. Equally, from a Weberian perspective, we might argue that despite surface stylistic changes, hierarchical power relations and structured inequalities remain in place.

In a study of occupational therapists carried out some years ago (Abberley, 1995), I suggested that the way that OTs work is evaluated and the way that the system requires them to offer evidence of 'success' in order to validate their work, leads them to define and place requirements upon their clients which disempower them. Even those individual OTs who are dubious of the ideology of vigorous self-reliance that largely constitutes their model of the rehabilitated client find themselves living out this ideology in their working lives, where their claims to professional status rest upon relatively independent, isolated and self-determined activity with individual clients. I argued that this did not happen as a result of conscious intention, but as a by-product of the way in which the therapist has to justify herself in order to achieve and retain 'professional' status. Thus the 'professionalisation' of occupational therapy, which enhances the status and enriches the work experience of an overwhelmingly female workforce, at the same time extends and intensifies the oppression of disabled clients (also predominantly women).

This would, I think, suggest that many of the 'caring professions', which provide better status, reward and so on, for a largely female workforce have to be abolished or at any rate substantially transformed from a directive to a collaborative relationship with clients (Leonard, 1997). So I think that the very developments which apparently reduce the oppression of women workers in the 'care industry' serve to increase the oppression of disabled people who are the objects of their labour. In a society where there are attempts to overcome disadvantage piecemeal it seems to me the tendency will be towards such 'zero-sum' adjustments, with the contingently strongest oppressed groups winning out at the expense of less well-positioned minorities. This is particularly likely, since groups becoming aware of their own oppression are probably disinclined to see themselves as also oppressors, as this seems to undermine a nascent and precarious positive collective self-image. This may lead to difficulty in coping with the ambiguity involved in recognising oneself as both oppressor and oppressed.

This is related to another issue: the increasing prevalence within health and welfare services of the requirement to evaluate and audit service delivery that inevitably leads to the need to produce operationalised criteria of success and failure. Following such writers as McKnight (1981) and Simpkins (1983), I doubt that this process results in any empowerment of the service consumer. McKnight argues that despite a possible recognition that individual problems have their genesis and meaning in the social, economic and political environment, services inevitably tend to abstract the recipient from that environment because of the individualised nature of the tools available to the practitioner, such that the recipient is defined as the problem and the professional the solution. Simpkins claims that although service providers are only too willing to claim credit for any success, failure tends to be presented as the fault of the recipient and Dowson (1990) argues that there are clear conflicts of interest involved in the providers of services also being the evaluators.

Analysing the interviews of OTs in terms of the theoretical perspectives outlined above, replies to requests to describe successful OT can be split into two main categories. Nearly half the interviewees mentioned client satisfaction as a major or sole criterion. Another kind of response, however, referred to therapist-centered, 'objective' criteria. Occasionally these were purely medical, but more often had a wider, task-based focus. 'You assess what the problem is, your short-term goal is reached. You set another goal. Your final aim is the achievement of realistic goals' (Abberley, 1995). Whilst the 'goal' here appears to be defined by the therapist, another response contains an element of mutuality, though apparently with the therapist in the ascendant. 'Where the patient agrees with you that goals have been achieved, though not all have the understanding to do so' (Abberley, 1995). Another provides objective criteria in terms of patient behaviour. 'In terms of outcome, the patient doesn't need me any more, they're taking responsibility for their own life. It's about quality of life' (Abberley, 1995). This latter is an interesting phrase. Whilst ostensibly referring to self-assessment, in some health discourse it has come to denote, as part of Quality Adjusted Life Years (QALY), an operationalised and external judgement which is supposed to be employed in the development of 'objective' criteria for the rationing of health care. Thus, to use the notion of quality of life in today's health service inevitably raises the question 'Who judges?'(Hahn, 2002): 'You've established targets and met them. Your ongoing task is to set goals and targets that are attainable. We can't allow people to fail' (Abberley, 1995). A limiting factor emerges here; if the patient 'can't be allowed to fail', then reality will tend to be defined in terms of what it is in the power of the OT to deliver. As another respondent put it, 'You arrive at where therapist and client wish to get to. But success for the patient depends on how realistic their expectations are' (Abberley, 1995). Part of the OT's task is here explicitly seen as the moulding of the client/customer to fit the OT's definition of reality. 'Even if difficulties haven't been overcome, the person has come to more of an acceptance of why they can't be. OT is problem solving – real success is when you overcome a problem' (Abberley, 1995). The 'problem' here would appear to be the client's 'unrealistic' expectations. Indeed, the client's view can also be 'wrong' in the opposite direction, as when 'Someone is pleased but it's not success, though a letter of thanks is lovely' (Abberley, 1995).

I am suggesting that, on the basis of this interview data, we can identify two kinds of expressed criteria being employed by OTs to identify success. One is client satisfaction, the other therapist-defined performance criteria. The two generally interact, and sometimes contradict. Where this occurs, the contradiction is resolved in favour of the therapist, and the adjustment of the client's view of reality is seen as part of the therapy task. Indeed, success in this is cited by some as a criterion of good work.

The OT is involved in a process of co-opting the client into his or her view of the situation, defined as 'reality', as an essential condition of carrying out the work. In OT theory this process is seen as educational and justified as such on the basis of the OT's superior objective knowledge. From a Foucauldian perspective, this ideological activity is more important for OT as a profession than any provision of equipment, and indeed takes precedence over it, since the latter could be, and is, done by the relatively untrained, and indeed by disabled people themselves, which constitutes a particular threat to professional status as presently constituted.

The difference is that the latter act in response to immediately expressed needs. For the OT, the desires of the client are processed through his or her superior knowledge of what is appropriate. Our previous interviews with disabled users of OT services indicated that, whether or not they expressed satisfaction with their experiences, it was only in terms of the provision of equipment that they envisaged making use of OT services in the future. In general, then, whilst clients expressed a desire for purely instrumental support, occupational therapy rejects the role of 'mere' equipment provider.

A significant feature of replies to a question about failure was how infrequently the responses laid responsibility at the door of the therapist herself. With failure reduced to the impossibility of doing everything, what is ostensibly an account of failure often ended up by saying that things could not have been different. True failure, in so far as it is acknowledged, tends to be attributed to forces beyond the therapist's control. These fall into three categories: lack of financial resources, 'the system' and, most significantly for a Foucauldian analysis, the customer/client. Some responses to the question about failure:

'Sometimes we don't get anywhere, they change their minds.'
'Clients sometimes have unreal expectations – sometimes things cannot physically be done.'
'I think of a lady who couldn't come to terms with her stroke. She wanted to die, therefore my treatment failed.'
'It could be that clients have unrealistic expectations.'
'It's not necessarily you that's failed if you've given them opportunities.'
'It's not you that's failed, especially with the elderly – we must be realistic.'
'I don't know that I've failed them. There are times when things have gone wrong, for example, patient degenerates or a relative undoes work. The patient has to choose.'
'The client may feel we've failed them when we think we haven't, for example, in stroke or carer problems.' (Abberley, 1975)

This is sometimes expressed in a more sophisticated form. 'I don't often see things in terms of failure. Hopefully I can say to them "we just don't seem to have achieved anything, it isn't a failure on either side", but just something that can't be achieved. For example, if what x wanted would make his medical condition worse, I couldn't give it to him. I hope I don't give false expectations. Clients sometimes hear what they want to hear. Family and carers can be more difficult than clients. There's high expectations of medicine today. OTs are in the middle' (Abberley, 1995). Another OT stated that 'There's the difficult area of young disabled men. I don't know if its failure, but you often get no or limited success. But that's turning it onto the client' (Abberley, 1995).

Even an assertion of the *rights* of clients can be employed to this effect. 'If they don't want to do it, that's their decision. Disabled people shouldn't *have* to be go-getters. It's not necessarily you that's failed if you've given them opportunities' (Abberley, 1995).

The complexity of the client's situation is seen as such that it is overdetermined to the degree that any intervention by the OT would inevitably have been inadequate and she should thus not be seen as having failed.

From the point of view of a theory of disablement as a form of social oppression, the activities of medical and welfare agencies are to be understood as key mechanisms through which this oppression can be produced and reproduced. For example, Zarb and Oliver, in their study *Ageing with a Disability*, argue that 'the statutory services that are available mostly create and reinforce older disabled people's dependency and frustrate their attempts to maintain control over their own lives' (1993: 66). They are, in the words of the chapter's title, 'dependency creating services'. The interviewed OTs seem to present success as theirs, with failure attributed to the consumer. In this way a disempowering view of disabled people is systematically produced and reproduced, since it is negative, not positive outcomes that the interviewees attribute to consumer agency. At the same time the emphasis on the power of human agents diverts attention away from the social structural constraints upon individual action. Thus, with failure goes the attribution of responsibility for that failure in a way that protects the OT, fairly low down in the hierarchical structure of health and welfare organisations, to disabled people, a group who consistently have less power than she does to define reality. A Weberian account seems to encapsulate the structural constraints which precipitate such collective behaviour, whilst Finkelstein, in his account of his recent experiences of bad practice at the hands of Professions Allied to Medicine (PAMs), seem to indicate a deskilling of the kind outlined in the work of Braverman (1974) as typical of late capitalism:

> Health and welfare practitioners appear to equate professional decision making with the technical duties reliant upon rule-following consistency ... Far from enhancing the status of the 'caring' professions, [PAMs] compliance with the de-skilling practice inherent in 'Modernising Social Services' will eventually completely destroy any vestige of 'professionalism' in the very best sense of the word. (Finkelstein, 1999: 4; see also Chapter 31)

Can things be otherwise? Some writers referring to the activities of those in the disability movement and the struggle for the full citizenship rights of disabled people argue that it can. Finkelstein contrasts the oppressive PAMs to a putative new democratic kind of support worker, prefigured in the activities of Centres for Integrated Living; 'CILs have ... seeded the momentum toward a new community based profession ... If this is to avoid the morass into which PAMs have fallen, then such a new profession will have to be a robust Profession Allied to the Community (PAC)' (1999: 2).

In a similar vein, Leonard voices the need for a renewed emancipatory project.

> The building of new forms of welfare ... develops ... as extensions of the groundwork of activities emerging from the collectivities which already exist in the new social movements ... Resistance to the disciplining power of the professional expert, for example, is transmuted into a practice which attempts to develop a prefigurative relationship between professional 'helper' and 'client' in which the interaction is characterized as 'subject to subject' and where distancing and objectification are expected to wither away. (1997: 173)

This 'would involve an abandonment of the urge to control and homogenize populations "in their own interests" and instead return to those values which form the critical emancipatory side of modernity: a belief in equality and justice' (1997: 178). Equally Wistow warns that 'The language of enabling will need to be replaced more fully by that of empowerment' (2002: 54) and that 'Successful independent living depends on social inclusion both to make it happen and to ensure it is sustainable' (Wistow, 2002: 55). He warns that, in contrast to those who can work in partnership with service users, 'Providers ... who can only provide *to* and *for* [users] will succeed in making very little contribution to the latter's empowerment' (2002: 59). Empowerment, the introduction to the report affirms, requires 'abandoning the consumerist approach ... and instead adopting a citizenship model, where rights to high quality, user-focused services are matched by appropriate roles and responsibilities for individuals and the wider community' (Kendall and Harker, 2002: 9).

References

Abberley, P. (1995) 'Disabling ideology in health and welfare – the case of Occupational Therapy', *Disability and Society*, 10 (2): 221–32.

Braverman, H. (1974) *Labor and Monopoly Capital*. New York: Monthly Review Press.

Dowson, S. (1990) *Who Does What?* London: Values in Action.

Finkelstein, V. (1999) *Professions Allied To the Community (PACs)*, 1 and 11. Leeds University Disability Studies Online Archives. http://www.leeds.ac.uk/disability-studies/archiveuk/finkelstein/pacall.pdf.

Hahn, H. (2002) 'Academic debates and political advocacy: the US disability movement' in C. Barnes, M. Oliver and L. Barton (eds), *Disability Studies Today*. Cambridge: Polity.

Hughes, G. and Ferguson, R. (eds) (2000) *Ordering Lives: Family, Work and Welfare*. London. Open University/Routledge.

Hughes, L. (2002) 'The workforce for social work and social care', in L. Kendall and L. Harker (eds), *From Welfare to Wellbeing – The Future of Social Care*. London: IPPR.

Kendall, L. and Harker, L. (2002) (eds) *From Welfare to Wellbeing – The Future of Social Care*. London: IPPR.

Leonard, P. (1997) *Postmodern Welfare – Reconstructing an Emancipatory Project*. London. Sage.

McKnight, J. (1981) 'Professionalised service and disabling help', in A. Brechin, P. Liddiard and J. Swain (eds), *Handicap in a Social World*. London: Hodder and Stoughton.

Simpkins, M. (1983) *Trapped within Welfare*. London: Macmillan.

Wistow, G. (2002) 'The future aims and objectives of social care', in L. Kendall and L. Harker (eds), *From Welfare to Wellbeing – The Future of Social Care*. London: IPPR.

Zarb, J. and Oliver, M. (1993) *Ageing with a Disability*. London: University of Greenwich.

37 Treatment at the Hands of Professionals
PETER BERESFORD

There are few areas of health and welfare activity as contradictory, ambiguous and politicised as current mental health policy. To make sense of it, it is necessary to examine its formal arrangements, its stated aims and some of the inconsistencies between them and the reality that service users experience.

Two big changes, representing a break from the past, have shaped mental health policy and practice over the last twenty or so years and look like shaping it for the foreseeable future. The first has been the closure of most of the old big Victorian institutions. The second has been the emergence of the mental health service users/survivors movement. Each has fundamental implications for both policy and practice and service users.

Care in the community

The ending of the old 'asylums' and the closure of hospital beds was linked to a move to a new philosophy – 'care in the community' (see Chapters 22 and 33). There were many reasons for this shift, both positive and negative. These included concerns about poor conditions and the denial of service users' rights, as well as a desire to save money by selling rather than maintaining rundown old buildings, maintaining people instead by prescribing major tranquillisers and other neuroleptic drugs associated with damaging (side) effects. Care in the community was based on a philosophy of people being able to stay in their own homes or live somewhere nearby in their 'neighbourhood' and have suitable support to do so. Care in the community was associated with the expansion of a wide range of 'community-based' services, including day centres/hospitals, supported housing, non-residential support workers, training and employment opportunities.

The community care reforms that led to the development of 'care in the community' were introduced by Conservative governments which were committed to an increased emphasis on private provision in health and welfare and the reduction of state intervention and expenditure. Their policies were based on a market approach and emphasised 'consumer choice' and involvement. Their argument was that the use of public services, including health and welfare services, should be seen in the same way as consumption of any other goods or services. Here was the meeting point of government with the other key new development: the emergence of the mental health service users/survivors movement.

The emerging service user/survivor movement

Building on the new opportunities for user involvement offered by care in the community, service user organisations expanded dramatically during the 1990s. A large and growing number (albeit a small proportion overall) of mental health service users/survivors have become involved in service user groups and organisations at local, regional, national and international levels. The mental health service user/survivor movement is concerned not only with self-help and mutual support, but also with collective action to reform the service system and make wider changes. There are now black and minority ethnic organisations as well as organisations for people hearing voices, with eating distress and who self-harm. As well as developing their own organisations, service users/survivors have had a growing involvement in and influence on traditional charitable organisations like Mind and in some cases such organisations, like, for example, the Manic Depressive Fellowship, have become user controlled (Campbell, 1996).

While both care in the community and the mental health service users/survivors movement have placed an emphasis on 'partnership', 'empowerment' and 'user involvement', they have often meant different things by them. The state and service system has predominantly been concerned with a consumerist approach to user involvement based on consultation and information gathering, comparable to the market research of commercial companies. Service users have been more interested in a democratic approach to involvement that challenges existing inequalities of power and offers service users an increased role in decision making over both their individual and collective experience of mental health and other services. The focus of user involvement in care and the community has been on improving the operational efficiency of the service system. The focus of user involvement in the mental health service user/survivor movement has been on improving the quality of people's lives. These are significantly different, sometimes conflicting goals.

There is another significant difference to be seen between these two developments. In relation to care in the community, this has more to do with political and media reactions to the policy than with policy intentions. Care in the community was essentially intended as a progressive and enabling policy. A key underpinning idea was that service users would no longer be subject to living or being 'treated' in institutions. An actual consequence of the policy, however, has been an increased emphasis in both political and media discussions, on service users as dangerous and a threat to the public. This development can most readily be understood by examining the development of 'care in the community'.

Service users and 'dangerousness'

Many service users and workers thought that care in the community might be a good idea in principle, but successive governments failed to fund it adequately or implement it properly in practice. For example, funds saved by the closure of long-stay psychiatric hospitals have largely not been spent on developing community-based mental health services, but used instead on other areas of health care given greater priority (Coppick and Hopton, 2000). Continuing problems of poor communication, co-ordination and integration between different departments and agencies at both local and national levels created additional problems. While the reality for some service users was being left without adequate or appropriate support, sometimes without a roof over their heads, sometimes isolated in poor-quality bedsits on stigmatised estates, this was not the issue that became the news story. Instead, the tabloid press attacked care in the community as defective in principle and accused it of leading to an increase in killings of members of the public by mental health service users. The definitive study of violence and homicides associated with mental health service users, published by the Royal College of Psychiatrists, actually showed no increase (instead a small fall) in such deaths since the implementation of care in the community (Taylor and Gunn, 1999). Evidence, however, has not been important in this debate so far.

This media preoccupation with violence rapidly had the effect of politicising mental health policy. Where the tabloids led, politicians seemed prepared to follow. Just before the 1997 general election, the *Sun* ran a banner headline over a two-page feature calling this 'The real election issue'. The then Labour Shadow Health Minister stressed Labour's support for further controls on mental health service users. One of the first acts of New Labour's Health Minister after the election was to announce that 'Care in the community is scrapped' (*Daily Telegraph*, January 1998). Since then (with a Green Paper, 1999; a consultation document, 'Managing People With Severe Dangerous Personality Disorder', 1999; White Paper, 2000 and Mental Health Bill, 2002) government has sought to increase the compulsory powers that can be imposed upon mental health service users both to extend these beyond the hospital and, in the case of people categorised as having 'severe dangerous personality disorder', prior to the commission of or conviction for any offence.

Thus three government concerns have dominated government mental health policy at the start of the twenty-first century. These are based on a view of:

- mental health service users as dangerous;
- the need to give top priority to 'public safety'; and
- the achievement of this by emphasising control and compulsory 'treatment'.

However, it would be a mistake to see this as the sum total of government mental health policy or philosophy. Indeed, this is what makes current mental health policy so complex and disturbing for mental health service users/survivors and their organisations. It may also explain their serious doubts and concerns about the nature of their present and future 'treatment' by the psychiatric system and its practitioners.

Policy pointing in two directions

Ideas of 'empowerment', 'involvement' and 'partnership' lie at the heart of government policy and pronouncements about mental health policy and practice. The emphasis on them has increased rather than decreased in recent years. They are highlighted in key policy documents like *A National Service Framework for Mental Health* (Department of Health, 1999), the appointment of a mental health Czar (2000) and the establishment of the National Institute for Mental Health in England (NIMHE) in 2002 to provide the knowledge base for policy and practice. There can be little doubt that many policy makers, managers and practitioners are committed to such values and goals.

The question, however, for both policy makers and service users is can you have a successful and supportive policy driven by what appear to be contradictory goals and values, both to compel and empower service users, to involve and control them? Policy and philosophy are both ambiguous and contradictory (Newnes et al., 2001). Service users and their organisations fear that the focus of policy will be on controlling people seen as a threat, rather than on ensuring support for the many more who want and need it but are not seen to pose any danger. They expect service users to try to avoid the mental health system, rather than risk being detained compulsorily. There are widespread fears that proposals for compulsion will have inadequate safeguards in practice and will discriminate particularly against black and minority ethnic people. The scale (and breadth) of concern has been reflected in the lobbies and demonstrations which service users have both organised and been involved in (Greater London Action on Disability, 1999, 2000, 2002).

It can only be expected that the emphasis on the threat and danger from mental health service users will increase the discrimination, barriers and exclusions which they face. These barriers are already substantial (Sayce, 2000). There are strong links between poverty, social deprivation and mental health service use. People with mental health problems are identified as having the highest rate of unemployment among disabled people (Bird, 1999; Mind/BBC, 2000). If the aim of mental health services is ideally to provide support and help people live their lives, a complicated and stigmatising benefits system leaving people without an adequate or secure income has the opposite effect and is damaging for their wellbeing and self-esteem. The government's flagship welfare to work policy, with its slogan of 'Work for those who can [work] and security for those who can't' is frequently problematic for mental health service users who want to be in paid employment, but who *also* may need continuing help and support.

The problems of provision

Acute (hospital) services, particularly in the big cities, are associated with poor conditions. They are frequently unsafe for women service users, who are still placed in mixed wards. Mental health service users report problems accessing adequate, appropriate and reliable support services. They are much more likely to be offered neuroleptic drugs than the 'talking' and 'complementary' therapies which service users experience more positively. The low status of mental health service users and services means that there are continuing problems of funding, staff recruitment and retention. While the integration of health and social care in mental health was envisaged as a route to improved services and service co-ordination, service users have real concerns that it will undermine social understandings of their distress and reinforce traditional (unhelpful) medicalised individual understandings of their situation and experience. This is also reflected in new government interest in and emphasis on the idea of 'recovery', which is explicitly based on a medical understanding of madness and distress. Service users are understandably concerned that the only services they may access are those provided through extended compulsory powers of mental health legislation, based on the chemical and mechanical approaches about which service users have particular worries and fears.

During the 1990s, two parallel routes to access mental health services developed. These were care management and the care programme approach. The first was operated by local authority social services departments, the second under the national health service. The new emphasis on integration in health and social care has brought these two approaches closer together. Both are intended to ensure that service users receive a careful assessment of their needs and a suitable plan for their support, both of which they are meant to be involved in shaping. Multidisciplinary community mental health teams have also developed to increase the involvement of service users and to work in a more holistic and co-ordinated way. However, service users so far have had little effective involvement in the development of policy and practice at a broader level. While it has been a central focus of their activities, mental health service users and their organisations have so far had very limited success in reforming the service system.

Different ways of understanding

Service users and their organisations are now increasingly arguing for different ways of understanding and responding to their situation, because existing 'treatment' can often be worse than their original distress. A survey of people with mental distress carried out by the Mental Health Foundation found that different things helped different people at different times. Neuroleptic drugs did not work for everyone. They affected people differently, weren't enough on their own and were often prescribed without information about their unwanted effects. People wanted to have a holistic approach to their support, which took account of all aspects of their life, including the material, emotional and spiritual. They wanted their own expertise about themselves to be valued and to have choices in the 'treatment' they were offered (Faulkner, 1997). The user-led Strategies for Living project has found that some of the supports and activities that people find most helpful are acceptance, shared experience, emotional support, finding meaning and purpose, feeling secure and safe, pleasure, relaxation and having a reason for living (Faulkner and Layzell, 2000).

Mental health service users are placing an increasing emphasis on user-led, non-medicalised alternatives to provide the kind of support they want. These include complementary therapies and personal survival strategies. This has also encouraged service users/survivors to campaign for and develop their own non-medicalised crisis and out-of-hours services, including safe houses and refuges, help lines staffed by survivors, peer counselling and advocacy schemes and so on. These are valued by service users, but still only exist on a small scale. Mental health service user/survivor organisations have also developed their own advance directives and crisis card schemes so that individuals can specify in advance what they want to happen and who they want contacted if they have a bad time and don't feel able to take control.

Mental health service user/survivor organisations are now paying more attention to combating the discrimination that they face and adopting the kind of rights-based approach to securing support and countering prejudice which the broader disabled people's movement pioneered. This has been encouraged unintentionally by government attempts to increase compulsory provisions for 'treatment', which have led to more campaigning and direct action by service users/survivors (GLAD, 2002). Mental health service users/survivors are paying increasing attention to safeguarding their rights and beginning to make stronger links with the disabled people's movement. They are looking at how they can use the Disability Discrimination Act (1995) and Human Rights Act (1998) to safeguard their rights. The Disability Rights Commission has responded to this by setting up a Mental Health Action Group, which includes a majority of service users/survivors.

Many mental health service users/survivors are eligible for 'direct payments' (Community Care (Direct Payments) Act 1996), which put disabled people in control of the support they receive. So far very few mental health service users/survivors are getting direct payments, but the numbers and interest are rapidly growing. They offer a valuable way of getting the kind of non-medicalised support that many service users/survivors value. They offer a practical basis for preventive support. Many mental health service users/ survivors are keen to get back into employment, but they continue to face major obstacles. Government emphasis on employment as an obligation, rather than a right, poor conditions in the labour market, and the frequent failure of the benefits system to enable people to move flexibly in and out of work as their changing situation demands, all make this unnecessarily difficult. Evidence is already growing, however, that where the contribution of service users/survivors is valued and supported, they have much to offer (Snow, 2002).

Some mental health service users/survivors reject the idea of 'mental illness' as damaging and stigmatising. For others, it is the only model for understanding their situation that they have been offered. Service users/survivors are now, however, beginning to explore a *social model* of madness and distress that could challenge medicalised individual models of 'mental health' which still predominate and require service users to prove mental 'incapacity' to get benefits or support (Beresford et al., 2002). This perhaps offers one of the most hopeful bases for transforming attitudes towards, and services for, mental health service users/ survivors. Like the social model of disability before it, it may offer service users a way of understanding their experience in relation to the barriers and discrimination they face and highlight more clearly the priorities and strategies that will most effectively overcome them.

References

Beresford, P., Harrison, C. and Wilson, A. (2002) 'Mental health, service users and disability: implications for future strategies', *Policy and Politics*, 30 (3): 387–96.

Bird, L. (1999) *The Fundamental Facts: All the latest facts and figures on mental illness.* London: Mental Health Foundation.

Campbell, P. (1996) 'The History of the User Movement in the United Kingdom', in T. Heller, J. Reynolds, R. Gomm, R. Muston and S. Pattison (eds), *Mental Health Matters: A Reader.* London: Mamillan.

Coppick, V. and Hopton, J. (2000) *Critical Perspectives On Mental Health.* London: Routledge.

Daily Telegraph (1998) 'Care in the Community is Scrapped', 17 January.

Department of Health (1999) *A National Service Framework for Mental Health: Modern Standards and Service Models.* September. London: Department of Health

Faulkner, A. (1997) *Knowing Our Own Minds: A survey of how people in emotional distress take control of their lives.* London: Mental Health Foundation.

Faulkner, A. and Layzell, S. (2000) *Strategies For Living: A report of user-led research into people's strategies for living with mental distress.* London: Mental Health Foundation.

GLAD (1999) 'New Mental Health Act … Direct from Hell', *Common Agenda Newsletter*, Special Green Paper Edition. December. London: Greater London Action on Disability.

GLAD (2000) 'MPs meet with survivors', 29 March, *Common Agenda Newsletter*. May/June: 1–2. London: Greater London Action on Disability.

GLAD (2002) *Common Agenda Newsletter*. October. London: Greater London Action on Disability.

Mind/BBC (2000) *Mental Health Factfile.* January. London: Mind.

Newnes, C., Holmes G. and Dunn, C. (eds) (2001) *This is Madness Too.* Ross-on-Wye: PCCS Books.

Sayce, L. (2000) *From Psychiatric Patient to Citizen: Overcoming Discrimination and Social Exclusion.* Basingstoke: Macmillan.

Snow, R. (2002) *Stronger than Ever: Report of the First National Conference of Survivor Workers UK.* Stockport: Asylum Press.

Taylor, P. and Gunn, J. (1999) 'Homicides by people with mental illness: myth and reality', *British Journal of Psychiatry*, (174): 9–14.

38 Diagnosis and Assessment in the Lives of Disabled People: Creating Potentials/Limiting Possibilities?
MAUREEN GILLMAN

Whilst diagnosis and assessment are acknowledged as problematics in the lives of disabled people, there is no denying that the vast majority of disabled people have been subject to such processes during their lives. Oliver and Barnes suggest that definitions of disability can be divided into two groups: 'Official definitions produced by professionals and academics, and those developed by disabled people and organisations controlled and run by them' (1998: 14). It may be more comfortable from a social model perspective to separate impairment, and its associated practices of assessment and diagnosis, from disability. These practices are, however, very powerful discourses that shape identities and control often scarce resources.

Diagnosis

Diagnosis can be defined as a system of analysis of people's lives based on the specialist knowledge and expertise of professionals. It is a tacit agreement within particular professional areas to make sense of certain phenomena or events in a certain way (Gergen et al.). In the field of health care, the notion of diagnosis is complex. Some forms of diagnosis would be welcomed if not demanded by individuals and generally regarded as helpful. These include identification of life-threatening illnesses or broken limbs. Even good professional practices leading to an accurate and life-saving diagnosis, however, can have detrimental effects in terms of the medicalisation of a person's life.

In contrast, other types of diagnosis may be regarded as stigmatising and unhelpful, and may lead to impoverished lifestyles and exclusion from mainstream society. Examples include classification of mental illness such as schizophrenia and identification of bio-genetic profiles such as Down's Syndrome. For example, Goble discusses the impact of diagnosis on people with learning difficulties and suggests that:

> A key component in their historic and continued oppression is the medical profession's assumption of the powers of definition, classification and diagnosis on the basis of criteria such as IQ, adaptive behaviour and bio-genetic profiles or 'syndromes'. (1998: 834)

People with learning difficulties are the subjects of the medical (and other) professions' attention and theorising and are objectified as 'cases' and 'problems' (Gillman et al., 1997). Learning difficulties has come to be seen as an illness or disease and is a professional specialism in the fields of psychiatry, social work and psychology. The construction of diagnostic classification systems, amongst other functions, serves to mark out the boundaries of professional territory.

There is an assumption that diagnosis is based on the 'certainties' of scientific rigor and formal knowledge. However, such certainties do not stand up to close scrutiny. For example, Goodley asserts that:

> Assessment techniques for challenging behaviour are low in validity and reliability, simplistic and inappropriate. Assessment also ignores the cultural and social processes that help to shape others' reactions to challenging behaviour. (2000: 42)

Some diagnostic procedures and instruments can be seen as inappropriate and unreliable. In recent research (Gillman et al., 2000), hearing tests were frequently criticised by participants:

> 'I didn't think the hearing tests were very good for somebody who had a learning disability ... You had to sit at a machine and press this if you heard a ring ... How was he going to do that? But they said that there was nothing wrong with his hearing.' (2000: 398)

Similar difficulties were experienced by some participants when visiting the optician. Such examples highlight how diagnostic systems are often based on the normative assumption that everyone is able to read or comprehend speech.

Scope for confusion also exists in the area of mental health. Gravestock et al. (1996) put forward the view that standard diagnostic criteria for classification of mental illness are of limited use when assessing people with learning difficulties. For example, it is impossible to diagnose schizophrenia in people with limited communication who cannot put their thoughts into words (James and Mukerjee, 1996).

Despite the fallibility of diagnostic systems, once a diagnosis is made, it tends to be seen as an established, objective truth. Green et al. reported that most people in their study who were diagnosed with glaucoma were taken by surprise by the diagnosis and had not noticed any problems with their vision. They go on to say that:

> Some recalled a disjunction between clinical findings and their own experience: although tests indicated reduced visual fields, they perceived no problems with vision ... Only once they had been diagnosed could problems with sight be re-framed as 'symptoms' of glaucoma. The diagnosis itself attuned the patient to being sensitive to disabilities, and interpreting them as unusual and symptomatic ... (2002: 260)

Diagnoses are constructed in language and represent an agreement to make sense of certain phenomena according to particular theoretical models or frameworks. Diagnostic 'realities' are very much dependent upon the theoretical and ideological lenses through which professionals view phenomena. Korman suggests that:

> Diagnosis and assessment ... are determined ... from the theories that guide assessment and diagnosis. (1996: 282)

Here, Korman is making the point that diagnostic frameworks are not neutral but are founded on theoretical and ideological assumptions that organise what can be seen and, conversely, what should be ignored.

From this perspective it can be argued, for example, that we do not observe 'dysfunctional behaviour'. Rather, we observe behaviour that we label as dysfunctional, given a set of values that one holds as functional (Gergen et al.). From a social constructionist perspective, the outcomes of assessment and diagnosis are not representations of objective truth or reality about an individual, although many professionals act 'as if' this were so.

The acquisition of a diagnosis can open doors to resources and other forms of support (Sutcliffe and Simons, 1993). However, a family carer made the following point:

'Its like a double-edged sword. One thing is ... Do we need to label, and the second thing is unless you've got a label you can't access the Welfare State – education, housing ... Or whatever will meet your needs.' (Gillman et al., 2000: 402).

Similarly, research with people who had been diagnosed with glaucoma revealed that:

Some participants resisted registering as blind, or ... using a white stick in public. Thus, a potential key to independence is in itself perceived as stigmatising rather than enabling. (Green et al., 2002: 266)

Many disabled people and family carers seek a diagnosis in the belief that it would lead to an improved lifestyle and increased social support. A strongly-held belief in our society seems to be that diagnosis is benign and generally beneficial. Whilst this may be the case for some illnesses or conditions, many disabled people are substantially worse off as a direct result of receiving a diagnosis.

Take, for example, the classification or diagnosis of 'learning difficulty'. This is an overarching diagnosis that shapes identities and excludes people from mainstream society. Membership of this group has the potential to bring forth prejudicial and discriminatory attitudes in some professionals, which may lead to the disrespectful or dehumanising treatment of individuals who are seeking support. It may prevent access to certain treatments, such as transplant or dialysis. In addition, the label may lead professionals to 'look for' signs and symptoms of other 'conditions', such as mental illness and Alzheimer's disease, often resulting in a 'dual diagnosis'.

Professional diagnosis tends to exclude both the interpretations of those being diagnosed, and the systems of understanding and practices of negotiation that make it possible for stakeholders to arrive at shared meanings (White, 1997). Green et al. assert that:

Diagnosis thus does more than provide access to medical treatment – it also shapes the way in which sight loss is experienced and accounted for. ... an unexpected diagnosis had to be reintegrated within the stories participants told of their current strategies for coping and their concerns about the future. (2002: 265)

Working in partnership with disabled people in relation to diagnosis requires professionals to relinquish power by resisting the 'temptations of certainty' associated with diagnostic practices. If diagnosis is regarded as a hypothesis that is neither true nor false, but more or less useful, then consideration could be given to the efficacy of specific diagnoses in terms of the opportunities they create or the possibilities they limit. Viewing diagnosis as tentative or one of many possibilities affords those who are the recipients of a diagnosis the choice to accept or reject it.

Assessment

Assessment can be seen as an exercise in power. Professionals who hold most of the power in relation to the allocation of, often scarce, resources usually carry it out. Professionals control encounters with disabled people in a variety of ways: setting the agenda in relation to the information required to complete assessment forms; managing time to suit their diaries; framing and defining 'problems' and solutions on the basis of 'expert' professional knowledge; gate-keeping resources; and collaborating with other professionals. Assessment criteria and instruments are steeped in the characteristics of the individual model of disability and informed by definitions such as those contained in the Disability Discrimination Act 1995.

Services for disabled people are embedded in the discourse of rehabilitation (Finkelstein and Stuart, 1996). Barnes (1996) makes the point that while medical interventions may well be appropriate for minimising and monitoring the negative effects of impairment, they are inappropriate for dealing with disability:

> Professionals working within this perspective invariably pathologise the experience of impairment and in so doing compound the problems faced by disabled people; directing us into segregated special schools and sheltered workshops are two good examples. (1996: 43)

The dominance of the medical model can also be seen in relation to services for visually disabled people. Registration with the local authority as 'blind' or 'partially sighted' requires confirmation of diagnosis and a recommendation by a Consultant Ophthalmologist, whilst obtaining long-cane training or a guide dog requires written 'permission' from the disabled person's General Practitioner.

Social policies, dominant discourses in society and professional theories all influence and shape the 'assessment instruments' and criteria that are used to assess disabled people's entitlement to sources of support. Models and frameworks of assessment act as lenses or filters and dictate what can be taken into account and, conversely, what should be ignored. The possible consequences for disabled people of professionals adhering to models are identified by Hay, who suggests:

> When vested with authority of rank or role, it is almost inevitable that we bring our 'model' to bear on the person and family we are working with. We can override their perceptions of the world, and, indeed, are often trained to do precisely that. (2002: 13)

Assessment procedures tend to privilege information that is 'useful' to professionals, such as details of impairment or diagnosis. Such information allows professionals to slot people into categories which inform 'suitability' for services and resources. Pseudo-scientific forms of assessment tend to generalise about the expected 'effect' of impairment on an individual, thus excluding the disabled person's expertise relating to how their impairment actually affects them. Professionals need to listen to disabled people and recognise their expert knowledge about their conditions. This has implications for such issues as where and at what time of day assessments should be undertaken. Careful attention to disabled people's descriptions of how their impairment affects them can avoid oppressive assumptions that day-to-day variations in mobility and dexterity mean that they are lying or exaggerating (French et al., 1997).

Professional knowledge is invested with the status of truth because it upholds dominant discourses in society. In the field of welfare, professional knowledge and theories are concerned with personal growth, self-actualisation and overcoming personal adversity or deviance. Such notions are also consistent with current social policies, such as challenges to the so-called 'dependency culture'. Foucault (1977, 1980) maintained that professional theories and their associated practices, such as assessment and diagnosis, 'discipline' individuals and aim to reproduce 'acceptable' subjects who conform to societal 'norms'. Such norms may include notions such as 'independence', 'financial self-sufficiency' and 'productivity'.

Beresford and Holden (2000) assert that globalisation and its related economic constraints has become a key driver of public and social policy. It is at the heart of Labour's commitment to challenge 'dependency culture' and reliance on benefits. This is exemplified by Labour's determination to shift people from welfare to work. They go on to say that:

> Welfare service users can now expect to face an arbitrary combination of professional assessment, paternalistic welfare and compulsory employment. They are liable to categorisation as capable or incapable of work; deserving or undeserving. (2000: 983)

Policy makers are unlikely to have to witness the human costs of policy changes. A disabled person's life can be thrown into disarray when entitlement to resources and support is reduced or withdrawn. Interpretation and implementation of such policy changes are made by professionals who amend their assessment criteria accordingly. Hay discusses the frustrations experienced by disabled people and care professionals when coping with distribution of scarce resources:

> ... we are increasingly called upon to 'do more with less'. The public sector calls this 'managing expectations' – a painful euphemism for finding ways of not giving people what they need. (2002: 13)

What disabled people require in order to achieve or maintain desired lifestyles does not necessarily fit with professionals' perceptions of need. Entitlement to resources is inextricably linked to achieving productivity/employment and independence and often fails to take account of the personal dimension of need. For example, resources available under the 'access to work' scheme could provide a visually disabled person with resources at work, such as computer magnification software, CCTV system and a support worker. Similar equipment required at home for so-called personal use, however, has to be funded by the individual or a bursary from a charity.

Beckett and Wrighton (2000) make the point that there is a real difference enshrined in law and policy between personal individual need and need for enablement in a social world. Although the rhetoric of service provision for disabled people is claimed to be 'person centred' and therefore responsive to need, a distinction between 'need' and 'want' is a barrier to entry to the social and public world. Beckett and Wrighton assert that:

> Adequate response would need assessment that values both public and private activities equally. This is intrinsic to a social model of disability... (2000: 998)

The social model of disability and professional practices

The social model of disability questions the professional dominance over disability and supports experience over expertise, and self-help and collective action over professional intervention and personal adjustment. Professionals can work in partnership with disabled people by adopting a position of 'determined advocacy' in supporting disabled people to participate and define their own needs (Oliver and Sapley, 1999). Professionals should share power by sharing expertise; for example, by avoiding language that excludes, such as jargon, and by sharing information about sources of support. Active participation of disabled people should be encouraged in relation to report writing and writing in case files. In this way, the voices of disabled people will be heard and represented in official files and documents.

While professionals may well feel constrained by their agency role or the administrative procedures required in carrying out an assessment or diagnosis, there usually remains some degree of flexibility in which professionals can look for opportunities to work in partnership with disabled people (French et al., 1997). This can be achieved by professionals seeing themselves as a resource in terms of expertise, information and advocacy so that disabled people can work towards achieving their desired lifestyles. The following steps can be seen as a guide to professionals embarking on assessment with disabled people:

> Clarify the goals towards which the person aspires.
> Identify the barriers which may prevent the realisation of these goals.
> Work toward removing the barriers. (French et al., 1997: 55)

Perhaps in attending to the knowledge/power discourses in practices of diagnosis and assessment, professionals could critically evaluate and deconstruct assessment models, diagnostic procedures and case recording practices. This may well require a radical move toward collaboration/participation with disabled people and a recognition that the subjects of such processes are stakeholders in the enterprise.

References

Barnes, C. (1996) 'Visual impairment and disability', in G. Hales (ed.), *Beyond Disability: Towards an Enabling Society*. London: Sage.

Beckett, C. and Wrighton, E. (2000) 'What matters to me is not what you're talking about – maintaining the social model of disability in private negotiations', *Disability and Society*, 15 (7): 991–9.

Beresford, P. and Holden, C. (2000) 'We have choices: globalisation and welfare user movements', *Disability and Society*, 15 (7): 973–89.

Finkelstein, V. and Stuart, O. (1996) 'Developing new services', in G. Hales (ed.), *Beyond Disability: Towards an Enabling Society*. London: Sage.

Foucault, M. (1977) *Discipline and Punish*. Harmondsworth: Penguin.

Foucault, M. (1980) *Power/Knowledge: Selected Interviews and Other Writings*. London: Hanover Press.

French, S., Gillman, M. and Swain, J. (1997) *Working With Visually Disabled People: Bridging Theory and Practice*. Birmingham: Venture.

Gergen, K., Hoffman, L. and Anderson, H. 'Is diagnosis a disaster? A constructionist trialogue', draft of a chapter for inclusion in F. Kaslow (ed.), *Relational Diagnosis*. New York, NY: Wiley. (http:/www.swarthmore.edu/socSci/Kgergen1/index.html/accessed 2003)

Gillman, M., Heyman, B. and Swain, J. (2000) 'What's in a name? The implications of diagnosis for people with learning difficulties and their family carers', *Disability and Society*, 15 (3): 389–409.

Gillman, M., Swain, J. and Heyman, B. (1997) 'Life history or case history: the objectification of people with learning difficulties through the tyranny of professional discourses', *Disability and Society*, (12): 675–94.

Goble, C. (1998) '50 years of NHS involvement in the lives of people with learning difficulties: a cause for celebration?', *Disability and Society*, 13 (5): 833–835.

Goodley, D. (2000) *Self-advocacy in the Lives of People with Learning Difficulties*. Buckingham: Open University Press.

Gravestock, S., Bouras, N. and Holt, G. (1996) 'Quality monitoring in community psychiatry of learning disabilities services: current, planned and future approaches', *British Journal of Learning Disabilities*, 24: 95–8.

Green, J., Siddal, H. and Murdoch, I. (2002) 'Learning to live with glaucoma: a qualitative study of diagnosis and the impact of sight loss', *Social Science and Medicine*, 55: 257–67.

Hay, M. (2002) 'Disabled by denial', *Human Givens*, 9 (1): 13–19.

James, D.H. and Mukerjee, T. (1996) 'Schizophrenia and Learning Disability', *British Journal of Learning Disabilities*, 24: 90–94.

Korman, H. (1996) 'On the ethics of constructing realities', *Human Systems*, 7: 275–82.

Oliver, M. and Barnes, C. (1998) *Disabled People and Social Policy*. New York, NY: Addison Wesley Longman.

Oliver, M. and Sapley, B. (1999) *Social Work with Disabled People* (2nd edn). London: Macmillan.

Sutcliffe, J. and Simons, K. (1993) *Self-Advocacy and Adults with Learning Difficulties*. Leicester: The National Institute of Adult Continuing Education.

White, M. (1997) *Narratives of Therapists' Lives*. Adelaide: Dulwich Centre.

39 Tragedy Strikes Again! Why Community Care Still Poses a Problem for Integrated Living
MARK PRIESTLEY

This chapter highlights some of the key differences between community care and integrated or independent living. The experience of community care policy over the past decade suggests some important tensions between traditional discourses of disability, based on dependency, individualism and segregation, and the challenge of an independent living approach, based on full participation and equality. Ultimately, the participation of disabled people in managing their own affairs also challenges some deeper cultural values about disability and citizenship in society. A more detailed anaysis of the arguments is presented in *Disability Politics and Community Care* (Priestley, 1999).

A needs-led agenda for community care?

British disability policy has been traditionally dominated by an ideology of disabling cultural values. In particular, policy makers and those in the 'caring' professions have often viewed disability in terms of personal tragedy, the impaired body and otherness. These core values have been translated into mainstream services that are often preoccupied with care, medicalisation and segregation (at the expense of civil rights, participation and social integration).

The introduction of new arrangements under the 1990 NHS and Community Care Act suggested a move away from professionally-defined solutions, based on institutional living arrangements, towards community-based solutions, based on self-determination and the greater involvement of service users. In particular, the White Paper *Caring For People* emphasised the importance of proper 'needs-led' assessments. Indeed, the Audit Commission argued that the assessment process was so central to successful community care implementation that 'Authorities will rightly be judged by the quality of this process above all else' (Audit Commission, 1993: 9).

Initial guidance suggested that care management and assessment would help to achieve policy objectives by 'promoting individual choice and self-determination' (DoH/DSS, 1990: para. 3.3). The stated intention was to recognise the individuality of people's needs by making the wishes of users central, and by bringing the locus of decision making as close as possible to the end user. This has been consistently reflected in specific guidance for care practitioners. There have, however, been considerable reservations about how far this has been achieved. In practice, care assessments are also constrained by the need to ration scarce welfare resources within finite budgets. Rationing affects people in two ways. First, there may be restrictions on the total number of hours allocated to a package of support. Second, there may be restrictions on the kinds of support for which care assessors can allocate resources.

Good-quality home support services should provide help with a wide range of ordinary living tasks including personal assistance, domestic help and social or emotional support. However, changes in the move from home help to 'home care' focused service provision on limited 'personal care' tasks, while district nursing visits became restricted solely to 'nursing tasks'. Thus, for example, Jenny Morris (1993) showed how statutory domiciliary services are not generally available for assistance with activities outside the home and that they often fail to support participation in personal and family relationships.

Disabled people within the movement for independent/integrated living have consistently argued that support services should extend beyond the confines of care at home and enable them to take part in work, leisure, travel and family life. From this perspective, confusions between 'needs' and 'wants' are often misplaced. Without support to travel, to pursue social contacts, and to take part in the life of their communities, many disabled people face the risk of isolation and segregation within the home. Any service that is limited to medicalised personal care and 'essential' domestic assistance in the home has more in common with an ideology of care that undermines the citizenship and civil rights of disabled people. Thus:

> The ideology of caring which is at the heart of current community care policies can only result in institutionalization within the community unless politicians and professionals understand and identify with the philosophy and the aims of the independent living movement. (Morris, 1993: 45)

The practice of care assessment and management is not simply a technical 'gate-keeping' mechanism – it defines disabled people's needs in a very particular way. Value-laden purchasing decisions can perpetuate the myth of 'care' over independent living by focusing resources on personal care and limited domestic chores at the expense of support for social integration. Thus, care assessments all too frequently consolidate the social segregation of disabled people in their own homes, rather than challenging their enforced dependency.

Self-assessment and peer support

By contrast, the values of the disabled people's movement offer a significant counter-culture. In particular, the professionally dominated discourse of 'care' has been consistently challenged by the emergence of independent living projects under the control of disabled people themselves (De Yong, 1981, 1983; Davis, 1993; Davis and Mullender, 1993).

Since the early 1980s, a variety of self-managed personal assistance schemes have been developed by disabled people. Some, like Project 81 in Hampshire or the Kingston Independent Living Service, resulted from the personal struggles of individuals to gain control over their own affairs. Others have been led by established organisations of disabled people or centres for independent/integrated living (such as those in Avon, Southampton, Greenwich and Derbyshire). Often, they have involved local social services departments or voluntary organisations, such as the Wiltshire Independent Living Fund (WILF), Voluntary Action Sheffield, The Pendrels Trust in Coventry, Fairdeal in Leicestershire, the Norfolk Independent Living Group, or Merton Social Services Department.

The goal of self-managed support is to bring choice and control closer to the end user. The way in which the schemes operate, however, varies considerably. Some are 'direct payments' schemes (see Chapter 33), but the majority have used 'third-party' organisations or trust funds to broker funds (Zarb and Nadash, 1994). For example, in Barnet and Hackney, care brokerage schemes were run by disabled case managers. In Merton, personal assistants were employed directly by the Social Services Department (pending the implementation of direct payments legislation). In Derbyshire, personal support workers were employed by the Derbyshire Centre for Integrated Living (DCIL) under the direction and control of the end users.

Speaking at a conference organised by Coventry Independent Living Group (CILG), John Evans, chair of the British Council of Disabled People's Independent Living Committee, argued that:

'There ought to be no compromise regarding self-assessment; it is fundamental to the empowerment of disabled people. It is critical in terms of the assessment process that self-assessment is the starting point in enabling disabled people to determine their lifestyles.' (Barnes et al., 1995: 3)

This is no simple process. Many disabled people have been historically disempowered by dependency-creating welfare services and may lack the confidence or knowledge to make informed choices about the support they need. Simply asking people what they want is not a sufficient guarantee of user involvement. Thus, Personal Assistance Support (PAS) schemes are crucial in preparing potential personal assistance users for their community care assessments and supporting them through the process itself. Effective use of personal assistance depends on the quality of support that people receive when organising their package (Kestenbaum, 1993; Zarb and Nadash, 1994; Simpson and Campbell, 1996).

Support for self-assessment varies, but it can include meeting other disabled people and learning about their experiences, developing self-assessment skills, and drawing up a personal assistance plan. Proper planning prior to a formal community care assessment is in the interests both of the consumer and of the purchasing authority, since it cuts down on unnecessary social worker involvement and is more likely to lead to an effective and enabling use of resources. However, the provision of intensive individual support can be time consuming and potentially costly. PAS schemes need to draw on capable and experienced support workers committed to working intensively with potential users. Some schemes have to rely on the goodwill of existing personal assistance users for this function; others are able to utilise well-developed organisations with premises and paid staff.

Developing peer support in self-assessment is important because it provides positive role modelling for inexperienced personal assistance users and creates an empathic environment for the exploration of integrated living options. Although it has been difficult to win financial support for such initiatives, the provision of supported self-assessment is entirely consistent with the general drift of government policy. From what we have learned over the past ten years, it is clear that established organisations of disabled people, and particularly Centres for Independent Living (CILs), are well placed to develop peer support and back-up services for disabled people who want to manage their own affairs.

'Case' management and self-management

Initial guidance on community care policy stressed that users and carers should play an active role in implementing their 'care plan', and there is ample evidence that disabled people have welcomed the opportunity to take more control over their own lives through self-management. Within the movement for independent living, much emphasis has been placed on securing the resources with which disabled people might manage their own affairs through direct/indirect payments. The success of the Independent Living Fund and local self-managed support schemes prompted a sustained campaign by disabled people's organisations for direct payments legislation, and the introduction of the 1996 Community Care (Direct Payments) Act made this option available to many more disabled people. The permissive nature of the legislation, however, means that local authorities can still choose not to exercise their powers and there is evidence of political resistance to the principle in some areas.

One of the main attractions of self-managed assistance schemes is that they allow for more flexibility in the timing and content of support when compared to service provision (Zarb et al., 1996). However, making choices can also be a tricky business. Many disabled people have been historically denied the opportunity to make the sort of everyday life decisions that non-disabled people take for granted in our society. Past experiences of institutional care, 'special' schooling, 'protective' families, physical 'treatments' and chemical restraint have all contributed to this disempowerment. In addition, it is important to remember that ordinary choices become financial choices when people rely on paid assistance to facilitate them. For personal assistance users, everyday choices about the use of their time (cooking, cleaning, gardening, walking the dog) may become commodified choices about the use of scarce financial resources.

In this context, it is worth noting that people with additional personal resources (for example, savings and earnings) or alternative sources of support (from family, friends, volunteers) may have fewer of these difficult decisions to make. This is the case for non-disabled people, too. Disabled people in Britain, however, are more likely to live in low-income households and are significantly less likely to be able to draw on such resources. Consequently, significant numbers of disabled people without personal financial resources remain dependent upon the decisions made by community care assessors. Flexibility is clearly enhanced by self-managed personal support schemes, but real self-determination and life choices are still a function of personal income and familial capital for most people.

Self-managed support schemes *on their own* cannot solve all the problems. Without adequate resources for peer support, advocacy and organisational back-up, the effect is simply to devolve the difficult decisions of rationing from the care assessor to the end user of the service. Those without additional personal resources are then placed in a position of self-regulation and surveillance, forced to impose upon themselves the values of a welfare system that prioritises 'care' and 'treatment' over social integration and participatory citizenship.

Conclusion

For many disabled people, resources for personal support continue to depend upon professional assessments of 'need', from which they and their organisations have often been excluded. Encounters between disabled people and community care assessors show that there are often considerable differences of opinion about the priorities for assistance with everyday living. Consequently, personal assistance users may find themselves caught between the self-empowering values of independent living (arising from the politicised disabled people's movement) and the disabling values of a community care system that often maintains traditional values of care, individualism and social segregation. Rationing decisions that accept people's 'needs' for physical care and limited domestic help, while rejecting demands to support integrated social activities as 'wants', legitimise some of our most disabling cultural values. Thus, as Jenny Morris concludes:

> The aim of independent living is held back by an ideology at the heart of community care policies, which does not recognise the civil rights of disabled people but instead considers them to be dependent people and in need of care. (1993: 38)

The fact that disabled people and community care assessors come to the encounter with different agendas and expectations is not surprising, but it is something we should continue to question. In challenging the ideology of 'care', the movement for independent/integrated living has focused attention on the development of self-managed personal support schemes that bring resources under the control of disabled people themselves. Such schemes offer vital support to those who wish to manage their own affairs. They also bring greater choice, control and freedom to those who use them. Their success still depends upon the purchasing decisions of commissioning authorities and community care assessors. The challenge for organisations within the movement for independent/integrated living is to demonstrate the value of self-assessment and self-management within the competitive market for 'social care'. The challenge for care managers and assessors is to find ways of purchasing innovative packages of support that increase participation, social integration and citizenship, rather than simply reproducing care and dependency.

References

Audit Commission (1993) *Taking Care: Progress with Care in the Community.* London: Audit Commission.

Barnes, C., McCarthy, M. and Comerford, S. (1995) '*Assessment, Accountability and Independent Living: Confirmation and Clarification of a Disability Led Perspective*'. Report of a conference organised by Coventry Independent Living Group (CLIG) and Coventry Social Services Department. Coombe Abbey, Coventry, 23–24 May.

Davis, K. (1993) 'On the Movement', in J. Swain, V. Finkelstein, S. French and M. Oliver (eds), *Disabling Barriers – Enabling Environments.* London: Sage/Open University Press.

Davis, K. and Mullender, A. (1993) *Ten Turbulent Years: A Review of the Work of the Derbyshire Coalition of Disabled People.* Nottingham: Centre for Social Action, School of Social Studies, University of Nottingham.

De Yong, G. (1981) 'The Movement for Independent Living: origins, ideology, and implications for disability research', in A. Brechin, P. Liddiard and J. Swain (eds), *Handicap in a Social World.* London: Hodder and Stoughton.

De Yong, G. (1983) 'Defining and implementing the independent living concept', in N. Crewe and I. Zola (eds), *Independent Living for Physically Disabled People.* London: Jossey Bass.

Department of Health, Department of Social Security, Welsh Office, Scottish Office (1990) *Community Care in the Next Decade and Beyond: Policy Guidance.* London: HMSO.

Department of Health, Department of Social Security, Welsh Office, Scottish Office (1989) *Caring for People: Community Care in the Next Decade and Beyond*. London: HMSO.

Kestenbaum, A. (1993) *Taking Care in the Market: A Study of Agency Homecare*. London: RADAR/DIG.

Morris, J. (1993) *Community Care or Independent Living?*. York: Joseph Rowntree Foundation.

Priestley, M. (1999) *Disability Politics and Community Care*. London: Jessica Kingsley.

Simpson, F. and Campbell, J. (1996) *Facilitating and Supporting Independent Living: A Guide to Setting up a Personal Assistance Support Scheme*. London: Disablement Income Group.

Zarb, G. and Nadash, P. (1994) *Cashing in on Independence*. Clay Cross: British Council of Organisations of Disabled People.

Zarb, G., Nadash, P. and Berthoud, R. (1996) *Direct Payments for Personal Assistance: Comparing the Costs and Benefits of Cash Services for Meeting Disabled Peoples' Support Needs*. London: Policy Studies Institute for British Council of Organisations of Disabled People.

40 The Global Economy of 'Care'
CHRIS HOLDEN

The notion of care has been a contentious one for disabled people, and other chapters of this book provide a critique of this notion (see Chapters 30, 31, 33 and 39). Whilst acknowledging these critiques, this chapter examines the development of market-type arrangements for the delivery of care services in the UK. The services discussed are mainly those provided in residential and nursing settings – referred to as 'long-term care', although services to support people in their own homes are also increasingly provided by for-profit agencies in the UK. The chapter explains how market arrangements have led to a shift away from state provision of care services towards for-profit and voluntary providers, how the influence of large and internationalised corporations is growing in the sector, and why these types of providers are likely to continue to expand throughout the world. It concludes by exploring some of the possible implications of these developments for disabled people.

The marketisation of care

Ever since the social services provisions of the NHS and Community Care Act (1990) were implemented in 1993, social care services for adults in the UK have been delivered through a 'quasi-market'. 'Quasi-market' is the term given to the type of arrangements that have been established in countries like the UK whereby the purchasing of services is sep-arated from its provision. So, under the terms of the NHS and Community Care Act (1990), social services are paid for by local authority social services departments, but may be provided by a range of different organisations, including state agencies (usually local authority providers), private for-profit providers and voluntary organisations. The com-missioning section of the social services department therefore contracts with each of these providers to pay them a specified fee for a specified package of services. Whilst these ser-vices are free for many users, unlike health care, they are means-tested, which means that a fee is usually charged to those who are deemed able to afford it.

Over the last decade, direct provision of care services by local authorities has been con-siderably reduced, and replaced by care provided by 'independent' providers (the umbrella term for for-profit and voluntary providers). There are many reasons for this. In the decade prior to the implementation of the NHS and Community Care Act (1990), long-term care for older people in independent homes was paid for unconditionally by the then Department of Social Security (DSS) (for those who passed the means test). This encour-aged local authorities to sell their own residential homes, as they could raise money from such sales and could pass the cost of supporting people on to the DSS. The implementa-tion of the purchaser–provider split in 1993 was accompanied by a Special Transitional Grant' (STG) to help authorities meet the costs of their new responsibilities. However, the government stipulated that 85 per cent of the STG must be spent in the independent sector. Furthermore, the purchaser–provider split introduced a new culture into social services departments, whereby they no longer expected to be the main providers, but would instead become assessors and purchasers of care provided by others. Although initially local authorities tended to display a preference for purchasing from not-for-profit providers, over time this preference has dissipated as authorities have got used to dealing with for-profit organisations. Thus independent provision has become the norm in long-term care services and is rapidly spreading throughout home care services.

Initially, for-profit provision in long-term care was overwhelmingly dominated by small providers, many of whom were 'husband and wife teams' motivated as much by a desire to provide a service as to make a profit. Whilst small providers continue to make up the majority of provision, since 1996 there has been a rapid process of concentration in the market. A series of mergers and acquisitions between the larger providers in 1996–97 initiated this process of concentration. Since then a number of factors have combined to accelerate the process still further. These factors relate mainly to the costs of provision. Large providers are much more economically efficient than small providers, since they can make use of economies of scale. These economies include both those obtained from purchasing supplies in bulk at a discount, as well as those obtained from building larger homes which are relatively cheaper to run. Large providers are also able to borrow to fund their expansion, or to raise money by selling their properties to real estate companies and then leasing them back. Thus large providers have been in a much better position to absorb recent increases in costs than small providers. Many of these large providers are becoming increasingly internationalised (Holden, 2002a).

The costs to providers have risen in recent years as a result of a number of factors (Holden, 2002b). In 2002 the government introduced new National Minimum Standards for long-term care homes and a new body for the whole of England to ensure their implementation, the National Care Standards Commission. Although the government signalled its willingness to be flexible in the introduction of the new standards, the perception that they would impose significant new costs led some providers to exit the market. The government has also introduced regulations governing working conditions that will affect the care sector, such as the National Minimum Wage and the Working Time Directive, both of which have added to the labour costs of providers. The fee levels paid by local authorities have generally been insufficient to allow small providers to meet such costs, thus increasing the tendency towards concentration of ownership and provision. Although the commitment to increase health spending announced in the 2002 budget will provide some extra resources for social services departments, the logic of the market is likely to continue to favour large corporate providers, especially since the dramatic rise in house prices in some parts of England gives small providers an added incentive to sell up.

The internationalisation of care

The degree to which corporate providers are involved in the delivery of care services in any given country will depend on the structure of the welfare state in that country. Welfare systems which are based upon state provision of services do not provide many opportunities for the involvement of private companies, whilst those countries that have a history of large-scale private provision offer extensive opportunities to such companies. The direction of change in most countries, however, is away from provision directly by the state and towards private provision, although the pace of change varies greatly from country to country. The development of the 'mixed economy of care' in the UK since the 1980s is a good example of a shift from a primarily state provided system to a marketised one, which in this case was driven initially by the neo-liberal ideology of the Thatcher governments. As already explained, this was achieved through the implementation of the purchaser–provider split, but this is not the only means by which private providers may be involved in care provision. Each country has its own particular form of welfare state, and reforms to these different systems may also take a variety of forms. The USA, for example, has always had a system which is based on the principle of private insurance, backed up by state insurance for the poor and for older people. Such systems offer at least as much scope for the involvement of private companies as the UK quasi-market system.

The trend towards greater private involvement in care services in advanced capitalist countries is mainly a result of policies freely chosen by national governments. These governments may be motivated by neo-liberal ideology, as Thatcher's were, or by pragmatic or political concerns. It has been argued in recent years that governments in fact have little room for maneouvre in today's 'globalised' economy, and that the need to compete in the world market forces them to reduce state spending and adopt more market-friendly policies (Mishra, 1999). This is an important debate, to which we are unable to do justice here, but it is important to note that emphasising apparently external constraints allows governments to legitimise unpopular policies which they intended to pursue anyway.

Whilst the governments of advanced capitalist countries do have choices about the policies they follow, the governments of poorer countries are often coerced by institutions controlled by the richer and more powerful countries. The countries of Eastern Europe and the former Soviet Union, which since the end of the 1980s have been undergoing a profound transition from bureaucratically planned economies to capitalist ones, have often been pushed into premature or inappropriate pro-market policies by Western-dominated institutions and by their own national elites. Whilst many of these countries' welfare systems currently remain state-provided ones, the trajectory of change is once again towards more market-friendly arrangements. The still poorer developing countries of the world, many of which have huge debts to Western banks, are even more vulnerable to pressure from international institutions.

The two most important international institutions are the International Monetary Fund (IMF) and the World Bank. Both of these were set up at the end of the Second World War to help rebuild the world economy, both of them are effectively controlled by the advanced capitalist nations, and both of them adhere to essentially neo-liberal ideas (although there is some degree of debate both between and within them about the correct types of policy to follow – see Deacon, 2000). These two institutions offer poor countries the debt relief and development funds which they desperately need (sometimes under the label of 'Structural Adjustment Programs'), but in return demand that governments follow their neo-liberal policy prescriptions. Amongst an array of other policies, these usually involve privatisation and the opening up of the economy to the multinationals of the advanced capitalist world.

Added to the policies of the IMF and the World Bank are the activities of the World Trade Organisation (WTO). The WTO was set up in 1995 to take forward the process of trade liberalisation which, until then, had been negotiated through the General Agreement on Tariffs and Trade (GATT). GATT involves countries agreeing to systematically reduce tariffs (import taxes) and other barriers to free trade. Whilst GATT was focused mainly on trade in manufactured goods, the WTO has now turned its attention to the liberalisation of services through the General Agreement on Trade in Services (GATS). The barriers to trade in services identified by the WTO include such things as state subsidies, rather than simply tariffs, and have significant implications for welfare services. Welfare services provided by the state in a non-competitive environment are exempt from GATS. However, where services are provided in a competitive environment, which arguably they are within UK-type quasi-market arrangements, as well as in more traditional market environments, they are particularly vulnerable to being interpreted as falling within the provisions of GATS (Price et al., 1999: 1890). The full application of GATS to such services would mean that all foreign providers would have equal access to care markets on the same terms as domestic (private or state) providers, thus further facilitating the internationalisation of care provision.

Currently, countries can choose whether they want to fully include particular sectors of the economy within the provisions of GATS (or to use GATS terminology to 'schedule' them), but trade talks are likely to increase pressure for new sectors to be liberalised, including welfare services. The advanced capitalist countries of the EU and the USA are particularly keen to force developing countries to open up their public services to Western multinationals. Taken together, the activities of the IMF, the World Bank and the WTO can only increase the privatisation and internationalisation of care services across the world, particularly in developing countries.

The Implications of a global economy of care

This process of internationalisation reflects the growing internationalisation of the world economy more generally. The internationalisation, or 'globalisation', of the world market is a process which has been in train at least since the nineteenth century, but has gathered particular pace since the 1980s. In that decade, Foreign Direct Investment (FDI) by multi-national firms began to grow at an even faster rate than international trade, whilst the speed and volume of financial flows to buy and sell shares, bonds and currencies grew to an extent where it was widely believed that no single government could control them. During this period, FDI by service firms has been growing even faster than that by manufacturing firms. Although still in the relatively early stages when compared to the huge multi-national producers of cars or pharmaceuticals, the internationalisation of care firms and other welfare providers is likely to increase.

Internationalisation in sectors such as care services tends to take the form of FDI rather than trade. This is because services are 'consumed' at the point of 'production' – a care provider must set up a residential home in the community where people live, or send its employees to users' homes, whereas pharmaceuticals, for example, can be produced in a single location and then exported to other countries. Research indicates that some large providers of long-term care actively seek new markets outside of their home countries (Holden, 2002a). Whilst such providers may currently account for a minority of provision in a country like the UK, they are likely to have a disproportionate impact on the nature of care delivery, since they are leaders in terms of innovation, whether in marketing techniques or in their internal organisation. Such providers usually compete aggressively with domestic providers, and thereby set up an incentive for other organisations to emulate them in order to retain or extend their share of the market. This is likely to affect not-for-profit and voluntary organisations as much as other for-profit enterprises, the largest of which have increasingly begun to operate in a similar manner to corporate providers (Holden and Beresford, 2002: 203).

The process of the internationalisation of care services is also facilitated by the internationalisation of Western conceptions of 'care'. The development of capitalist industrialisation in the West played a key role in the generation both of impairment and of dominant conceptions of disability (Holden and Beresford, 2002: 193). Western notions of disability have been transposed to the rest of the world, often without due regard for indigenous cultures and understandings. Mike Oliver (1996: 127) has argued that, just as industrialised societies created their own category of disability, they also created an industry to service it. The internationalisation of Western notions of disability and 'care' thus provides the cultural and ideological basis for the export of commercial care services to other parts of the world by Western companies.

Three possible implications of the provision of care services by large corporations have been identified (Holden, 2002b). First, these developments tend to involve a process of merger and acquisition, whereby large firms merge with each other in an attempt to enhance their competitive advantage or acquire smaller less profitable firms. This can impact negatively upon residents, since in the process of merger some care homes will be closed down, whilst others will experience a change of internal regime as the acquiring firm attempts to integrate the new units into its particular way of working. Such disruption can be very upsetting for residents, and in the worst cases may result in fatalities for older people. Second, large firms usually implement their own internal quality assurance regimes, which allow them to exert control over the various units within the organisation and to market the care they offer as a single 'brand'. Each firm thus wants to assure potential residents that, wherever they are in the country, they can expect the same level of care from any home belonging to that firm. This may be consistent with high standards of care by some definitions, but it tends to lead to standardisation of services – an outcome which does not sit easily with the notion of 'community care'. Finally, depending on the particular welfare arrangements in any given country and the nature of the care market, it is possible for local monopolies to arise. Monopoly provision undermines the supposed benefits of competition, and places a greater responsibility upon regulators to ensure high standards of provision. It would be ironic indeed if the final outcome of quasi-markets was to replace the target of neo-liberal reforms – state monopoly – with private monopolies.

The marketisation and internationalisation of care services is likely to increase in most countries in the coming decades as a result of the factors discussed in this chapter. This has particularly profound implications for disabled people in developing countries, where the adoption of Western notions of care and the private provision of that care may lead to extreme inequalities. If for-profit provision of such services becomes the norm, it will prove very difficult to reverse this trend in favour of other, more socialised, methods of provision, since the existence of international agreements like GATS will lock countries into a set of institutional arrangements premised upon neo-liberal ideas. It is important that disabled people and their allies respond to such developments in a pro-active way, using the influence of their own international networks to ensure that emerging forms of provision genuinely meet their needs.

References

Deacon, B. (2000) 'Globalization: A Threat to Equitable Social Provision?', *Social Policy Review*, (12): 250–71.

Holden, C. (2002a) 'The internationalization of long term care provision: economics and strategy', *Global Social Policy*, 2 (1): 47–67.

Holden, C. (2002b) 'British government policy and the concentration of ownership in long-term care provision', *Ageing and Society*, 22 (1): 79–94.

Holden, C. and Beresford, P. (2002) 'Disability and Globalization', in C. Barnes, L. Barton and M. Oliver (eds), *Disability Studies Today*. Cambridge: Polity.

Mishra, R. (1999) *Globalization and the Welfare State*. Cheltenham: Edward Elgar.

Oliver, M. (1996) *Understanding Disability: From Theory to Practice*. Basingstoke: Macmillan.

Price, D., Pollock, A.M. and Shaoul, J. (1999) 'How the World Trade Organization is shaping domestic policies in health care', *The Lancet*, 354 (9193): 1889–91.

Part V
Creating A Society Fit For All

41 Disability and Social Exclusion in the Information Society
BOB SAPEY

The social model of disability is an analysis of a process of marginalisation, oppression, discrimination, exclusion, or in other words disablement, that affects people with impairments. A significant feature of the social model is that disability is considered to be a product of industrialisation. This does not mean that prior to the industrial revolution people with impairments were valued and always included, rather that the scale of the very specific demands of a new form of economy led to the construction of particular social responses to impairment, notably a hegemony of care and segregation. The purpose of this chapter is to consider whether this particular process of disablement will continue within the informational economy that began to emerge over the last quarter of the twentieth century or whether the process of exclusion will take another form.

Disability as a product of industrialisation

The link between industrialisation and disability is a fundamental aspect of the social model of disability. Ergonomically, the requirements of new working environments of the industrial revolution excluded many people, especially those with physical impairments, from employment. While the most common characterisation of this demand is of children being employed to undertake tasks within textile mills because adults were too large to clamber within the machinery, the process of disablement as it exists today was generated by the use of these new productive technologies (Finkelstein, 1980). At the same time, the demands of the production process on workers meant that families had less opportunities to assist relatives who were impaired and alternative forms of care needed to be found. The dominance of medicine and its claim to expertise in the area of impairment led to this care being provided in hospitals and other similar settings, which in turn led to institutionalisation and segregation being the shared experience of disabled people (Oliver, 1990).

Borsay (1998) argues that this analysis may not accurately reflect the intentions and practices of hospital-based medicine, which sought to rehabilitate disabled people back into the workforce, but what is clear is that the provision of institutional care – in workhouses, hospitals and nursing homes – steadily increased from the mid-nineteenth century and throughout the twentieth century. Schorr's (1992) analysis of British welfare suggests that the numbers of people entering such places only declines when the provision of pensions increases the relative spending power of dependent people. So whilst the rehabilitative project of modern medicine may have had inclusive intentions, these have had minimal effect without complementary social security provisions. The result of this is that rehabilitation services have been widely criticised by disabled people for individualising the socially constructed problems they face. As Brechin and Liddiard say:

> ... disabled people are faced with impossible social, financial, housing and environmental difficulties, and are then offered a piecemeal welfare system of professionals and services to help them adjust to and cope with their unacceptable circumstances. (Brechin and Liddiard, 1981: 2)

This combination of being excluded from the mainstream economy whilst being offered segregated forms of living led to what Finkelstein (1980) has termed 'a hegemony of care'. Unlike many others who may have been excluded due to lack of skills or character, disabled people were considered to be deserving of some form of state support. Indeed, Oliver (1990) has argued that the need to separate the undeserving from the deserving was instrumental in distinguishing disabled people from others, hence defining disability as a social category. The development of medicine and its desire to gain power by co-opting areas of social life such as disablement (Oliver, 1990) provided the state with a means of looking after the deserving, namely care, that was distinguished from other forms of relief. By the time disabled people began to develop the social model analysis in the latter half of the twentieth century, the idea that they needed care had become so ingrained in our ways of thinking about the world that it appeared to be beyond question – it had become hegemonic. The social model of disability and its rejection of care in favour of civil rights began to question the unquestionable and in so doing brought about a paradigm change in the way we think about disability.

Exclusion from the mainstream economy is predominantly achieved by exclusion from employment and through inadequate levels of other forms of financial help, such as state benefits. Research on employment and disability in the UK has shown that disabled people are far more likely to be unemployed than non-disabled people, and that if they are in employment they are likely to be in lower paid and less valued occupations (Barnes, 1991). This is also true of the USA (Sapey, 2000), and in both countries there is a greater likelihood of unemployment amongst disabled women, disabled people from ethnic minorities or amongst those with less education. This exclusion arises because of barriers that are both structural and attitudinal: the design of employment and the assumptions made by employers that disabled people would be unable to perform as efficiently as non-disabled people.

In 2001 there were just over 7.1 million disabled people of working age in the UK and they made up 19.3 per cent of the working-age population, almost 1 in 5 (Smith and Twomey, 2002). However, less than half (47.9 per cent) were in employment as compared with 81.2 per cent of the non-disabled population. Almost the same number of disabled people were classed as economically inactive, although nearly one-third of this group would like to work. Overall, the percentage of disabled people who were either seeking employment or would like to work was 23.6 per cent, while for non-disabled people it was about one-third of this at 8.6 per cent. (See Chapter 29.)

Smith and Twomey also report that while disabled people make up 1 in 5 of the working age population, approximately 1 in 3 households of working age contain at least one disabled adult. It is here that the exclusion from the economy can be more clearly seen in terms of its effect on household income. The Family Resources Survey 2000–2001 (cited in Smith and Twomey, 2002), which takes into account state benefits as well as earned income, shows that in terms of income distribution, approximately 25 per cent of households with a disabled adult were in the lowest quintile and this figure gradually falls to about 14 per cent in the highest quintile. For households without a disabled adult the position was the reverse, rising from around 14 per cent in the lowest quintile to nearly 30 per cent in the highest. This is probably the clearest indicator of the inequalities that arise due to the exclusion of disabled people from the economy. So whilst the impact of policies and practices which have accompanied industrialisation is clear, what is of interest at this point in history is whether the changes taking place within the economy, especially in terms of the informationalisation of work, are having an impact on the nature of disablement.

Informationalisation

Many sociologists speculate that we are in the process of post-industrialisation. This may have different meanings or be used in different contexts, such as to explain the rise in importance of information and data, changing production processes or to analyse the changing structures of modern organisations. Castells (1996), however, uses the term 'informationalisation' to describe:

> ... a specific form of social organization in which information generation, processing, and transmission become the fundamental sources of productivity and power, because of new technological conditions emerging in this historical period. (1996: 21)

His interest is not so much with what went before as with the nature of the new economy that has been emerging over the last quarter of the twentieth century. This is an information economy that may be capable of existing in its own right. It is, of course, interlinked with the industrial economy in just the same way that the industrial economy was interlinked with the agricultural economy, most obviously through activities such as the production of farm machinery, but information technologies also generate new markets for themselves. The most obvious examples are our thirst for information via the Internet and its link to sales of home computers, or the widespread sale of mobile phones, so commonly used to let others know where you are when they already know. In this sense the term 'post-industrialisation' may have explanatory limitations in the same way that 'post-agricultural' would have been inadequate to describe the process of industrialisation. These terms take as their base of reference what went before, whereas industrialisation and informationalisation describe new forms of production and of social organisation.

The importance of examining the impact of these changes on disabled people arises because part of Finkelstein's (1980) analysis of the creation of disablement under industrialisation is that the rise of new technologies would lead to a third phase in which people would be freed from the constraints of their impairments. Oliver (1990) felt that this was too optimistic and that it is necessary to examine the power relationships that govern the use of new technologies. The potential for benefit certainly exists and within the technological literature there is a widely shared optimism that developments can and will lead to positive outcomes. There is evidence to suggest, however, that little has yet changed in terms of disabled people's access to work. Elsewhere (Sapey, 2000), I have examined employment data, particularly from the USA, which indicate that disabled people are more likely to be found in employment in the agricultural sector than the industrial, and more likely to be in the industrial sector than the informational. While this is necessarily a crude analysis due to the fact that data are not collected or organised in these sector categories, the trend is nevertheless clear – what appears to be happening in the new economic sectors is a continuation of disabled people being one of several groups who are excluded from valued fields of employment. Whilst that reflects a similar operation of power as in the past, Roulstone (2002) argues that these processes cannot be fully understood or acted upon without understanding the changing nature of employment.

One of the significant aspects of the changing nature of employment is the move towards employers requiring people to have higher academic and vocational qualifications. The Confederation of British Industry (Edelsten and Bell, 2002) reports that 29 per cent of firms will recruit fewer people without qualifications over the next three years, while some 47 per cent expect to recruit more graduates. This trend is consistent with the growth of an informational economy in which knowledge workers are likely to be in greater demand, and with the contraction of the industrial economy through the dispersal of unskilled work to other parts of the globe where labour costs are lower. However, the Department for Work and Pensions (Grewal et al., 2002) report that disabled people are twice as likely to have no qualifications, that they are likely to leave school at a younger age, and when they do have qualifications, they are less likely to be academic ones. The impact of such trends is likely to be a negative one for many disabled people seeking entry into the mainstream, as opposed to the social security, economy.

Changing Welfare

Informationalisation, like industrialisation, also has a role to play in structuring the welfare system and in so doing the social problems that system is intended to deal with are liable to be redefined. The most obvious change in recent times in this respect is the rise in popularity in both academic and political circles of the term 'social exclusion'. This term may mean a number of different things and is liable to be used in different ways, so it is necessary to be clear about what I mean by 'social exclusion' in this context. First, it is linked to exclusion from paid employment within the legitimate economy and second, it involves a reduced entitlement to alternative support from the welfare system, especially in terms of social security. In the USA, for example, some states have experimented with withdrawing financial support from single parents, usually mothers, encouraging them into employment or, failing that, other forms of financial dependence, notably the black economies of drug trafficking and pornography. At the same time, child welfare surveillance is strengthened so that parents are more closely policed (Grover and Stewart, 2002).

While this is not yet occurring on any large scale in the UK social security system, the rhetoric of this approach was present in the parliamentary arguments used by the Labour government to explain the withdrawal of One Parent Benefit and the lone parent premium element of Income Support (Grover and Stewart, 1999), and in their arguments for the integrity tests for invalidity benefit (Harris et al., 1999). It is possibly a sign of the success of disabled activists and campaigners that the Disability Discrimination Act and the Disability Rights Commission have been strengthened so that employers are being more consistently challenged over the exclusion of disabled people from employment, while the stick of reducing benefit entitlement to individuals in conjunction with the new deals on employment has yet to be effectively wielded. As Roulstone (2002) warns, however, there are limits to what can be achieved through the anti-discrimination legislation approach and the strength of the momentum of globalised capitalism will take more than the Disability Rights Commission to ensure that disabled people are included. Thus it appears that some of the elements of an increased exclusion from employment are in place, but that for the time being the rhetoric of individual responsibility and reduced social support is on hold, thus sustaining the hegemony of care.

Abberley (2002) is critical of the focus of discourses of social exclusion on employment. He is concerned that traditional political theories, be they Marxist or neo-liberal, are inadequate to resolve the problems of disablement because of their emphasis on the value of a person's productive skills and ability. This, he argues, will leave many disabled people socially excluded if the only route to gaining respect is via employment, and he seeks to examine how it may be gained through the valuing of non-productive roles. Sennett (2003), who has been concerned with the impact of new forms of production upon those working within them, has examined the issue of respect in some depth, not necessarily in relation to disabled people but certainly in relation to welfare. His concern is that the tendency in the more individualistic world we live in today is for respect to be associated with self-reliance so, while people who seek support because of their neediness are certainly going to gain attention, it is only when they are no longer needy that they are likely to gain respect. As with Abberley, he is also concerned about the limitations of egalitarian approaches which argue that mutually respectful behaviour will emerge from an equalisation of material conditions:

> This expectation is psychologically naïve. Even if all unjust inequalities could be removed in society, people would still face the problem of how to shape their worse and their better impulses. I don't suggest accepting or accommodating inequality; rather, I argue that in social life as in art, mutuality requires expressive work. It must be enacted, performed. (Sennett, 2003: 59)

This places an emphasis on action at a personal or cultural level, rather than leaving the responsibility solely with structures and institutions. Indeed, if one examines the current practices within the social welfare system, it is possible to detect these individualistic impulses. There has been a strong commitment from the government to the use of new technologies in the delivery of social care (Department of Health, 2000a) and this has had an impact on the nature of the care that is then provided. On the one hand their intention is that a focus on information will mean that welfare recipients are better informed and as a result more in control of how their needs are met (Department of Health, 2000b), and this is supported by the promotion of new approaches such as direct payments and the requirement for local authorities to work more collaboratively with disabled people. On the other hand, at a local level the impact of informationalisation is tending to change the priorities of social services agencies so that the outcomes of social care are now focused more on the collection of data about their clients, rather than the delivery of a material service to them (Huntington and Sapey, 2003). This surveillance approach in combination with a degree of reluctance by social workers to engage with direct payments (Dawson, 2000) does cast doubt on whether current practices would indeed lead to greater respect being afforded to disabled people by those within the welfare system, let alone by those outside of it. Furthermore, while there has been a shift from institutional to community-based care, the move away from material services may reflect a reduction in the hegemony of care.

The question I am interested in is whether these changes in the economic sphere have in any way changed the nature of disability, and at the moment it would appear from the evidence that rather than liberating disabled people, new technologies have created forms of work and welfare that may be more exclusionary than those of the industrial era. In terms of social security, disabled people are still deemed to be deserving, though, as Abberley (2002) argues, there would need to be a democratisation of the system for it to begin to afford respect. That respect also appears to be lacking in the practices of social care, although there may be more evidence of it being present in the rhetoric of government. Thus changes are taking place, but in a way that appears to reinforce and strengthen the nature of disablement rather than diminish it.

References

Abberley, P. (2002) 'Work, disability, disabled people and European social theory', in C. Barnes, M. Oliver and L. Barton (eds), *Disability Studies Today*. Cambridge: Polity.

Barnes, C. (1991) *Disabled People in Britain and Discrimination: A Case for Anti-discrimination Legislation*. London: Hurst.

Borsay, A. (1998) 'Returning patients to the community: disability, medicine and economic rationality before the industrial revolution', *Disability and Society*, 13 (5): 645–63.

Brechin, A. and Liddiard, P. (1981) *Look at this Way: New Perspectives in Rehabilitation*. London: Hodder and Stoughton.

Castells, M. (1996) *The Information Age: Economy, Society and Culture: The Rise of the Network Society*. Malden, MA: Blackwell.

Dawson, C. (2000) *Independent Success: Implementing Direct Payments*. York: Joseph Rowntree Foundation.

Department of Health (2000a) *Information for Social Care: A framework for improving quality in social care through better use of information and information technology*. London: Department of Health.

Department of Health (2000b) *A Quality Strategy for Social Care*. London: Department of Health.

Edelsten, M. and Bell, J. (2002) *Employment Trends Survey 2002: Measuring Flexibility in the Labour Market*. London: Confederation of British Industry.

Finkelstein, V. (1980) *Attitudes and Disabled People: Issues for Discussion*. New York, NY: World Rehabilitation Fund.

Grewal, I., Joy, S., Lewis, J., Swales, K. and Woodfield, K. (2002) *'Disabled for Life?' Attitudes Towards, and Experiences of, Disability in Britain*. London: Department for Work and Pensions.

Grover, C. and Stewart, J. (1999) 'Market workfare: social security, social regulation and competitiveness in the 1990s', *Journal of Social Policy*, 28 (1): 73–96.

Grover, C. and Stewart, J. (2002) *The Work Connection: The Role of Social Security in British Economic Regulation*, Basingstoke: Palgrave.

Harris, J., Sapey, B. and Stewart, J. (1999) '"Blairfare": third-way disability and Dependency in Britain', *Disability Studies Quarterly*, 19 (4): 360–71.

Huntington, A. and Sapey, B. (2003) 'Real records, virtual clients', in E. Harlow and S. Webb (eds), *Information and Communication Technology in the Welfare Services*. London: Jessica Kingsley.

Oliver, M. (1990) *The Politics of Disablement*. Basingstoke: Macmillan.

Roulstone, A. (2002) 'Disabling pasts, enabling futures? How does the changing nature of capitalism impact on the disabled worker and jobseeker?', *Disability and Society*, 17 (6): 627–42.

Sapey, B. (2000) 'Disablement in the informational age', *Disability and Society*, 15 (4): 619–36.

Schorr, A. (1992) *The Personal Social Services: An Outside View*. York: Joseph Rowntree Foundation.

Sennett, R. (2003) *Respect: The Formation of Character in an Age of Inequality*. London: Penguin.

Smith, A. and Twomey, B. (2002) 'Labour market experiences of people with disabilities', *Labour Market Trends*, 110 (8): 415–27.

42

From Universal to Inclusive Design in the Built Environment[1]
ROB IMRIE

One of the more significant problems for disabled people relates to physical obstacles and barriers in the built environment. Many commercial and public buildings are inaccessible to wheelchair users, while few buildings provide appropriate design features to enable people with a range of sensory impairments to move around with confidence and ease. Accessible public transport is a rarity, while most housing lacks basic adaptations or design features to facilitate independent living for disabled people. Likewise, high streets are littered with street furniture that make ease of movement difficult for vision-impaired people, while uneven pavements and lack of kerb cuts render independent wheelchair use more or less impossible. Physical barriers, then, prevent disabled people's ease of access to a range of places, and are implicated in denying disabled people the right to determine where they want to go. As some have argued, this is tantamount to an infringement of disabled people's civil liberties (Barnes, 1991; Imrie and Hall, 2001).

Research suggests that the perpetuation of inaccessible environments is related to architects' lack of understanding of the diverse design needs of disabled people, and the reluctance of developers to incorporate appropriate design features into buildings (Imrie, 1996; Imrie and Hall, 2001). Most architects have little or no knowledge of impairment, and are rarely called on to think about designing for the needs of disabled people. Design education rarely raises disability as an issue, and the building regulations tend to treat designing for disabled people as an 'add-on' rather than integral to good building design[2]. Part M of the Building Regulations, which sets legal building standards for designing for disabled people in England and Wales, replicates the usual stereotypes about disability. Its definition of disability is impairment-specific, and disabled people are seen as a discrete population that require 'special treatment'. Impairment tends to be understood as ambulatory or mobility deficiency, which focuses architects' attention on wheelchair users at the expense of other disabled people (Imrie, 1996).

These pejorative attitudes towards, and understanding of, disability have pre-empted the development of alternative ways of thinking about, and responding to, the design needs of disabled people in the built environment. The most far-reaching perspective, to date, is that of universal design (UD), the focus of this chapter. In seeking to evaluate the importance of UD, as a means of solving problems faced by disabled people by physical barriers in the built environment, I divide the chapter into three. First, I describe the origins and principles of UD. Second, I develop the argument that the principles of UD, while laudable, fall short of providing the basis for an inclusive architecture, or an architecture that is sensitised to the bodily needs of disabled people. I conclude by suggesting that the principles of UD be aligned to a political agenda that challenges entrenched values and practices of property agents and actors and the hierarchical social relations of property development.

Figure 42.1   The key principles of Universal Design

Principle	Description
Simple and intuitive use	The use of the design is easy to understand regardless of the user's experience, knowledge, language skills, or concentration levels.
Equitable use	The design does not disadvantage or stigmatise any groups of users.
Perceptible information	The design communicates necessary information effectively to the user, regardless of ambient conditions or the user's sensory abilities.
Tolerance for error	The design minimises hazards and the adverse consequences of accidental or unintended fatigue.
Flexibility in use	The design accommodates a wide range of individual preferences and abilities.
Low physical effort	The design can be used efficiently and comfortably and with a minimum of fatigue.
Size and space for approach and use	Appropriate size and space is provided for approach, reach, manipulation and use, regardless of the user's body size, posture or mobility.

Source: Center for Universal Design, 1995

The principles of universal design

UD has its origins in the USA and it has spawned a range of research initiatives and practical applications (see Salmen and Ostroff, 1997; Steinfeld and Danford, 1999; Weisman, 1992, 1996). As Figure 42.1 suggests, UD is a social movement underpinned by a range of foundational principles. Foremost is its concern with integrating disabled people into society by making products, environments and communication systems usable to the greatest extent possible by the broadest spectrum of users. Impairment is not seen as unique to a specific population, but as intrinsic to the human condition (Zola, 1989). UD seeks to respond to everyone, regardless of whether or not they have an impairment, or, as Greer notes:

> ... improved design standards, better information, and new products and lower costs make it possible for design professionals to begin designing all buildings' interiors and products to be usable by all people all of the time instead of responding only to the minimal demands of law that requires a few special features for disabled people. (1987: 58)

UD is part of a broader awareness of the limitations of architectural processes and practices, which are more concerned with aesthetic issues than those of building use. A range of research indicates that the human subject, or the user of buildings and the wider built environment, has often been reduced to a specific type or even ignored in Western (or modern) architectural theories and practices (Marble, 1988; Tschumi, 1996). The most influential architectural theories and practices fail to recognise bodily and physiological diversity, and there is a tendency for architects to design to specific technical standards and dimensions which revolve around a conception of the 'normal' body. For most architects, this is based on classical conceptions of the fit and able body. The body, in this view, is little more than an object with fixed, measurable, parts; it is neutered and neutral, that is, without sex, gender, race, or physical difference.

Such conceptions are anathema to UD, which conceives of the body as neither fixed nor static but as fluid and ever changing. The body, as a dynamic entity, requires an architectural or design process which is able to anticipate changes in physiological and other needs. In particular, the proponents of UD are critical of compensatory approaches to architecture, or where accessibility is added 'to otherwise inaccessible objects and standard designs' to compensate disabled people for their functional limitations (Connell and Sandford, 1999: 35). Accessible design is seen as demeaning and drawing attention to a person's impairment with the potential for stigma and social exclusion. As Steinfeld (1994: 3) argues, it provides little more than a token response. Steinfeld further notes that 'accessible design acknowledges that people with disabilities have a right to access and use of products and environments, but it doesn't go far enough because it doesn't express social integration' (1994: 4).

In contrast, UD, so it is claimed, seeks to integrate the accommodation of disability with the basic concept of the design by sensitising the environment to the broadest possible range of bodily shapes, dimensions and movements. The objective is to draw attention away from people's impairment as a source or site of difference to minimise the possibilities of social ostracism. There is also a recognition that the design of buildings, and other products, ought to enhance, rather than inhibit, 'the changing abilities of humans throughout their life-span' (Salmen and Ostroff, 1997: 3; see also Steinfeld and Danford, 1999). UD is seen as a complex process which requires an integrative, team approach to transcend the limitations of any one perspective or professional viewpoint. As Salmen and Ostroff note, 'designers cannot get … information from books, databases or design criteria alone' (1997: 6).

Such views underpin UD's support for equitable use or the development of design that does not disadvantage any group of users. The reduction of energy expenditure is a core principle or, as Steinfeld (1994) notes, people need an environment that eliminates unnecessary expenditure of effort. As Steinfeld amplifies: 'this can be achieved by organising space and designing devices to simplify the task of using them … useless movements should be eliminated' (1994: 2). Likewise, the illegibility of the built environment, and related products, is a constraint on their use and UD seeks to simplify environments by the use of colour and texture contrasts. While Steinfeld (1994: 3) acknowledges that not all environments will be usable by all people from the beginning, a remit of UD is promoting the flexibility, adaptability and interchangeability of fittings and fixtures.

Some limits to universal design

The principles of UD are important and, potentially, progressive in seeking to restore disabled people's self-esteem, dignity and independence, while encouraging the development and implementation of user-friendly design. However, it is difficult to see how far transformations in disabled people's lives can occur without the development of a social or political programme for change and, in this respect, the core philosophies of UD ought to be developed further. Its principles are apolitical in that there is little, explicit, recognition of the interrelationships between the social, technical, political and economic processes underpinning building and design. UD proceeds largely on the basis that environmental change is a matter of developing and implementing a technical or design solution. Facilitating access, for universal designers, is about adaptation from one type of design to another, reconfiguring the fixtures and features of a building and developing new procedural mechanisms for deploying resources and their management.

A technical and procedural response is, however, partial because it leaves intact the social and attitudinal relations that influence the form and content of design. Given that the attitudes of developers, architects and other property professionals are usually indifferent towards the needs of disabled people, there is no reason to suppose that technical adaptations, in and of themselves, will significantly change the lives of disabled people. Gleeson (1999) goes further in arguing that assistive technologies are no more than corrective mechanisms or a means to transform disabled people into 'normal' human beings. The objective is 'to integrate people with disabilities into the mainstream' (Center for Universal Design, 2000: 1). However, for Linton (1998: 58), such mainstreaming, which is core to the principles of UD, revolves around standards set by the dominant majority, or those allied to a definition of disability as 'not-normal' or 'abnormal'. In this sense, impairment, as far as UD ideas are concerned, is regarded as something to be overcome or to be eradicated, rather than to be accepted as an intrinsic feature or part of a person and their identity.

UD also appears to be totalising in its message of wanting to cater for all within the context of its design solutions. Its proponents claim, however, to be able to accommodate difference and variation by using adjustable and interchangeable design elements and designing spaces that can be easily customised. Some have raised doubts about such solutions and, as Hind has noted:

> ... there are so many different types of sight loss and you can't create 'access for all'; universal design is not possible – there are too many contrasts and types with visual impairment and also depth of vision varies so much – you can get two-dimensional vison and distance just goes and you have to re-educate yourself about your environment. (1996)

In this sense, UD may be promising much more than is technically achievable or feasible. It is also unclear as to how conflicts between different types of users, with contrasting design needs, can be accommodated within the overall ethos propagated by UD. For instance, can a singular design respond to all types of vision impairment?

UD is characterised by a particular conception of the user as a consumer or customer of design products. As Ostroff states, 'in universal design, where the needs and limitations of users may be unfamiliar, the designer can learn a great deal from the experiences of the potential consumer' (2000: 1). The customer analogy is, however, problematical because it does little to challenge or change the design professionals and their position as knowledgeable experts. As Salmen and Ostroff suggest, 'designers must listen to and hear from perceptive spokespeople who can articulate the needs and responses of people of all stages of life' (1997: 6). Users are seen as consumers of a service, and only active in its production through market-based testing or exercises similar to those carried out by large private corporations prior to the development of their latest product. Thus, for Salmen and Ostroff, a legitimate exercise is that 'designers must involve the future users, the customers of the design, through universal design reviews' (1997: 6).

For Salmen and Ostroff (1997: 6), UD is able to make 'designer, user and building owner more sensitive' to the needs of disabled people, yet they do not say how such sensitivity will be acquired or applied in ways which will guarantee a change in developers' and designers' perspectives and practices. They also suggest that the process of UD should be 'representative, user responsive, and participatory'. While these are laudable aims, it is not clear how they will be achieved. In part, this is because UD focuses too much on the architectural profession *per se*, and not on the social and political realities that impinge on their work. Indeed, architects are one of many actors and/or institutions involved and implicated in the development of the built environment, and a fuller understanding of the architect's role requires a broader understanding of development and design processes (Imrie and Hall, 2001). As Knesl (1984) suggests, architecture is pre-determined by political and economic power, including laws, statutes, codes and corporate clients.

Towards an inclusive design process

UD is characterised by general principles that few would disagree with. They are meaningless, however, unless wedded to policies and practices that challenge the realities of property development and design dynamics. Economic and cultural rationales and values drive these realities and, in doing so, the needs of diverse users of the built environment are often overlooked (Imrie and Hall, 2001). An inclusive design process is required, or one whereby a transformation takes place in the social relations of the development and design process. Foremost, law and legal principle, in relation to access to, and the design of, buildings, has to be strengthened. The building regulations and the Disability Discrimination Act (1995), an alleged piece of civil rights legislation, are part of a lineage that does little to challenge the prejudices of developers and architects. There are too many get-out clauses and exemptions in law to expect anything other than the continuation of practices which treat accessible design as an 'add-on' or part of compensatory design.

Attaining inclusive design will also require a genuine democratisation of the development process, far removed from the consumerist perspective of participation envisaged by UD. The latter does not challenge the vested interests or hierarchies of the development process. In contrast, an inclusive process will seek to draw inspiration from design philosophies that have, at their fulcrum, an understanding of design as a reciprocal process between designer and those that use the built environment. Such ideas were formative in the writings of John Turner, who developed the notion that the property professional ought to be an enabling practitioner or 'one who is not only a reflexive listener but also an active collaborator with the client' (1987: 273). As Bentley suggests, 'the problem, therefore, lies not so much in the fact that designers feel they are experts, as in the kinds of experts they believe themselves to be' (1999: 239).

Note

1 This chapter is based, in part, on the reproduction of material contained in Chapter 1 of Imrie, R. and Hall, P. (2001) *Inclusive Design: Designing and Developing Accessible Environments*. London: Spon Press. The author would like to thank the publisher, Spon Press, for permission to reproduce parts of this book. My thanks are due to Sarah Fielder and Marian Hawkesworth for their helpful comments on the chapter.

2 A similar regulation exists in Northern Ireland (Part R), which came into effect on 1 April 2001. In Scotland, there is no separate regulation relating to disability and access, although there are substantial references to access issues in Parts M, Q, and S of the Scottish Building Regulations. Access to housing is primarily covered in Part Q.

References

Barnes, C. (1991) *Disabled People in Britain and Discrimination*. London: Hurst.

Bentley, I. (1999) *Urban Transformations: Power, People and Urban Design*. London: Routledge.

Center for Universal Design (1995) *Principles of Universal Design*. Buffalo, NC: North Carolina State University: Center for Universal Design.

Center for Universal Design (2000) website: www.design.ncsu.edu/cud/index.html accessed 2003.

Connell, B. and Sandford, J. (1999) 'Research implications of universal design', in E. Steinfeld and G. Danford (eds), *Enabling Environments*. London: Kluwer Academic. pp. 35–57.

Disability Discrimination Act (1995) *Code of Practice: Rights of Access to Goods, Facilities, Services and Premises*. London: Department of Social Security.

Gleeson, B. (1999) 'Can technology overcome the disabling city?', in R. Butler and H. Parr (eds), *Mind and Body Spaces: Geographies of Illness, Impairment and Disability*. London: Routledge. pp. 98–118.

Greer, N. (1987) 'The state of the art of design for accessibility', *Architecture*, January, 58–60.

Hind, F. (1996) Interview conducted by R. Imrie with Fiona Hind, Rehabilitation Officer with the Society for the Blind, Leicester, 12 August.

Imrie, R. (1996) *Disability and the City*. London: Paul Chapman.

Imrie, R. and Hall, P. (2001) *Inclusive Design: Designing and Developing Accessible Environments*. London: Spon.

Knesl, J. (1984) 'The power of architecture', *Environment and Planning Design: Society and Space*. 1: 3–22.

Linton, S. (1998) *Claiming Disability: Knowledge and Identity*. New York, NY: New York University Press.

Marble, S. (1988) *Architecture and Body*. New York, NY: Rizzels.

Ostroff, E. (2000) 'Mining our natural resources: the user as expert', *Adaptive Environments* website: www.adaptenv.org accessed 2003.

Salmen, J. and Ostroff, E. (1997) 'Universal design and accessible design', in D. Watson (ed.), *Time-saver Standards for Architectural Design Data: The Reference of Architectural Fundamentals*. New York, NY: McGraw Hill. pp. 1–8.

Steinfeld, E. (1994) 'The Concept of Universal Design'. Unpublished paper presented at the Sixth Ibero-American conference on accessibility, Centre for Independent Living, Rio De Janeiro, 19 June.

Steinfeld, E. and Danford, G. (eds) (1999) *Enabling Environments*. London: Kluwer Academic.

Tschumi, B. (1996) *Architecture and Disjunction*. Cambridge, MA: MIT.

Turner, J. (1987) 'The enabling practitioner and the recovery of creative work', *Journal of Architectural and Planning Research*, 4 (4): 273–80.

Weisman, L. (1992) *Discrimination by Design*. Chicago, IL: University of Illinois Press.

Weisman, L. (1996) 'Diversity by design: feminist reflections on the future of architectural education and practice', in D. Agrest, P. Conway and L. Weisman, (eds), *The Sex of Architecture*. New York, NY: Harry N. Abrams. pp. 273–86.

Zola, I. (1989) 'Towards the necessary universalising of a disability policy', *The Milbank Quarterly*, 67 (2): 401–428.

43

The Disability Movement: Some Observations
LEN BARTON

In this brief chapter I will be very selective over the issues and ideas that are examined. The intention is to provide a stimulus that will encourage the reader to explore further this very important topic. I will identify some of the key factors informing the development of the disabled people's movement, and highlight some of the agendas they have pursued and some of the challenges that they are currently facing. I will particularly focus on the UK context and give priority to the views of disabled people. This is their movement and their voices need to be listened to. In attempting to write their own history, disabled people have provided a wealth of insights into the processes of thinking and action that have characterised these developments (Campbell and Oliver, 1996; Charlton, 1998).

For an adequate understanding of the motivations behind such developments, it is essential that we begin to recognise and understand the extent and degree of the discriminatory and exclusionary barriers that disabled people encounter both individually and as a group. These include attitudinal, economic, structural conditions and relations that have contributed to the appalling and unacceptable situation in which, as Barnes so powerfully contends:

> ... the lifestyle of the overwhelming majority of disabled people is characterised by poverty and social isolation. (1996: x)

This depressing and offensive global perspective in which disabled people's self-worth, opportunities and experiences have been negatively affected in systematic ways, provides the context in which the pursuit of inclusion and the adoption of alternative perspectives based on human rights needs to be understood.

One of the emerging concerns in relation to disabled people is that of representation and the expression of their voice. This interest in the perspectives of disabled people is motivated by a recognition that both as individuals and groups they have been excluded from decision making over a range of issues relating to the quality of their lives.

Some disabled analysts view the disability movement as an example of a new social movement in modern societies (Oliver, 1990; Hasler, 1993; Shakespeare, 1993). The disability movement serves two main functions: an internal one, creating a context for solidarity and mutual support; and externally, for campaigning for anti-discrimination legislation, independent living and a barrier-free society.

In a crucially important book, Campbell and Oliver (1996) explore the social and political contexts within which, over a relatively brief period of time, disabled people have gained in strength as a new social movement, against enormous odds. These they maintain include: chronic under-funding, a lack of faith in the viability of the new movement by many professionals, policy makers and politicians and serious opposition on the part of those organisations for disabled people. Added to these is the general disabling environment presenting various barriers in terms of meeting and organising.

This is really serious business in which disabled people are involved through their organisations at a regional, national and international level in struggles to capture the power of naming difference. An emancipatory meaning of difference is one of the goals of a movement concerned with social justice. This involves challenging definitions and assumptions that legitimate and maintain relations and conditions that marginalise and exclude, and replacing them with definitions which engender inclusion, dignity and solidarity.

By challenging a subordinate and dependent role, refusing to acquiesce to a stigmatised social identity and developing a sense of pride in who they are, the disability movement is mounting a serious challenge to overcoming ignorance, prejudice and discrimination. The motivating force for this is clearly orientated in the hope of a future society, which as Morris advocates:

> ... celebrates difference, a society which does not react to physical, sensory or intellectual impairments, or emotional distress with fear and prejudice. We want a society that recognises the difficulties we face, but also values us for what we are. (1992: 28)

In their writings and everyday discourse, disabled people organisationally and individually describe their activities in terms of a *struggle*. It is a battle in which there is no room for complacency and such political discourse is a reminder of the stubbornness and pervasiveness of that which is being opposed: it highlights the degree of commitment required by those engaged in such efforts; it reinforces the social nature of their activity and thus the importance of social bonding and solidarity; and it assumes that there are no easy, quick, slick answers to these complex and contentious issues.

Social model of disability

One of the major achievements by disabled people has been the development of a social model of disability (see Chapter 1) A key turning point in the development of the social model of disability in Britain was the definition of disability developed at a meeting of the Union of the Physically Impaired Against Segregation (UPIAS) in 1976:

> In our view, it is society which disables physically impaired people. Disability is something *imposed* on top of our impairment by the way we are unnecessarily isolated and excluded from full participation in society. Disabled people are therefore an oppressed group in society.
>
> Thus we define *impairment* as lacking part or all of a limb, organ or mechanism of the body; and *disability* as the disadvantage or restriction of activity caused by a contemporary social organisation which takes no or little account of people who have physical impairments and thus excludes them from participation in the mainstream of social activities. (1976: 14, my emphases)

This perspective has since been broadened to include all impairments, physical, sensory and intellectual, and is the official position of the British Council of Disabled People. (The British Council of Organisations of Disabled People was created in 1981 and is now called The British Council of Disabled People.)

Recognising the centrality of institutional, ideological, structural and material disabling barriers within society is fundamental to a social model of disability. The value of the social model is most clearly outlined in the statement by Hevey, in which he acknowledges the ways in which he had internalised his oppression. He likens his experience to that of a religious conversion, or 'Road to Damascus' encounter:

> I had internalised my oppression. As a working class son of Irish immigrants, I had experienced other struggles but, in retrospect, I evidently saw epilepsy as my hidden cross. I cannot explain how significantly all this was turned about when I came into contact with the notion of the social model of disabilities, rather than the medical model which I had hitherto lived with. Over a matter of months, my discomfort with this secret beast of burden called epilepsy, and my festering hatred at the silencing of myself as a disabled person, 'because I didn't look it', completely changed. I think I went through an almost evangelical conversion as I realised that my disability was not, in fact, the epilepsy, but the toxic drugs with their denied side-effects; the medical regime with its blaming of the victim; the judgement through distance and silence of bus-stop crowds, bar-room crowds and dinner-table friends; the fear; and not least, the employment problems. All this was the oppression, not the epileptic seizure at which I was hardly (consciously) present. (1992: 1–2)

This is about the development of a politics of identity in which personal and collective pride and motivation are essential features of this process (see Chapter 5). This emphasis has been captured by Wood in the following powerful way:

> Discovering our identity as disabled people is very, very important. It's still important today, otherwise people won't value themselves. I think this is probably the biggest success that the movement has been able to point to. It is our movement, nobody else owns it. We know who we are. (1996: 124)

The social model of disability provides an emancipatory way of conceiving the relationship between the individual and society and of the importance of socio-economic conditions and relations in terms of understanding the position and experiences of disabled people in society.

It is important to be clear as to what a commitment to a social model of disability means and involves for individuals and organisations of disabled people. They are not arguing for sameness, or to become as normal as possible, nor are they seeking an independence without assistance. Their vision is of a world in which discrimination and injustice are removed, including stereotypes, ignorance and fear. They are desirous of the establishment of alternative definitions and perceptions based on a dignified view of difference.

Globalisation

We are witnessing a fundamental transformation of technological, social and cultural change. The explosion of technological infrastructures involving telecommunications, information systems, microelectronic machinery and computer-based transportation has contributed to the globalisation of markets (Bauman, 1998). Whilst globalisation is a disputed concept, it is important to recognise, as Carnoy maintains, that the essence of globalisation is 'a new way of thinking about economic and social space and time' (2000: 45). In the contemporary world, immense movements of capital are dependent on information, communication and knowledge that are part of the global market.

In a discussion of globalisation, Hallak argues that it produces two contradictory phenomena:

> ... standardisation and diversification. Standardisation of eating habits, clothes and cultural products tends to produce growing similarities in the living conditions of societies. On the other hand, diversification strives to preserve the multiple facets of society by promoting access to the diverse features of world heritage. (2000: 25)

In this highly intrusive, competitive world, globalisation is creating new forms of inequality, as Hallak also forcefully reminds us:

> Globalisation engenders exclusion, the development of economic and social differences, aggravation of conflicts between groups of different identities, the dislocation of societies and the dissipation of commitments to universal solidarity. (2000: 27)

This dependency can be viewed most vividly with regard to disabled people and the impact of globalisation. Indeed, Hurst contends that the 'global information network does not address the concerns of disabled people' (2003: 166), due to factors of irrelevancy, inaccessibility and negative images. Disabled people, Hurst continues, have experienced an increase in their isolation, disempowerment and segregation.

However, important developments have taken place. For example, the birth of Disabled People's International, which became in 1992 a human rights association and which now has over 160 national assemblies (Hurst, 2003). This organisation is committed to establishing links with other organisations of disabled people, including the British Organisation of Disabled People and Disability Awareness in Action, in order to pursue global justice. Through this means, greater numbers of disabled people, individually and organisationally, have begun to appreciate that they have a role to play beyond the level of national contexts.

Through, for example, the collective endeavours of national and international organisations of disabled people, the positive use and impact of the Internet and e-mails is beginning to be developed and felt (see Chapters 8 and 23). Concrete facts, information, and experience are being directly shared between disabled people in different cities and countries. This is providing a wealth of collective knowledge, understanding and insights which can be used to meet the demands of various campaigns, policy developments and their implementation. This again has educative, mobilising and encouraging functions.

Conclusion

It is important to recognise that disabled people are not a homogeneous group. Nor are the developments related to the emergence of a disability movement part of a linear process of improvement. Nor is the social model fixed in tablets of stone. All social movements entail tensions, disagreements and the disturbing process of critical self-engagement. The disability movement is no exception. Currently within the British Organisation of Disabled People there are serious arguments taking place over the future and purpose of the organisation and over the nature and function of the social model of disability (Finkelstein, 2002a, 2002b; Hurst, 2003; WECODP, 2002).

Nor should debate and dialogue of this nature be seen as unhealthy or counter-productive. It is an essential aspect of the creative process of change in which the questions of fundamental values and future hopes are of central significance. What is objectionable is when the exchanges are about personality slamming, status, control and individual or factional vested interests.

As you continue to confront and raise questions relating to disability and the quality of the lives of disabled people, do remember the importance of the organisations of disabled people and their relationship to the disability movement. Remember the centrality of the voices of disabled people whose words are powerfully echoed in the following ways:

> Nothing About Us Without Us!
> Choices and Rights in our Lives!
> Piss on Pity!

References

Barnes, C. (1996) 'Theories of disability and the origins of the oppression of disabled people in Western society', in L. Barton (ed.), *Disability and Society: Emerging Issues and Insights*. Harlow: Addison Wesley Longman.

Bauman, Z. (1998) *Globalization: The Human Consequences*. Oxford: Polity.

Campbell, J. and Oliver, M. (1996) *Disability Politics: Understanding Our Past, Changing Our Future*. London: Routledge.

Carnoy, M. (2000) 'Globalization and educational reform', in N.P. Stromquist and K. Monkman (eds), *Globalization and Education: Integration and Contextualisation across Cultures*. Oxford: Rowman and Littlefield.

Charlton, J.I. (1998) *Nothing about Us without Us: Disability, Oppression and Empowerment*. Berkeley, CA: University of California Press.

Finkelstein, V. (2002a) 'The social model of disability reappraised', *Coalition*, February, 10–16.

Finkelstein, V. (2002b) 'Separate! You have nothing to lose except your careers', *Coalition*, November, 8–9.

Hallak, J. (2000) 'Globalization and its impact on education', in T. Mebrahtu, M. Crossley and D. Johnson (eds), *Globalization, Educational Transformation and Societies in Transition*. Oxford: Symposium Books.

Hasler, F. (1993) 'Developments in the Disabled People's Movement', in J. Swain, V. Finkelstein, S. French and M. Oliver (eds), *Disabling Barriers – Enabling Environments*. London: Sage.

Hevey, D. (1992) *The Creatures Time Forgot: Photography and Disability Imagery*. London: Routledge.

Hurst, R. (2003) 'Conclusion: enabling or disabling globalisation?', in J. Swain, S. French and C. Cameron (eds), *Controversial Issues in a Disabling Society*. Buckingham: Open University Press.

Morris, J. (1992) *Disabled Lives: Many Voices, One Message*. London: BBC.

Oliver, M. (1990) *The Politics of Disablement*. Basingstoke: Macmillan.

Shakespeare, T. (1993) 'Disabled people's self-organisation: a new social movement?', *Disability, Handicap and Society*, 8 (3): 249–65 (Special Issue).

UPIAS (1976) *Fundamental Principles of Disability*. London: Union of the Physically Impaired Against Segregation.

West of England Coalition of Disabled People (2002) 'Disabled People's Parliament', *Newsletter*, (50): 3–9 (Bristol).

Wood, R. (1996) Interview quoted in J. Campbell and M. Oliver (1996) *Disability Politics: Understanding our Past, Changing our Future*. London: Routledge.

44 Genetics, Disability and Bioethics[1]
HELEN CAPLAN

The affluent First World in which we live is an ever more acquisitive and individualistic society. In such a society where advertising encourages consumption, and media images show aspirational figures of beauty, strength and wealth, there is an emphasis on striving for the finest goods that money can buy. This has extended to health care and childbirth. A Western perspective places the emphasis on individual autonomy and this, coupled with a view that there is a right to have a child, has aided the push for assisted reproduction. But it is no longer enough to have a child, rather one must strive for the perfect child. As families are in general smaller, more personal investment is made in the children that people do have and so the search is on for the 'perfect baby'. In this push for perfection, tests are employed to check for embryo quality. In this climate of opinion, many disabled people feel threatened as their very existence is being questioned.

As prenatal testing for genetic and chromosomal defects are the most prevalent of the techniques available to the medical profession, and as these techniques worry disabled people the most, I am going to concentrate on the implications they have for disabled people. There are also tests which are offered to children and adults. In all cases, although we can discover abnormalities, at present we do not have many treatments or cures. Adults can choose whether to take a test, in the full knowledge of all its potential implications. In the case of Huntington's disease, life insurance will be refused and there is no treatment currently available. For children there is often a reduced level of consent to undergo tests, depending on the age of the child. The difference in prenatal testing is that a decision is being made for someone who is not yet born. This decision may result in death if abortion is chosen.

Pregnancy and birth are very personal, but societal attitudes affect the experience. Testing for impairment is promoted as scientific and value free, but it is done in a climate which is often hostile towards those who are seen as different. Disabled people are starting to speak out about testing and this can only improve the level of debate. Whether it changes practice remains to be seen.

A brief outline of testing

Before examining reasons for the expansion of testing, it is important to look at the types of investigation that are offered. In cases where techniques are offered to a group of people who have not been identified as being likely to bear impaired children, then this is classified as screening. Testing occurs when a familial history suggests that an impairment may be found or a carrier status may be discovered. Also, it may follow screening if positive results are discovered. Some screening methods give an indication that impairment may be present and this is called the 'risk factor', whilst others are diagnostic.

A pregnant woman may be offered a variety of investigations in order to determine whether she is carrying an impaired fetus. The most commonly offered screening techniques are ultrasound scanning and a blood test to determine levels of alpha feto-protein and two other pregnancy related hormones. The former is used to indicate whether the fetus is growing normally or if abnormality is present. Recently it has been used to detect Down's Syndrome is some cases. The latter gives an indication of whether chromosomal or genetic impairments are present. The most frequently offered test is amniocentesis, whereby fluid is taken through a needle from the amniotic cavity in the uterus of a pregnant woman. It is performed at around 16 weeks into the pregnancy. Chorionic Villus Sampling (CVS), whereby cells are taken from the placenta using a needle guided by ultrasound, is sometimes offered and is performed at around 10 to 12 weeks. As there are additional risks with CVS, such as a higher rate of miscarriage than with amniocentesis, many centres do not offer it.

The emphasis on screening has created enormous stress for women and their partners and has resulted in women being unable to enjoy their pregnancies. Until all the tests are complete a woman is experiencing what Katz Rothman (1994) has called 'the tentative pregnancy'. Women reported to her that they felt unable to announce their pregnancies in case they needed an abortion following a positive test result. Some decided to have tests even though they would not abort for any reason, but here the risk is that if an impairment is found the child is considered in those terms rather than as an individual.

This is indeed a common experience for disabled people, being regarded in terms of a 'condition' rather than as an individual with wants and needs. It is so common to be labeled as a Down's child, instead of being seen as Alice or Fred. By encouraging screening, what image of disabled people is being promoted? If the test has as its purpose the elimination of the potential disabled person, then the suggestion is that life as a disabled person is not worthwhile. Clearly, looking at the lives of existing disabled people this is generally untrue (see Chapter 5). So, if impairment is not the negative force it is often portrayed as, why is this message not reaching the wider public? Why is it not enough for disabled people to value our own lives? Why must we pass other people's tests as well? There are many reasons for this and in a short chapter I am unable to discuss them in detail, but the existence of tests does lead to a questioning of what counts as normal.

The growth in screening

Since it poses so many difficulties, the question needs to be asked: Why has this emphasis on screening come about? Farrant (1985) identified powerful groups who had interests in expanding prenatal screening. In the mid to late 1970s, the government needed to develop screening services due to general economic restraint. In 1977 the Department of Social Security published a paper entitled *Reducing the Risk: Safer Pregnancy and Childbirth*. This shows an economic bias as the following passage indicates: 'because caring for the handicapped can impose great burdens on our society, the prevention of handicap ... in addition to its other benefits may save money' (cited in Farrant, 1985, page 99). Obstetricians have always been interested in technological innovation as it enhances their status as a speciality and helps them to achieve control over women and midwives. What Farrant terms the 'new techno fix' gives them control in the early stages of the pregnancy as they are able to interpret the test results. In the late 1970s, the proposed cuts to maternity services could be avoided because obstetricians could argue that money was needed to fund testing. Since the government favoured testing, they had to agree to its being funded. Geneticists saw the possibility of NHS funding for their work and an increase in research possibilities. At the time of the push forward in screening, much of their work was funded outside the health service. The medical supply industry saw that they were in a position to make large profits from manufacturing obstetric ultrasound equipment. Pharmaceutical companies make profits from supplying kits for maternal serum Alpha Feto Protein (AFP) tests.

Reporting on a survey carried out by the Institute for Social Studies in Medical Care, Farrant (1985) notes that of the obstetricians questioned, 85 per cent thought that a national screening programme to detect neural tube defects was beneficial. They thought that screening was good for individual women as they could avoid the birth of a disabled child and good for society as a whole in terms of saving money. Spallone (1989) points out that whilst obstetricians see themselves as protecting fetal interests, this is only true of non-disabled fetuses.

With so many powerful groups pressing for screening programmes, it is not surprising that they have expanded so rapidly. The availability of screening has coincided with a shift in childbirth trends. Many women are having children later and families are in general becoming smaller, so expectations have changed. If a couple decide to have only one or two children they may invest certain hopes for their futures and this can result in a view that impairment would prevent these hopes being realised. This may not be true because the couple concerned may know very little about a possible impairment. They may under-estimate what their potential offspring could achieve.

The ethics of abortion

There is an increasing interest in bioethics in the 'problems' created by disability. Taking a broadly utilitarian stance, many ethicists suggest that it would be better for society if dis-abled fetuses were not allowed to progress to term. As we now can frequently detect abnormality, we should in turn prevent it. Since prevention means ending the life of the fetus, that should be done. McGee gives the example of Trisomy 18 as a disease that must be avoided: 'There can be no question that a couple who determines that their infant is sure to suffer and die incurs special responsibilities, and among these responsibilities may be one to abort. From time to time genetic testing will suggest a duty to abort' (1997: 93). There is an implication in this that one also has a *duty* to take a series of tests. If abortion is morally acceptable, then, the argument goes, in the case of impairment, we have a valid reason to do it. Of course, not all philosophers agree that abortion is acceptable and some adopt a sanctity-of-life view, based on the moral position that an embryo has the same sta-tus as a fully-grown human being. Others believe that it is acceptable in certain circum-stances. I do not propose to rehearse all the arguments for and against abortion. Suffice it to say that if we believe abortion is at least acceptable, then it is consistent to say that it is acceptable on the grounds of impairment. What it is not, is inevitable.

There is a new technique that avoids the need for abortion. It is only available for a limited number of conditions. It is called pre-implantation genetic diagnosis (PGD) and uses *in vitro* fertilisaton techniques. After several eggs have been collected from the ovary, they are fertilised in a test tube. The resultant embryos are checked for disease and poten-tial impairment with one or two being implanted in the womb provided that they are free from disease and impairment. For those who believe that once fertilisation has taken place a human being has been created who merits the same moral status as a child or adult, the problem of destroying something sacred persists. For others, there is the problem of selecting an embryo to continue its existence whilst discarding the remaining embryos.

Decisions, decisions

It is highly unlikely that screening will cease, so it is important that counselling is done in an unbiased way. The views of disabled people need to be taken into account. After all, if a balanced picture of disability is to be achieved, then those living with impairments have valuable contributions to make to the debate. At present, any pregnant woman is unlikely to have access to disabled people with impairments similar to those present in her fetus. If she were able to discuss the affects of impairment with someone experiencing it, then her view on proceeding with the pregnancy might change. A purely medically-based view can never show the richness and diversity of a life. Certainly, information concerning screening needs to be given by outsiders to the medical system so that a social dimension can be added. It is difficult in the clinical environment of a hospital to move away from a medical model.

Genetics and the future of testing

In the UK, there is a tension between those researching into the human genome and many in the disabled people's movement. The fear amongst disabled people is that the more the wider society knows about genetic impairment, the less tolerant we will become of difference and that abnormality will always be screened out. Is this necessarily the case? It may be possible to manipulate a fetus's genetic coding in such a way as to prevent certain future impairments. Many people would welcome that, seeing it in the same light as vaccination. Others feel that it is a step too far, in that it changes the very fabric of life. As scientists delve into which problems have a genetic basis, they find that genes are at least partially responsible for the way we are mentally and physically. All of us are endowed with 'faulty' genes which may cause us harm in the future. In the USA, a prevalent term amongst disability activists is 'temporarily abled', as many people will become disabled at some point in the future. Given that, why are some people so intolerant to difference? Do they sense that they may join the 'others', that is, those who are disabled?

I think that the testing culture is so entrenched that we cannot go back. Therefore we must use the technology to empower people, by providing knowledge regarding future children. We can do one of three things:

- *confuse*, that is, make someone unclear about whether to continue the pregnancy;
- *alarm*, that is, this child will have so many problems it is not worth continuing the pregnancy; or
- *truly inform*, that is, these are the impairments we have found and this is what can currently be done to assist you and this child if he or she is born.

Also, we need to remember that most impairments are not genetic in origin and that illness, the environment, accident and poverty play their parts. By concentrating on genetic causes of impairment, we can fail to change the social and environmental conditions in which people live. We should be looking to clean up polluted waters, make working practices safer and take all steps to minimise the risk of famine and epidemics. In addition, Jones (1994) reminds us that whatever we do, evolution will ensure that new mutations of genes will occur and that therefore new impairments will arise. By improving people's chances in life through education and improved nutrition, to give two important examples, we improve their chances of living longer and often healthier lives, but in time they will die, probably from genetically-linked disease such as cancer or heart failure. Some of their children will have genetic diseases and the chances increase if people mate within their own ethnic group. He points out that, for example, many people from Pakistan, now living in the UK, marry cousins, thus increasing the chances of passing on genetic disease. Also, more disabled people are finding partners and having children and some of these children will inherit genetic impairments.

We will never eradicate impairment and therefore we need to improve the society we live in by educating the public concerning disability and improving access in its widest sense to all those living with impairments. Unless disabled people play a full role in society, they will always be on the margins. We need to exert influence on policy makers to make sure that there are safeguards against genetic discrimination. At present, genetic tests, apart from the one for Huntington's disease, cannot be used by insurers to discriminate with the exception of policies greater than £500,000. We must be vigilant and work to keep the present rules in place to prevent further conditions being added to the list. If possible, removal of Huntington's disease as a bar to insurance should be worked towards. Whilst I am not denying that certain diseases shorten life, insurance is a collective responsibility.

The present abortion law is eugenic in that it has no limit to the age at which an impaired fetus can be aborted. This should be changed as it is grossly unjust, since it suggests that an impaired fetus is less morally worthy than one free of impairment.

Our genetic future?

If nothing is done to change current practice, then we may move from the modification or eradication of 'faulty' genes using gene therapy, towards genetic enhancement. In the latter case, we add on extra qualities to our future offspring's genes, such as enhanced senses and greater intelligence. Harris (1998) thinks that if it becomes safe to do so, then we should go ahead with it as it improves the life chances of our children.

Genetic tests for minor impairments and treatments to enhance will, I suspect, only be open to a wealthy few. But it will create further division in an already divided society. Those who cannot access tests may feel they are missing something. They may be missing something which is less valuable than they thought. Mistakes will be easy to make, both about the sorts of lives future people will live and the effect that genetic manipulation will have. How would we be able to predict what a person in the future would regard as a fortunate inheritance? Parents cannot anticipate what their children will judge to be valuable. Those like Harris, who favour positive genetic manipulation, are making assumptions about how a future human race should be in order to be an improvement on this one. Genetically-based medicine, if proven to be safe, will be a valuable addition to our lives, but genetically modified people may not be an improvement on the random system we have now.

Note

1 Sections of this chapter have previously appeared in *Community Practitioner*, January 2001.

References

Farrant, W. (ed.) (1985) 'Who's for amniocentesis?', in H. Homans (ed.), *The Sexual Politics of Reproduction*. Aldershot: Gower.

Harris, J. (1998) *Clones, Genes and Immortality: Ethics and Genetic Revolution*. Oxford: Oxford University Press.

Jones, S. (1994) *The Language of the Genes*. London: Flamingo.

Katz Rothman, B. (1994) *The Tentative Pregnancy: Amniocentesis and the Sexual Politics of Motherhood*. London: Pandora.

McGee, G. (1997) *The Perfect Baby: A Pragmatic Approach to Genetics*. Lanham, MD: Rowman and Littlefield.

Spallone, P. (1989) *Beyond Conception: The New Politics of Reproduction*. London: Macmillan.

45 Legislation and Human Rights
RACHEL HURST

When discussing legal protection for disabled people, there has been much talk of 'human rights', 'civil rights' and 'anti-discrimination legislation'. Although these three themes share a similar objective, if we want a world where every human being, irrespective of who they are, can be treated equally, without discrimination and with dignity and freedom, we need to realise that these three areas are not the same.

The concept of human rights has been around for as long as there have been philosophers and thinkers. Human rights are all those rights that are inherent in an individual's humanity – her or his right 'to be born equal in freedom and dignity' (United Nations, 1948), to personal integrity and self-determination. Human rights are seen as fundamental, as above man-made laws; they exist whether there are national laws to uphold them or not. They are universal and they are indivisible. It is states who should uphold them and it is individuals who should expect them.

Civil rights are what individuals or groups of people can expect from a country's law or code and are interpreted by the courts. Unlike human rights, civil rights only exist if they are protected within law (Light, 2000).

Freedom from discrimination is just one of the fundamental human rights. Anti-discrimination legislation ensures that this right, through civil rights laws, can be enforced and requires changes in the behaviour of both individuals and the systems and structures of society. Because anti-discrimination legislation requires social change, none of the laws upholding non-discrimination give it as an absolute right. It is always qualified by the effect that these changes might have on an employer or service provider. This is where the term 'reasonable accommodations' or 'reasonable adjustments' comes in. This is to ensure that the right of a service provider or employer to run the business profitably or without undue hardship will not be damaged by the right of the disabled person to protection from discrimination. It is a compromise that has been accepted – the alternative would be no anti-discrimination legislation at all as the burden would be too great on society to change. It is important, however, that disabled people are involved in setting guidance as to what is deemed 'reasonable'.

Human rights

In 1948, the Universal Declaration of Human Rights was agreed as an urgent response to the Holocaust and the Nazi atrocities of the Second World War. The Universal Declaration and the resulting Covenants on Civil and Political Rights (1966) and the International Covenant on Economic, Social and Cultural Rights (1966) form the International Bill of Rights. The Covenants and the other international human rights instruments all guarantee that rights will be exercised without discrimination of any kind, although, with the exception of the Convention on the Rights of the Child, disabled people are not specifically mentioned but are one of the groups of people covered through the term 'or other status'.

Enforcement of these international human rights instruments is through specific monitoring committees which look at reports from member states on a regular basis and produce written comments on the state's progress. There is no international court through which violations can be redressed, but the act of 'naming and shaming' through these publicly available comments has been effective. The monitoring committees all accept written evidence from non-governmental organisations (NGOs) in respect of country reports. This provides a useful opportunity for civil society to ensure that the monitoring committee gets to know the real situation – not just the governmental viewpoint. It is particularly important that disability NGOs are involved in this process to ensure that monitoring committees focus on the specific rights of disabled people. It has been through NGO involvement that we have discovered how member states commonly exclude the rights of disabled people. In a recent meeting of the Committee on the Rights of the Child, a country reported that they now provide free education to all children. When specifically pressed by the Committee, at the instigation of a disability NGO, as to whether the term 'all' included disabled children, the country's representative said that disabled children were not included as they were not considered children!

As well as the human rights conventions, there have, at the international level, been many declarations on the rights of Disabled People (1975), on Mentally Retarded Persons (1971), on Persons with Mental Illness and the Improvement of Mental Health Care (1991). In 1982, the United Nations produced the World Programme of Action concerning Disabled Persons, which set out recommendations to member states on how they could implement the full and equal participation of disabled people in society (Degener and Koster-Dreese, 1995).

In 1987 there was an attempt by Italy and Sweden to introduce a convention on the rights of disabled people, but it was not initiated. Instead, the UN General Assembly agreed the Standard Rules on Equalisation of Opportunities for Disabled Persons in 1993. These Rules were a refinement of the World Programme of Action, but were not a mandatory instrument, nor did they have any formal enforcement mechanism within the regular UN system. Using voluntary funds, a Special Rapporteur was appointed to monitor member states' use of the Standard Rules and the Rapporteur was supported by a Panel of Experts of representatives from the international NGOs representing disabled people. The Standard Rules have proved useful as a lobbying tool and as guidance. They are more concerned with how society is structured, however, than on the individual disabled person's right to humanity.

The most important trigger for world acceptance of disability as a human rights issue was the report *Human Rights and Disabled Persons*, by Leandro Despouy (1993), Special Rapporteur of the Sub-Commission on the Prevention of Discrimination and Protection of Minorities. In this report, Despouy provided conclusive evidence that disabled people's rights were systematically denied and that the existing human rights instruments, although including disabled people, were not being used in reference to them. Despouy pressed for an international convention. Despite this, it was only in November 2001 that a convention was mooted through a resolution to the UN General Assembly. An *Ad Hoc* Committee has been set up to examine the proposition and propose mechanisms for implementation.

The UK and human rights

In the UK, we are not only subject to the international human rights instruments, but also to the European Convention for the Protection of Human Rights and Fundamental

Freedoms (1950) and now to our own Human Rights Act (1998), which gives rights and freedoms guaranteed under the European Convention on Human Rights. The European Convention is enforced through cases taken through the European Court of Human Rights. This can be done by individuals or institutions once all available legislation has been used in the European country concerned. The Human Rights Act is enforced through the UK courts. Cases under the Human Rights Act can only be taken when the state or a state agency has violated a right – it is not possible to take a case against an individual or a private company. This is the same for all human rights instruments.

The European Court has been used very effectively by disabled people. The Human Rights Act less so. The Disability Rights Commission (see below) is still not able to take cases under the Human Rights Act, and many of our lawyers are not used to working either in the field of human rights or disability and so cases are often not deemed to be eligible or have poor outcomes.

Civil rights

Before 1970, most legislation in the UK was based on social services and health and community care systems. Either disabled people were not seen as part of other civil rights legislation – for instance, people with learning difficulties were not afforded the same right to education as other children under the 1944 Education Act – or there was 'special provision', in itself often discriminatory, as evidenced by the quota systems in employment, in existence in Europe since the 1920s (Cooper, 2000). The 1970 Chronically Sick and Disabled Act gave disabled people support to ensure that they had accessible housing and technical assistance, though, because of the wording of the Act, they did not have a right to these services and were dependent on local authorities for implementation. It was not until 1986 and the Disabled Persons (Services, Consultation and Representation) Act that the word 'rights' was actually used with regard to disability legislation, but that Act has never been fully implemented by government.

There was also other legislation that sought to protect society rather than disabled people – laws such as the Mental Health Act (1983) and laws to protect those who are without capacity to understand the nature, purpose and effects of a particular proposal or situation. Although the Disabled Persons (Services, Consultation and Representation) Act specifically tried to address the right of disabled people to an independent advocate or representative, it was just those sections of the Act which were never implemented. Even now, draft bills out for consultation are widening the powers of the courts and the medical profession to control decisions regarding people with mental health problems and those without capacity to make decisions. The latest Mental Incapacity Bill, which, among other things, sought to ensure compulsory treatment in the community as well as in hospitals, has met with considerable opposition in recognition that it would be in contravention of the Human Rights Act.

Anti-discrimination legislation

Since the early 1980s, disabled people in the UK believed that the only way that they could obtain their civil rights was through anti-discrimination legislation. From 1983 onward, there were 13 private members bills all supporting civil rights for disabled people. Each bill activated intense lobbying from the Disability Rights Movement, which reached its peak in 1994 causing media coverage and parliamentary resignations. As a result of this, the government very quickly, and with no open consultation, introduced the Disability Discrimination Act (DDA) 1995. This Act was seen as deeply flawed: it had a medical definition of disability and did not cover crucial areas of disabled people's lives, such as transport, education and local authority policies. The employment section did not cover employers with under 20 staff. It provided justifications for discrimination in some areas and was not enforceable.

The Labour Party Manifesto of 1997 openly committed them to full and enforceable civil rights for disabled people. When they won the election on 1 May 1997, the disability lobby set about ensuring that they fulfilled their manifesto commitment. Unfortunately, progress has been slow. The government formed a Disability Rights Task Force which, at the end of two years, produced 156 recommendations for amendment to the DDA. A Disability Rights Commission was set up by Act of Parliament and started work in 2000, providing support to disabled individuals in obtaining their rights under the DDA and allied legislation (though not the Human Rights Act). The duty on providers of goods and services and employers not to discriminate did not come into force until 2000 and at that time there was also a duty not to make a service or employment less accessible to a disabled person. The duty to bring down physical barriers and to provide reasonable adjustments does not come into force until October 2004. Similarly, although in 1999 it was announced that the DDA would cover transport and small employers, the small employers do not have to comply with the legislation until October 2004, and there are still no dates fixed for transport compliance.

On 22 January 2003, the Minister for Disabled People announced that a new Disability Bill would be introduced in the Queen's Speech in the autumn, after consultation. This Bill is supposed to enlarge the definition of who is eligible under the DDA and to fulfil the recommendations of the Disability Rights Task Force. Meanwhile, a Special Education Needs and Disability Act (2002) was introduced to extend protection from discrimination to education.

European Union legislation and influence

Before 1993, neither the European Parliament nor the European Commission saw disability as anything other than an issue of rehabilitation and social care and provision. The concept of rights, equalisation of opportunities and independent living were merely words, sometimes bandied about, but with no political or legislative support. In 1993, Disabled People's International – Europe, funded by the European Commission, celebrated the first International Day of Disabled Persons, 3 December, with a parliament of disabled people held in the Hemicycle of the European Parliament. Where normally the MEPs debated issues, there were 440 disabled people with leaders of the European Commission and Parliament debating the resolution:

> … invites the Community institutions and the Member States of the European Community to take practical steps to guarantee the human rights of disabled people by the adoption or adjustment of legally binding instruments, and to adopt and to ensure implementation of the UN Standard Rules on the Equalisation of Opportunities for disabled people. (DPI, 1993)

The commissioners and leading parliamentarians signed Affirmations of Commitment to this resolution and it was passed unanimously. This event was to have a profound effect on the European Union, as did the Treaty of Maastricht (1993). This revision of the Treaty of Rome changed the concept of the European Union from just a common market to one providing for a European social dialogue, including an Agreement on Social Policy. This was adopted by all member states except the UK.

By giving social partners (employers, trades unions and NGOs) a voice in introducing a new basis for action, there was considerable pressure put on the institutions of the EC to introduce the notion of protection from discrimination. This Agreement allowed disabled people's organisations – notably Disabled People's International – Europe – to push for the adoption by the European Union of the UN Standard Rules. They were formally endorsed by the Council in its Resolution of 20 December 1996 on Equality of Opportunity for People with Disability.

Further lobbying from the social partners, including disabled people's organisations, resulted in Article 13 of the Treaty of Amsterdam (1997), which provides for appropriate action to combat discrimination based on sex, racial or ethnic origin, religion or belief, disability, age or sexual orientation. This enables the European Union to help national and local agencies to do much more on the fundamentals of integration and rights, including the rights of disabled people.

Using Article 13 as a starting point, the Council adopted, on 27 November 2000, a comprehensive anti-discrimination package consisting of a Directive establishing a general framework for equal treatment in employment and occupation and a Community action programme to combat discrimination (2001–2006). The Directive provides a legislative framework for legally enforceable employment rights, including provisions on a number of key issues such as protection against harassment, scope for positive action, appropriate remedies and enforcement measures. More importantly, the Directive also adopts the duty of reasonable accommodation, which implies the adjustment of the workplace to meet the needs of a disabled person. It was this directive that put pressure on the UK government to abolish the exemption of small employers from the DDA.

In order to fulfil its commitment to citizenship, the Commission adopted, on 12 May 2000, a Communication *Toward a Barrier-Free Europe for Disabled People* in which it commits itself to developing and supporting a comprehensive and integrated strategy to tackle social, architectural and design barriers that restrict access for disabled people to social and economic opportunities (Hurst, 2001). An initiative to bring in a Directive to support this communication has just been launched by the European Parliamentary Intergroup on Disability and the European Disability Forum.

With European legislation regarding disability rights being so much more comprehensive and radical than the DDA or the new Disability Bill, there is little doubt that the proposed Directive could make a profound difference in future implementation of rights for disabled people in the UK.

Way forward

As was said right at the beginning – there is still confusion over the difference between human and civil rights. Disabled people and their organisations have for a long time fought for civil rights and have learnt that legislation covering these rights is only as good as the comprehensive nature of the law, the enforcement mechanism and the understanding and judgements of the judiciary.

We are now learning that, because of:

- new genetics;
- a cost-cutting health service with (for many disabled people) inappropriate and discriminatory health care;
- judgements on our quality of life as not worth living, resulting in involuntary euthanasia of disabled babies and older people and of 'Do Not Resuscitate' notices put on patients of all ages;
- non-custodial sentences given to people who kill their disabled family members because they are considered 'mercy-killings';
- the lack of access to justice because of prejudicial views of disabled people (especially of those who do not use verbal communication); and
- the abuse and violence suffered by disabled people both at home and in institutions (disabled children alone are seen to suffer at least three times as much abuse as non-disabled children);

it is imperative that we ensure that our human rights are at the top of the legislative agenda and that there are proper enforcement mechanisms in place both nationally and with regard to the UN instruments (Light, 2002).

To quote from Leandro Despouy in his UN special report, *Human Rights and Disabled Persons*:

> It might appear elementary to point out that persons with disabilities are human beings – as human as, and usually even more human than, the rest. The daily effort to overcome impediments and the discriminatory treatment they regularly receive usually provides them with special personality features, the most obvious and common of which are integrity, perseverance, and a deep spirit of comprehension and patience in the face of a lack of understanding and intolerance. However, this last feature should not lead us to overlook the fact that as subjects of law they enjoy all the legal attributes inherent in human beings and hold specific rights in addition. (1993: 1)

References

Cooper, J. (ed.) (2000) *Law, Rights and Disability*. London: Jessica Kingsley.

Degener, T. and Koster-Dreese, Y. (eds) (1995) *Human Rights and Disabled Persons*. Amsterdam: Martinus Nijhoff.

Despouy, L. (1993) *Human Rights and Disabled Persons*. Geneva: Centre for Human Rights.

DPI (1993) *Agenda and Report of the European Disabled People's Parliament*. London: DPI–Europe.

Hurst, R. (2001) *Briefing Paper on Europe, Legislation and Disability*. London: Disability Awareness and Action.

Light, R. (2000) *Civil Rights Law and Disabled People*. London: Disability Awareness and Action.

Light, R. (2002) *A Real Horror Story: The Abuse of Disabled People's Human Rights*. London: Disability Awareness and Action.

United Nations (1948) *Universal Declaration of Human Rights*. New York, NY: United Nation.

Index